Praise for

VOICES OF A MASSACRE

"Once again the lesson must be learned that not all massacres are reported and acknowledged as the brutal and systematic killings that they are. What geopolitical reasons are there for having kept the history of the Great Massacre of 1988 in Iran from being told? This indispensable volume, *Voices of a Massacre*, takes the reader through that history, exposes the well-constructed oblivion to which this history has been consigned, and assembles the testimonies of political prisoners and those who mourn their losses. It documents the various arduous efforts to appeal to the government, the media, and international authorities to recognize and condemn this crime, and weaves together the acts of resistance among those who are fighting for this history to be told and known. This is an urgent and belated book that draws on multiple archives to establish the systematic death-dealing of the late 1980s in Iran, as well as the unforgivable and complicitous silence on this period of lethal violence. That history is established through many voices and genres, all of which constitute a living testimonial, a collective act of mourning, and a resounding call for justice."

> JUDITH BUTLER, Maxine Elliot Professor of Comparative
> Literature, University of California, Berkeley, and author
> of *Precarious Life* and *The Force of Nonviolence*

"Nasser Mohajer writes for the same reasons as George Orwell—'desire to see things as they are, to find out true facts and to store them up for the use of posterity.' This is an invaluable testimony to the shameful 1988 prison massacres that the authorities denied, regime historians tried to vaporize, and many others either minimized or glossed over its medieval essence. The Inquisition that oversaw the mass executions was not only horrific but also unprecedented in the whole of Iran's long history."

> ERVAND ABRAHAMIAN, Distinguished Professor Emeritus of Iranian and
> Middle Eastern history and politics, Baruch College and Graduate Center,
> City University of New York, and author of *A History of Modern Iran*

"*Voices of a Massacre* is a testament to the human capacity to resist, survive, remember, and respond ethically to others—even at the very limit of what a person can bear. It is gut-wrenching and difficult to read, and that is precisely why we must read it, as slowly and carefully as necessary to absorb what has happened and to grasp what must be done. The book is a truly amazing achievement."

LISA GUENTHER, Queen's National Scholar in Political Philosophy and Critical Prison Studies, Queen's University, Kingston, and author of *Solitary Confinement: Social Death and Its Afterlives*

"*Voices of a Massacre* is an unsparing account of *Untold Stories of Life and Death*, vital for understanding the cruelty of the Islamic Republic of Iran, yet unique in presenting human qualities of resistance, hope, despair, and fear under the condition of imprisonment. Through insightful narrations one can imagine and sense people's desire for survival when pushed to life's extremes. An agonizing, but not-to-be-evaded read."

SHAHRZAD MOJAB, Professor, University of Toronto, and author of *Revolutionary Learning: Marxism, Feminism and Knowledge*

"*Voices of a Massacre* is a valuable response to the 'duty of memory.' Through both analysis and testimony, it provides a profound series of reflections on the shocking 1988 mass killing of political prisoners that continues to cast a long shadow on the people of Iran. By surfacing the historical truth, this unique collection helps confront the culture of denial and impunity that stands in the way of a better future built on the supremacy of human rights."

PAYAM AKHAVAN, Professor of International Law, McGill University, and author of *In Search of a Better World*

Voices of
a Massacre

Untold Stories of Life and Death in Iran, 1988

Compiled and edited by
Nasser Mohajer

Foreword by Angela Davis

ONEWORLD

A Oneworld Book

First published by Oneworld Publications in 2020

Copyright © Nasser Mohajer 2020
Foreword © Angela Davis 2020

A CIP record for this title is available from the British Library

ISBN 978-1-78607-777-6
eISBN 978-1-78607-778-3

Typeset by Tetragon, London
Printed and bound in Great Britain by Clays Ltd, Elcograf S.p.A.

Oneworld Publications
10 Bloomsbury Street
London, WC1B 3SR
England

Stay up to date with the latest books,
special offers, and exclusive content from
Oneworld with our newsletter

Sign up on our website
oneworld-publications.com

MIX
Paper from
responsible sources
FSC® C018072

To the memory of the thousands of Iranian prisoners of conscience who were massacred in the summer of 1988 solely due to their beliefs

Contents

Acknowledgments

The initial idea for this book emerged through discussions Nima Mina and I had some ten years ago in Mistral Restaurant in Paris. The long journey that resulted from those discussions has been more challenging than I could have dreamed at the time. It has required establishing contact with survivors and bereaved families; gaining access to untapped sources; translating first-person accounts from Persian and other languages into English; and fact-checking, editing, and proofreading the various pieces of this compilation as it came to life and evolved over time.

Years of extensive research and publishing on the penitentiary system of the Islamic Republic of Iran, and my acquaintance with many different kinds of ex-political prisoners from the 1980s, allowed me access to the perfect pool of individuals to share stories of living through the Great Massacre. I would like to take this opportunity to thank all my fellow travelers for their contributions to this volume, and to salute their patience as they awaited its appearance. The most difficult component of the project, however, was to find seasoned researchers, translators, editors, and proofreaders who were willing to collaborate with me in this essential and long-overdue endeavor to painstakingly excavate the dark past. I was fortunate indeed to receive the unequivocal encouragement and indispensable assistance of many gifted colleagues and friends who agreed to share their various areas of expertise.

The critical phase of translating texts from Persian into English was the meticulous work of Roxana Fard, Sina Navaie, Maryam Jazayeri, F. Amini, Ali Hojat, Maliheh Razazan, Cyrus Bahramian, Aram Nozad, Hedayat Mahdavi, and Yasmin Jayhoun. These dear friends, to whom I am deeply grateful, paved the way for my beloved friend and colleague Gerald William Swanson (1942–2017), professor emeritus of political theory at York University, to start on the editing process. I miss Bill's enthusiasm and his congenial presence, which I so appreciated as we worked closely together in Paris and Toronto during two summers.

With Bill's passing, the editing of the texts, a task which had expanded over the course of his long illness to incorporate new dimensions of the massacre, fell solely onto my shoulders. It was during this difficult time that Isabella

Maz and Fereydoon Farhadi stepped in and offered their editorial skills to help bring this book into being. I won't be able to forget their kindness and valuable contributions. After some time, my dear old friend Katherine Sigman was able to step onto the scene for a short while, and then Laura Gorjance honored me by taking up the task of fine-tuning my finished drafts of the texts. Laura's editing skills, coupled with her unbounded kindness, have been like fresh air to me. My sincere gratitude to her for all her unconditional help.

I would also like to express my profound appreciation to Lale Behzadi, Azam Nourullahkhani, and Banafsheh Massoudi, who provided me with several important documents. As always, Banafsheh Massoudi was essential in laying out the first draft of the manuscript. I cannot continue without acknowledging the contributions of Shohreh Mahmoud and Shokoufeh Sakhi in fact-checking some of the testimonial narratives. The task on Shokoufeh's shoulders before Bill fell ill was essential. Even after that she did whatever she could to make this project possible. I can't thank her enough. Sima Nouri, Pari Farrokh, Sina Navaie, and Behzad Ladbon contributed greatly with their meticulous proofreading. I am earnestly thankful to each and every one of these dedicated souls.

Several very dear friends and colleagues accompanied me throughout this expedition, assisting me in various forms and in numerous fields: Ali Hojat, Sima Nouri, Aram Nozad, Shahram Aghamir, Shohreh Mahmoud, Maliheh Razazan, and especially Kaveh Yazdani and Siavush Randjbar-Daemi. I am also immensely gratified and indeed indebted to dear Professor Angela Davis who did me the great honor of writing the foreword of this book. My acknowledgment of the support granted to me by all these committed humanists would not come close to completion without mentioning my wife, Mahnaz Matin. She has been my rock throughout years of working on this project, providing essential moral and intellectual backing as I came to terms with a topic whose very existence highlights the fact that the world we are living in is gripped by extreme injustice.

Last but not least, I should express my deepest appreciation for Oneworld, especially Novin Doostdar and Jonathan Bentley-Smith, who bore with me throughout this journey. Alan Bellinger, my copy-editor, deserves an abundance of gratitude for his excellent suggestions and fine modifications to the manuscript.

Despite the essential assistance I received from these friends and colleagues, and my heartfelt gratitude to each and every one of them, I remain responsible for any shortcomings or inaccuracies contained within this volume.

A Note on Translation and Transliteration

In translating oral testimonies, interviews with former political prisoners, state officials, and "religious authorities," I have sought to be faithful to the voices of those who bore witness rather than alter the wording of their accounts to adhere to the traditional standards of written English.

Unless otherwise indicated, all translations from Persian, French, German, etc. were undertaken by the contributors to this volume.

As there is no consensus on a comprehensive and conclusive method of Persian–English transliteration and the anglicization of Persian words, I have used a modified version of the system of transliteration employed by *Encyclopædia Iranica*. Furthermore, I have done my best to remain true and get as close as possible to the contemporary pronunciation and current phonetics of the dominant intonation, dialect, accent, and diction in Iran (in the light of classical Persian poetry). I have also tried to present a standardized and unitized English spelling of Persian words, even when citing direct quotations from English-language sources, in order to engender a sufficient degree of consistency. Moreover, Arabic words and terms have been persianized. However, in exceptional cases, where a term or concept has already entered the English lexicon, I have maintained the Arabic transliterations (e.g. jihad, surah, Iftar).

I have abstained from using diacritical marks, except for the < ع >, which has been transliterated with < ' >, as in Shi'ite and shari'a. The word < ق >, < ق >, or < غ > has been transliterated with a < q >, as in Qom and Qurban. Ezafe-constructions (connecting two or more words through an unstressed -e and -ye) have been transliterated with an < e >, as in Bang-e Raha'i, and < ye >, as in Cherikha-ye Feda'i-ye Khalq.

Foreword

ANGELA DAVIS

Pernicious examples of state violence that produce (and reproduce) collective trauma also generate demands for memorialization that can imprint the memory of the trauma on the historical record, while assuaging our sense of incredulity in the face of such violence. Käthe Kollwitz's 1924 lithograph *Nie wieder Krieg* (Never Again War) calls out for a collective memory of the pain and violence of war and at the same time announces a mandate that mass brutality should never be repeated. In his 2010 *Geometry of Conscience*, an installation on the grounds of the Museum of Memory and Human Rights in Santiago de Chile, Alfredo Jaar memorialized those whose lives were lost or forever damaged by the Pinochet coup and dictatorship. In Buenos Aires, in the Parque de la Memoria, there is a Monument to the Victims of State-Sponsored Terrorism during the military dictatorship, 1969–83. And finally, over 150 years after the putative abolition of slavery in the US, there are new and innovative efforts to memorialize the foremothers and fathers of many of us who continue to struggle for an end to racism today. In 2006, the Toni Morrison Society celebrated the author's seventy-fifth birthday by inaugurating its Bench by the Road Project. This project was a response to Morrison's reflections on the absence of memorials to slavery:

> There is no place you or I can go to think about or not think about, to summon the presences of, or recollect the absences of slaves... There is no suitable memorial, or plaque, or wreath, or wall, or skyscraper lobby. There's no 300-foot tower, there's no small bench by the road...[1]

Thus far, the Society is responsible for the installation of twenty benches, including in Harlem, Paris, and Fort de France, Martinique.

---

1   https://www.tonimorrisonsociety.org/bench.html, accessed February 4, 2020.

But there are also instances of exceptionally virulent state violence that have been subject to official cover-ups and for which there has never been the opportunity to publicly and internationally memorialize those whose lives were systematically, ruthlessly, but also covertly extinguished by the state. One of the most dramatic examples of unacknowledged, large-scale state terrorism is the 1988 Massacre of political prisoners in Iran. Estimates regarding the numbers of those subject to extrajudicial execution range from 4,000 to more than 10,000. Neither those executed nor their families were informed of their fate. Nasser Mohajer's *Voices of a Massacre* is a much-needed collection of narratives and writings by survivors, family members, researchers, and others who are determined to prevent the erasure of this massacre from the historical record.

As a longtime political activist in the US, my own trajectory has been deeply influenced by progressive and radical resistance in Iran. Some of my most prominent political memories involve solidarity efforts in the 1960s directed against the Shah of Iran. I was involved in the German Socialist Student Organization in 1967 when Benno Ohnesorg was killed by the police in Berlin while participating in a rally against the Shah, and I still have vivid recollections of the intense fear evoked by SAVAK—in the US, in Europe, and, of course, in Iran. At that time solidarity with progressive movements inside Iran was a crucial dimension of contemporary anti-imperialist practices. If we then challenged US military incursions in Vietnam and stood in solidarity with the Vietnamese people, we also challenged US support for the Shah and stood in solidarity with the Iranian people. Given this history, should we not be self-critical today regarding our failure to serve as effective allies of progressive movements that refuse to permit the rulers of the Islamic Republic to continue their cover-up?

As a scholar whose research interests revolve around the emergence and evolution of the prison industrial complex and the central role of structural racism, and as an activist who has helped to organize numerous actions and campaigns over the years asserting the human rights of prisoners, I count myself among those who are especially concerned about the politics of the proliferation of prisons under the Islamic Republic of Iran. The official refusal to admit governmental responsibility for the 1988 Massacre is linked to the increased use of the prison as an apparatus of repression. Thousands of people are currently behind bars in Iran, and while we know that the United States claims the highest rate of incarceration in the world, Iran, which also has a high rate of incarceration, has come to rely on prisons and executions as a response—amongst other repressive measures—to pressing social, economic, and political problems.

As a former political prisoner who once faced the prospect of execution by the state and whose life was saved by a massive international solidarity movement, I am deeply troubled about the fact that we in the US—particularly those of us who see ourselves as allies—have not more closely followed the situation of political prisoners in Iran. Granted, it is true that an official and extensive cover-up of the 1988 extrajudicial execution of thousands of political prisoners prevented even family members of the executed from discovering the fate of their loved ones. As readers of *Voices of a Massacre* will learn, many were under the impression that their relatives were on the verge of being released—especially those who had been imprisoned for such relatively minor acts as distributing opposition literature or being in the company of those who were known to be members of oppositional political groups. Some had, in fact, already completed their sentences. It was also the case that prisoners, who witnessed the disappearance of their imprisoned comrades, were sometimes under the impression that the disappeared had been released or moved to another facility. From the Death Commission that interrogated prisoners and handed down decisions on those who were to be summarily executed to the mode of execution—often mass hangings—and the clandestine burials of the bodies, an almost impermeable cloak of secrecy obstructed the circulation of knowledge regarding this massacre that is so vast that it continues to strain our imagination today.

However, as *Voices of a Massacre* underscores, that cloak was first perforated by the tenacity of family members who refused to believe that they would never learn the fate of their loved ones and who would not temper their resolve to learn where their relatives were buried. Thanks to the passionate obstinacy of family members of victims and survivors, and thanks to the work of Iranians both within the country and those, like Nasser Mohajer—political exile and scholar of modern Iranian history who has meticulously and consistently researched and documented the Islamic Republic of Iran's prison system—living abroad, the truth regarding the massacre has slowly trickled out. Like the Mothers of the Plaza de Mayo in Argentina, the Mothers of Khavaran have taken the lead, demonstrating the strength, political acumen, and perseverance that we have witnessed in other women's formations that have developed in response to similar political conditions. The Mothers were among the first to call for information regarding those who had been disappeared, and because of their insistence the mass graves in Khavaran

Cemetery were discovered. Largely due to their persistence in attempting to find their loved ones and to identify those officials who were responsible for the extrajudicial executions, the gates to the Khavaran Cemetery were locked in 2004. Five years later, authorities bulldozed the cemetery.

The regime's response to the Mothers of Khavaran—and to others who continue to press for information about the massacre and who insist on the right to memorialize the victims of IRI state terror—is an indication that they continue to feel threatened by ongoing efforts to extricate the 1988 Massacre from the shroud of official secrecy. The subtitle of Amnesty International's 2018 report *Blood-soaked secrets* is *"Why Iran's 1988 prison massacres are ongoing crimes against humanity."* Amnesty International's focus on one of the most heinous chapters of state violence in Iran's recent history is further prompted by the ongoing official campaign to repress the commemorative efforts of survivors, families, and human rights defenders, and to demonize the victims and distort the facts about the extrajudicial execution of political dissidents in the 1980s. It is all the more relevant as many of those alleged to have been involved in the 1988 enforced disappearances and extrajudicial executions hold or have held positions of power in Iran. They benefit from a continuing atmosphere of secrecy and impunity in the country. The report persuasively argues that the crimes of enforced disappearance committed by the Iranian state are not only situated in the past but continue until such time as the authorities "fully disclose the truth about the fate of the individuals concerned and the location of their remains."[2]

The Iran Tribunal—a people's tribunal modeled after the Russell Tribunal, organized in 1966 by Bertrand Russell and Jean-Paul Sartre to investigate US war crimes in Vietnam—which included such renowned international jurists as John Dugard, Michael Mansfield, and Patricia Sellers, had already found the Islamic Republic of Iran responsible for flagrant human rights violations. Their verdict, released on February 5, 2013, declared that:

(I) The Islamic Republic of Iran has committed crimes against human-ity in the 1988–1989 periods against its own citizens in violation of applicable international laws;

(II) The Islamic Republic of Iran bears absolute responsibility for the gross violations of human rights against its citizens under the International Covenant of Civil and Political Rights; and,

---

2 *Blood-soaked secrets* (London: Amnesty International), p. 9.

(III) Customary International law holds the Islamic Republic of Iran fully accountable for its systematic and widespread commission of crimes against humanity in Iran in the 1980–1989 period.[3]

There may be those who argue that these events took place long ago and that there is little to be done today, but the fact that it has been more than thirty years since this atrocity took place is an even more compelling reason why an international solidarity movement is needed to support the demand to render the Islamic Republic of Iran accountable for past as well as ongoing acts of repression. Current governmental authorities are responsible for the continued repression of those who want answers and who want to be able to mourn and memorialize those who were subject to extermination and summarily buried in mass graves simply because they opposed the theocratic regime. As challenging as it has been to begin to tear away the cloak of secrecy, this story of flagrant repression is now clear. While the actual magnitude of the massacre still remains to be confirmed and many more specific details will continue to be revealed, voices of this massacre call out to us. We cannot remain silent.

---

3 *Prosecutor vs. The Islamic Republic of Iran: Judgment,* Article 170, p. 52.

Preface

NASSER MOHAJER

History, despite its wrenching pain,
Cannot be unlived, but if faced
With courage, need not be lived again.

MAYA ANGELOU

This book is about a massacre that occurred in the summer of 1988 inside the prisons of the Islamic Republic of Iran (IRI), as the result of a fatwa, or religious edict, issued by the Supreme Leader Ayatollah Ruhollah Khomeini. Those slaughtered, estimated to be between 4,500 and 5,000, were women and men, young and old, Muslims and Marxists who were serving their sentences, some even scheduled for release.[1] The vast majority were survivors of the waves of mass executions initiated on June 20, 1981, following the ousting of Abolhassan Banisadr, the first President of the IRI, by Islamic fundamentalists. The exact number of victims of these waves of executions between the middle of 1981 and late 1983 is not known. Estimates fluctuate between 5,000 and over 10,000.[2] However, the arbitrary mass detention of members and sympathizers of an array of political parties of the time is well established:

> [T]housands of political prisoners were held because of their non-violent political or religious beliefs or activities, or their relationship with people who had engaged in opposition to the government. Arrest, detention and legal procedures all appeared to be arbitrary. Detainees were held for long periods before being charged and when trials did take place they lacked the safeguards which would ensure a fair trial.[3]

---

1 Amnesty International Index: MDE 13/118/2008, August 19, 2008, p. 1.
2 According to the Iranian state media of the time, a considerable number of those executed were under the age of eighteen.
3 Amnesty International, Iran, Report 1983, p. 305.

The survivors of the mass executions of 1981–83, the majority of whom became victims of the 1988 massacres, were subject to ideological indoctrination in addition to undergoing harsh physical and psychological torture. Some repented, embraced Islam, and became collaborators of their jailers. Some committed suicide, or lost their sanity and never regained their mental health. Most of the detainees, however, stood fast, enduring pressure and pain without succumbing to the whims and wishes of their wardens. This resistance and perseverance were perceived by leading prison officials and state authorities as a disgraceful defeat. In fact, it was through their penitentiary system, as ordained by shari'a (Islamic law), that the IRI leaders first encountered the bitter taste of defeat. This defeat epitomized the unfeasibility of returning to the Age of the Prophet Mohammad, and crafting the ideal of Madinat al-Fadilah,[4] in a semi-developed country such as Iran. But the Islamic fundamentalists did not admit defeat; instead they opted for revenge.

This revenge, long-planned and meticulously plotted, was inflicted on non-conformist prisoners of conscience immediately after July 18, 1988, when the IRI was forced to accept UN Resolution 598, which stipulated a ceasefire in the eight-year war with Iraq. In effect, this decision, which Ayatollah Khomeini likened to "drinking from the chalice of poison," also marked the defeat of the strategy of "exporting the Islamic Revolution" to other so-called Muslim countries, a strategy regarded by the leaders of the IRI as the pre-condition for establishing their ideal Muslim community in Iran. Accepting the ceasefire and the UN Resolution also meant ending the war economy, the state of siege, and the extreme restrictions imposed on the social and cultural activities of Iranian people under the pretext of the war. It also meant abandoning the policy of self-reliance, ending the isolation of Iran from the "world of arrogance," opening the borders of the country, and re-establishing relationships with small and big "Satans." The influx into such a social environment of thousands of avowed dissidents who defied the theocratic state, even under torture, was clearly a grave peril that the IRI had to quell in advance through pre-emptive action.

The heinous crime began on July 28, 1988, and continued until late August of the same year, under total secrecy, behind closed doors and with extensive deception. The military incursion of the Iraqi-based National Liberation Army (NLA), the armed wing of the People's Mojahedin Organization of Iran (PMOI), became an excuse for the sudden lockdown of detention centers

---

4 Refers to the city of Madina, originally Yathrib, where the Prophet Mohammad instituted the first Muslim Community.

and the severance of all channels of communication of prisoners with the outside world. Soon prisoners were being retried by a board of four in inquisition tribunals. They had no comprehension of what was happening and were entirely unaware that certain types of responses regarding their faith or organizational affiliation would send them straight to the gallows. It was weeks before the other prisoners realized that their cellmates had not been relocated as they had assumed, but had in fact been executed following the verdict of the board of four. They also learned later that non-Muslim female political prisoners had been horrendously tortured to make them embrace Islam, though in vain.

The families of the victims were kept in the dark too, and were deceived into thinking that their imprisoned loved ones were alive and that visits would resume in a short while. It was two months before they heard the shocking news, when they were summoned by prison officials to formally receive the belongings of their loved ones in the waiting rooms of penitentiary facilities. The bereaved families immediately started to spread the news, and thus became the initial source for dissemination of the reality of the massacre. Through their courageous and relentless efforts, it was learned that many of the bodies of the executed communist prisoners were buried at the dead of night, in individual or mass graves in what the Shi'ite theocracy called the "Cemetery of the Damned," later informally named the Khavaran Garden by the democratic opposition. It was also due to the arduous collective action of the families that the identities of 1,345 men and women who perished during the summer of 1988 were tracked down and presented to the Special Rapporteur of the United Nations Human Rights Commission, Amnesty International, Human Rights Watch, and other concerned organizations.[5]

The disclosure in March 1989 of three letters written by Ayatollah Hossein Ali Montazeri was a watershed in the struggle to establish the reality of the massacre.[6] Two of the letters were written to "his Auspicious Presence, the grand Ayatollah Imam Khomeini," and one to members of the board of four. Besides vividly depicting the contours of the massacre and Montazeri's vehement opposition to Khomeini's fatwa, the letters also reveal that "several thousand" were executed "in a few days" by the "majority decision" of the board members.[7] These letters, which resulted in the dismissal of Ayatollah

---

5 *Bang-e Raha'i*, The Organ of the Center to Support Political Prisoners (inside Iran), nos 8 and 9, August and September 1989.
6 See Appendix A, "Theocracy Memos."
7 Ibid.

Montazeri as *Velayat-e faqih*[8] (Supreme Leader) in waiting, shattered all doubts regarding the dimensions of a national crime, though the details were still indeterminate. It was only years later, following the flight of some of the survivors of the Great Massacre, that particulars of the crime became known. Soon after escaping the IRI and taking refuge in European countries or North America, the survivors started revealing the inferno they had been through. The testimonies they provided to human rights organizations such as Amnesty International and to some parliamentary committees, the interviews they gave to expatriate Persian-language media outlets, scholars, and researchers, and the speeches they made to gatherings and in meetings of the Diaspora and others, enabled concerned individuals, artists and human rights activists to comprehend some aspects of the Great Massacre. Prison memoirs also shed light on many dark corners of this horrendous event and contributed to a better understanding of how the massacre had been carried out in different detention centers. Based on data, descriptions and narratives provided by former political prisoners, Iranian researchers, political analysts, writers, and artists in exile have produced a number of articles (mainly in Persian and English) on the massacre.[9] A few scripts, documentaries, and movies have also been made, including *Born in Evin* by Maryam Zaree, 2019, and *Morgen sind wir Frei* (Tomorrow we are Free) by Hossein Pourseifi, 2019 (both in German),[10] together with some short stories, songs, and even lyric poems and dances.[11]

---

8 See the Glossary for more information on this and other terms.

9 Two of the best studies on the subject in English are Ervand Abrahamian, "Mass Executions of 1988," in *Tortured Confessions: Prisons and Public Recantations in Modern Iran* (Berkeley, California: University of California Press, 1999), pp. 209–28, and Kaveh Shahrooz, "With Revolutionary Rage and Rancor: A Preliminary Report on the 1988 Massacre of Iran's Political Prisoners," *Harvard Human Rights Journal* 20 (2007), pp. 227–61.

10 Others include *Khavaran Documented* by anonymous (Tehran, 2005), *Madaran-e Khavaran* (Mothers of Khavaran) by Nasser Mohajer (Berkeley, 2008), *Those Who Said No* by Nima Sarvestani (Stockholm, 2014), *The Tree that Remembers* by Masoud Raouf (2002), *Budding Grief* by Pantea Bahrami (2015), *The Secret Fatwa* by Delnaz Abadi (2018), and *Sie Erinnert Sich* (She Remembers) by Parastou Forouhar and Thomas Giefer (2018).

11 Films and documentaries are particularly helpful in sowing the seeds of truth and justice in the public memory. Nonetheless, we still lack artistic works such as Joshua Oppenheimer's masterpiece *The Act of Killing* (2012), on the mass killings in Indonesia (1965–66); *Tadmor* (2016) by Monika Borgmann and Lokman Slim, on the Tadmor prison massacre in Syria (1980); and *The Silence of the Others* (2018), Almudena Carracedo and Robert Bahar's magisterial documentary—executively produced by Pedro and Agustín Almodóvar—dealing with Spain's "Pact of Forgetting" (*El Pacto del Olvido*) imposed by the state a few months after the death of Francisco Franco. Through the relentless struggle of the bereaved families and the advocacy of human rights activists, this pact was finally replaced by the 2007 Law of Historical Memory.

Observing the anniversary of the Great Massacre has become a tradition among the Iranian opposition in exile, who hold memorial events at the same time that the families and friends of the massacred gather in Khavaran Garden, or in their private residences if barred by the security forces of the IRI from assembling in the Garden. Despite all these endeavors, this episode, unprecedented in Iran's modern history and recognized as a crime against humanity by Amnesty International, the UN Commission on Human Rights, and the Parliament of Canada, among others, has received scant attention in the US, Europe, and elsewhere. A case in point was the total silence of the international mass media on the thirtieth anniversary of the Great Massacre, which was roughly contemporaneous with the Tiananmen Square Massacre. The *New York Times* editorial is telling:

> Here is an anguish and a mission shared by many people around the world scarred by great atrocities, whether survivors of the Holocaust; or relatives of the "disappeared" in Argentina; or those who carry the memories of the Soviet gulag, the Armenian genocide in Ottoman Turkey, the Khmer Rouge killing fields of Cambodia, the massacres in Rwanda or any of the other mass murders of modern times.[12]

The absence of Iran from discussions of more or less similar tragedies is one of the reasons why this project, *Voices of a Massacre*, was undertaken. The book's foreword is written by the distinguished scholar and ex-political prisoner Angela Davis. Professor Davis, who popularized the term "prison-industrial complex," has written extensively on penal systems and is at the forefront of the worldwide prison-abolitionist movement. She emphasizes that the historical record of the 1988 massacre needs to be buttressed by a collection of first-person narratives and writings to tear down the "cloak of secrecy" around this flagrant crime by the IRI.

In Chapter One, the present author provides a narrative of the massacre based on the testimonies of political prisoners and bereaved families; prison memoirs; assertions and declarations by the leaders of the IRI; available documents from the archives of entities such as the British Foreign Office,

---

12 "China cannot erase Tiananmen," *New York Times* (International), June 4, 2019. Among other mass killings and massacres of the last quarter of the twentieth century, mention should be made of the Tadmor prison massacre (1980), and the mass killings in East Timor (1970s and early 1980s), El Mozote in El Salvador (1981), Guatemala (1981–83), "Gukurahundi" in Zimbabwe (1983), "Wagalla" in Kenya (1984), and Somalia (1987–89).

Amnesty International, and UN bodies concerned with human rights; and the news outlets of the IRI and its opposition. As will be seen, these documents at times highlight the indifference of some Western governments to the early reports of the massacre, due to their desire to avoid placing into jeopardy the resumption of political and diplomatic ties with the IRI. Chapter Two then provides eyewitness accounts and testimonial narratives, by five women and four men of various political persuasions, of events that unfolded in the prisons. Chapter Three is a survey of how the massacre was carried out in cities other than Tehran, and includes the testimony of one of the survivors of Vakilabad prison in Mashhad. The next chapter is devoted to the efforts of the bereaved families to find out why and how their dear ones were executed, where they were buried, and the discovery of mass graves in the "Cemetery of the Damned." It also describes the founding of the Mothers of Khavaran movement and the struggle to thwart the destruction of the Garden of Khavaran, which is crucial evidence of a historical crime.[13] Chapter Five covers the testimonies of the sons and daughters of the executed: how they lived through and experienced the tragedy; their struggle to unearth the truth; and the steps they took against historical oblivion. An epilogue to this chapter contains three articles describing the different approaches and attitudes adopted by the bereaved families and survivors towards strategies for seeking justice against a Theocracy that is not accountable and that has striven to conceal the crime, hiding it with impunity as a state secret.

At the time of writing, no other monograph on the Great Massacre of 1988 exists. The massacre is discussed at some length in Ervand Abrahamian's *Tortured Confessions: Prisons and Public Recantations in Iran* (1999) and Geoffrey Robertson's *The Massacre of Political Prisoners in Iran, 1988: Report of an Inquiry* and in his *Mullahs Without Mercy: Human Rights and Nuclear Weapons*. The present book offers a more focused and in-depth perspective on the Great Massacre.

This volume contains contributions solicited by this editor and specifically written for this book. Three of these, the accounts of Mehrdad Neshati Melikiyans, Nasser Kh., and Mahnaz Saida, were originally oral

---

13 Such personal suffering is comparable to the plight of relatives of the mass executions of the Franco era in Spain. As the *New York Times* reported on September 24, 2019, Ascension Mendieta, who lost her father to Franco's killing squads at the age of thirteen, devoted the following eight decades of her life to tracking down his remains and ultimately fulfilled her desire to be buried alongside him.

interviews conducted by the editor and subsequently rearranged as testimonial narratives.

The approach used throughout this book is that of presenting a contextual perspective through historical chronicle, political analysis, and legal review. It is inspired by the work of several scholars on the role of narrative in furthering historical and personal memory. As noted by Paul Ricœur:

People do not remember in isolation, but only with help from the memories of others... and they preserve their own memories with help from commemorations and other public celebrations of striking events in the history of their group.[14]

Ricœur further focuses on the role of the historian in this regard:

Speaking about memory necessarily means speaking about forgetting, because one cannot remember everything. A memory with no gaps would be an unbearable burden; it is a cliché to say that memory is selective. Narrative structure, which memory and history have in common, confirms this law of the necessity of forgetting. A narrative always consists of only a limited number of events, selected in the operation of narrative composition. The methods of academic history merely raise this necessary selectivity to the level of a strategy for, respectively, understanding and explanation.[15]

The present project also draws on the concept of "living testimony," as espoused by the prominent filmmaker Steven Spielberg, which gives voice to victims of modern genocides. The University of Southern California's Shoah Foundation, which he founded, has in recent years gone beyond its original remit of the Holocaust to record material on other mass killings in recent world history. Here too, unlike the foundation's other efforts and findings, the Great Massacre of 1988 in Iran is not documented through currently available audiovisual sources. Anyone wishing to engage on such a project would have to produce a careful narrative combining the testimonies of affected and bereaved families, news and reports from the opposition journals, leaks of information from within the IRI elite, and

---

14 Paul Ricœur, "Memory, forgetfulness, and History," in Jörn Rüsen (ed.), *Meaning and Representation in History* (Berghahn Books: New York/Oxford 2009[2006]), p. 11.
15 Ibid., p. 16.

material deriving from international organizations and Western government archives.[16]

The biggest challenge, however, is the IRI authorities' resolve in concealing the truth about this state secret and the truth of the massacre. Unlike the previous round of mass killings, in 1981–83, during which lists of those executed were regularly published in daily newspapers and during evening news bulletins, the 1988 Great Massacre have been systematically denied by nearly all factions and personalities of the post-Khomeini era. The publication of Ayatollah Hossein Ali Montazeri's memoirs on the Internet in 2000 pierced the state *omertà* in this regard. Montazeri's continued high standing within the Iranian polity and society following his estrangement from the IRI meant that his explicit description of Khomeini's involvement in the massacre was read closely by a broad stratum of Iranian society, which had become interested in politics again following the emergence on the scene of Hojat al-Islam Mohammad Khatami in 1997. Sixteen years later, Ayatollah Montazeri's son Hojat al-Islam Ahmad Montazeri made use of the Internet again to publish the only substantial non-print source to date, a long audio recording of his late father's dialogue with members of the board during the massacre. Ayatollah Montazeri is heard stating that the IRI would be forever tainted by the ongoing crime.

The publication of the audio prompted a coordinated reaction within the IRI establishment. A week after Ahmad Montazeri's initiative, the head of the judiciary, Hojat al-Islam Sadeq Larijani, urged the rest of the political elite to "come to the scene and shatter these devilish whispers."[17] He also stated at that time that the *Monafeqin*—the term widely used within the IRI nomenklatura to describe the PMOI—of the 1980s were "worse" than the Daesh/ISIL of the present, and declared that the IRI should not permit a "distortion of history" by allowing the "disasters caused by the *Monafeqin*" to be forgotten.[18] The IRI elite closed ranks around Larijani and vehemently supported his directive.

Despite this, the state-imposed taboo on discussing the 1988 Great Massacre has progressively weakened in recent years. During the presidential

---

16 In the latter case, some material has been released only very recently, such as the British Foreign Office's dossiers on Human Rights in Iran in 1988, which shed considerable light on the attitude of British diplomats towards the emerging news of the massacre.
17 Sadeq Larijani, remarks on August 16, 2017, as reported on www.farsnews.com/printable.php?nn=13950525000961.
18 Ibid.

campaign in the spring of 2017, President Hassan Rouhani made thinly veiled references to the role of his main opponent, Hojat al-Islam Ebrahim Raisi, as a board member during the crackdown. Many Rouhani supporters framed participation in the contest as a choice between "reformism" and someone with the blood of thousands of political prisoners on his hands. Hojat al-Islam Mostafa Pourmohammadi, a key member of the board of four, had gone on to hold high public office in the decades following the massacre, serving as interior minister to Mahmoud Ahmadinejad and justice minister to Hassan Rouhani. On July 25, 2019, he presented a mendacious account of the rationale behind the killings of the *Monafeqin* and his role in the purge, but finally accepted and recognized that such a historical event had indeed occurred. This caused an uproar among human rights activists. For example, Amnesty International stated:

> Recent statements by Mostafa Pourmohammadi, advisor to Iran's head of the judiciary... defending the mass extrajudicial executions of 1988 provide shocking confirmation of the authorities' willful flouting of international human rights law both at the time and now a stark reminder of the sense of impunity that senior officials linked to the killings enjoy.[19]

Unlike Pourmohammadi, Ebrahim Raisi, currently the head of Iran's judiciary, has never talked about his role in the killings. The increasing perception, among observers of Iranian politics both inside the country and abroad, is that he is one of the leading contenders to succeed Ali Khamenei as Supreme Leader. His celebration as an equitable judge by prominent personalities such as Foreign Minister Mohammad Javad Zarif confirms that the IRI continues to pretend and portray the massacre as a pre-emptive act of "self-defense" against the "challenge" posed by the thousands of political prisoners who, in the summer of 1988, refused to defer to its authority despite having suffered years of infernal existence in Iranian prisons.

Pourmohammadi's remarks came in the midst of a concerted effort within various spheres of the IRI to construct a detailed counter-narrative, framing the massacre as part of an ongoing confrontation with the opposition throughout the 1980s. This effort included the creation of award-winning cinematic films such as *Majara-ye Nimruz*, or "Midday Affair," which was

---

19 Amnesty International Public Statement, July 30, 2019.

steered by the Islamic Revolutionary Guards Corps (IRGC), who acted as consultants in providing an account of the hunting down and annihilation of that segment of the PMOI leadership which was based inside Iran at the end of 1981. The counter-narrative also included the publication of extensive "histories" of radical organizations such as the People's Feda'ian and PMOI, which were in significant part sourced from prison interrogations conducted under duress in both the pre- and post-revolutionary eras. As such, the IRI has sought to turn the tables by claiming that the opposition was the instigator of political violence during the 1980s and to seize control of the narrative concerning this dark age of contemporary Iranian history.

Over time, the narratives of members of the IRI intelligence community have converged on a number of points. The remarks made by the long-serving intelligence minister Hojat al-Islam Ali Fallahian in July 2017 contained a scenario that had in part been previously alluded to by Hojat al-Islam Larijani and later reiterated by Hojat al-Islam Pourmohammadi. This scenario had three main components: first, reduction of all political prisoners of different persuasions to the ranks of the PMOI, as if there were no communists or partisans of other political trends and tendencies in jail. Second, that the PMOI were worse and more dangerous than Daesh/ISIL and that they were "nothing more than criminals and terrorists."[20] And third, that the Mojahed prisoners were planning a riot, with an insurrection to follow in coordination with the PMOI forces that were to invade Iran with the support of the Iraqi military.[21] This scenario received the tacit endorsement of the Supreme Leader Khamenei, who asserted on one occasion that those who pass judgment on the 1980s have to exercise vigilance so that "martyrs and executioners do not change places."[22]

The main task of this volume is not, however, to expose lies or uncover secrets. It seeks instead to embody what Primo Levi defines as the "Duty of Memory,"[23] the objective being to gain insight into the historical reality and portray the subtle details of the "policy of cruelty" implemented by the IRI throughout the 1980s. In the words of Lynn Novick, co-director with Ken Burns of the mesmerizing ten-part documentary on the Vietnam War:

---

20 *Mosalas* (weekly), July 25, 2019.
21 www.mashreghnews.ir, July 19, 2017.
22 http://www.iran-newspaper.com/?nid=6512&type=0.
23 Primo Levi, *The Drowned and the Saved* (Summit Books, 1988), p. 53.

It is a shortcoming and self-humiliating to constantly say that they have lied; there is no doubt that they have lied. But what we really want to do is to show what has happened.[24]

Therefore, it is imperative that we prevent the massacre from being consigned to oblivion. With history erased and this crime against humanity obscured from the gaze of current and future generations, what was "perpetrated yesterday could be attempted again tomorrow."[25]

---

24 *New York Times* (International) September 15, 2017.
25 Primo Levi, *The Drowned and the Saved*, p. 53.

Chapter One

IN HINDSIGHT

The Great Massacre

NASSER MOHAJER

Although thirty years have elapsed since Ayatollah Khomeini ordered the purge of political prisoners throughout Iran, the Great Massacre of 1988 is still an open file. All past and present leaders of the Islamic Republic of Iran (IRI) have maintained a policy of silence about this crime, and any reference to this atrocity is considered a political taboo by the Islamists in power. Yet, because of the surviving political prisoners, who fled Iran and landed in Western Europe and North America in the 1990s, as well as their families who stayed in Iran and fought to unearth the facts of this heinous crime, we now know that following Ayatollah Khomeini's fatwas of 1988, all political prisoners were re-interrogated and retried in inquisition-like tribunals. Thereafter, thousands were taken blindfolded to the gallows and thousands flogged, day after day, to submit and succumb.

"Cleansing" of the incarcerated was carried out in total secrecy. Not only were the detainees kept in the dark about the task of the commission that re-interrogated them, and the process of re-interrogation, but the authorities also refrained from revealing the burial sites of the executed, and forbade their families from holding public memorial services. Hence, many aspects of this massacre are still obscure. We still do not know the exact number of men and women killed during that bloody summer. We still do not know where they were buried. We still do not know why the IRI decided to undertake such a "cleansing" measure. And we still do not know the names of all the officials involved in the preparation and implementation of the deadly fatwa.

Accurate answers to these questions may never come to light as long as the IRI is in power. Yet, personal narratives of ex-political prisoners who survived the Great Massacre make it possible to reconstruct the events as they unfolded in summer 1988 in Tehran's two notorious prisons, Evin and Gohardasht. The political context and the chain of events at the time help us understand and allow us to draw rational conclusions about some of the underlying motives behind this crime, unprecedented in modern Iranian history.

THE PRETEXT

On July 18, 1988, it was reported that Hojat al-Islam Ali Khamenei, then President of the IRI, had notified Javier Peréz de Cuéllar,[1] secretary-general of the United Nations, of Iran's acceptance of UN Security Council resolution 598 and the truce with Iraq. The news astounded political observers, as the IRI had resisted all international mediations throughout the eight-year war with Iraq, insisting on continuing the Jihad (holy war) until the overthrow of the "infidel Ba'athist regime of Saddam Hossein" and conquering of the city of Karbala as the springboard to "liberate Jerusalem from the occupying Zionist regime." The surprising news was confirmed when Ayatollah Khomeini publicly endorsed the assertions of Ali Khamenei:

> ... on accepting the Resolution which, in fact, has been quite a bitter and unpleasant problem for all, me in particular..., due to certain events and factors, which I refrain from mentioning at this moment, I have given my approval to the Resolution and ceasefire... Making this decision was more deadly than taking poison. I submitted myself to God's will and drank this chalice of poison.[2]

This was on July 20. On July 25, the People's Mojahedin Organization of Iran (PMOI) dispatched its Iraqi-based armed forces to the western border of Iran. The PMOI's National Liberation Army (NLA) crossed the borders to deal the "final blow" to the "Reactionary Islamic Regime."[3] As part of an overall strategy named *Forough-e Javidan* (Eternal Light) Operation, the PMOI called on the people of Iran to "rise up."[4] Yet, neither in Tehran nor anywhere else in Iran did people heed the Mojahedin's call to take to the streets! Ignored by the masses and cornered in the western zone of Iran, they were quickly and

---

1 Javier Pérez de Cuéllar (b. 1920). Peruvian diplomat. Served as the UN secretary-general from 1982 to 1991. Prime Minister of Peru from November 2000 to July 2001.
2 *Resalat* (newspaper), Tir 30, 1367 (July 21, 1988).
3 PMOI, *Newsletter*, 3, The *Forough-e Javidan*.
4 PMOI, *Newsletter*, 4, The Great *Forough-e Javidan* Operation.

brutally crushed in Karand[5] and Eslamabad[6] by the combined forces of the *Pasdaran* (Revolutionary Guards), the *Basij* (the Islamic militia), and other irregular armed bands and vigilantes. Some 1,263 NLA militants were killed[7] in what the regime called the Mersad Operation.[8] Dozens of Mojahedin were captured and immediately executed on the spot and many dispatched to Evin and Gohardasht prisons.[9]

With the suppression of this three-day operation came vengeance.[10] The social base of the IRI in general, and the Iranian Hezbollah (Party of God) in particular, deeply upset about the outcome of the war and heartily despising the *Monafeqin* (hypocrites), flamed the anti-PMOI fever into frenzy, roaming the streets of big cities, calling for the execution and annihilation of the "Mojahedin breed," and taking the law into their own hands. They even arrested ex-Mojahedin, who had been imprisoned, served their sentences, and stopped political activism once released.[11] The prevailing mindset of the supporters of the regime is described in the three instances given below.

First, a Tehran daily reflecting the views of the "hardliners" of the Islamic fundamentalist state wrote: "We request that his Great Holy leader confront the criminals vigorously and get rid of them at once and forever."[12] Second, during the Friday prayer of Tehran on August 16, Chief Justice Ayatollah Mousavi Ardebili claimed:

> ... they don't know that people consider them inferior to animals. People are totally against them. There is immense public pressure on the judiciary as to why they are not executed. A number of them are in prison... people say that every single one of them must be executed.

5 Karand: A small Kurdish city in the province of Kermanshah that fell into the hands of the Mojahedin in their 1989 military excursion into Iran from Iraq.
6 Eslamabad-e Gharb, originally Harounabad, is a Kurdish city of 89,000 inhabitants in Kermanshah Province. Eslamabad was conquered by the Mojahedin forces in July 1988.
7 The Final Report of the NLA Headquarter, *Monthly Showra Newsletter*, 43–44, Shahrivar 18, 1364 (September 9, 1988).
8 A name given by the IRI to the military operation to crush the Mojahedin.
9 *Islamic Republic Newspaper*, Mordad 12, 1367 (August 3, 1988). See also the report produced by the UN's Social and Economic Council on the human rights condition in the Islamic Republic, October 13, 1988.
10 "Why the IRI Succumbed to Ceasefire and the Outlook of Peace Negotiations." *Aghazi-No*, Shahrivar 1367 (August 1988).
11 Declaration submitted to the 45th meeting of the UNHCR by Amnesty International, January 1989. See also the report produced by the United Nations Social and Economic Council on the human rights condition in the Islamic Republic, October 13, 1988.
12 *Resalat*, Mordad 12, 1367 (August 3, 1988).

On the one hand, the judge has to deal with a number of problems...
On the other hand, there is the pressure of public opinion. Most of
all, I should thank these wretched beings who have made our task
easy. We put dozens of them on trial. Files are brought in and taken
out. I regret that only one fifth of them are dead. I wish they would all
be wiped out so that this problem would be solved once and for all.[13]

Third is this quotation from a petition signed by "thousands of people from
Arak" (an ancient city 260 kilometers south of Tehran):

We ask the people in charge of the judiciary to punish these heartless
Monafeqin to the highest degree; to punish those who have taken refuge
abroad and are involved in espionage activities against the system in
Iran and are shamelessly attacking Iran's militarily, spilling the blood
of the children of this nation and were captured in the recent Mersad
Operation to be brought to justice and not to tolerate or forgive.[14]

As disingenuously as the procession organized and staged by the grey eminences of the Islamic theocracy, vengeance was on the move and genocidal
mania escalated, with imprisoned Mojahedin throughout detention centers in
Iran summoned to the inquisition tribunals and hundreds sent to the gallows.

THE BACKGROUND

We now know that Ayatollah Montazeri was behind the 1984 prison reforms,
the pinnacle of which was the dismissal of Assadollah Lajevardi,[15] the chief
prosecutor of Tehran, known as the "Butcher of Evin." However, forbearance
or abstention from indoctrinating prisoners of conscience was not condoned
by the principal authorities of the IRI. By mid-1986, the rift between Ayatollah

---

13 *Resalat*, Mordad 15, 1367 (August 6, 1988).
14 Ibid.
15 Assadollah Lajevardi (1935–98), a former lingerie peddler who joined the Islamic
Coalition Party and took part in the assassination of Prime Minister Hassan Ali Mansour
in 1966. After serving 18 months in prison, he returned to political–religious activity and
was arrested again for attempting to blow up the Tehran office of El-Al, the Israeli airline.
After the February Revolution of 1979, he was named the chief prosecutor of Tehran and
in 1981 the warden of Evin prison. Discharged in 1984, he was appointed as the head
of the Organization of Iran's Prisons in 1989 and held that position till February 1998.
Lajevardi was assassinated by two members of the PMOI in Tehran Bazaar on August 23,
1998, on the tenth anniversary of the Great Massacre.

Montazeri and Ayatollah Khomeini became insurmountable. The schism, though, at that time was invisible to many except the higher echelons of the politico-religious establishment. It became visible only after Ayatollah Montazeri was removed from the position of Khomeini's "heir apparent." Two years prior to the massacre of the political prisoners, Ayatollah Khomeini had written to Ayatollah Montazeri:

> I request that you consult the pious men who know about the country's affairs. Then put that into effect so as to not, God forbid, harm your reputation, which would harm the reputation of the Islamic Republic. The irregular release of some hundreds of *Monafeqin* was granted by the order of a committee, whose sympathy [toward *Monafeqin*] and good intentions have led to an increase in the number of explosions, terrors, and thefts.[16]

In the turbulent and troubled days following the military excursion of the Mojahedin, the same point was raised by Assadollah Lajevardi:

> Unfortunately, the manner in which the *Monafeqin* have been dealt with during the past years has been against the interests of Islam. According to the information at hand, most of the people who were set free from prison in the name of *tavab* [repentant] rejoined the *Monafeqin* and a number of them perished in the Mersad Operation. From 1981 until the end of 1984, when the *Monafeqin* were harshly dealt with, they couldn't even attract ten people to their organization, but then after the *Monafeqin* were treated with slackness and leniency, and their members were set free as repentant. Because of this release [of prisoners], we are witnessing the attacks on Eslamabad and Karand... Who is really responsible for shedding the blood of the innocent Basijis [the Islamic militia] who were martyred by the *Monafeqin* and now landed in heaven?[17]

The authority Assadollah Lajevardi is alluding to as "responsible for shedding the blood" of the murderous forces of the IRI is Ayatollah Hossein Ali

---

16 Letter of Ayatollah Khomeini to Ayatollah Montazeri. *Political Memoirs of Mohammad Reyshahri* (Tehran: Institute of Political Studies and Research, 1990), 3rd edition, p. 46.
17 *Islamic Republic Newspaper*, "People's Views on the Recent Crimes of the *Monafeqin*," Part 2, Mordad 15, 1367 (August 6, 1988).

Montazeri, who was publicly disgraced, deemed *persona non grata*,[18] and stripped of all political power awhile before Lajevardi was reinstalled as head of Iran's prisons in the winter of 1998. The pejorative term *Monafeqin* was again utilized for dissidents, thereby adding fuel to the fire. The leadership of the IRI was well aware that the employment of this derogatory term made it easier to justify repression. The documents at hand leave no doubt that the ruling cabal had long considered the extermination of steadfast opponents as the order of the day, if they were forced to accept the ceasefire with the Iraqi regime. They were aware that some rules and regulations would have to be relaxed, and a range of social, political, cultural, and even foreign policies would inevitably have to be modified or altered in the post-war period.[19] Evidence also reveals that the plan included assassination of both the *"Monafeq"* and *"non-Monafeq"* dissidents inside and outside of the country.[20]

Thanks to the efforts of the political prisoners who lived through the nightmare of the Great Massacre, we are now able to construct the chronicle of one the most dreadful crimes of the last quarter of the twentieth century.

THE SCHEMA

It seems to me that it was in the winter of 1987 that the regime finally made its decision... between November and December 1987, all the prisoners were re-interrogated, one by one: 'Do you still believe in your organization? Do you accept the legitimacy of the Islamic Republic? Do you say your prayers?' According to the answers given, the prisoners were divided into different groups. The changes continued with the transfer of prisoners. In the fall of 1987, all the prisoners with life sentences were moved from Gohardasht to Evin prison; they would be kept in separate wards as well...[21]

---

18 *Keyhan Newspaper*, "Ayatollah Montazeri's Speech in the Gathering of Qom Theology Students and Clergies," Tir 8, 1367 (June 29, 1988).
19 "Ja-ye an ast ke khoon mouj zanad dar del-e lal" (On the Massacre of Political Prisoners), *Aghazi-No*, Azar 1367 (November 1988). See also N. Mohajer and V. Tabrizi, *Aghazi-No Bulletin, special issue on Salman Rushdie*, Spring 1993.
20 See also Showra, *Revue Mensuelle du Conseil National de la Résistance d'Iran*, p. 47, April/May 1989.
21 Saiid Homayoun, "And a River of Blood Flows Off the Masses," *Ettehad-e Kar*, 23, Shahrivar 1370 (August 1991).

Sometime later:

> They separated all the Mojahedin from the leftist prisoners. In fact,
> they divided the prison into two areas. The first area, which included
> wards 1 and 2, was exclusively for the Mojahedin. The far end of the
> prison, which included the wards connected to the auditorium, was
> the second area and exclusively for the leftist prisoners. In order to
> confuse the prisoners about the layout and the organization of the
> wards, they changed the numbering of the wards as well. For instance,
> they numbered the section of the Mojahedin and the left-leaning pris-
> oners differently, splitting each into two main groups and separating
> the prisoners according to the length of their sentences. Prisoners who
> were sentenced to less than 10 years, were placed in special wards.
> Prisoners sentenced from 10 to 15 years were all put into one ward...
> while prisoners with sentences of 15 years to life, were all taken to Evin.
> In addition, those who had accepted to take part in staged interviews
> and make "confessions" were placed in Ward 14. Concurrently, all the
> "*Mellikesh*"[22] prisoners were transferred to Gohardasht prison and
> were housed in Ward 10.[23]

And yet later:

> A few days before the announcement of accepting UN [Security
> Council] resolution 598 and Khomeini's speech in which he likened the
> acceptance of ceasefire with Iraq to drinking from a chalice of poison,
> I was walked to a section of the prison clinic which was exclusively
> for the sick prisoners in solitary confinement. There, I saw lots of
> bags stacked on top of each other. On one of the bags, I saw Hossein
> Qalambor's name and concluded that probably he and some others...
> had been transferred from general Ward 316 to solitary confinement.
> This all happened at the same time that the daily 45-minute sessions
> of fresh air were eliminated. The situation had become very bizarre.[24]

22 Prisoners who had served their sentences and were still incarcerated because they
refused to participate in staged interviews or make a pledge to support the Islamic
Republic of Iran.
23 Nima Parvaresh, *What Happened to Us in 1988*? (Paris: The Ad-Hoc Committee, on
the anniversary of the massacre of the political prisoners in Iran, 1995), pp. 2–3.
24 "Bitter Feelings and Awakened Conscience," *Kar* OIPF (Majority), 44, Mehr 8, 1371
(September 1992).

IMAM'S VERDICT

Indeed, it was a bizarre situation, and Ayatollah Khomeini took the utmost advantage of it by putting his plan into action. In response to Ayatollah Montazeri, he proclaimed:

> As the treacherous *Monafeqin* do not believe in Islam; as whatever they say is stemmed from their deception and hypocrisy; as they have become apostates of Islam, according to the claims of their leaders; as they wage war on God and are engaging in classical warfare in the western, northern, and southern parts of the country with the collaboration of the Ba'athist Party of Iraq, and also spying for Saddam [Hossein] against our Muslim nation; as they are tied to the World Arrogance[25] and have inflicted foul blows to the Islamic Republic since its inception, it follows that those prisoners throughout that country who remain steadfast in their position of *nifaq* [dissension] are considered to be *muharib* [waging war on God] and are condemned to death.[26]

This verdict was not made public and was never mentioned by anyone in the politico-religious establishment, except for Ayatollah Montazeri. The latter saw the massacre of political prisoners as not in the long-term "interest of Islam, the revolution, or the country, nor beneficial for the prestige of the *Velayet-e faqih* [Guardianship of the Islamic Jurist] or the Islamic Republic."[27] Thus, during that very bloody July, to "absolve" himself from religious duty, Ayatollah Montazeri wrote two private letters to "Imam Khomeini" and one to a religious judge, Hojat al-Islam Hossein Ali Nayyeri. The letters surfaced months later, after the carnage:

> About your Excellency's order to execute the existing *Monafeqin* in the prisons: the execution of the arrested in the recent event has been accepted by the society and the people. There doesn't seem to be any negative effects. However, execution of the existing prisoners

---

25 Euphemism for "American imperialism" in the lexicon of the Islamic Republic of Iran.
26 Ayatollah Hossein Ali Montazeri, *Matn-e Kamel-e Khaterat-e Ayatollah Montazeri, be hamrah-e Peyvastha* [Memoirs of Ayatollah Montazeri; full text, with attachments], (Union of Iranian Editors in Europe, 2nd edition, January 2001, Appendix 153), p. 520.
27 See Appendix A, "Theocracy Memos," letter from Montazeri to Nayyeri and the "Death Commission."

(those who are serving or have completed their sentences) in the present situation, to begin with, will be perceived as hatred and vengeance...[28]

It was also through these letters that we first learned that Ayatollah Khomeini had appointed Hojat al-Islam Ali Nayyeri as the shari'a judge for the Inquisition Tribunals and asked him to immediately examine the cases of the "counter-revolutionaries" in order to determine who should be executed. Yet again, it was through these letters that we came to know the identities of the other members of these kangaroo courts: Morteza Eshraghi, Tehran's prosecutor; Ebrahim Raisi, deputy prosecutor; and Mostafa Pourmohammadi, who was then the Intelligence Ministry representative in Evin prison.[29] We also learned through these letters that the verdict could not be based solely on the decision of the judge, the prosecutor, or the Minister of Information; the majority's approval was required.[30]

Much later, when the prisoners' contact with the outside world was resumed, we found out many details of those inquisitorial courts and realized how the executions were being ordered. For instance:

> In determining who should be executed, not only the interrogators, the wardens and their deputies, but also the prosecutors voiced their opinion. Even the *Pasdars* [Revolutionary Guards] were influential in deciding whose life would have to be taken and whose would be spared.[31]

As to the legal proceedings, it was clear from the onset that even those who had served their sentences and were about to be released—whether Mojahed or Marxist—would have to appear before the Tribunal and might be condemned to death. This point is addressed in Montazeri's letter to Nayyeri, the shari'a judge: "Furthermore, the execution of those without recent activities is to question all judges and their past judgments. On what grounds do you execute someone who had not been sentenced to death (before)...?"[32]

---

28 Ibid., Montazeri's first letter to Khomeini.
29 Ibid., Montazeri's letter to Nayyeri.
30 Ibid., Montazeri's first letter to Khomeini.
31 "Among Those Bloody Days," *Kar* OIPF (Majority), 274, Shahrivar 20, 1368 (September 11, 1989); and Saiid Homayoun, "And a River of Blood Flows Off the Masses," *Ettehad-e Kar*, 23, Shahrivar 1370 (August 1991).
32 See Appendix A, "Theocracy Memos," letter from Montazeri to Nayyeri.

THE EXECUTIONS

There were certainly some criteria for executions of political prisoners. It seemed that any male prisoner who remained steadfast in his opposition to the IRI and was not willing to bow to pressure met the criterion to be executed. In the case of women, they decided to take the lives of the Mojahedin women and to break the spirit of the "apostate" Marxist women. They established the same rules and regulations for both male and female inmates in Evin and Gohardasht prisons.

On July 27, they took all the television sets out of the wards and stopped the prisoners' access to newspapers and to fresh air (*havakhori*).[33] They also suspended the prisoners' family visits until "further notice." They even prohibited sick prisoners from going to the infirmary.[34]

On July 28, 1988, the Tribunals went to work. They started with Mojahedin, men and women. They took them out of their cells blindfolded, lined them up in the hallways, and took them one by one into a room that was to become the interrogation chamber and the headquarters of Nayyeri, Eshraghi, Raisi, and Pourmohammadi. Then, they began their inquest: "Do you still believe in the *Monafeqin*? Are you willing to give a public interview in the presence of other prisoners and condemn the organization you are affiliated with?" And the interrogations did not stop there.

In his second letter to Ayatollah Khomeini, Ayatollah Montazeri cites some examples of these interrogations:

> Three days ago, a shari'a judge from one of the provinces was saying—the intelligence chief or the prosecutor, I can't recall which one—was trying to ascertain if a prisoner was still holding fast to his beliefs. He asked the prisoner if he was prepared to condemn the *Monafeqin*. The prisoner said: "Yes." He asked him: "Are you willing to give an interview?" The answer was "Yes." He then asked: "Are you willing to go to the front to fight in the war with Iraq?" The answer was "Yes." "Are you willing to walk over landmines?" The prisoner said: "Are you implying that all those who are willing to go to war are ready to

---

33 A prison idiom referring to allowing the prisoners to spend thirty minutes to an hour a day in open air in the prison yard.

34 Nima Parvaresh, *What Happened to Us in 1988?*, pp. 18–19. See also *Haghighat-e Sadeh* (Simple Truth), Independent and Democratic Organization of Women in Hannover, Germany, 1995, vol. 3, pp. 125–6; and Azar Nasim, "No Death Have I Feared," *Noghteh*, 6, Summer 1375 (July 1996), pp. 55–74.

walk over landmines?" The interrogator concluded: "So it is obvious that you are still holding on to your political beliefs and are steadfast in your positions..."[35]

Execution was undoubtedly the punishment for the prisoners who were steadfast in their opposition to the IRI. However, before the execution, they were allowed to write their last testaments:

> In the afternoon, one of the guys who had been checking the ward in front of ours realized that someone was tapping a message by Morse code through the window of one of the cells... it was a brief and clear message: "In the unjust court, the amnesty commission of the regime has convicted me to death, and I will be executed in a few minutes. They've brought me here to write my last testament..."[36]

Ironically, the executions began with the Mojahedin women: "They executed all Mojahedin women, except for one who was in solitary confinement..."[37] The massacre began in Evin on July 28 and in Gohardasht on July 30. It went on until August 15, with short interruptions. It recommenced in Evin on August 28. The members of the "Death Commission," who had posed as an "Amnesty Commission," now turned their attention toward the leftist prisoners:

> The communist prisoners, who were in separate cells, were unaware of the massacre of Mojahedin... The inmates of Ward 7 in Gohardasht had seen Davoud Lashkari through the fence carrying a load of thick rope to the surrounding areas inside the prison compound. On another day, the inmates of Ward 8 had seen a stack of slippers, and on the following day, they saw a truck covered by tarpaulin with a few Revolutionary Guards on top of the truck securing the ropes. It looked as if there was a cargo of meat under the tarp... One day, the inmates of Ward 6 saw through the fence a number of prisoners queuing to use the outdoor toilets. Five Revolutionary Guards and Davoud Lashkari, the man in charge of executions in Gohardasht prison, surrounded them in a

---

35 See Appendix A, "Theocracy Memos," second letter from Montazeri to Khomeini.
36 Iraj Mesdaghi, "The Epic of Resistance in Khomeini's Torture Chambers," *Iran-Zamin Weekly*, 101, Tir 14, 1375 (July 14, 1996).
37 Mesdaghi, *Iran-Zamin Weekly*, 101.

strange manner. Through the fence, the blindfolded faces of the inmates could be discerned. They were waiting in line with pale and gloomy faces. There was a murmur in Ward 6, "They are the ones sentenced to death!" Only the inmates of Ward 20, because of where their cell was situated, had clearly seen through their bathroom fences that the Revolutionary Guards were carrying the dead bodies of the executed to the trucks parked in the prison yard.[38]

The time had come for the prisoners affiliated with an array of left-wing organizations to be "eradicated." On August 28, they called several names and told the prisoners to put on their blindfolds, get out of the ward, and line up in the hallway:

> They took the guys, one by one, into one of the side rooms connected to the ward in front of ours. Sitting there was Davoud Lashkari along with a few Revolutionary Guards interrogating the prisoners. Those who asserted that they were not Muslims and that they didn't say their prayers were seated on the left side of the hallway, and the ones stating they were Muslims were seated on the right side of the hallway. Those on the right side of the hallway who refused to pray were taken to solitary confinement to be beaten with cables until they acquiesced. At each praying time—morning, noon, and night—they received twenty lashes. Those inmates who agreed to pray were taken to Ward 8. The ones seated on the left side of the hallway were taken in groups to the first floor (the administrative section of the Gohardasht prison). There, in a room, the same interrogations were repeated in front of Eshraghi...[39]

More questions were asked, such as "Do you still believe in your organization? Will you agree to a public interview? Will you cooperate with us and give us information?" At this point, if any of the inmates' responses was still negative, they would be seated on the left side of the entrance-way and later would be sent in groups to the slaughterhouse. No matter to which leftist group, organization, or party they belonged—Peykar, Razmandegan, Sarbedaran, Ranjbaran, Kumeleh, Sahand, Sazman-e Vahdat-e

---

38 *Rah-e Kargar*, Editorial, Second Period, 29, Mordad–Shahrivar 1374 (July–August 1995).
39 Nima Parvaresh, *What Happened to Us in 1988?*, pp. 17–18.

Komunisti, Feda'ian (Minority), Rah-e Kargar, Feda'ian (Majority) or the Tudeh Party—

> they were taken to the *Hosseiniyeh* [place of worship] to be hanged. Some were crying and some cursing... Some smiled and hopelessly waited for the last seconds of their lives. Some of the guards were competing with one another to perform the executions in hope of a greater oblation. A smaller group of guards were restless and traumatized from seeing so many corpses. Some of the inmates fought back and attacked their captors but were beaten fiercely. The executions were conducted very quickly.[40]

The slaughterhouse in Gohardasht was the auditorium, while in Evin it was the parking lot of the prosecutor's office. The condemned were hanged in both prisons.[41] Once the Mojahedin women were dealt with, it was the leftists' turn in Evin. It was early September:

> They summoned a number of [female] inmates from each room—this time all leftists—to go for interrogation. Then the prison authorities came for the prisoners' bags and belongings. Three individuals were removed from our room. They took a number of inmates from every room... Two or three weeks had passed before the first group of leftists returned. Up until that time, we had no clue as to what was happening to them. They were... placed in the adjacent room. For the first time, we learned from this group about the Death Commission (via Morse code, of course). They explained that a special commission... had come to prisons. In addition to being asked to identify themselves and explain their charges, they had been asked whether they prayed or considered themselves Muslims. If the inmates responded with a "No" or refused to answer the questions altogether, the Death Commission concluded that they were *Murtads* (apostates) and issued the punishment accordingly... Five sets of lashes within twenty-four hours, corresponding to five daily prayer sessions... Next, they informed us that most of them had endured fourteen days of lashing before they broke down...[42]

---

40 Hormoz Mottaghi, "Life After 1988," *Noghteh*, 6, Summer 1375 (July 1996).
41 Conclusion based on common features of many reports.
42 Shokoufeh Sakhi, *Speaking for the Dead: Survivor Accounts of Iran's 1988 Massacre* (New Haven, Connecticut: Iran Human Rights Documentation Center, 2009), pp. 32–3.

A few of the female leftists in Evin had gone on hunger strike, and one committed suicide. No one died under torture and only one leftist woman was executed: Fatemeh Modaresi (Fardin), a member of the Tudeh Party. However, not even one Mojahed woman came back from the sanatorium's solitary confinement cells.[43]

Ultimately, we found out that they had executed almost all female Mojahedin prisoners who were *Mellikesh*. With the exception of three or four, all intransigent female Mojahedin were killed.[44]

It was only after the resumption of prison visitations that the depth of the tragedy became known to the prisoners.

DEATH TOLL

All the wards in all detention centers went through the same "housecleaning." According to numerous accounts, only two Death Row inmates in Evin outlived this inferno and did not perish in the Great Massacre. Out of 1,100 prisoners in Gohardasht, only some 200 survived.[45] More or less, the same scenario played out in other major cities of Iran: Kermanshah, Shiraz, Isfahan, and so forth. It is almost impossible to furnish an accurate number of men and women who lost their lives in that carnage, due to the IRI authorities' total silence on, and obstruction of, any investigation into this crime. The lack of accurate figures is the reason why some independent researchers, like Ervand Abrahamian, only speak about "thousands who were executed in that 'calculated planning'."[46] In spite of this fact, some survivors of the Great Massacre, as well as Amnesty International, have calculated that between four and five thousand men and women were killed during that bloody summer.

It is important to note that in September 1989, exactly a year after the Great Massacre, a grassroots association in Iran, blossoming out of the struggle of the bereaved families during the bloody summer and fall of 1989, disclosed a list of 1,345 victims of the "national catastrophe of 1988." The association acknowledged that they had not yet acquired the names of

---

43 Shokoufeh Sakhi, "The Taste of Mortadella" (this volume).
44 Sakhi, "The Taste of Mortadella."
45 Saiid Homayoun, "And a River of Blood Flows Off the Masses," *Ettehad-e Kar*, 23, Shahrivar 1370 (August 1991).
46 "Punishment by Death in Iran," Amnesty International, January 1989; Ervand Abrahamian, *Tortured Confessions: Prisons and Public Recantations in Modern Iran* (Berkeley, California: University of California Press, 1999), p. 218.

many of the "people's martyrs slain in cold blood."[47] Soon after this list was published, one of the Iranian opposition journals in exile published a list of 1,387 names of the perished prisoners. The journal also warned that the list "is still unfinished and incomplete. It may also contain some inaccurate data due to lack of independent research."[48]

The secrecy of the executions, covert transportation of the slaughtered prisoners, and concealed burials in unknown mass graves, coupled with measures to hide from view the IRI's blood-spattered hands, make an accurate accounting of the fallen impossible. It should not be forgotten that the IRI has never admitted the existence of mass graves of the victims of the 1988 Massacre anywhere in Iran.

THE END OF WAITING

For days, weeks, and months, the distraught families of political prisoners waited at the prison gates, asking for news about their loved ones. Some were hopeful and thought they would be able to see them. Some feared a humanitarian catastrophe had occurred and that the birds would never sing again. Many had brought money and the deed to their houses with them, to obtain a signed receipt (which was an indication that their loved ones were alive). What did they then receive? A resident of Saltanatabad received a note, in the shape of a ten-dollar bill, which said: "Brother... Please attend on... at... o'clock in Saltanatabad Kommitteh. Signed, Saltanatabad Kommitteh."[49]

The family members residing in Tehranpars, Naziabad, and other zones of Tehran received similar letters. This was during the second half of November, 1988. Then, "On the designated day, from 6 a.m. on, there was a hubbub in front of the Kommittehs of 'Golsahra' (on Saveh Road), Zanjan (Zanjan Avenue), Khavaran (near the Golestan Khavaran), Naziabad, Tehranpars and... At 9 a.m. they called the first names in 'Golsahra Kommitteh.' After a long and excruciating wait, finally one person came back with a bag. A second bag was given to a father... a third bag... a fourth bag."[50] The bags containing the belongings of their loved ones was conclusive proof that they were dead.

---

47 *Bang-e Raha'i*, The Organ of the Center to Support Political Prisoners (Inside Iran), 1, Aban 1368 (October 1989).
48 *Kar* OIPF (Majority), 321, Mehr 16, 1369 (September 27, 1990).
49 *Cesmandaz*, 6, Summer 1368 (1989).
50 *Bang-e Raha'i*, 1.

That experience set off the movement of the families of the executed political prisoners. They took actions such as sit-ins in front of the Ministry of Justice, gatherings in front of the judiciary, and collecting 370 protest signatures for an appeal to the United Nations High Commissioner of Human Rights, as well as contacting activists and organizations outside of the country. The Iranian immigrant and exiled communities in the diaspora responded immediately and effectively. They contacted internationally known human rights organizations, the press, political parties, progressive intellectuals, and all concerned individuals the world over in order to inform the public and also raise awareness and sympathy about the "national catastrophe" in Iran, the dimensions of which no one yet knew. This worldwide campaign finally led to a reaction from European and American human rights organizations, international media, political parties, a few governments, and the European Parliament. They demanded that the Iranian government allow a UN investigative committee to inspect the conditions in prisons.[51]

The IRI leaders' reaction to this wave of concern and queries was deceitful and devious. They categorically denied the extermination of political prisoners in custody. They claimed that the executed were either captured on battlefields in the western border cities of Iran, or else were associates of the *Monafeqin* inside the detention centers, responsible for instigating prison riots in case the "Eternal Light Operation" proved victorious.[52] This political ploy was masterfully promoted by two of the leading IRI officials in public speeches in Tehran. Two examples are characteristic: In a question-and-answer session at Tehran University, a student who seemed to be a supporter of Ayatollah Montazeri asked Hojat al-Islam Khamenei, President of IRI: "Why is the Islamic Republic uninterested in human rights issues and forbids entry of the United Nations experts to investigate the suspicious executions in Iran...?" Ayatollah Khamenei answered:

This question sounds like the questions asked by the foreign media... about the executions, the mass executions in Iran; it has the same implication, of course, the *Monafeqin* radio says the same thing. In our Islamic Republic we have execution as a form of punishment... those inside prison with links to the *Monafeqin* who embarked on

---

51 See Appendix A.
52 The latest example is the assertion of Ali Fallahian (former Minister of Intelligence) in an interview with the state-affiliated Tarikh Online website on July 9, 2017. See the interview at www.youtube.com/watch?v=TXCtDzTqzHU, accessed October 10, 2019.

an armed attack inside the territory of the Islamic Republic, in your opinion, how should they be treated by us? Should we pamper them and give them a treat with sweets and candies?[53]

Hojat al-Islam Ali Akbar Hashemi Rafsanjani's assertions are noteworthy as well. Then the second-highest ranking strongman of the IRI, he retorted:

This false and strange propaganda that the *Monafeqin* have recently orchestrated in Europe and Western countries about a few thousand of their forces being executed in Iran is to justify to the world the loss of their members in the Mersad Operation... There are always elements who can't be dealt with in any other way but to be put down. We must crush these people. There must always be a state of fear for such traitors and unrighteous people.[54]

Not only the "traitors and unrighteous" were subjected to a state of terror, but their grieving families also had to undergo cruel treatment. Yet, "the Politics of Cruelty"[55] didn't stop the families from pursuing their just cause of seeking the truth. They had scores of unanswered questions burning in their hearts. There was a quest for answers, "an unquenchable thirst in the darkest of nights." They put it in words in an open letter to Ali Akbar Hashemi Rafsanjani:

Finally, after months of waiting, the prison gates were opened, but we couldn't even visit our spouses, fathers, children, and our loved ones at their graves. Your criminal republic is not only involved in a mass killing of prisoners, but also refuses to reveal where they are buried. In many cases, it used the financial bonds and bail posted by the families, along with serious threats, to ensure that the relatives would not hold funerals or any other ceremonies for the victims. This is one of the basic rights of every human being... Was this your gift to the suffering people and the anguished families of the political prisoners on the occasion of ending the destructive eight-year war... ?[56]

53 *Resalat*, Azar 16, 1367 (December 7, 1988).
54 Ibid., Azar 12, 1367 (December 3, 1988).
55 Title of a book by Kate Millet, subtitled "An Essay on the Literature of Political Imprisonment," Vintage, 1994.
56 "The Message of Solidarity," *Newsletter of the Committee in Solidarity with Political Prisoners in Iran*, 2, Shahrivar 1368 (September 1989).

They concluded by asking Rafsanjani the following questions:

1. On what grounds did you kill them?
2. In which court, by which committee, and according to which written law were they executed?
3. Why were the prisoners who were sentenced long ago and who had already served their sentences suddenly exterminated behind closed doors in a matter of two to three months?
4. Why do you refuse to publish the real number of the victims of this massacre and evade publicly answering the explicit questions from people and the families of the political prisoners?[57]

To date, none of the heads of the IRI have been willing to answer these questions. The chapter of the 1988 Massacre of the political prisoners in Iran is still open, and the last word has not been uttered.

---

57 "The Message of Solidarity," *Newsletter of the Committee in Solidarity with Political Prisoners in Iran*, 2, Shahrivar 1368 (September 1989).

Chapter Two

VOICES OF SURVIVAL

This Is a Warning: "We Plan to Kill You"

MAHNAZ SAIDA[1]

In December 1981, when I was arrested on a charge of affiliation with the PMOI (People's Mojahedin Organization of Iran), I was fifteen years old and in my second year of high school. In a trial that was over before you could even blink, I was sentenced to five years of imprisonment and an additional five years of probation. I was released near the end of winter 1986, but I was required to report either weekly or biweekly to a Kommitteh (the regime's unofficial parallel police) in Vosoogh Ave, one of the major Kommittehs in Tehran, as did many political prisoners. We had to report on our daily activities, associates, and opinions on national and foreign affairs.

One day in November 1987, after the typical questions, the chief interrogator closed his notebook and said, "Today I want to talk to you about something serious. I want to tell you that we're planning carnage. We have a slaughter and purge plan. We plan to kill you."

"What do you mean?" I said. "I don't understand."

"Let me tell you something. I can see that you're not even twenty, yet you've spent five years in jail. I know you think I'm telling you lies, that I'm bluffing to scare you. I know all this. But what I'm telling you is true. I'm warning you. There's a list of all the people who have not collaborated with us."

"You mean I'm on your list even though I have already served my sentence and wasn't even given one day of remission?"

---

1 Mahnaz Saida was born in Tehran in 1966. Like thousands upon thousands of teenagers of her generation, she joined the demonstrations and marches against the Shah's regime in the turbulent years of 1978–79. She continued her political activities as a sympathizer of the People's Mojahedin Organization of Iran (PMOI) after the 1979 Revolution. She was apprehended in 1981, sentenced to five years of imprisonment, and released in 1986. Her second arrest in 1988 led to three years of imprisonment and ten years of probation. She is a survivor of the Great Massacre of 1988. Mahnaz fled Iran in 2001 and has lived in Switzerland ever since.

"Exactly."

"Well, how are you planning to kill me?"

"For instance, on the street. Or on a road. This is a new plan. Believe me! Your name's on this list and I don't want your name there."

"What exactly do you want from me?"

"Collaboration."

"Well, if you really have good intentions and want to save me, write that I've collaborated. I'm not interested in politics anymore. I'm going to high school and I will be graduating soon."

"It's not as easy as that. We need some evidence to show that you've collaborated with us. Something real."

"You know, I can't do this. I can't even think about it. I'm not up to it!"

I left the Kommitteh bewildered. It was quite obvious from his tone that he was telling the truth. What could I do? I told myself, "I'm living an ordinary life and going to high school. I have no political activities whatsoever. But they're still threatening me openly and blatantly. I don't want to sacrifice my life for nothing. I'm doomed to extinction here in Iran. I must flee the country."

At the time the PMOI had operatives who would contact released political prisoners who wanted to join the National Liberation Army and smuggle them to Iraq. I decided to do this, and preparations were made for the journey. However, on the day of my departure, in January 1988, I was arrested at the airport.

After interrogation, I was transferred to Evin prison and interrogated again by the Prosecutor's Bureau. I was in solitary confinement for two or three months. In April 1988, I stood trial. Nayyeri, the shari'a judge, asked me, "Why are you back?"

Returning to prison, especially for Mojahedin women, was a serious offense. Those who were arrested and incarcerated again were called "repeat offenders" (*mojaddadi*). To reduce the term of my imprisonment, I had to bargain with Nayyeri. "What else could I do other than flee the country?" I said. "You even went so far as to lay a trap for me!"

I told him about my last interrogation at the Vosoogh Kommitteh. We argued for about an hour. Nayyeri completely denied the existence of such a plan.

"There's not a shred of truth in this," he said. "We have courts, we have judges. How is it possible to kill someone who's living her life and doing her studies just like that—for no reason?"

"The interrogator's words were serious," I insisted, "and I took them seriously. I had no other choice than to escape. I didn't want to get killed on the street."

My insistence was useless. Nayyeri sentenced me to three years of imprisonment and ten years of probation. I was transferred to the ward. There I saw some friends I had been with before and told them about the regime's plan to exterminate all political activists. To some friends I said, "The country is in turmoil; it's pregnant with events. Political organizations can't remain silent under such circumstances. The PMOI has certainly planned some operations. We should take some things seriously, and the regime's plans to eliminate the opposition is one of them." I also talked about my fears and worries with Hamdam Azimi, a woman with clear views about the political situation of the time. From the very beginning of my incarceration, I was trying to convince my friends that the regime was planning to slaughter us.

In August 1988, we had already heard on the radio about the ceasefire with Iraq. We all knew some changes were underway, but we had no idea what those changes would be. One night, around eleven or eleven-thirty, Zahra Falahat's name was called over the loudspeaker. In the ward, rumor was that Zahra Falahat was one of the operatives of the PMOI and that she had helped some supporters of the organization flee the country. Zahra associated with no one in the ward. She spent most of her time studying Arabic. I think she was in Cell 9 of Ward 2, where "repeat offenders" were held. Zahra began to pack her things up with sangfroid. But the voice on the loudspeaker was impatient: "Ms. Zahra Falahat report quickly to the ward's control desk, in full hejab!"[2]

It was 11:30 p.m. No one was ever taken for interrogation at such an hour, especially those whose interrogations had finished. Zahra Falahat's interrogation was over, and she was "awaiting a trial verdict," which meant the court had yet to rule on her case. Calm and poised, she left the ward with a smile. She gave her ethnic Baluchi dress to one of her friends before she left. Zahra leaving the ward gave many of us the premonition of disaster.

A couple of days later, female Islamic Revolutionary Guards (*pasdars*) raided the ward. Anxious and furious, they rummaged around—checking under the beds, in the inner folds of the bags, everywhere. We had curtains and behind them we had installed some small shelves. You could not put anything behind those shelves. But the *pasdars* even searched behind those

---

2 Hejab is the Islamic covering of a woman's entire body other than the face and hands.

too. In the end, they took away the televisions and shut off the radio news broadcast. We were kept completely in the dark. But somehow we learned about the PMOI's military expedition to Iran, though we knew nothing about the details.

From that day on, almost every day a few prisoners were called for interrogation. Throughout this time we were constantly trying to understand what was going on. My friend and I thought there must be a massive operation out there, which would explain why the guards were so agitated.

Soon after, from one of the locked dormitories in the ward downstairs where nonreligious prisoners were held, we heard the news that a new squad had arrived at the prison. Some of the girls had heard the *pasdars* laughing loudly as they said to each other, "Did you see how she danced on the gallows?" They mentioned some prisoners by name, including the names of prisoners who we later learned were hanged the next day.

The girls downstairs had passed on the information upstairs. We had an ominous feeling, but no proof yet. When they called someone for interrogation, they did not ask the person to bring along her stuff. And yet, not a single one of those called had returned. Had we become blind and dumb?

The very first week they called my name along with some other "repeat offenders." Prison officials were especially irritable when it came to some of the prisoners in Cell 9 of the ward upstairs. My name was called out, along with eighty-seven others. We were all taken to the ward's administration area where we waited for more than one hour. Among us was Azadeh, a cautious and independent-minded girl whose father was a dentist. "Last night I dreamt that I was in my father's office," she said. "My father was going to treat my teeth. But as soon as he turned on the light, all the lights went out." Parvin trembled at this and her expression suddenly fell. Parvin, who later fled the country and joined the PMOI abroad, was good at interpreting dreams and also divined through the interpretation of the Odes of Hafez[3] (a form of divination using the Divan of Hafez in which passages are chosen at random and the future foretold from them). Azadeh asked Parvin, "What's the divination of this dream?" Parvin dodged the question. Once Azadeh was taken back to the ward, Parvin said softly, "Azadeh's dream was not good. Darkness is not a good omen."

---

3 Hafez Shams al-Din Mohammad (d. 1389) is considered one of the greatest classic Persian poets and the undisputed master of a lyric form named *Ghazal*. His mysticism, metaphors, and poetic "ambiguity inspired controversy as to whether his works suggest mystical longing or describe amorous liaisons." *The Oxford Dictionary of Islam*, p. 102.

This dream and its divination made the atmosphere even heavier. There was a feeling that something momentous was about to happen. But what? Nobody knew. Sometimes we were overcome by hopefulness and would say, "It's nothing. They just want to transfer some of us to Gohardasht prison. They are trying to figure out the hierarchical organization within the ward."

I was not optimistic. I could sense the onset of the slaughter. The Haji who was responsible for the admission and discharge of the prisoners usually would deliver one document and receive another from the senior guard. The first document dealt with the delivery of the prisoner and the second one indicated to where the prisoner was being transferred. At that time, the senior guard was a woman named Rahimi. She was an older woman who appeared kind, but was in fact ruthless. With a glib tongue, she tried to run the ward tactfully. Prisoners referred to her as "a wolf in sheep's clothing." As the Haji was about to deliver the prisoners, Rahimi pushed me forward. "Here, take her. She is the worst *Monafeq* [hypocrite] of all."

"But I don't have the papers to take this girl," the Haji said. "Where should I take her?"

"Take her with the others."

The Haji had no choice but to take me. I waited for the others outside the ward. The *pasdars* were seen in every corner and kept a watchful eye on us. As soon as anyone raised her head or moved the slightest bit, they would beat her up. The Haji was religiously not permitted to touch unrelated members of the opposite sex as they were not *Mahram*. The prisoners were in chadors (Islamic full-body cloaks) and blindfolds, so it was difficult to recognize anyone. When they were taking us out of the solitary ward, I realized that another group of prisoners were also waiting. They were probably from the communal ward adjacent to the solitaries. When we left the building, we encountered yet another group of prisoners who were waiting in line. They lined us up behind the others. We had to hold on to the chador of the person in front of us and follow her. We were under strict surveillance. Such high-security control was surprising. The *pasdar* accompanying us shouted aggressively: "Keep your heads down! Don't talk!" If they heard the slightest sound, they would hit the suspect hard on the head.

They took us to Building 209, formerly Evin's dispensary. Building 209 had a large steel door. The door opened and we entered a hallway filled with girls (and a few guys, if I remember correctly). The dense crowd was a clear indication of an extraordinary situation.

They lined us up along the wall. We were all forced to stand, as there was not enough room for anyone to sit. We waited for an hour or two. This time was unlike the times before when you could peek from under your blindfold or whisper to your neighbor. The *pasdars'* attitudes were unusual. One by one, they called out our names. Finally, my turn came.

They led me into a room. I was told to remove my blindfold, and when I did, my eyes fell upon Nayyeri—the same religious judge who had tried me a month or two earlier. Two people were sitting on his right and two on his left. Two people were standing on either side of me too. The windows were covered with dark military blankets. It was a terrifying setting. It certainly did not look like a courtroom. Nayyeri asked me my name.

"Mahnaz Saida."

"Offense?"

"*Monafeqin.*"

"Will you give an interview?"

The only line I had clearly drawn for myself from the very first day I entered prison was not to collaborate under any circumstances. Till that day I had always refused to give an interview. But that horrifying setting and the constant fear that never left me after the last interrogation in Kommitteh Vosoogh—a fear with which I lived and had transmitted to my friends too— caused me to say, "Yes, I will give an interview."

"Will you sign a letter of repentance?"

"Yes."

"Go outside. There's a text. Sign it."

They took me to a small cubicle. The text was short. "I, ..., who have been arrested on a charge of affiliation with the *Monafeq*, hereby declare my abhorrence toward all counter-revolutionary groups."

I didn't understand why I had to condemn the other groups, but I signed the text anyway and left the cubicle. After waiting in that swarming hallway for a while, they took me to a solitary cell. I was alone in the cell, but after a while, they brought in two more prisoners: Nasrin, whose family name I don't remember, and Makhsoos Bokhara'i. They had also been interrogated and had given the same responses as me. In that moment I learned how the executions and purges were taking place.

That night I could not sleep. Around three in the morning I heard noises; sporadic cries. Then I heard cell doors open and slam shut. I woke my cell-mates. "There are strange noises. I guess something's going on!"

We were all ears. "That's Halwaie's voice," one said.

Mojtaba Halwaie was the military commander of the prison and head of the execution squads. Makhsoos knew him well. We quickly put on our scarves, chadors, and thick black socks, and sat waiting. Usually as they approached a cell, the guards would shout, "Cell! Observe your hejab!" This time, however, they barged in without any warning. They probably expected to find us asleep and without the hejab—giving them an excuse to harass and torment us even more.

There was a female guard accompanying Mojtaba Halwaie. Her appearance surprised me. She was around twenty-seven years old, wearing make-up: mascara, kohl, and her *maghnae* (an Islamic scarf for women) was well back on her head under the chador. What did a guard with an appearance like that want from us at three o'clock in the morning?

Halwaie was dressed in full military uniform. He was wearing combat boots and had a gun at his waist. He was surprised to see us ready. Irritated, he asked our names hurriedly, then our offenses. "You got away with it tonight," he said, shaking his head as he was leaving our cell. "But tomorrow is another day."

As soon as Mojtaba left, we started a discussion about what he meant by "you got away with it." Were we going for interrogation again the next day? Was it possible? We had no idea. But we were certain that tragedy was headed our way. Halwaie had given us his message.

We were in that cell for a week before they transferred us downstairs to Ward 1 with the locked dormitories. We were fifteen or sixteen inmates brought there from various cells. News of our arrival reached the girls in Ward 2. I realized that many girls from our ward were missing. But there were still some inmates who held on to the belief that soon the girls would return in groups.

For two or three weeks after our return to the ward, the doors remained locked. We were allowed to use the washrooms only three times a day. The guards treated us very rudely, much worse than before. "You got away with it, but you're dreaming!" they kept saying.

We felt that it was not over yet. The sense of being suspended between life and death behind those closed doors was constantly with us. After two or three weeks, they returned us to our former ward, Salon 2, which was very sparse. When they took us, we were many. When we returned, we were only a few. The atmosphere was heavy, very heavy. The twenty to thirty inmates who had survived were those who had never had "issues" in the ward. They weren't die-hard *tavabs* (repentants), but they got along well with the *pasdars*.

Some of the survivors were not affiliated to any political group, and one or two were royalists.

We asked each other, "Who did they take? How did they take her? How did she go?" Question after question. Those who had not gone through interrogation asked, "The ones who have returned, how did they return? How come they were brought back? Where are the others?" We had no answers. We were almost certain that the ones who had returned were the only ones who had not been sentenced to death for one reason or another. Maybe they had been more on the alert than others. Maybe they had capitulated. Maybe they were lucky. Maybe...

Prisoners who had been taken in groups were returning one by one. A ward holding 150 to 200 prisoners was reduced to 70. The ward was bare and gloomy, and the feeling that something terrible was going to happen prevailed.

Eventually, newspapers were allowed in the ward. They brought back the television and, without any prior notice, we were called to the *Hosseiniyeh*. Going to the *Hosseiniyeh* was mandatory. The guards would look in all the rooms to make sure that no one had remained in the ward. The market for interviews was booming. After a few sessions at the *Hosseiniyeh*, we found out what was going on: prisoners were being taken for interviews in alphabetical order.

"Introduce yourself. What is your offense?"

If you were a supporter of the PMOI they would ask, "If we arrested Masoud Rajavi, your leader, would you finish him off with a bullet?"

If the prisoner responded, "You haven't arrested him yet," they would say, "Right now we're going to execute some of his supporters and sympathizers. Go downstairs and finish them off!"

What was even more horrifying is that a few prisoners actually succumbed to this pressure.

One day they called me to give an interview. I was not expecting it. They asked what my offense was, and then, "Would you kill Masoud Rajavi?"

"No."

"Why not?"

"I'm not a murderer and I don't like the thought of killing people."

The *Hosseiniyeh* shook with shouts of, "*Monafeq!*" "*Monafeq!*"

"You won't kill him because you're still a *Monafeq*."

The behavior of the person sitting up there, together with the crowd in the *Hosseiniyeh*, frayed my temper and nerves to an absolute minimum. The only thing that came to my mind was, *Masoud Rajavi is an idea, an ideology. You can't kill an ideology with guns and bullets, you can only fight against it with a new way of thinking.* I didn't know what would happen next. The *Hosseiniyeh* was once again shaking.

"Down! Get lost!" the interviewer said.

I went back to my place.

"Why did you say that?" one of my cellmates whispered.

It was a strange feeling. I felt that such singular moments crystallized the innocence, endurance, and legitimacy of many inmates. "It's just as well to be hanged for a sheep as a lamb! I'm fed up. Fed up with these programs too. What else can they do?"

I remember the day I was sitting with Azadeh, such a calm and quiet girl. Azadeh said, "If we have to pay the price for our people's liberation, what are our lives worth? Let's give our lives!" I will never forget the ring of her voice. Or Hamdam's: "Look Mahnaz, if you stay alive, and I hope you will, bear witness! Testify. Tell them how they took groups of us, what they did to us."

The echo of such words is unforgettable. I can still see the smile that accompanied such words, invigorating the ward. Such composure and willingness to accept one's own death, merely in the *hope* of freedom for one's people. That's all. For years they had endured torture and the cruelty of prison life. I don't know if they could see the possibility of a fundamental change and a bright future for the country. But they had great hopes and did not fear death. May God bless them!

Despite all this, there were still some girls in the ward who doubted the executions. They believed that there were still many inmates in solitary confinement. For people like me, however, it was as clear as day that they were all gone.

One day the guards came to our stagnant and gloomy ward and said, "Go to the workshop. You must work."

A large number moved toward the workshop, among them many who had previously refused to go there. They did not want to give any excuse to the *pasdars*.

After a while, Zamani came to the ward's Control Desk. At that time Zamani was the representative of the Ministry of Intelligence in the prison. I had never had direct contact with him but had heard he was rather blunt. He was one of the main architects of the slaughter and purge of political prisoners. Zamani was feared by everyone, and it was generally believed that we should be watchful in our dealings with him.

Every day he spoke with a group of prisoners. Gradually, I suppose he came to know everyone. Then he gave furlough to some prisoners, whether they had asked for a leave of absence or not. The ward was no longer what it had been. We did not have the same spirit. The absence of our friends was conspicuous, but we were not permitted to even mourn or cry. The few *tavabs* who had remained in the ward reported our every movement to further their own cause. For instance, a girl named Jamak had become even more collaborative than before—hoping to be granted a pardon by reporting on us. And she succeeded.

What horrid days!

TRANSLATED FROM PERSIAN BY NILOO

Summer 1988

ANAHITA RAHMANI[4]

Summer 1988 started with a peculiar calm. The prison, to a great extent, had been freed from the upheaval of 1981–82. Our daily routine was specifically set: English and French language courses, the physics of Einstein's theory of relativity, the psychology books of Pavlov, and newspaper articles about the socio-economic conditions that would circulate around the group page by page. We read them carefully so that we might see an indication of the struggle in some corner of the world, or to understand any reference as to what new decisions the state would make regarding political prisoners. We went for walks in the open air for part of the day, we jogged, and we played with a cloth ball that we had made ourselves.

But those were hard days for Soussan,[5] a particularly beautiful young woman who had caught the eye of interrogator Zamani. He brought her in for interrogation every day, each day using a different excuse. Her political opinions and ideas were investigated. Zamani was part of the Intelligence Division and played a significant role in the interrogations of political prisoners before their executions. Through physical and psychological pressures he tried to push Soussan to write a "statement of recantation." But Soussan resisted. In the beginning she defended her ideas, but later she adopted a policy of silence. Every time she came back from interrogation, we would encircle her and ask questions. With a bruised body and tired mind, she answered our questions about the news of the "Interrogation Division" and the information that had been exchanged. In one of the interrogations, Zamani had told her, "A dangerous situation is awaiting the prisoners. Many

4 Anahita Rahmani was born in Tehran in 1958. With a BS in Social Science, she lives in Canada. She is an activist with the Communist Party of Iran (Marxist–Leninist–Maoist), the March 8 Women's Organization (Iran–Afghanistan), and the Council in Support of the Iranian People's Movement. Currently, she is a social worker and a student in Social Science at the University of Ryerson.
5 The names of all potentially vulnerable people have been changed, as here.

of them are to be killed. It would behoove you to issue your statement of recantation right now and save your life." We laughed at these threats. We believed strongly that Zamani was trying to trick and scare Soussan into a statement of recantation. We were immersed in our own world and were largely clueless as to the disaster that was unfolding around us. Even though we had seen indications of an evolution in the situation, we couldn't have imagined the terrifying reality that was awaiting us.

During this period I was deeply involved in serious studies with my circle of friends, who were more or less of the same ideological persuasion. We had reduced texts to small handwritten copies. We read them carefully and took meticulous notes, then had lively discussions about every detail and came up with good questions. We asked ourselves how, in the future society, we could develop Iran's backward economy without dependence on oil or multinational corporations. Could we develop technologically and boost the economy without giving rise to class divisions? Could we take, as a model for developing Iran, the road that revolutionary China—not the current capitalist China—took? We were concerned with how we were going to deal with political dissidents and our political enemies in the future society. We should not let any of our enemies be arrested. We wanted to destroy the prisons altogether. No, it would be better to transform the prisons into museums so that people would know at what extraordinary cost despots and reactionaries were overthrown and the new society was charted and built. But did the country need so many museums while there were still not enough hospital facilities and laboratories for the citizens? We thought we would just convert a *few* of the prisons into museums—just to keep people from forgetting the past! But was it not better to think of the path to revolution instead of charting the outlines of the future society that we would build *after* a successful revolution?

∼

The prisoners, known as *Mellikesh*, were separated from the rest of us. Soussan was among them. During visitations we heard that the men's division had been divided more extensively. During the month of Ramadan they sent some of the PMOI to solitary cells and brought others to our division.

In spring 1988, Hosseinzadeh, the prison warden, summoned *all* of us, men and women, and individually asked us several questions: First name? Last name? Organizational affiliation? Do you believe in your organization? What is your opinion on Marxism? Do you believe in God?

As to the last question, when the prisoners responded with a firm "No," he said, "We will show you!"

What did he want, or what could he "show" us? We had seen the bloodshed of 1981 and 1982. Those were the days when they sentenced fifty to sixty people to death after a quick question-and-answer session. Those were the days when the IRI's "repentance factory" was working at full capacity. Those were the days when the repentants turned the prison wards into a real hell and reported our every move to the prison guards. We had held out against this earthly hell; what else could Hosseinzadeh have to show us that we hadn't already seen? On the other hand, the political and social climate of 1988 had changed fundamentally since 1981 and 1982. The opposition movement, which was so strong then, was now crushed and had withdrawn into exile. We couldn't see a rationale for another round of bloodshed.

After eight years of a destructive war with Iraq, the Islamic Republic of Iran (IRI) finally submitted to the ceasefire codified in UN Security Council resolution 598. On July 20, Khomeini appeared on television and, as he put it, drank this "chalice of poison." On July 25, the PMOI launched their military operations under the name *Forough-e Javidan* (Eternal Light). On July 27, the regime announced that military forces had knocked out and crushed the *Monafeqin* (hypocrites). Thus, under the direct mandate of Khomeini, the execution of thousands of political prisoners became the order of the day. But at the time we were clueless.

There were, however, a number of obvious changes. All of a sudden, the prison visits were halted, which was unprecedented. They no longer gave us newspapers, and the television was removed from our division. After that, they took no one to the infirmary. We were completely severed from the outside world.

～

One night they summoned three Mojahedin. They never returned. Maryam Golzadeh Ghafouri was one of those three. They were the first group taken for execution. A few days later, they took another group of Mojahedin from our division. One of them, Farzaneh Zia Mirza'i, returned anxious and distraught. Had they made a mistake, or had they returned her to the division deliberately? She went straight to her friends to tell them what she had seen and heard. She was still describing the events that had occurred when the guards summoned her again. They took her to a courthouse, where there were several men and women sitting in rows waiting behind the closed door of the court room. Before taking them into the court room, the guards gave the prisoners a sheet of paper on which to write their opinions on the institution of the *Velayat-e faqih* in the IRI's political structures, on the Mojahedin Organization, and on the Islamic Republic. They generally convinced the prisoners that a trial was not on the horizon for them and that these questions were simply for the purposes of general information. However, in the court proceedings, the shari'a judge asked them a different set of questions and, right then and there, a judgment was issued. All those who identified themselves as a Mojahed or referred to the Mojahedin as anything other than *Monafeqin* weren't asked any more questions but were simply put on the list of those to be executed. However, the prisoners who were on the execution rolls were dealt with in such a way as to convince them that they were going to be transferred to Gohardasht prison.

They summoned the last group of Mojahedin from our division, but this group returned after a few hours. Prisoners who were lined up at the door of the courthouse were so great in number that their turns never came that day. Some of them were very optimistic and saw the chance for freedom as a real possibility. Some of them even put on their best clothes and played ball in the prison yard during the open-air periods. We couldn't or didn't want to believe the horrific reality that was unfolding. After a few days, the prison officials finally took them for execution. For the final farewells, we all stood in the hallway. It was a painful moment. Some people preferred not to come forward to say goodbye. But before being led away, Shoorangiz Karimi kissed everyone on the cheek. She had a peculiar smile on her face. When we embraced each other, she said in my ear, "Don't forget that dying is easier than living well and continuing the struggle." She had said this to me once before, when my execution order was reduced to a life sentence and I was embracing my fellow prisoners with joy and they were congratulating me. For a moment I felt a slight shudder run through my entire being.

But Mehrangiz, Shoorangiz's sister, left us with a strangely jolly spirit as if she were going to a party. Her complexion, which was always pale because of her heart condition, was rosy that day. She calmly kissed everyone on the cheek and left. She was a supporter of the Arman-e Mostaz'afin Organization, but because she didn't want to continue living without her friends, she identified herself as a Mojahed in the court, and that very night she was executed along with her sister and her friends. But the rest of us who had leftist tendencies and affiliations still held out the hope that we would soon see them again.

~

One night we heard the sound of a female guard crying in the prison guards' room, which was adjacent to our cells. Another guard was consoling her, saying, "The *Monafeq* has to die. Just like their lives, their deaths are a headache for us. Did you see how they held hands as they were hanging from the nooses? They clasped hands so tightly that when the Brothers came to take them away, they had to break their hands to separate them." This frightful news spread throughout the prison. A heavy silence befell us. Exercise and games were halted. We withdrew into ourselves. We could not find calm even in our sleep. Often the sound of whimpering and suffering echoed throughout the room. We never found relief from the thought of what they would do to us. Was the bloodshed that had begun restricted to the Mojahedin or was everyone going to be caught up in it? We still had no news of the leftist male prisoners who had been sentenced to death. It was a strange circumstance. The prison authorities regularly came to our division and asked us questions that we had to answer with either a "yes" or a "no." Once they came during lunch and asked us, "Do you perform *namaz* [daily prayers]?" "Will you give an interview?" We all gave the same reply: "No."

It was clear to me that if they came to our division to take away the leftists, I would be among the first because I had a life sentence. In those days I was like someone who lived in the clouds and tried every day to put even more distance between myself and the ground. I was immersed in my own beautiful dreams and sublime thoughts. I thought about the kinds of mistakes we had made in our struggles, and how we could avoid them in the future. These thoughts were pleasurable for me, as if I were leisurely debating with my lover. I had attained such a state of mind that I didn't really see the tumult going on around me. I don't know if this was a conscious choice or a subconscious defense mechanism. I concentrated on the writings and poems of Mao Zedong that I had written meticulously in miniscule size. Mao's statements strengthened my spirit for struggle and resistance. In my dreamland I made plans for a truly beautiful world that we were working for, and chalked out its broad outlines in the tableau of my mind. One day a very close friend asked me, "How can you study under these circumstances when they can come for your life any moment?" I just looked at her. During that period, I myself didn't know that perhaps by concentrating on my own goals and longings I was managing my fear of death. I just continued looking at her and she didn't ask me anything else.

One day, Akbari, the guard and head of the division, came and read out my name along with two others and ordered us to gather our belongings and exit the division. The one thing that the three of us had in common was that in our first trials we had been sentenced to death, but in our second trials our sentences had been reduced to life in prison. All of the prisoners stood in line to say their goodbyes to us. Was this the last time we were to see each other? It was a heavy atmosphere. Some cried. I tried to look persistently into their eyes. I didn't want to tear my eyes from them. The guard shouted at us to go faster. I gathered my things and left the division quickly. They took me to an isolation cell. Later I found out that during that period they were busy executing leftist male political prisoners. I heard the guards marching past, their boots hitting the ground, and they chanted "death to the *Monafeq* and death to the godless." I was waiting for my turn. I paced around the cell for hours and thought about Behrouz, my husband, who had been killed under torture in 1982.[6] Remembering the epic story of our lives and the death of people like Behrouz, I felt good about myself: it felt good that I had resisted prison pressure and had not surrendered; it felt good that I had not traded with these criminals, selling out the people's interests in return for my life.

∾

I don't remember how many days I was in the cell, but they finally returned me to the division. Everyone surrounded me. They were all happy to see me. They asked about the Mojahedin. We couldn't and didn't want to believe that they had all been executed.

It was toward the end of August that they came for us leftist women.

---

6 Behrouz Fathi was one of the leaders in the armed insurrection of Sarbedaran. This movement began in August 1981 with Sarbedaran forces positioning themselves in the forest areas of northern Iran. Despite immense efforts and sacrifices of the Sarbedaran and the people who supported them, the insurrection was defeated. Behrouz was not killed then, but many leaders and fighters lost their lives or were arrested while retreating and later were executed. A few months later, in summer 1982, the nationwide organization of the Union of Iranian Communists (UIC) was completely broken up by the security forces of the IRI. At this sensitive juncture Behrouz, along with other comrades, took up responsibilities at the leadership level and organized the Fourth Council of the UIC in the liberated areas of Kurdistan. A few months after returning to Tehran, Behrouz and Anahita were arrested on the Karaj Highway. See Appendix B, "Union of Iranian Communists."

News reached us that some of the *Mellikesh* prisoners who had been in isolation cells had been summoned and asked questions about their ideology,
and had been sentenced to five lashes at each of the five *namaz* (prayer)
times, which added up to twenty-five lashes per day. The first lashes were
administered at 4 a.m. The prisoner's cell was opened during the morning
call to prayer; they brought the prisoner into the hallway, laid her on a bed,
lashed her five times, and then returned her to the cell. The second round
was at noon. The third was at 4 p.m. The fourth was at 8 p.m. The last round
came just before midnight. After a time, a few of the prisoners who couldn't
withstand the lashes, under this vicious torture, agreed to perform *namaz*
and were taken to Division 2 where all of the prisoners did *namaz*. Shortly
thereafter, they summoned several people from our division. They took
them to court and asked them whether they did *namaz*, whether they were
Muslims, and other questions along these lines. Everyone answered, "No,
we are not Muslims and we do not do *namaz*." The shari'a judge issued his
verdict right there, and ordered that those prisoners be flogged until they
either repented or passed away. In response to this sentence, the prisoners
decided to go on a hunger strike. Accordingly, the next group of prisoners
who had been sentenced to flogging announced the dry hunger strike.

There was severe psychological pressure on us. Everyone tried to keep
busy with some kind of work. At night, we all gathered in one room in the
division and "read novels." Laleh, for example, described the novel *The Road
to Calvary* by Aleksey Tolstoy for us. She narrated the book so thoroughly
and paid such attention to each detail that it was as if we were reading the
book ourselves. (Years later, when I read that book myself outside prison, I
really became aware of the extent of Laleh's diligent work.) The pressures of
prison were severe, but we were no longer the young and immature people
we had once been. By now, each of us had become tempered steel, and we
were not broken under the lashes and death around us in the prison. We
mocked and laughed at the prison guards, who we did impressions of and
made jokes about.

∽

There were some among the prisoners who were keeping it all inside and
choking on their pain. Little by little, they withdrew into themselves. Mahin
Badouie was one of them. She had been put in a "coffin," which prisoners
agreed was the most tormenting of all tortures, for ten months and had not

surrendered.[7] When the head of the Qezel Hesar prison was replaced, Mahin was transferred to our division. Within the division, she lived an isolated life. She ate alone and walked alone. After a time, she stopped talking altogether. Her eyes and beautiful face were always anxious and worried. In those days, in summer 1988, she was always very distressed and disturbed. She was in a division where every few hours prisoners were taken in groups to be flogged, and this was an intolerable pressure for her. We were all worried about her. Some of her friends looked after her without her noticing. On several occasions, when she was attempting to slit her wrists in the bathroom, they stopped her. The last time, she resisted vehemently and pulled out one of the veins that she had cut. The other prisoners quickly told the guards what had happened and they took her to the prison infirmary. There she slit her wrist for the last time and ended her life. The prison guards had made no effort to save her.

The suicides continued. The unsuccessful suicide attempt by Fariba, who had also been a political prisoner under the Shah and thus had years of "experience" behind her, was unexpected for everyone. She tried to kill herself by taking a large quantity of pain killers and sleeping pills which she had collected bit by bit from others over time. We summoned the division guard. They had anticipated such an event, and they took her to the infirmary inside the building, on the first floor. (At that time, taking prisoners to the central infirmary was forbidden.) They returned Fariba after a few days. Her friends said that she had tried to kill herself in protest of the floggings. When Rafat, a Mojahed, committed suicide by eating hair-remover cream, nobody was surprised. Sometime before then, they had taken her from our ward to Division 2. (Her brother had killed himself the year before.)

It was about the middle of October when we got news that the prison warden had been replaced. The new warden came to our division to investigate

---

7 The "coffin," which was also called grave, resurrection, casket, cage, box, and hell, was an innovation of Haj Davoud Lashkari in 1983. It looked exactly like a coffin, built in different sizes primarily for women political prisoners. They had to lie in their coffins, which severely limited their movements from dawn to dusk for months. The prisoner subject to this torture had to eat her or his meal while sitting in the coffin. "According to prison officials this place was a Resurrection fabricated by the Islamic Republic to review prisoners' past actions and hold them accountable for their sins. A *Hell* modeled in the divine *Resurrection*, it was administrated by 'torture officials'. They also used the term Grave indicating burial of the dead, to simulate Shi'ite concepts of *Pressure* in *First Night of Grave and Transition World...* . This environment aimed to completely reincarnate victims through a set of convoluted processes. The reincarnated victim would have no resemblance to her former self." Iraj Mesdaghi, *Torture in the Name of Allah*, translated and edited by Sepehr Manouchehri (Pezhvakeiran Publishing, 2018), pp. 143–4.

and said, "If you want something, tell me." We were silent. After that, they returned the television to our division and gave us newspapers. The warden also visited the rooms where prisoners were taken five times each day to be flogged, told them they would no longer be flogged, and asked them to end their hunger strike. In the end, they returned these prisoners to the division. Among them, Nadeen and Mahtab were worse off than the others. They had become emaciated. They had been flogged twenty-two days in a row—a total of 550 lashes—and during that time, they had been on a hunger strike. In the last week of their hunger strike, they frequently lost consciousness. Perhaps the astounding resistance of these hunger strikers along with the suicide of Soheila Darvish, who was said to have hanged herself, influenced the policies of the prison guards and dissuaded them from continuing their ruthless suppression and brutal torture.

It was toward the end of October that the visits began again. But visiting days were not happy days. The family members who came to visit told us the names of some of the people who had been executed. Each time a prisoner came back from a visit, she brought back with her more and more of these names. Families cried and begged for the prisoners to compromise and save themselves. But we had withdrawn into a state of stupor along with outrage and spite. It was as if we had passed through a furnace of death and torture, with immense pain in our hearts for our fellow prisoners who we had lost. Fear of death had been replaced with *laughter* at death mixed with deep resentment toward all the cruelty and baseness around us.

In this way the summer of 1988 concluded.

I spent another three years at Evin moving from division to division, from cell to cell. Sometimes they grouped us with regular prisoners. Sometimes they put me in a cell with a mentally ill prisoner. I didn't hear any more laughter in prison, and no one played ball in the open-air walks anymore. But in the isolation cells, during long stretches, the sound of singing and of revolutionary songs came from the other prisoners in nearby isolation cells and in the sanitarium, and reminded me of the persistent and strong pulse of life. In 1991, I was released from prison on the basis of a leave called "leave connected to release."[8] And this is how my eight years in prison passed.

TRANSLATED FROM PERSIAN BY MARYAM JAZAYERI

---

8 They did not officially release me and others who refused to sign any document before being discharged. So they gave us a "leave," but they never made us go back to prison or even file monthly reports.

He Held His Head Up

NAZLI PARTOVI[9]

I try with all my might to keep the lump in my throat from bursting into tears, but the pressure is more than I can imagine. I hold my hands over my mouth and face just to make sure that it looks normal and so no one can see the condition I'm in. I quickly walk past my cellmates who are sitting down to have lunch, and go to the toilet. I cover my mouth with one hand and my glasses with the other so that they won't get damaged. In prison if your glasses break, it is a total disaster; it would take a month or more to have them fixed or to get new ones. I take off the glasses automatically without thinking and put them in a loose pocket of my trousers.

I struggle desperately to control my emotions and not to cry. There is a strange feeling inside me; I don't want anyone to see the depth of my

9 Nazli Partovi was born in 1956 in Tehran. Her older brother, Mohammad Ali Partovi, a first-generation member of the Organization of Iranian Peoples Feda'i Guerrillas (OIPFG), took part in the attack on the gendarmerie post in Siahkal on February 8, 1971, and was captured by SAVAK right after the military attack. He was brutally tortured and sentenced to life imprisonment.

After graduating from high school, Nazli was accepted to Gilan University, where she obtained her bachelor's degree in industrial management in 1978. She was politically active while at university and participated in the 1979 Revolution against the Shah's dictatorship. After her brother Mohammad Ali was released from prison in late 1978, they joined the Sahand Group. Both were arrested in 1982 in a massive raid by the IRI's security forces. Once more, Mohammad Ali was sentenced to life and Nazli to twelve years of imprisonment. In 1988, Mohammad Ali was condemned to death by the Death Commission and immediately executed. After eight years and three months, Nazli was released from prison and fled Iran in 1993, seeking political asylum in Sweden. She continued her studies and received her master's degree in nursing and has been working in that profession for over twenty years. As a veteran political prisoner and a survivor of the Great Massacre, her public testimonies, lectures, interviews, and essays have contributed to a better understanding of the way in which the IRI's prisons operated in the 1980s. Nazli's mother, Maliheh Birang (known as Mother Partovi), one of the prominent figures of the Mothers of Khavaran (see Chapter Four), died on January 19, 2013.

grief. Until that moment, I had not let any of the prison wardens or the Revolutionary Guards read in my face that I had lost him, but every cell in my body is in pain from his loss. I don't want my cellmates to see the turmoil I'm in, maybe because no one knew him as well as I did. No one loved him as much as I did. No one had seen the depth of his ocean… or maybe it is my selfishness that even the grief of having lost him should belong only to me.

I need to release the explosion that is building inside me, but what can I do? How *would* I do it? Thinking of him makes me mad. His face, his look, his voice, his innocence flash before my eyes. I think of him walking with his limp but with his head held up going to the gallows. I wish I could know what he was thinking in those final moments. When I was subjected to mock executions in the last moments before "death" thinking that I was going to die, my life and its best moments flashed before me. I am sure it was the same for him.

It was before the beginning of the mass murders when news of the assault by the Mojahedin from across the Iraqi border into Iran broke—and Khomeini drank from his so-called cup of poison (as he described it), finally complying with UN Security Council resolution 598 and proclaiming an armistice with Iraq—that they took the televisions from each ward. They cut all our ties with the outside world. All visits with relatives were halted, and they stopped giving us newspapers. No one would even be taken to the infirmary.

When they brought the televisions back to the wards, it was as if they somehow wanted to show us that the carnage had ended and that life was going to return to its normal routine. I managed to keep my composure until I was caught that day. We were sitting around the lunch cloth on the floor. The television was on playing loud music. There was a joyful song that had taken over the whole ward. But the damn music felt like an avalanche that invaded my whole body and soul, breaking my composure. Joy? I had forgotten that there was joy and beauty in this world. And I, who could not but laugh at any happy occasion, was shocked at my own reaction—torn in realizing the contradiction between the beauty of that song and the immensity of my sorrow.

Until then, I had put a barrier around myself so that my sorrow would stay in my heart; so that one day, when I was ready and saw fit and no one was around, I could just let go and cry as much as I wanted. But that song just blew me away. Every cell in my body was shattered, each fiber shaking.

I locked myself in the bathroom so that I could get a hold of myself, swallow my pain, and keep my composure. I washed my eyes with cold water and put my glasses on so that the redness in my eyes would remain invisible. The danger had passed, the music had come to an end, and conversations had resumed in the ward. I took a newspaper and hid my face behind it.

In his heart I am sure that he had remembered each and every one of those he loved, and in total grief he knew that he would never see them again. He had wanted to tell them so much but would never be able to do so. I just know in my heart that in the last moments of his life, holding his head up, he only let them see his pride, not his agony.

Shahla, who had been one of the first in the ward to see her family after visitations had resumed, came running up, throwing herself at me. In a tearful voice she said that they had executed her husband, Hamid, and my brother, Mohammad. "Your mom and your sister are here to see you. Your sister knows of your brother's execution, but your mother doesn't know anything."

Shahla had heard all this from her mother and sister, who had been in touch with my family. At that time, many of the prisoners' families had close ties with one another. In fact, we, the political prisoners, had become like a large family whose pain we all suffered and whose joy we all celebrated.

Briskly, I distanced myself from her and said it would have been suspect if they had not been executed. The blow from hearing this devastating news was too strong to contemplate. I tried to run away from her, from all others, and from myself. It was at that moment that they announced my name on the intercom, summoning me to go visit my family—the perfect time to run away from the horrific news I had just heard.

When I got to the booth, I had a strange feeling. I had a lump in my throat. I saw my mother on the other side; she looked strange and there was pain written all across her face. Once in a while, though, you could see a spark in her eyes. She told me some families had been notified of the death of their loved ones but, fortunately, my family had not heard anything about Mohammad.

My head was spinning and I did not know what I was doing or saying. I just told her that we all must stay strong and accept reality. After our conversation was over, she handed the receiver to my sister. Since I knew that my mother could not hear me on the receiver, in broken words and in bits and pieces, in such an excruciating way that I cannot even remember, I told my sister that I knew the truth and realized that she, my mother, didn't know it. My sister said, "During one of our last visits, Mohammad told me that the situation in prison wasn't okay, but I tried to calm him down and told him, 'This is one of those winds that will pass'. But he disagreed with me and said, 'No, this is not just a wind. This is a thunderous lightning that will strike, taking all of us with it'."

I still do not know whether it was us who tried to hide our faces from our mother or whether it was she who tried to ignore the *pain* she saw on our faces. Whatever it was, our visit ended in sorrow, with tears in our eyes and a thousand wounds in our hearts. I was cold and numb. That only changed sometime after they brought the television back into our ward.

TRANSLATED FROM PERSIAN BY F. AMINI

A Taste of Mortadella: Reflections on Massacre and Resistance[10]

SHOKOUFEH SAKHI[11]

Does the distance of some thirty years clarify reflection, obscure sequences of events, illuminate meanings, and render names and dates suspect? Yes. Do any of these affect the essence of the matter? Not in the least. What then are these experiences of memories and how can I communicate them to you? Muddled by the daily remembering and forgetting of the intervening years, momentous events and minute details jostle one another with the familiarity of nocturnal repetition, with the poignancy of the return or death of a friend, with the stubbornness of a constant heart. With all this and so much more, it may be best to begin this remembrance of summer 1988 with the bare facts and let the reminiscences tell their own story as they unfold.

Iran is a country with many large prisons. In Tehran of the 1980s, there were two main prisons in the city and two larger ones in the suburbs. In summer 1988,

---

10 I must thank all the cellmates and friends who helped me in this work through hours of conversations reviewing and remembering the historical nuances of the events of summer 1988. I could not have done this without their participation. I also must emphasize that this is not a historical record but rather my account of that historical event.

11 Dr. Shokoufeh Sakhi is currently a member of the Pathologies of Solitude research network, a project hosted at Queen Mary University of London. She has a doctorate in political science from York University, Toronto, with a specialization in political theory and philosophy. She acted as executive committee director (2013–14) of the Iran Tribunal Foundation investigating the Iranian state's crimes against humanity in the 1980s. She also testified as an ex-political prisoner at the Iranian People's Tribunal hearings (2012). Among many documentaries, she participated in *The Tree That Remembers*, a 2002 production of the National Film Board of Canada. Her most recent publication is *Ethical-Political Praxis: Social Justice and the Resistant Subject in Iran* in *Iran's Struggles for Social Justice* (Basingstoke, UK: Palgrave, 2017).

I am in Evin prison. More precisely, I am in Ward 1 of the three women's Wards of the Amoozeshgah compound. Amoozeshgah is composed of two three-story buildings: women prisoners were held in Wards 1, 2, and 3 of one building and the men in Wards 4, 5, and 6 of the other. Each Ward has six large cells. Aside from that, each Ward has its own rules and regulations depending on the level of the prisoners' repentance and collaboration, or their lack thereof. In summer 1988, I am in Cell 1 of Ward 1. All six cells in this Ward are kept locked at all times, without access to the toilet or running water. Here, in Cell 1, I live with, at various times, between twenty and thirty other prisoners. Ward 1, for the most part, holds prisoners who are kept beyond the completion of their official sentences, the Azadi-ha.

I am a petite 24-year-old woman with short hair and a round face, wearing a large pair of broken glasses sewn together with threads. My five-year sentence ended on August 12 of the year before, 1987.

I remember a day in July...

Friday or Saturday, July 29 or 30, 1988

The door opens. A guard's head appears: "Hejab," she orders, and closes the door. One of us starts distributing chadors. The Mojahedin have their own stash and they distribute theirs. Mandatory when males are present, we are still busy putting the chadors on when the guard opens the door again: "Hurry up, cover yourselves and sit down."

We seat ourselves against the walls around the Cell. I find a spot across from the women who have been arrested in relation to Mojahedin (that is, the People's Mojahedin Organization of Iran, PMOI) and wonder what is going on this time. Yesterday the guards removed the television sets from the three women's Wards.[12] This morning the guards refused to give us our ration of two daily newspapers, and now there are officials here.

The Cell is ringed by veiled women sitting on the floor. I know their hearts are thumping like mine as our faces assume the usual artificial coolness, with the usual variety of underlying approaches to such contact. Some dare the presence of the officials, some avert their eyes; some say we are not here, you don't see us; some say see us, yes, we are here, in your face. A few whisper under their breaths; another one's lips hint toward a smirk; some even feel playful, challenging the officials' presence, while others remain serious, grand,

---

12 We had secret contact with the rest of the Cells in Ward 1 and the other Wards in the women's section in *Amoozeshgah*.

and proud. It seems we all sense the proximity of some event; we all maintain our usual façade, but intensified anxiety is the rule. Minutes pass. The muffled sound of a commotion in the hallway slips through the locked door. In the Cell silence takes over, broken only by an isolated cough here and there.

Something is up.

The women's legs, torsos, arms, shoulders, and heads—except for their naked faces—are buried under the layer of chador: homogenized bodies, officially nonexistent, except as passive, shameful loci of retribution and correction. Yet I see the shoulders, the arms; whole bodies move and with them the various fabrics, some patterned, some pure black, cease their collusion with the regime and come to life. The two sides of the fabric meet in front of the women's bodies, random openings and closings, an arm coming out and going back inside, a restless foot sticks out, a knee bends beneath the body, stretching the fabric like a plastic wrap leaving a rounded trace; the fabric comes to life, testifying to the presence of a living body, yes, a contained and disciplined body, but one with a rebellious and patient soul beneath the cover.

The door opens revealing a group of men and the female guards giving way for the Warden to enter first. "Take off your shoes before entering," dares say one of the day workers sitting near the door.

The Warden and his cronies, four or five men in all, enter the Cell. The head guard holding tight onto her black chador locates herself by the door jamb. The men sit on the floor by the door.

"Your name and charge?"

No matter the stage of our sentences, from the time they arrested us to the day they killed us, let us go, or we got away, we were identified not by what we had allegedly done, but by reference to the political groups and lines of thought with which we were affiliated or sympathized. Even here they could not use criminal discourse in dealing with us—not "saboteurs," not "terrorists." So, whenever they wanted us to identify ourselves, they asked our name and our political/ideological affiliation; hence, the question as to "charge" or "accusation."

"Your name and charge?"

The Warden directs his head toward the prisoner, who, seated immediately to his right, is staring hard at her knees. My cellmates seated along this side of the Cell are all Mojahedin. We know the drill. Counterclockwise, one by one, we are to say our names and the name of the political organization we are accused of belonging to. The woman with the fixed stare speaks, or doesn't speak, or must have spoken, but what she says, or doesn't say, puts time out of sync for a moment. I don't so much hear her as think I remember *having* heard her.

"So-and-So, Mojahedin," she says, and in the space left by the sounds of her words comes the more than usually tense, more than usually mechanical response of the next along the wall: "So-and-So, Mojahedin"; and so on, a repeating echo confirming my first sense of something impending just out of reach, something foreboding.

My own suddenly more focused awareness is apparent in the rest as we each do our turn: "So-and-So, Peykar," "So-and-So, Aqaliyat," "So-and-So, Sahand," and so forth.[13] We proceed through the litany, also mechanically, as the import of what has just taken place adds itself to the accumulation of small signs we have been detecting.

Hmm... the Mojahedin are taking a collective position. What does it mean?

Such was the experience of Evin at the time: they—from the Warden down to the lowest guard—did everything in their power to avoid giving us any clue about anything; we became attuned and adept at interpreting the slightest traces of information. Here, however, to anyone who had been around a while, the clue was not at all subtle. Except for "Mojahedin," the litany of organizational names given on that day consisted of different leftist-Marxist organizations. We, the leftists, had always responded to our charges with these names. Not so with the Mojahedin.

Although for the past year or so there had been a resurgence of direct confrontation and resistance among some of Mojahedin sympathizers, as a rule, from 1981 and the first wave of mass executions, many of those who were arrested and accused in relation to the PMOI, identified themselves not by the actual name of their organization but by the derogatory name the state had given them: Monafeq *(hypocrite).*

To comprehend the stunned aura of the Cell that comes back to me after all these years, it's necessary to get a sense of the significance of this reversion in the response. This simple re-appropriation of the literal name of their organization in the context of the Iranian Islamic prison system meant nothing less than taking back, recovering, their political identity. Instead of their long-standing tactical repentance and identification of themselves through the use of the state's discourse as politically resigned testimonies to its power, they were bringing what was left of themselves out of hiding, changing fundamental strategy, turning to fight.

---

13 See Appendix B.

In fact, as we know now, this outright change in the political stance of the prisoners occurred in synchrony with the organization's assault on the western front, named by the PMOI Forough-e Javidan (Eternal Light) Operation. A week previously, on July 18, Iran had accepted UN Security Council resolution 598 which had finalized a ceasefire in the eight-year war with Iraq. The Mojahedin hoped and evidently believed that, with the Iraqi military support they were expecting, the people would join forces with them and they would march across the country and enter the capital in a matter of days.

All this perspective comes from hindsight, of course.

"Your name and Charge."

"So-and-so, Mojahedin." "So-and-so, Sazeman." "So-and-so, Razmandegan." "So-and-so, Aqaliyat"... and on around the Cell.

Eyes fixed in an unselfconscious glare, the Warden glowers at each in turn; the skin on his face is tight. The faces he encounters, to the exact contrary of his attempt at a penetrating presence, have drained in the direction of studied neutrality. Various degrees of stubborn inwardness compete with a need to withdraw, to disappear. The outcomes of the struggle, different from woman to woman, are apparent. As each speaks, I sense behind the heightened mechanical qualities, still, like the faces, something of the individual: voice tones to match the averted eyes, the touch of daring, the hints of pride still tracing themselves subtly across the faces, though all smirks are gone: we have trained ourselves to show the foe the least fear, anxiety, or agitation we can manage. Seething anger, a need to strangle us on the spot, betray themselves through the simultaneously bitten-off and nonchalant sarcasm of the Warden's words: "This is the end of our benevolence, the end of taking it easy in our prisons." He manages a dramatic pause before hitting us with the punch line. "From now on, you're getting the prison of 1981."

As it would eventually turn out, even the threat of the more extreme insecurity and unpredictability, the utmost punishment, torture, and summary executions of 1981 did not prepare us for the experience of the prison regime of 1988.[14]

∾

---

14 See Chapter One of this book for the timeline of political suppression and mass executions during the 1980s.

He points to two leftist prisoners, one of them the day worker who told him to take off his shoes, tells them to join all the Mojahedin supporters, and jabs his thumb toward the door. "Put on your blindfolds and move." They are all to be taken away. The Warden and the other men file out. The chief guard stands by the door and says, "Hurry up, grab your blindfolds and get out."

I am watching... *we* are watching a rush of hesitant movements entering the bodies of our cellmates, who are getting up, each going to their stuff, fumbling for their blindfolds. Defiance and readiness! One by one they pull down their blindfold before stepping out of the Cell. Before closing the door, the chief guard's head appears again. "Pack up all of these women's stuff." She manages to get both glee and disgust into her tone. Her eyes sparkle with a sadistic glint. She is jubilant. This is her day.

We don't have to look at each other to know that everyone feels the change in the Cell, the new emptiness, the heaviness. Just like that, in the blink of an eye, two of our leftist and all our Mojahedin cellmates are gone. What is the meaning of this particular event? What could it be? Once again, we are left with traces. This is not just a separation of the Mojahedin from the prisoners; that has happened before, and this feels stranger. Besides, they took leftist cellmates too. Maybe they are being taken to solitary cells; we can at least hope that is the explanation, the destination. But what was the meaning of the reference to 1981?

Someone suggests that the guard's grinning face made her look like she was constipated. Most of us manage a not entirely empty laugh. But we don't feel much in the mood. In a matter of a minute someone who has been living with you for months or years is transferred to another prison, Ward, or Cell—or for execution. Most of the time it is as it is now: we don't know which it is to be. We set to work, packing the clothing and personal belongings of our friends and cellmates. We are experienced at this task: as much as possible, emotions are kept at bay and attention is focused on packing the things most necessary for survival in solitary cells or worse conditions. We deftly hide the illegal items as inconspicuously as possible in the corners of their bags or among their personal stuff.

We finish, kneeling or squatting on the cell floor. When they are finally ready, we stack the bags neatly by the door. We are sure from the noises in the hall that many others are being taken from adjoining cells as well. Eventually the noises die down and we are left in silence with no real idea of what has just happened.

∽

Memory? What an evasive thing it is! Thing? What an ethereal experience! Experience? What an event it is to remember! I used to wish that some form of hypnotic suggestion would make it possible to get at some objective truth, that finally it would be possible to pick up a pair of tweezers and extract the scattered images and voices from my soul, line them up, and call them "history." But now I know that history is not made up of a series of discrete events, like beads on a string, each leading to the next and the whole thing being history. *No, it is* meaning, *meaning always intimately related to now—and it should be. These memories, here and now, appear in my reflections as snapshots, as cherished and painful experiences, as meanings.*

We climb up the iron shelf that covers the east wall. The shelf blocks the cell window that would open on the space behind the building. We try to get our ears as close as possible to the outside. It is a minute or two after midnight. I crouch on top of the shelf and extend my neck. My friend hushes everybody. "Listen," she says, "they are taking them for execution. I hear men singing the 'Internationale'."[15] Straining, I, too, hear something. Is it some scuffling, maybe men's voices? Or, I *think* I hear voices... but do I? We are all frozen stiff on the shelf, midway climbing up, or squatted down on the floor trying to capture a sound wave that might be sneaking into our Cell through cracks in the iron-shaded window behind the massive iron shelf. One thinks she heard noises coming from the direction of the solitary confinement building (they called it *Asayeshgah*, the "relaxation spa"!). Another thinks she heard guards barking commands. One is sure she hears nothing and then thinks maybe she does. Another hears chanting. Silently, an image flows into our minds: the guards taking a group of our comrades from the male solitary section for execution, blindfolded, each one's hand on the shoulder of the one ahead of him, chanting and singing the "International," marching to their deaths. Slowly we retrace our steps, resume our sleeping places on the spread blankets on the floor. It is quiet now.

All we can do is wait.

∽

---

15 A socialist anthem that has been a standard of left-wing movements since the late nineteenth century.

How many days has it been since they cut us off from everything outside our Cell? It was Friday, July 29, during the afternoon toilet break that the guards took the Cell television and our ration of state-run newspapers. They even cut off the annoying loudspeakers which had broadcast propaganda from the state-run radio station, updating their latest military triumphs. Now there is no visiting with family, no letters, no packages, no money received from the outside; no visits to the prison's clinic, no matter the emergency. We're being sucked toward a black hole... what black hole? Why all this secrecy? Not even in 1981 did they act so mysteriously.

A few months before, maybe it was in spring or winter 1988 (or was it 1987?), they had turned one of the guards' rooms into a registration office. One by one we were taken into the room, re-fingerprinted, and each of our pictures retaken (this time with each of us wearing a number plate). They asked if we had any distinguishing marks on our bodies and gave us a questionnaire to fill out. Were we Muslim or not? Did we pray or not? Did we accept Khomeini as the Supreme Leader and did we believe in the Islamic Republic? We, the leftist prisoners of Wards 1 and 3, who were known as *sar-e moze-i* (uncompromising), declined to respond to such questions, insisting that our beliefs and faiths were our own private affairs and that the state had neither the right, nor indeed the power, to prosecute our consciences. We refused to participate in their interrogations. Beyond the few of us who replied with a direct "No," our response to ideological and positional questions such as these was, "I have no reply." The regime, of course, did not consider this a legitimate position. In fact, political and ideological conversion and compliance of the political prisoners was the main objective of the prison system; hence, the category *Azadi-ha*. The response, "I have no reply," was an act of direct resistance.

The interrogator told us on that occasion not to worry about the consequences of our responses since this interrogation was only for prisoner reclassification and prison reorganization, encouraging us to respond "truthfully." Who did they think would answer those sorts of questions? Who did they think would believe them? What did they take us for? Fools? Imbeciles? They couldn't be that stupid, so why were they doing this? Clearly, it was not merely an ideological census.

Tuesday, July 26

Today is our Ward's turn for family visits. The loudspeakers spit out military tunes as the broadcaster announces the state's heroic military engagement with the *Monafeqin* on the western front. Our families rush into the visiting hall, anxious and excited to spot their daughters behind the glass wall. We, on our side, are standing in our separate cubicles, with one hand on the glass and the other waving. Every second counts. We cannot ask what is happening out there directly, but some of my cellmates have become experts in lip-reading, so while one parent talks on the phone receiver the other one lips out news of the outside world.

We are back to our Cell trying to build up a narrative from the bits and pieces we have picked up. A week ago, Khomeini proclaimed his acceptance of UN Security Council resolution 598, which halted the eight years of what Khomeini had called the "God-sent bliss." And now the Mojahedin's militia is marching through some western cities of Iran. This means something critical: some parents have been ecstatic, wanting to believe that the end of the war might mean less pressure on their children, or maybe even amnesty. We listened incredulously.

Ceasefire, the end of war without victory. The PMOI's military excursion. Our parents' faces: excited, want-to-be-optimistic, yet nervous and shaky. Khomeini declaring the necessity of drinking from the goblet of hemlock and accepting the UN Security Council resolution. The prison guards' eyes burning with resentment, watching us for slight signs of happiness at the news of their defeat. In our Cell, none of us leftists share the optimistic analysis. Suspicion is the general mood—that and anticipation of something ominous that we cannot yet grasp. One of my friends recalls the brightened faces of our Mojahedin cellmates a few days ago when they read about the attack in the newspaper: "You can hear the footsteps of the revolution" one of them had said. If only that were true. But we remember 1981: then the Mojahedin prisoners had gone to sleep every night for months with their belongings stored under their pillows, to be ready always when the hand of the people opened the prison doors.

❧

Memory, memories: images, voices, senses come and go—rushing into each other, making a mess of facts, realities, and imaginings. It's chaos. So I can't—and I don't want to—pick them apart and line them up one after another like soldiers. I refuse.

"Make a straight line. Put your hand on the shoulder of the one in front of you, grab her chador, and move. One after the other! Don't move your head around; keep in line. Head down. I'll break your neck." *Thump* goes the muffled sound of knuckles hitting a skull wrapped in a layer of fabric.

My images are not orderly. They are all present at the same time. Now here and one, now there and another.

We bang at our door; we bang and bang hoping in vain that they will open it so we can get a glimpse of those we can hear being taken away. A guard yells, swearing at us from behind the closed door. Another guard shouts insults as she prods the blindfolded women to form an orderly line. We bang again complaining that we can't wait any longer for our long-overdue toilet time. Maybe a guard will open the door to get us to shut up...; it works. The door opens and one of us immediately gets into a shouting match with the guard to distract her so others can try to get the attention of any of the blindfolded women in the hallway; a chin turns and then is lifted toward our door. Something is mouthed. The guard in the hallway notices; our door is shut violently; a stream of insults and threats spit from her mouth.

It is quiet now for a few moments, then the same guard opens our door again: "You pitiful, miserable, filthy pieces of garbage, why are you in such a hurry? It'll be your turn soon enough." Her nonchalant tone makes one shiver. "For your efforts, you'll be the last cell to get to the washrooms today." The door shuts.

∾

Cell 2 has become a transit station. It fills up with voices, with movement, and then it is vacated and turns quiet. We hear a new group of prisoners enter. A friend of mine and I hear our personal code signals being tapped on the wall. This can only mean one thing: it is our friend from our previous Ward. We rush to the wall, facing each other. I stick my left ear and she her right one to the wall, and I tap back:

"Hi, what's hap—"

"A 'special commission' is re-trying all of those arrested in relation to the Mojahedin."

Her tapping breaks up and picks up again, and then breaks up and picks up again. We on our side try to calm her down. She tells us that whoever answers "Mojahedin" to the charges is sent to solitary.

"They are going to kill us all," her hairpin taps on the wall.

"No, no, they can't do that, maybe only those who are already on death row."

We tap back hurriedly but she interrupts again.

"What should I do?"

We know what she means: she is not ideologically with the Mojahedin anymore, though that is how she is still charged.

"Can't you tell them that you are a leftist now and not a Mojahed—"

Tap, tap, tap... "No, no, no... doesn't matter. I can't bring myself to say or do what the regime wants me to. They'll demand cooperation."

Trapped. She is utterly and absolutely trapped; we are utterly and absolutely trapped. She scrapes the wall aimlessly.

What she says, what she doesn't say, explodes across the Cell. The moment echoes like ancient and fateful boot steps along an empty stone hall, carrying news of an already perpetrated catastrophe. But it's the old familiar being there and not being there: mechanically, as the import of the moment and of the small signs we had been recognizing for weeks settle inexorably into the vacuous space. We don't recognize it; we can't, because while we are there, we are not there; we don't exist; we have never existed.

We try to find something to say; we start to scratch something, but she interrupts: "It's only that it's a pity that I'm going under for what I no longer believe." We listen; we hear; we feel her hair brushing on the wall as she moves to adjust her ear; we hear the thin sound of the hairpin searchingly scraping.

Did we really understand the extent of the disaster? Could we make it out? After years of imprisoning their oppositional forces, after rendering ridiculous "judgments" and absurd sentences... to now pick up the scythe and just kill them? No, we couldn't. And yes, we felt its approach, but we were too alive to experience our death. They killed her. She never made it out alive. But still, she was mistaken. It doesn't matter what they thought she was dying for. She went for the right reasons, not to give them what they would take by force, what they tortured and murdered for.

The last thing we hear from our friend is the sudden sound of the hairpin sliding on the wall as she pulls herself away at the sound of the guard opening the door.

She goes. The Cell is emptied. They're all gone.

Have you ever seen a panther caged in a zoo? Sometimes it paces in a straight line: back and forth, back and forth, back and... And we paced in our rib cage, in our minds; we paced the Cell floor back and forth, back and forth, and again. What else could we do?

What would you have done?

~

The guards can't help themselves: they are different now. The sharp edge of hatred and frustration in their expressions has given way to a dull, distant mockery. They don't get agitated much with our constant complaints about lack of access to toilets or need for medical attention, nor do they find much enjoyment in looking for little excuses to put more pressure on us. We see in their sideways glances, the narrowed eyes, the smirks curling an upper corner of lip, we see, in their lack of response generally, just how insignificant our existence has become to them. Sometimes, we even spot a momentary instant of pity in one or two of them! What do they see when they look at us, we wonder.

Because Islam requires daily ablutions, we are allowed to use the washrooms four times a day, unless the privilege has been withdrawn for punishment. These days we can't be sure when they'll open the door. It must be around six o'clock in the morning and a few of us are already awake waiting for it. Suddenly we hear the outer door into the Ward open. We hear the guards rushing in. One of them comes directly to our door and opens it. "Hurry up, finish it quickly," she orders.

A middle-aged guard is running toward their washroom at the end of the hallway, clutching her stomach and throwing up. The third guard goes to her assistance. They try to joke their way through it. I glance around the hallway as I stall by looking for a pair of slippers: both shifts' guards are here at the same time. They are loud and hyper, hysterically laughing. As I stroll toward the washroom, I see the one who got sick leaning on another guard. Her face is convulsed; she whimpers that she cannot bear it anymore. The head guard scolds her in her usual artificial way: "Haven't you heard Haj Agha (the Warden) say that everyone has to be present? Everyone must participate." Another guard turns back toward one of my cellmates who is very obviously watching them. "What are you looking at? You'll be dangling soon yourself." She sneers as she noisily drags her slippers on the floor. They rush all of the Cells, one after the other, in and out of the washrooms, and then they leave again: *to be present, to participate.*

Back in our Cell, we wonder what it is that all of them, all the prison personnel, have to take part in. What do they do or see which is making even them sick to their stomachs, which is making them so edgy, not being their usual selves?

I don't know how much death one can take in. We saw the signs. We heard the guards' blatant promises that our turn would come too. We could sense, almost smell, the death. They were saturated in it. Again, there were moments of pity in some of their faces. Yet we were alive and had to live: pacing the length of our Cell, talking, joking, dreaming, hoping, and waiting. And they did come, but slowly, ever so slowly.

∾

One morning a guard calls three of our cellmates to get ready for interrogation. Here it is; it is our turn now. As usual, one of us is eavesdropping at the door. She hears the guard go to the other Cells and call names to get ready. We help our friends. Everybody's face is a silent question mark: Why her and not me; why me and not one of the others; why these three? And interrogation? Interrogation for what? One of the three cracks a joke as she fixes her chador in place.

I remember only that we laughed, that her face opened up in her laughter, her vivid eyes anxiously running from one face to another, as she said goodbye. But I don't remember the joke.

The door opens. "Hurry up, put your blindfolds on and come out," the guard says casually. There are other blindfolded women in the hallway. We know them. This group is all chosen from our category, the leftist *Azadi-ha*.

Weeks are passing. Two more groups have gone so far. We hear through our network that several leftist women have been taken from the upper Ward. Why are they so slow in dealing with us?

∾

It is more than two months since we were cut off entirely from the rest of the world. We haven't seen it, but fall has arrived.

The guard opens the door to the adjacent Cell, Cell 2; we hear it turning on its hinges. The Cell has been left empty for a long time... Footsteps and the muffled voice of a woman talking to the guard... sounds familiar. We are

all ears, silently tracing the guard's dragging slippers leaving the main corridor. One of our cellmates taps on the wall. Someone taps back the familiar
identification code. Aahh, she is one of the three cellmates who were taken
away from our Cell. We are ecstatic; they are alive; they are back; they are
here; they live! Our Cell transforms into a ball of anxious happiness, buzzes
with laughs, jokes, cheers, comments, questions.

"Hush kids!" someone warns. Now you can hear the rapid code-tapping
running through the cement wall. One of us is standing watch by the door;
a couple of women position themselves in a way that blocks the peephole
view on our friend tapping the wall; the rest quietly sit here and there or
pace the length of the cell. We wait for the news. We find it strange that they
have brought our friends to Cell 2, since they've been doing everything to
prevent us from contacting and communicating with other prisoners. They
knew we would easily communicate through the codes!

By the tightening lines on our friend's forehead, by her contracted body
language, and by the frequent breaks in the rhythm of her taps, we can sense
the stifling effect of the news. Whatever the reason for our friends' return, it
is not a reason for celebration.

The news turned out to be that they were taken to the Solitary Ward,
Asayeshgah. One by one they were questioned by the "special commission."
In addition to their official "charges," the commission asked them if they
were Muslim or not, if their parents were Muslim, and if they performed
the daily prayers. As always, they answered, "I have no reply." The commission declared our friends *Mortad* (apostates) and, in accordance with their
interpretation of Islamic principles for female *Mortads*, condemned them
to a regimen of five lashes five times a day, at each prayer time, unto death
or acceptance of Islam.[16]

For two weeks our friend and her other two cellmates have been lashed
five times a day. The guards have set up a bench in the middle of the corridor of the Solitary Ward where prisoner after prisoner is laid face down and
receives the lashes. Every guard participates in the lashing, collecting their
god's blessing for punishing an apostate. As time passes and the prisoners
do not break down, the male guards join the torturing crew. Their hits carry
more force, and perhaps more conviction! For fourteen days our friend and

---

16 It must be emphasized that at different historical moments, Islamic principles and
their application had been (as they still are) interpreted differently. For example, there
were leftist women in the early 1980s who, charged with apostasy, were not only tortured
but also executed.

the others endured the lashes. What finally broke them down, she said, more than the inability to endure the five lashes at each session, was the anticipation of the next round. Every dawn, noon, afternoon, evening, and late at night the guards were at their door, taking them out again. She and her cellmates discussed their situation: through the prisoner network, tapping with other solitary cells, they had the suspicion that many of the Mojahedin who were taken from our Ward had been removed from the solitary cells too. All the signs pointed toward the worst possibility. They could not see an end. She tapped that they were oscillating between committing group suicide and complying with the ruling of the special commission. After holding out for two weeks, they opted for the latter.

Yet, this was not, of course, the end of the story. It almost never is. When the goal is not retrieving information, but destruction of identity and its reformation, capitulation under torture is generally just the beginning—as it was here. After submission in words, they demanded submission in deeds: perform the prayers or get more lashings. When the goal is psychic annihilation and assimilation, the spirit must be broken: a guard would sometimes come to the Cell and demand that they pray in front of her and, at other times, she would assume the position of religious leader herself, lining them up behind her and directing the rite. Prayer itself became a ritual of submission to the guard, the prison, and the regime it represented. Meanwhile, they could hear other prisoners being transferred to the Solitary Ward and being tortured. The anxious anticipation of the time for prayer and the sound of a Cell door opening, footsteps ending somewhere in the middle of the corridor, the bench creaking under the prostrated body, the mocking insults and thump, the carefully extended pause... the next thump... thump... thump... thump...

So, bringing back this group of prisoners from the Solitary Ward and locking them in the adjoining Cell was no accident. They wanted us to hear what was waiting for us. They were trying to soften us up, "tenderize" us, hoping to achieve our submission more efficiently, saving both time and effort. To take us all through the torture process would have required a huge amount of labor and many solitary Cells; to take us a few at a time would take a long, long time. How much more time could they spare to break down two or three hundred leftist, noncomplying,[17] "inferior" female prisoners?

---

17 I repeat the term "noncomplying" because this number is not the actual statistic for all female prisoners with a leftist "accusation," just as those who were arrested in relation with Mojahedin comprised a larger number than those who were considered by the regime what today would be called Mohareb, enemy combatants.

It is midday and time for our afternoon toilet. Today's cell-designated workers have everything prepared and ready for the door to be opened. The woman with latrine duty and the one in charge of water are standing by their buckets three or four paces away from the door, chatting with the girls charged with dishes. The dirty dishes racked in a basket sit between the two girls; the basket's handles have been mended and sewn together many times with pieces of rags and plastic. A little further along, another two are sitting at the edge of the Cell's single army bunk bed with their shrunken brooms ready in hand. It is crucial not to waste the first ten minutes of group bathroom time. During this time the door remains open to transport our stuff to the washroom area. This is when the Cell's day workers sweep the floor, taking advantage of the open door to vent the Cell and dust. As always, the *ezterrary-ha*, the ones with weak kidneys or bladders, are gathered by the door, ready to jump out and run. The door cracks open slightly. "Stay put. No washroom yet," the guard says and opens the door further. She glances around casually and stops at a face. "You, come on out with your chador and blindfold." It has been a while since the last time they took someone from our Cell. Our attention turns toward our cellmate, being with her and helping her to get ready. We are, of course, apprehensive for her, but sometime later, well after our turn at the toilet, she is returned unharmed!

The moment she steps in through the door and pulls off her blindfold, everyone springs up and crowds around her. Walking her to a corner, we all sit on the floor as one body. After a pause and in a tone of disbelief, she says, "I had an internal visit with my brother." She stares out at us in blank wonder as she plays with her blindfold, wrapping it around her fingers and unwrapping it again. "What? No way!" "How come?" "How was he?" "Why?" "How are the guys?" We can hardly contain ourselves. Her chador is still lingering on her shoulders, but with each agitation in her narrative it slides down her torso and finally drops and lies still around her on the floor. She tells us that she and a few other comrades from other Cells and other Wards were allowed an "internal visit."[18] She says her brother has recently been transported, along with the remaining male prisoners, from nearby Karaj's prison, Gohardasht,

18 On some occasions and with various motives, the prison officials allowed prisoners whose first-degree relatives (i.e. husband, wife, brother, sister, parent, or child) were among prisoners and in the same prison to have a supervised visit. These visits were known as "internal," being internal to the prison.

to ours. Silently, we listen to the news. As in Evin, Gohardasht's visiting times, television, newspapers, and so forth had been cut since late July. He told her how they all had been questioned by Khomeini's "special commission"; how he and his cellmates believed with the war ending, there would be a general amnesty for the prisoners. He told her how wrong they were; that almost all prisoners arrested in relation to Mojahedin were hanged; that many, many, many of the leftist men were hanged; that he was alive only because he told the Council he was a Muslim.

Not many Gohardasht prisoners were left alive, same as at Evin.

For leftist male political prisoners who were ruled apostate the penalty was death, while for leftist female prisoners it was a regimen of five lashes five times a day, at each prayer time, unto death or acceptance of Islam. Aahh, the bitter irony of religious dogmas and rulings: in a belief system which considers women as creatures of emotions and irrationality, impressionable and incapable of rendering rational judgments (hats off to Aristotle!), being a female, though convicted of apostasy, saves one from execution. We were saved, most of us, by the same sex-apartheid dogma that considered us inferior to men and that hanged our male comrades who said "No" or refused to reply.

Nobody interrupts her; listening but not hearing; hearing but not registering. She tells us that her brother cannot believe that we are still *sar-e moze-i*, that we are not even considering giving in. Are we naïve or just stupid? he'd asked her. He told her that he and others who said they were Muslim but did not pray got twenty lashes five times a day, right at each call for prayer, till they all conceded. Twenty, five times a day! How could they last more than a couple of days! He was adamant that the regime will not stop torturing and killing until we have either complied or are all dead. Sitting there listening, I realize this means that until we completely give up, are neutralized and neutered, or are dead, that the real options here come down to which form of obliteration we choose. But the brother, she tells us, takes another view, begging her to change her position. After all, if they, our male comrades, could not resist the torture, what chance did we women think we had?

The Cell feels hot. Everyone has a lot to think about. The news comes to us as something that we have really known for some time, as something that we could not quite fathom. Even now, with our suspicions confirmed, we have difficulty with the reality of it. Most of us have been in prison for the last six or seven years; we have witnessed and undergone a variety of physical and psychological tortures, long-term solitary confinement, months of experimental sensory deprivation, and so on. We have gone through the time of mass executions, the three years of 1981–83, to which the Warden has promised to take us again. But even that was nothing like this. To be executed after all these years. To have been among those to whom historical chance had conveyed the responsibility of sustaining resistance against annihilation; to have sustained it only to be annihilated anyway?

The air is stagnant and feels heavy in our chests. We think and talk among ourselves. It seems very peculiar that after all of their careful efforts to isolate us from any source of information, to prevent our piecing together any sense of what is coming and what to guard against, now, all of a sudden, they literally deliver news to our cells: first they locked our tortured friends in Cell 2 and now this "internal visiting." The Cell is abuzz with groups of two, three, or four gathered here and there mulling over what they just heard. The odd woman walks by or sits by herself in a corner silently pondering, assessing.

I wonder now, did we recognize then, just how clever and cunning the prison officials had been all through the months leading up to summer 1988? Or was it only later that we became aware of the extent of the enemy's strategic intelligence? I don't really remember. The fact is that they maximized the realization of their desired outcome in the shortest possible time. First came the extreme seclusion: prison segregated from outside, prison from prison, ward from ward, room from room, cell from cell. They covered up the nature of the "special commission" and the outcomes of their verdicts, even from the very prisoner being tried, the prisoner who never knew whether the verdict sent him or her to further torture or to hanging until immediately before the event. Only then, finally, after the massacre was all but completed, did they restore the opportunities to communicate and so deliver this news to the last remaining resistant, openly noncomplying prisoners. The news, passed on by our trusted and dear friends and comrades, was the news of our imminent end, of the futility of our being, of the inevitability of their total power. Perhaps, beyond contingent motives, they hoped we women, the inferior species, would, as a group, fold, lie down, and submit as soon as we heard the fate of our male counterparts. Actually, in any case, they did admit later that in this they had underestimated the leftist women.

∽

Trying to remember...

At the moment, I just remember that a lot happened from then on. Around this time the guards' office on our floor turned into a part-time interrogation room, frequented by the Warden and prosecutors. Some of the guards were transparent in their impatience at our continued existence, reminding us that we would soon join those who were not there anymore. Uncertainty dominated our days.

∿

Wednesday, October 19

The Cell door opens and a guard's head appears. "Write a letter to your parents and tell them to come to a visit on Tuesday, November 8." She drops a bundle of letter forms in the middle of the Cell and the door shuts again. It takes us a few seconds to comprehend what is happening, then one of us rushes for the forms. Later in the day the door again opens a crack and an extended arm tosses in a newspaper. We are allowed a newspaper again! It can't have all ended: we are still here. We read that the Mojahedin's military march into Iran from the western front has been suppressed.

Tuesday, November 8

From early morning the Cell has been filled with excitement and impatience. Contradictory feelings of happiness, sorrow, anticipation, pain, anxiety, and disbelief roll and boil inside everyone, and we know our parents outside are in no better condition. Everyone has her chador and blindfold ready at hand. The first people are called out. We wait for news, afraid of what we might hear.

Throughout the day each of us comes back with bits and pieces of news we have gathered from our family or exchanged secretly with prisoners in our visiting group from the other Cells. Once again, the Cell opens out to the world beyond the door. More prisoners have received apostate sentences. Some were tortured for days before giving in. One girl from our Ward, an *Azadi-ha*, cut her wrist open but was prevented from dying by the guards and put back on the torture bench. A few days later, she submitted too. Another one, from Ward 3, hanged herself from her Solitary Cell window by tying her chador around her neck. However, a group of prisoners from Wards 1 and 3 have resisted—survived the lashes without giving in. They are back to their Ward after weeks of torture, barely able to walk, with faces hard to recognize, but triumphant. They responded to the torture with a hunger strike and, in the last week, with a dry strike: no food and no water. It has happened, though it feels impossible to believe: some of us did resist unto death... and live.

Outside, parents are bewildered and frightened. Some who have heard from others about the visiting date, but have not received letters themselves, are gathered behind the doors. Their pleas to get a visit with their daughters and their questions about their whereabouts are rudely rebuffed by the visiting office's personnel and guards.

Here they are, my mom and dad with their fear-stricken and tired faces. My little son is not with them; I was hoping to see him today. They look older, smaller since the last time they were here. I try to reassure them that I am fine and nothing has happened to me. They plea once more for me to accept and do whatever the prison wants. I smile, tell them not to worry; I am who I am. They know that none of us can talk much: our visiting areas are tapped, our conversations overheard. I ask them to take care of themselves and my son.

Under pretense of asking about my brother, I ask them about a comrade friend of mine. He had been a leftist student activist when he was arrested in 1981 and received a life sentence. He is in Gohardasht prison.

I don't know now what I was hoping to hear; I probably didn't know then, but I know I could not stop crying when I heard he was alive.

I am sobbing; I see my parents' puzzled faces, hear their words that he is alive, he is okay, and I hear my own blabbering. If he is alive, it means he is broken... he is done, finished. Tomorrow when he and those like him are released, they will have to claim that what happened to us here was our own fault. They will have to justify themselves. Why can't I control my crying? Would I rather have heard that he was executed? I don't believe it.

I did not want him gone. That day, I realize now, I mourned him. I mourned my comrade, my dear friend. I had known him since I was a little girl and throughout the revolution. He was spirited, thoughtful, committed, proud, and a faithful Marxist revolutionary. I could feel the blows landing on his body and soul. I could sense the mush that remained of him. I grieved his absence.

~

And no, it did not end for us. We were still present, the last couple of hundreds of sar-e moze-i, *noncomplying leftist women. My head is full of images: lined up prisoners all covered in black and blindfolded, grabbing the chador of the one ahead of them and following the male guard to the interrogation building: more threats, more questions, more threats.*

One late fall day (or was it early winter?) all of the *Azadi-ha* from three Cells in Ward 1 and a number of prisoners selected from Ward 3 are ordered to pack their belongings and be ready for transportation. They load us into buses and take us to Gohardasht prison. There, they send us all into a public Ward, one previously occupied by male prisoners. Gohardasht's Warden, giving his blessing to us, says, "Here is where everything began and here it is going to end. This is the end for you." He asks if any of us have been given lashes and one says she has received them to the end. He says, "They did not end! We stopped them, and we will start them up again whenever we feel like it!" Then, with mockery he adds, "Here is where we hanged all of your 'jewels'." Happy with his pun, he steps outside of the Ward. (*Gohar* means "jewel" and *dasht* means "field": Gohardasht is "field of jewels.")

I do not remember what else he said. But I do remember that, rather than frightening, it just felt so unreal being in that Ward, walking, sitting, eating, sleeping, living in those Cells and hallway; places that belonged to others, filled only a few months ago with our male comrades. The experience of being in that Ward is inexpressible. Even now, so many years later, awareness, presence, and acknowledgment are still arriving—though I don't imagine there will be a time when they have fully *arrived. To say that it was surreal doesn't begin to get at it, actually diminishes the experience of being in a Ward where all occupants, everyone without exception, was suddenly plucked from life. As for ourselves, there we were, in a borrowed space on borrowed time.*

Pieces of men's clothing lie scattered here and there. There is the odd slipper, a sock. Every piece of scrap paper, the smallest object we find, is a treasure; holding it is holding onto a life, preventing it from vanishing into nothing. We are here; we know what has happened here. Sometimes it feels as if we are there with them, them with us, that we can feel and hear all the daily hustle and bustle of the hundreds of men. It is like there is a temporal and spatial corridor between us. And we flow through this corridor. *Does that make any sense to you?*

A friend walks toward me and a couple of others standing by a Cell door talking.

"Who wants a taste of Mortadella?"

Her mischievous eyes brighten up her bony face as she shows us her "find." She's holding a jar containing bits of feta cheese soaked in salt water, pieces of dried bread crumbs, and a small container of garlic powder.

"Here, try it."

She gives us each a piece of bread.

"Soak it in the cheese water and then sprinkle it with garlic powder... Now, eat it!"

She looks at us with delight.

"Aha! Oh yeah," I say, "it does taste like Mortadella. I can't believe it."

"Didn't I tell you? Want more?"

∽

Today when I look back I see that the prison wanted to defeat us, to break our spirit by taking us out of our familiar space and putting us in the space saturated with the absence of thousands of resisting souls, with death. And that is precisely what did not *happen: we were alive, stubbornly, insistently alive, unwilling to go out and meet death before it came to us, unwilling to be cowed by it. We spent our first hours organizing our daily lives. We set up our routines, resumed life from where it had been interrupted: readings, drawings, telling stories, debating political and philosophical topics, studying... and we added daily walks up and down the huge hallway. We joked about the possible interrogations and came up with secret signs to let each other know whether we had received a death sentence or solitary confinement.*

It arrives. Interrogation. We are all wrapped in our chadors and blindfolded, lined up with our backs to the wall of the big main corridor, waiting for our turn to be taken into one of the rooms. To make it difficult to talk among ourselves, each is placed against the wall four or five steps from the one to the left and the one to the right. When each exits the interrogation room, she is placed against the opposite wall. Peeking from beneath my blindfold, I see that none of those who come out of the interrogation room show the signal for hanging (four fingers dangling) or the signal for solitary (one finger wagging by itself). I am taken in. A voice says, "Pull up your blindfold." The prison Warden and an Evin prison prosecutor are sitting behind a desk with papers and files in front of them. "Name and charge?" the prosecutor asks. I say my name and the name of the leftist organization I was affiliated with.

"Do you pray?"

"No."

"Are you Muslim?"

"I have no reply."

The Warden looks more closely. "I know you. You were here last year with the rest of your bunch!"

I say nothing.

"So you already know that we mean business here. We are good people. We want to let your parents know what finally happened to their daughter. What's their phone number?" He smiles; his face wrinkles at his hypocrisy.

"We don't have a phone." I give them my parents' neighbor's number instead.

The guard takes me out. I sit on the floor by the wall where the guard leaves me. Is this it? I look around. Very soon the last of us will have been in and out. Fear creeps in: So this is how it ends? Quietly, I whisper to a friend sitting to my right. She has responded similarly to the questions. But why aren't they separating anyone from the line; does it mean that we all gave similar responses? Have we all finished it right here? I say to myself, patience Shokoufeh, patience; don't get ahead of yourself; don't forget who you are. Everything will become clear when the last one comes out.

We are all back in our Ward, exhausted yet pumped with adrenaline. The Ward fills with noises. We can't sleep until we have fully briefed each other, interpreted every little thing and tried to translate it into a tangible prediction. The Ward unravels by dawn, exhausted. The night after, we hear from the loudspeakers that in honor of the anniversary of the 1979 Revolution, on February 11, Khomeini will grant amnesty to a large group of political prisoners.

Later in the week, we are loaded into a bus again and taken back to Evin, to the care of our much surprised and deeply annoyed old guards. They cannot believe that we are still alive; we can't either. One complains to the man who delivers us to the female guards: "Why didn't they kill them? Believe me, nothing would happen outside, not even a ripple on the water, if they kill these ones too."

◦

Yes, memory is a tricky and faulty thing. The distance of thirty years clarifies reflection, obscures sequences of events, illuminates meanings, renders names and dates suspect; this and so much more. But does it really matter whether experiences from different days are misremembered and presented as contiguous, or whether the expression on someone's face on a particular occasion showed a vacant stare rather than the anxious one remembered from another time? Not in the least. In the telling, as close as memory allows to the actual events, truth is contained in the poignant remembrance of the face of a cellmate being taken away to be shot or hanged, the solidarity against the prison regime expressed in a stern and determined face, the feeling of the so called "amnesty parade" by the broken men and women prisoners through the streets of Tehran in compliance with the powers that had crushed them.

One snowy night they take all of us from Wards 1 and 3 to Evin's central office. They line us up against the wall. The building is crowded with prisoners and guards. Eventually, after standing there for a while, we sit down, leaning back on the wall. Finally, a man attends to our line. He asks cheerfully, "How many of you want to go home tomorrow?" No one says anything. He rewords his question: "Who wants to be freed tomorrow?" Again, no answer. His voice registers a tinge of agitation: "Which one of you is ready to request an amnesty from Imam Khomeini?" He becomes more agitated. "Those of you who are ready to participate in a march tomorrow to be freed immediately after, right there on the spot, stay where you are; and those who want to stay here and be executed move to the wall across the hallway." As I pull myself upright, I see from beneath my blindfold my friend's slippers and black chador moving into getting-up position and walking to the other side. Every one of us stands up and walks to the opposite wall. I wish I could see the guard's face now!

◦

We have read in the newspapers that to defy the international outrage about the mistreatment of political prisoners in Iran, political prisoners are going to demonstrate their support for the regime in Tehran on February 11, 1989. They will gather in front of the parliament building and from there they will march to the United Nations office. The event is to be called the *Caravan-e Azadi*, the "Freedom Caravan."

None of us women from Wards 1 and 3 took part in the parade. Later, I heard that only about twenty of the leftist men who had survived the slaughter refused to participate.

Thus ended the regime's efforts in summer 1988. It eliminated a large population of Mojahedin and successfully destroyed the Iranian leftist movement for decades to come. Those who were not killed that summer, especially among our men, individual by individual, left with deeply wounded identities. We, the leftist women, were sent home some years later on temporary passes to give our families a last chance to convince us to capitulate. Some of us took that opportunity to escape, as I did with my son. We, the remaining handful of leftist women and men, are the remainders of that imprisoned revolutionary generation. Since 2000, however, we have witnessed the birth and presence of a new generation of leftist students and civil activists, among elsewhere, in the universities and prisons of Iran.

Reynaldo Galindo Pohl's Inspection of Evin Prison

LALEH MASTOUR[19]

I hear the wheels of the food cart coming to a stop outside my cell. The door opens. It's *pasdar* Taleghani: dinner, lentil soup. After she hands me the soup, she bends down to grab a sheet of paper from the bottom shelf of the cart. "Write your letter," she says, passing me the blank paper. "We'll collect it after dinner."

I am seized with excitement. I don't know what to do, what to write, or who to write to.

It is exactly three months that I have been in solitary confinement without any access to communal facilities. And now, suddenly, I am given permission to write to my family! What does this mean? If I am granted the right to communicate with my family by letter, then why am I not back in my previous ward with my fellow inmates? I don't have much time to think about these ifs and buts; I must focus on writing my letter and getting it done as soon as possible.

I write a draft on a piece of cardboard. Then I carefully transfer the final version to the letter form. The letter is addressed to all my family members, my loved ones. It is brief and in keeping with the self-censorship forced upon us. I read the letter a couple more times. I couldn't have written it any better.

Suddenly my cell door opens. It's *pasdar* Taleghani. With the letter in hand, I take a long stride toward the door.

"Quickly gather your belongings and get ready."

"Why? Where? What about my letter?"

"We will collect the letters later. Now you must hurry up and collect your things." She closes the cell door abruptly.

---

19 Laleh Mastour was arrested in 1982. She survived the Great Massacre of 1988 but had to endure prison for another three years. She was released on bail in 1992. Feeling threatened, she left Iran in 1995 to reside in Europe.

I am rather perplexed: first the sheet of paper and now I am told to gather my belongings, indicating a transfer procedure, implying that my three-month solitary confinement has come to an end. Throughout this solitude, they never told me *why* I was condemned to solitary confinement or how long would it last.

I listen intently through the crack in the door—to the voices of other prisoners noisily talking to each other across the gaps in their doors.

"So, they've told you to gather your belongings? Me too!"

I hear bustling noises mixed with laughter. This is a new atmosphere. It is not the sound of a solitary-confinement ward; not the usual hushed silence, thick and painfully mysterious. I hear the sound of opening cell doors mixed with the sounds of hurried movements. It is apparent that some are moving their belongings to the entrance of the ward. Some, still locked inside, are banging on their doors. Finally, my cell door opens and I step into the corridor with the bag in my hand. I notice a few of my fellow cellmates with their blindfolds pushed up to their foreheads, carrying their bags and belongings, with lips open in a big smile, moving with quick strides verging on a run.

Pasdar Taleghani starts badgering us:

"*Khanoumha* [ladies], no talking. Pull down your blindfolds. *Khanoum* [lady], hurry up!"

I hear the voice of Amiri, the other *pasdar* coming from the entrance of the ward.

"*Khanoumha*, be quiet!" she says. "No talking! What's the matter with you!"

It seems like these two are the only guards present in this ward. Today, they both act with a relatively pleasant manner and it appears that they might have lost their usual control over the ward. I go to the entrance of the ward. It looks like a celebration. Blindfolds pulled up to foreheads like temple crowns, prisoners are hugging and kissing each other while exchanging news. A rose halo has settled on the pale and yellowed faces concealed from the rays of the sun for months. We're relishing in rediscovering one another and being together again, being free from the solitary cell and the (unwanted) solitude that comes with it.

The majority of the prisoners are *Azadi-ha*, by now months in solitary confinement. Subsequent to the mass executions and corporal and psychological tortures of 1988, some steadfast political prisoners, especially those without a conviction or verdict, continued to be subject to excruciating pressures. Now those same people, right here, in the isolation ward, have found the opportunity to revel in the victory of their resistance.

Mixed in with the laughter and clamor I detect some words: "United Nations... Human Rights... they want to inspect prisons."

I can't connect the dots between these words and what is happening, unable to comprehend the implication of this mass transfer. During the past three months, I have not set eyes on a newspaper and I have had no access to the news. Considering that my cell was close to the entrance of the ward and the guards' station, I was unable to communicate with my fellow prisoners. Those whose cells were located toward the end of the corridor were in a better position to communicate with one another.

The doors to most of the cells are now open. The corridor, lit with fluorescent lights, seems bright. In contrast, the space inside the cells looks turbid and bleak. I don't have any desire to set foot into a place where, until only a few minutes ago, I had to live for three full months. A feeling of sorrow, for myself and all of my fellow prisoners who dwelled in these cells, comes over me. My feeling of joy gets tangled with grief. I ask myself: How did we survive in these cells, how did we manage to live our lives in these dungeons? Nonetheless, this is where we were, where we lived, where we slept, where we spent our nights and days. How can I feel any dislike for the place that came to resemble a home and a refuge for me? But how can I feel any love for it? How? How can we love this turbid, foggy, dim, sickly space? This space removed us from the places we loved: society, streets, people, home, and family. It is only natural to be happy to leave this place behind and step outside.

I exit the ward. There are no barriers. It is now completely dark. I can't believe it. I move my blindfold up fully. I can see the glorious splendor of the sky and trees, unveiled under the night lights just as a free person could outside of the prison walls. Although it's the beginning of Bahman (late January), the weather is mild. After a few months in solitary confinement, breathing fresh air fills me with a satisfying sensation. I watch the carefully arranged rows of trees farther back at the foothill. Undoubtedly there are rows of barbed wire beyond these trees, obscured in the dark. In these moments of joy one can imagine that there is no barbed wire beyond these trees, that we can freely walk and walk until we reach the city streets. Oh, I wish that is how it was.

Buried deep in blissful reflection, I suddenly see three men appear from behind a building, a few meters from where I am standing. One of them is in civilian clothes, worry beads in hand, walking slightly ahead of the other two uniformed men.

"*Khanoumha!*" shouts the one in civilian clothes. "What are you doing here? Who gave you permission to come outside? *Yallah* [hurry up], all of you, go back to the ward, to your cells. Don't touch your belongings and bags. Fast. Hurry up!"

We are all shocked. The plan must have changed again. Maybe the female *pasdars* made a mistake and misunderstood the orders.

"This is Pishva," one of my fellow prisoners whispers, "the new head of the prison."

Obviously, changes have taken place in the prison administration as well. Pishva comes across more like a Haji Bazari[20] than an Evin prison chief administrator.

A police-like atmosphere takes over momentarily. We are all thrust back into the ward and to our cells. The female *pasdars* swiftly lock the doors to our cells, as if they have realized their roles once again and have resumed their duties. Yet again, we are in solitary confinement; this time we only have our chadors and blindfolds, having left the rest of our belongings outside. The atmosphere is intense and a deafening silence takes over the ward. A few minutes pass and once more the sound of opening cell doors echoes in the corridor, this time commanded by the chief administrator, the newly appointed prison boss, Pishva! They line us up in the area across from the ward. We are divided into two groups and are then transported to Ward 216, in two vans. At last with our belongings, we arrive at Ward 216 at around 10 p.m. where we are met with the typical aggression of the *pasdars* and with the routine physical examinations.

All the *Azadi-ha* are placed in Room 7 at the end of the ward, and including those already in Room 7, the number of prisoners is now approximately fifty. They then dispatch me and the other *sar-e moze-i* (steadfast) females to Room 5. The atmosphere of the room is peculiar. The prisoners who had already been in Room 5 tell us that in the past few days they had to be transferred twice because prison management came to paint the cell walls.

It is clear that the paint job is only superficial, with the intention of rendering a clean and light appearance to the prison cells.

"Haven't you read the newspaper?" one of my fellow cellmates says. "The UN Commissioner of Human Rights is flying to Tehran as we speak. He is scheduled to begin inspections of the prisons shortly and is demanding to meet with individual prisoners."[21]

---

20 Traditional and devout men of commerce who have made the holy pilgrimage to Mecca and whose base of operation is the pre-modern bazaar.
21 Reynaldo Galindo Pohl was the head of the special UN Human Rights Commission who visited Iran in 1989 and 1990 for the inspection of the Islamic Republic's prisons resulting in a report about the prisons and prisoners.

Aha, this is the reason behind the administration's frantic evacuation of the Solitary Ward. They want to exhibit the empty cells and say, "You can see that all our [solitary] cells are vacant, you won't find a single soul in there."

The prison administration has taken other measures as well, including the relocation of prisoners. The remainder of the "repentant" prisoners, those set to be released on the occasion of the tenth anniversary of the Islamic Revolution in Iran during the month of Bahman (January–February 1979), are being transferred to the general ward. Apparently, the prison administration plans to introduce them as the only remaining female political prisoners in Evin prison, while they have crammed us, the *sar-e moze-i* females, upstairs in closed rooms in Ward 3.

The conditions in the rooms of the *Azadi-ha* are truly deplorable. Within the main corridor right where our ward is situated, they have erected a wall that ostensibly separates our ward from the others, making it appear as if the corridor ends at the wall and that there are no rooms beyond it, indicating that our ward and we do not exist.

Our predictions are practically right. We later learn that the Special Representative of the UN Human Rights Commission, Reynaldo Galindo Pohl, was taken to visit the "repentant women." They also "showed" him that the solitary confinement ward was vacant, that only Maryam Firouz[22] and a few other nonpolitical prisoners were being housed there. Temporarily, the doors to the cells were left open to make it appear as if the prisoners could move freely within the ward. During these days the cells and prison stores were filled with fruits and food, and the quality was better than usual.

Our ward is completely quarantined. One could even say that we didn't exist in the minds of other prisoners, let alone that of Reynaldo Galindo Pohl and his entourage! Our only connection to the outside was the small door connecting the kitchen to our ward's corridor in order for us to receive food.

---

22 Maryam Firouz (1914–2008) was raised in a famous aristocratic family and was one of the leaders of the suffragist and feminist movements in 1940s Iran. In 1943, she married Noureddin Kianouri, who went on to become the leader of the Tudeh Party at the beginning of the 1979 Revolution. Despite vehement support, the Tudeh Party fell victim to the IRI, and Firouz, along with many female and male members of the Party, was arrested in 1982 and incarcerated in Ward 3000 (also known as Tohid penitentiary). After being transferred to Evin prison in 1983, she was confined in solitary cells in Ward 209 (which was turned into an infirmary). I vividly remember that two days before Norouz 1369 (March 19, 1990)—when I was still in solitary confinement—Pishva, the new head of Evin prison, tried to send her to the general ward. Firouz resolutely reacted against him and threatened that she would stage a hunger strike if that happened.

Pasdars have been ordered to avoid being ill-tempered and to behave gently toward us, to prevent any problems. Nevertheless, they are completely aware of their duties and continue to report all violations in detail to the prison administration. During outdoor hours, they keep a close watch on the prisoners through the windows of their stations.

Those exciting days came to an end with the conclusion of Reynaldo Galindo Pohl's inspections of the political prisons in Tehran. Although he was not permitted to visit our ward, I am convinced that he was aware of our situation and conditions—especially in light of our families' extensive efforts outside the prison to provide information on our actual living conditions. After the envoy's departure on February 7, I am dispatched to solitary confinement with another prisoner, whose name has also been recorded in the prison accounts, from the same ward. Shortly afterward, other individuals follow us to the same solitary cells. Four days from now, it will be February 11, the tenth anniversary of the Iranian people's revolution against the Shah. On this "glorious day," in the seventh year of my imprisonment, living isolated from my fellow prisoners and inflicted with a gloomy and desolate mood, I ask myself: "When will our moment come, the moment of rejoicing freedom; freedom for ourselves and for our people?"

TRANSLATED FROM PERSIAN BY A.F.

TESTIMONIES (MEN'S PRISON)

Chronicle of a Crime

IRAJ MESDAGHI[23]

Saturday, July 30, 1988 (8 Mordad)

This account begins on Saturday, July 30, 1988, in Gohardasht prison in Tehran. After breakfast, we noticed some newcomers to our wing. They had a lot of news and were eager to share it with us. The long-term prisoners at Gohardasht prison, many of whom had spent a long time in solitary confinement, had engineered a fourteen-inch Toshiba television to function as a sort of short-wave radio. It was used for listening to the Mojahedin station broadcasts and then passing on the information to other prisoners. We exchanged news about the Mojahedin's Liberation Army's Chehelcheragh Operation in Mehran, a western region of Iran.

---

23 Iraj Mesdaghi was born in Tehran in 1960. After finishing high school, he left for the United States for his university studies. In Los Angeles, he joined one of the branches of the Confederation of Iranian Students, which was vehemently against the Shah's regime. He returned to Iran in 1979 to participate in the revolution. With the downfall of the Shah, he joined the People's Mojahedin Organization of Iran (PMOI). Mesdaghi was arrested and detained twice in 1981 (the first time for about forty days) because of his association with the PMOI, and was subjected to torture. He was tried and sentenced to ten years of imprisonment and spent the next decade in Evin, Gohardasht, and Qezel Hesar prisons. He is one of the survivors of the Great Massacre of 1988. Following his release, in 1994, he fled Iran and sought political asylum in Sweden. Mesdaghi resumed his political activities in exile by exposing human rights violations in the IRI. *In Between Life and Death* (2004), a four-volume memoir of his ten years of imprisonment in the IRI's jails, is considered to be one of the most detailed eyewitness testimonies against the atrocities of the IRI. Mesdaghi's other books include *On the Hemp Rope* (prison poems) (2006), *Hell on Earth—Qezel Hesar Prison* (2008), and *Violation of Fundamental Rights of Labor in Iran* (2010). He is featured prominently in Nima Sarvestani's acclaimed documentary *Those Who Said No*, which concerns the massacre of political prisoners in Iran. This diligent political activist and writer has testified, on the crimes against humanity committed by the IRI, before international forums including the UN Human Rights Commission, European Parliament, and international labor organizations.

I was assigned the role of lookout because of my cell's location. I had to lie on the floor and peer through the gap underneath the door where I could see reflections of people approaching. I would warn the others by flushing the toilet. As soon as the information exchange started, only I had the right to use the toilets and flush.

Suddenly I panicked. I flushed the toilet several times, and everything grew quiet. A moment later, my cell door opened and several prison guards came in looking nervous and agitated. They ordered me to cover my eyes with my blindfold and follow them out.

I immediately assumed that the guards had appeared because they had found out about today's contact and knew what was going on. Then I noticed that the doors to *all* the cells were open and *all* prisoners had been called out. This meant that the guards did not know about our communications after all. I breathed a sigh of relief.

Having arrived on the first floor, we were lined up against the wall. A few minutes later, I saw from beneath my blindfold that the head of Gohardasht prison, Davoud Lashkari, was walking toward us. He asked why we were lined up there. Who had ordered it? One of the guards answered, "Saeed" (the officer in charge). Lashkari angrily told them to return us to our cells immediately and wait for his order. So, we were all taken back to the wing.

I could sense that something was not quite right. Once the guards had left, I climbed up onto the toilet to look through the cell window; I saw a yellow Mercedes-Benz parked in front of the prison gate.

As I was stepping down from the toilet, my cell door suddenly opened. Again I assumed, as I had earlier, that I had been under surveillance. But, as before, I was wrong. This time it was Lashkari himself followed by a few prison guards.

"What are you charged with, Mr. Iraj?" he said mockingly.

"Mojahedin." I waited to see how he would react.

He did not show any negative reaction. He simply asked me to put on my blindfold and follow him. He did the same with the seven others who had been taken to the solitary block with me. A few minutes later, we were back in the wing. Lashkari and his guards were being especially accommodating to us, and this surprised me. Previously, they would probably have reacted with anger or even disgust to the term "Mojahedin," expecting me to use the insulting label of "*Monafeqin*."

The officer in charge of the wing asked Akbar Samadi what his charges were. When he replied, "sympathizer," rather than the derogatory term

"*Monafeqin*," the guard simply shook his head. Naïvely we attributed this new attitude to the possibility that they had actually changed their position on this issue and were backing down due to our long-standing and continued resistance to disowning our ties to the Mojahedin.

It is important to note that prisoners who were in open wards looked at things much differently than those of us who had been in solitary confinement. In many ways they had a broader and more realistic view of things. I, who had been in solitary (although surreptitiously in communication with prisoners from other wings), had become stauncher in my political positions to maintain a strong stance and continue my resistance. Perhaps more importantly, I had stopped relying solely on the apparent realities of my situation and instead trusted my gut instincts.

Later in the evening, a guard asked what Mansour Ghahremani's father's name had been. That sounded an alarm. Mansour had been one of the prisoners removed from the wing that morning. If he were still alive, I wondered, why was the guard referring to him in the past tense? Why wasn't Mansour himself being asked about his father's name?

It was only later that we learned that a massacre of prisoners had actually begun in Gohardasht at nine o'clock in the morning on Saturday, July 30. Apparently, we had been the first group to appear in front of the committee appointed by Khomeini, known to prisoners as the "Death Commission."

Those who were considered by the prison authorities to be staunch supporters of their political ideology would be the first to be tried. Since we had been put in the solitary cells as punishment, we were considered the most belligerent and were to be taken to the slaughterhouse first. They had put us in solitary cells in a segregated block for this purpose a few days before. It turned out, however, that Lashkari had already handpicked a group of eleven prisoners who had been transferred to Gohardasht from Mashhad just a few months before. It was this group that was to be the first massacred.

The massacre was supposed to be carried out in absolute secrecy so that the prisoners would not be aware of the execution process, the number of prisoners involved, or their own condition. Keeping the prisoners unaware of the plan would only be possible if the prisoners had no information about each other's situation. To achieve this objective, they needed isolation cells to transfer any prisoners leaving the wing and for those who became aware of the massacre. For this reason, they needed the solitary cells in the segregated block where we were.

On July 30 and 31, executions took place in a ditch behind a wall surrounding the prison building. We could see the vicinity of the ditch from the *Hosseiniyeh*. As the ditch was behind the prison area, however, the wall that separated it from the wings prevented us from seeing *inside* the ditch. The inmates had bent the slats on the windows and could witness what was happening. That evening, one prisoner saw Lashkari with a wheelbarrow full of rope.

We could see a lot of traffic into and out of the area which was quite unprecedented. Clearly, something terrible was taking place and we were all worried.

Since that morning, there had been a white Volkswagen station wagon repeatedly bringing some blindfolded young men in military uniform to the prison. We assumed that these young men were either the Mojahedin's National Liberation Army (NLA) soldiers who had been captured or soldiers who had rebelled during the battles. (No one ever saw them during or after the massacre, and their fate remains unclear.)

Sunday, July 31 (9 Mordad)

On Sunday morning, Ahmad Nooramin, Mehrdad Ardebili, and Hossein Bahri were called. Hossein Bahri had almost completed his prison term. Why him, we wondered, and not others with long-term sentences?

Soon after, Mehran Samadzadeh was called. After Mehran's removal, a sense of anxiety descended throughout the section. The guards had removed the television and stopped the sale of newspapers in order to prevent us from getting information about what was happening outside the prison. In spite of this, the prison authorities tried hard to pretend that nothing out of ordinary was going on.

Monday, August 1 (10 Mordad)

At about 10 a.m., during a routine inspection, Lashkari and the guards in charge of the wing collected the names of all prisoners who had a prison sentence of ten years or more. Apparently, they were classifying us according to the length of our sentences. Lashkari asked everyone with a sentence of ten years or more to sit down next to me. He then told the guard who was with him to write down all the names. I was the last one in the row.

"Enough!" shouted Lashkari before the guard had a chance to write my name. "Let's go to the next room."

"I was also sentenced to ten years," I protested, standing up. "So why didn't you write my name down?"

"Shut up!" he shouted, pushing me to the other side of the room. "It's not necessary!"

Then they rushed out of our room.

More than forty of the prisoners questioned by Lashkari that day did not return to the wing. They were transferred to Annexes 13 and 17. Our wing overlooked Annex 17. As soon as our friends arrived there, we communicated with them in Morse code, exchanging the latest information about how Lashkari and the *pasdars* had treated them. We were also in contact with a group of prisoners who had been transferred from Evin prison about three days earlier. They were on the third floor of the same block as Annex 17. They had also come to the conclusion that the real mission of the Commission was to sort out the steadfast prisoners and finish them off a few days after the killings had begun.

After dinner, we gathered in one of the section's two largest rooms, singing old and memorable tunes, reciting poetry, and chanting revolutionary songs. The empty place left by our departed friends weighed heavily. We didn't want to be crushed by the weight of that gloomy and terrifying atmosphere.

We were making the preparations for Eid-e Ghadir, one of the holiest ceremonies for Shi'ite Muslims, which would take place the following day. I was chosen as the Master of Ceremonies; therefore, I had to be very active in the preparations. A normally joyous celebration would have to be changed to a somber affair given that inmates had been martyred and that we had seen on television that a large number of militants involved in the *Forough-e Javidan* (Eternal Light) Operation had been killed. We also wanted to announce our readiness for whatever was to come. The prison choir was rehearsing a revolutionary song that had been composed inside the prison.

Tuesday, August 2 (11 Mordad)

At the ceremony on Tuesday, I recited three poems, two of which were about the dedication and fidelity of those who had been sent to the gallows and another one, "Mother," which was the last farewell of a revolutionary to his mother. After the ceremony, many of the prisoners requested a copy of this poem.

Wednesday, August 3 (12 Mordad)

Wednesday afternoon, Zein al-Abedin Afshoon, a prisoner from Karaj, was taken to the Commission. He returned to the wing after a short while. He explained that he had been taken to the first floor of the building, where the prison administration and courthouse were. There he had seen Nayyeri, Eshraghi and a few others not familiar to him. He was the only one who had returned to the wing. No one knew why.

The Morse code messages revealed that no one had returned to the annexes. Some of the wings and sections of Gohardasht had already been vacated. We were consoling ourselves with the thought that our friends had been transferred to other wings of the prison.

To our surprise, lunch that day was plentiful. We wondered why there was so much food at a time like this. We realized that this was because there were so many fewer prisoners to feed. I could not eat any more; I had lost my appetite.

Thursday, August 4 (13 Mordad)

On Thursday, only a few prisoners were left in Annex 17. One of the cells had become a gathering place where we sang songs and recited poetry.

Friday, August 5 (14 Mordad)

Our friends had been taken away without their personal belongings. We guessed that we, too, would sooner or later be transferred, so we packed up our things. We did not want our personal belongings to fall into the hands of the prison guards. A few prisoners were designated to pack the things of cellmates who had already gone and take them to the *Hosseiniyeh*.

We came upon the idea to use our loincloths or "longs" (a rectangular fabric made of cotton and hemp, with a black hue on a red background) as blindfolds. It could be used as a towel and a bandage, and the fabric was easy to see through. This worked very well and proved to be of great help to me and the other prisoners.

In the past two days, there have been no incidents and things have been relatively calm. It was clear that the Commission was not in Gohardasht. In the meantime, the Afghani workers were back. The Afghanis generally did the jobs that the *pasdars* were reluctant to do. It seems that some of them who did jobs around the prison had found out about the massacre. One of them had even tried to inform us about what was going on in the prison. At the first opportunity, he had run into the yard shouting, "They're executing the prisoners!"

Saturday, August 6 (15 Mordad)

Lashkari and some prison guards arrived in our wing. I was called first. Lashkari tried hard to persuade me to accept something. He had never treated me like that before. I wondered why his attitude had changed.

I could see a familiar *pasdar* through my blindfold. During my interrogations, I was badly beaten up, and this *pasdar* had actually rescued me by dragging me behind a cupboard pretending to beat me. Now, he was sitting next to Lashkari, occasionally making brief comments. Lashkari finally gave up on me and said, "Get out of here, you miserable old devil!" Together with a few other prisoners, I was sent to a cell in the wing where the *Mellikesh* were previously housed. This wing was used as the last stop for prisoners before trial.

After lunch, I laid down. Mohammad Reza Mohajeri (Agha Ali) had put his head on my chest and was pouring out his problems. He would have completed his prison term by September. Neither he nor anyone else could imagine he would soon be executed. Suddenly, the door opened and they called for me and Ali. I jumped with surprise. Along with Ali and a few others who were from other cells, we went downstairs to the place I had been taken the previous week. I sat down leaning against the wall. Looking around, I spotted a few familiar faces. Ali Haghverdi was among them.

Ali was suffering from a particular kind of headache, resulting from long hours of being held in a standing position and other tortures he had endured during the time of Haj Davoud. He often screamed and shook in his sleep. Two people had watched over him at night for over six months so that he would not have any attacks in his sleep. He had gradually gotten better. Now, apparently, he was on the verge of an attack. When he lit a cigarette to calm down, a guard who was watching us rushed toward him, grabbed the cigarette, and crushed it under his boot. The guard was aware of Ali's illness. For this reason, Ali was taken for the "hearing" ahead of schedule.

My heart was in my mouth when Nasser Mansouri was called. I couldn't believe he was among us. Nasser had been in solitary confinement since April 1988 for punitive reasons. Apparently, he had been under a lot of pressure.

He had refused to give information or to obey the orders of the prison guards and interrogators, and had attempted to commit suicide.

One evening in May, Nasser had broken the barred window of his cell and had jumped from the third floor. He did not die, but he was left totally paralyzed with a spinal cord injury.

The prisoners of Annex 13 saw that when the guards finally noticed Nasser's broken body, they kicked him around with their boots. Nasser was kept in the most wretched conditions in the prison hospital without proper medical care until August 6, when he was taken to the gallows on a stretcher.

I was anxious to know what was going on in the adjacent hallway. Mostafa Mohammadi Moheb, Qassem Seyfan, Mohammad Reza Mohajeri, and Mahmood Zaki went into the room, staying there only a few minutes each.

Mostafa Mohammadi Moheb had already experienced the atrocities of the regime in the most painful way in 1981. The interrogators had sent him off to the firing squad, although he had not had a trial yet. While being led to his execution, he had been ordered to carry a man on his back without knowing it was his brother. On the way, upon hearing the moans of the man, he realized that he was carrying his own brother who had been tortured so much that he was unable to move. Mostafa had then witnessed the execution of his brother. Afterwards, together with other prisoners who had also been taken to the scene of the crime, he had loaded the bodies of the slaughtered men onto trucks used for the transportation of meat. In 1981–82, thousands of prisoners were thus executed by the firing squads at Evin prison.

I was taken to the room immediately after Mahmood Zaki. Someone ordered me to remove my blindfold. When I did so, I was startled to see a room full of people. Panic-stricken at the sight of all those people staring at me, I nervously said hello. At first glance, I recognized several of them including Nayyeri, Eshraghi, and one named Raisi. Nasserian acted as a middleman and tried to create an atmosphere of fear. Pourmohammadi, a representative of the Intelligence Ministry, was there too, but I did not know him at that time. In fact, we didn't know any of the Intelligence officials. There were several thickset bodyguards and *pasdars* behind Nayyeri and Eshraghi in case of possible attack by any of the defendants.

I was about to sit before the Commission when Nasserian entered the room.

"Haji, the villain says he won't write it," he said to Nayyeri.

"But he agreed to write it when he was here," Nayyeri replied, seemingly astonished.

"It seems that he's changed his mind. He says he won't write it."

"In that case, take him back to his cell," snapped Nayyeri.

"Deceit" was the buzzword those days. Everything was based on subterfuge and hypocrisy. Even their smile was fake. On my way to the room, I had heard Mahmood Zaki and Nasserian arguing.

The composition of the Commission left no doubt in my mind that they were there to hand out death sentences. The hearing was nothing but a formality designed to support the false claim that there had been a real trial and justice had been done. Sitting before them, I saw Death watching me. I felt I had little to lose and I decided not to give in. In my mind, however, I carefully drew the lines that would prevent me from compromising myself or anyone else. The members of the Commission were looking at me maliciously, sizing me up, as if they were in a slave market looking for the fittest and healthiest slaves.

In response to their question about charges, I replied, "Organization."

"Which organization?" asked Nayyeri.

"The one that you know."

"Well, what's the name?"

"The name doesn't make any difference."

"Tell me exactly which organization you are talking about."

"Rajavi's organization [Masoud Rajavi, leader of the PMOI]."

"Would you seek pardon?"

"No, I've been sentenced to ten years, and I've already done seven years."

"What is your opinion about the Organization?"

"I have spent seven years in jail without any contact with them, so I can't have any opinion about them."

"We want you to condemn the actions of the *Monafeqin*," said Raisi.

"Condemning them has got nothing to do with me and I won't do it."

"Don't you know the *Monafeqin* have attacked the borders of the country?" shouted Eshraghi.

"So I've heard."

"Would you take a position on it?"

"No, it's none of my business. Besides, who am I to give an opinion or take a position on every issue?"

"How can you remain silent in spite of all the crimes they've committed?" he asked angrily.

"There are a lot of people like me in the society. When something happens, they quietly go home, keep to themselves, and wait for the dust to settle."

"Just write '*Monafeqin* have attacked the borders', and you'll be acquitted," said Nayyeri.

"I don't want to get involved in a dispute that's got nothing to do with me."

I don't know why they were haggling with me. Maybe because I had said "Hello" at the beginning. Or maybe, having already sentenced four defendants to death, they needed a break. Sadly, that meant in reality that the others had been sent to the gallows.

Why were they insisting so much? It flashed through my mind that perhaps they were not executing everyone. I had no knowledge of the fate of the others, so I had to leave a door open.

"If you free me," I said to Nayyeri, "I'll give a written undertaking that I'll never participate in political activities again."

"Why are you so stubborn? Go and write down a few words on a piece of paper and acquit yourself of the organization."

I held firm to my position.

"Get out of here!" Nayyeri said. "Write whatever you want!"

As I left the room, Nasserian gave me a recantation form in a childish handwriting.

"You have to write this down," he said.

"Haji said I could write whatever I wanted."

"No. You'll write whatever I *tell* you to write."

I realized then what the argument between Nasserian and Mahmood had been about: Nasserian had tried to force Mahmood to write a recantation letter, and Mahmood had refused. So, Nasserian had gone back to the court claiming that Mahmood would not write anything. In this way, he had sealed the death sentence of Mahmood. Now I knew better.

"I want to talk to Haji himself," I said.

For a moment Nasserian was taken aback—afraid that they would discover his stratagem for obtaining Mahmood's death sentence.

"Never mind," he said. "Write whatever you like."

I realized that they were in competition with each other for cruelty and violence. I wanted to inform Mahmood of my discovery as soon as I saw him.

I sat in the corridor of the court, facing the wall. Around me, some prisoners were sitting on chairs and others on the floor writing their *enzejarnameh* (recantation letter).

Introducing myself as a PMOI sympathizer, on a sheet of paper I wrote as follows:

Having severed my connection with the organization before my arrest, and having had no contact with the Mojahedin during my prison term, I hereby undertake not to participate in any kind of political activity after my release.

When he read the letter, Nasserian took the paper to Nayyeri in fury and transferred me to a hallway adjacent to the court. Death Row.

After an hour, the guard in charge of the visiting room came from the *Hosseiniyeh* wet with sweat. He was carrying a sack full of watches, blindfolds, and some money. Immediately afterward, another guard came out of the *Hosseiniyeh*, dragging his feet on the floor. He was holding the red "longs" of my fellow prisoners. It was as if I was hit by a thunderbolt. I managed to stifle my tears. My friends had just been executed.

Moments later, Mohsen Mohammad Bagher came on his crutches and sat next to me on the floor. (He could not walk due to a congenital disability.)

"What did you do, Mohsen?"

"I believe that death is just. I did not accept anything."

Gently, I held his hand. It was warm. I wanted to kiss it, but Lashkari was passing by.

Some prisoners who had not eaten anything asked for lunch. Lashkari mockingly said, "But, of course. We have ordered hot kebab for you. Please wait a few moments. Lunch will be ready soon!"

When one of the prisoners asked Nasserian when we would return to the wing, he laughed drunkenly. He began moving his arms in the air, trying to dance like a ballerina. He drawled his words and in a rhythmic tone said, "I don't know. I don't know."

At that moment, another group of prisoners were called. Mohsen jumped to his feet. Gently stepping on my hand as a way of saying his last goodbye, he smiled naughtily. They lined up. Yes, Mohsen walked on crutches, but with so much dignity. My heart followed them.

I did not know what to do. My whole body was on fire, and I was disheartened. My friends walked away in single file, forsaken by their companions. I was longing to kiss them on the cheek. Their names were like the blows of a sledgehammer on my head. Their voices echoed in my mind. One could not hear fatigue in their steps. They walked light-footedly.

Meanwhile, one prisoner who had been summoned to a hearing on August 3, and who had been in the death corridor all day, had become well aware of what was going on and was now trying to spread the word to others.

Faramarz Farahani said, "He said he'd been charged with being a member of the *Monafeqin*, but he didn't admit anything." Now I knew that when they said "take him to the wing," it actually meant "take him for execution." Nothing was uncertain and ambiguous anymore. I understood everything.

Assadollah Tayyebi was sitting opposite me, facing the wall. I asked him if he had already been tried and if he knew what was happening. He said he had been questioned by the Commission, but it was obvious that he had not understood what it was all about. I asked him if he knew that the Commission was there for the purpose of executing us. Assadollah answered that he had not gotten that impression from their questioning but had given the proper replies anyway. He had admitted to the charge of being a member of the *Monafeqin*, but he had refused to write the recantation letter which would acquit him of the Mojahedin.

I explained everything to him, emphasizing that he had already been tried.

"Are you serious?"

"Anyone who's missing has already been executed."

"Don't worry about it," he said, calm and poised. "It's too late for me now." He laughed bitterly as if to say, "Hopefully next time."

The last executions of the day took place at around seven o'clock in the evening, and Assadollah was among that last group. I was still gazing at the end of the hallway, the spot where I had seen my friends for the last time.

I saw Mohsen Vazin and then Adel Nouri in the death corridor. They said they had written a recantation letter. Adel said that it had not been an easy thing to do, but it was important to maneuver to save as many lives as possible. He was one of the most steadfast figures in prison. His will had not been weakened by years of solitary confinement.

Mohammad Reza Mohajeri was to be released in September. People like him could never imagine that the executions might affect them. It was a general belief at the beginning that probably everyone would be tried, and in the proceeding it would be judged that some prisoners were "not eligible to be freed" or their previous sentence had not been long enough.

At around 7:30 p.m. I was summoned for a second hearing. There was no one else but Nayyeri and Nasserian, who had brought me there himself. It appeared that Nayyeri had picked me as his final target for the day.

"What's this nonsense you've written here?"

"You asked me to stipulate that I would not participate in political activities, and that's what I did."

"Go and write a recantation letter. This is not acceptable."

I did not respond. I left the room. A *pasdar* handed me a sheet of paper. I wrote, in one line, the recantation letter.

"Is that all?" the guard asked.

"Yes." I handed it back to him.

He didn't say anything. I had once again cheated death.

Upon arriving at the new location, we noticed the presence of four Kermanshahi prisoners, three of whom had beards. One of the prisoners from Wing 1, the only wing with a television, was talking about the news and describing scenes from the *Forough-e Javidan* Operation that he had seen on television the previous week.

There were three Kermanshahi prisoners who were clearly *tavab* (literally meaning a person who repents a sin; they were collaborators with the prison establishment of the IRI). Mehdi, one of the prisoners, went on talking in a soft voice, describing the interview with Ali Shamkhani, the new commander of the Army of the Guardians of the Islamic Revolution (often called Revolutionary Guards), and the Friday Sermons of Mousavi Ardebili, the chief justice of Iran.

Meanwhile we discussed what we had to do with the three Kermanshahi prisoners, who were watching us the whole time. They were busy gathering information, and there was nothing we could do about it.

The annex to which I was taken with the Kermanshahi prisoners consisted of two rooms along with a bathroom and a shower. One of the rooms was big. We used the smaller room for communicating with our friends on the upper floor about the executions. We sent Morse code signals using the lamps. One person stood guard. We urged them to pass on the news to the Marxist prisoners too, and they promised to do so.

Sunday, August 7 (16 Mordad)

I woke up very early in the morning. Dariush Hanifehpour and another prisoner were sending Morse code signals to our old wing. The three Kermanshahi *tavabs* were up and sitting near the door of the annex.

"Those three shameless Kermanshahis are sitting there watching you!" I said. "Even the slightest report about our contacts with our friends upstairs would endanger the lives of those in Annex 17, and also the lives of our friends in the old wing."

"Take it easy," Masoud replied. "Let's hope for the best."

The prisoners in Annex 17 took a real interest in Masoud. First, he belonged to a new generation and his outlook was different from ours. Second, he had been arrested quite recently. Residing in Kermanshah, near the border in west Iran, he had been able to watch the "Resistant Television" programs, the Mojahedin Organization Broadcasting.

Monday, August 8 (17 Mordad)

Nasserian appeared in our section first thing in the morning. He was relieved to see the three Kermanshahis there, knowing that meant he would soon find his prey among us.

I talked with Mohammad Darvish Nouri, Hossein Feizabadi, Mohsen Vazin, and "DS," asking them if it would make sense to write a will in case of execution. We knew that prisoners were taken to solitary cells adjacent to the execution site to write their "last will and testament" before they were hanged.

The inmates' view on writing a testament, and its consequences, could be classified into two categories:

- A massacre was taking place. The regime was trying to document that the victims had undergone the legal procedures. Therefore, if we wrote our will, we were in fact legitimizing the massacre indirectly.
- It goes without saying that a massacre of sentenced prisoners was taking place. Public opinion condemned this massacre and felt it was by no means justifiable. Hence, writing a will or not would make no difference. Consequently, we should not refuse to write a will, if given the opportunity. Each would serve as a message to the people who read them in the future.

I agreed with both sides of the argument.

When I heard about the disappearance of my friends, I wavered in indecision: Should I stay or should I go? I thought about a book, *The Last Temptation of Christ*, which I had read some time ago. Nailed to the cross and awaiting death, Christ was ever mindful of life. Had I, like Christ, yielded psychologically to the temptation of staying alive? I recalled that Christ thought of marrying Mary Magdalene and having children with her while he was on the cross. Was it right to stay, or was I thinking like that because I wanted to stay alive? I was not afraid of death, but I was not ready for it either. Was there a difference between death and martyrdom? Was there a difference between involuntary death and welcoming death? What was the borderline?

Tuesday, August 9 (18 Mordad)

After breakfast on Tuesday, one of the three Kermanshahis claimed he was ill and needed to go to the dispensary. He spoke with the guard in charge of the wing and then left the wing quickly. It was obvious that the said prisoner had left the wing to report on us. The other two Kermanshahis were called just a few minutes later. Mission accomplished. Signs of worry and anxiety were clearly visible on the faces of prisoners who had conversed with them. A few minutes later, two other prisoners were called and both were moved very quickly out of the room. Right after that, they called the rest of us and moved us to the old *Mellikesh* wing. I felt I had saved my life from the Kermanshahis.

As soon as we reached the new cell, a prisoner and I started communicating in Morse code. He began communicating with the inmates of the two rooms across from our cell by sending signals in Morse code from underneath the door. There were fifteen prisoners in those two rooms, all of them Mojahedin supporters and *Mellikesh*. Ten days had passed since the beginning of the executions at Gohardasht, and these prisoners were still under the illusion that they had met with an "Amnesty Commission" rather than the Death Commission, and that they were engaged in legal procedures for their release.

We explained to them that Khomeini had issued a decree condemning all of us to death. The Commission was supposed to pardon a few of us and hang the rest. "If some of your cellmates are missing or you haven't heard from them for a while, consider them dead," we said. In the end, seventy of seventy-four of the *Mellikesh* Mojahedin were executed. Only two of the group we had addressed that day survived.

Around noon we heard some kind of commotion in the adjacent room. We learned that a few Marxist prisoners had refused to eat the prison food as a means of protest. They had been moved to our section for punishment. Their actions indicated that they knew what was going on. They mistakenly believed that the time was ripe for bargaining with the regime. I got in touch with them, briefing them in Morse code about what was happening.

The information I was giving was absolutely incredible to them, to the extent that they had difficulty understanding the words and asked me to repeat each sentence twice. From the way they were tapping on the wall, one could easily visualize the anxiety on the face of the person who was transmitting the message. They, in turn, informed us of the scenes they had witnessed within the previous few days. They told us of the Mojahedin prisoners from Mashhad who had been taken for execution down the ditch behind the wings. How gracefully and readily they had met their fate.

The full-scale execution of the Marxist prisoners began eighteen days later. Luckily, none of the Marxists transferred to our section perished. Unlike their comrades, they had gained an understanding of the situation in the last minutes. They really lucked out.

After lunch, I was summoned to court. Nasserian was waiting for me downstairs. I was led inside. Every member of the Commission was present.

Nayyeri spoke first. "What's this thing you wrote?" He tore up the sheet of paper angrily.

"Well, that's what you requested," I replied.

"Did I ask for just one line?"

"I don't know what you're talking about. You asked me to write two words, and even showed a two with your fingers. I wrote more than two words!"

He was taken aback by my reply. Nasserian, in the meantime, was writhing like a snake.

"Okay. Now go ahead and write the proper one," Nayyeri ordered.

Nasserian reluctantly led me out of the room and handed me another sheet of paper. It was only a few sentences. I do not know whose writing it was. Its content did not differ much from what I had written. But it was longer. I don't remember the exact words because I wasn't interested in memorizing it.

I wrote the text and mistakenly dated it August 6. At first, I wanted to cross it out, but then I changed my mind saying to myself, "What difference does it make? If they notice the mistake, I'll correct it. Otherwise, later they might think I wrote it on the sixth. It might even help me."

When I reached the Corridor of Death, I saw Manouchehr Bozorg Bashar. I had known him since 1983. His face was very agreeable. I was so happy and excited to see that he was still alive. As I did not expect to find *anyone* alive anymore, each time I saw a friend I felt great joy.

Ghanbar Nemati told me that the prisoners of the old Wing 1 had been tried earlier in the day and all of them had been executed. The prisoners of Wing 1 had had no notion of what was going on and, therefore, had not felt any alarm. A few prisoners from Evin had been transferred to their wing. They immediately understood the gravity of the situation and tried to warn everyone to be careful and cautious. Due to their far-sightedness, none of the prisoners from Evin who had been transferred to Wing 1 were executed.[24]

In Evin, too, the inmates of Saloon 6 in *Amoozeshgah*, who were considered new arrivals in comparison with other prisoners, underwent an emotional conflict upon hearing news of hunger strikes and other protest actions of the old prisoners. Contrary to their previous attitude in court, they had not accepted anything. Consequently, most of them were massacred.

As of August 6, everyone else had been fully aware of what was happening except the inmates of Wing 1. They were taken to court thinking that they were just being transferred to a new wing. Some prisoners assumed that the slightest negligence or hesitation would result in their return to the old section; thus, they had not accepted anything, and thirty of them were killed.

The members of the Commission were whitewashing the regime's crimes. Any sign of torture on the body of a victim could lead to his execution. One prisoner was in a very dangerous position that very day. Were it not for his alertness, he would undoubtedly have perished. In the course of the interrogations immediately after his arrest, he had been tortured while being restrained by handcuffs. One of his hands was partially paralyzed due to severe damage to the muscles and tendons. This fact could have been a good excuse for his execution. When asked about his arm during the hearing, he raised his good hand, claiming that he had recovered. He had done this with so much sangfroid and confidence that the team had not noticed his ruse.

In the afternoon I saw Raisi, the deputy prosecutor, sitting at his desk in the office across from the hearing room. There was a pile of paper money torn into small pieces on his desk. He was tearing up the pieces of money into yet smaller pieces with righteous indignation. Evidently, the prisoners had torn up their paper money just before the execution. Some had even smashed their wrist watches so that the guards would not be able to use them.

Nasserian himself had the responsibility of selecting the prisoners and taking them to the courtroom. I was wondering, "What if they take me back

---

24 Back in Evin, prisoners who had been housed in Section 6 of the *Amoozeshgah*, as newcomers relative to the others, when informed of the news of hunger strikes and other acts of disobedience by other prisoners, adopted a whole new tone and attitude. When confronted in the hearings, they were intransigent in their positions, refusing to comply. In the end, the majority of them were executed.

to the court? I have to leave this place as fast as I can." Through my blindfold, I could see everywhere. There was a line of prisoners ready to go back to the wing. Just one moment of negligence on the part of the *pasdar* would be enough for me to work out my plan. I approached the line and, in a split second, joined the last person. I put my hand on the shoulder of the person ahead of me and bent my head down to my arm, staring at the floor. I was thinking that if the *pasdar* noticed me, I would say, "But you said anyone who's finished get in line. I'm done. I've already done what Haji asked me to do." It was not a very good excuse, but it was the only thing that came to my mind at that moment.

I had my heart in my mouth when the line advanced. I did not know where it was going, but I was certain that it was not to Death Row. As it happens, we returned to our old wing. I said I was in Cell 8 and was sent there.

That day, the behavior of the Commission and the guards was markedly different. They were no longer playing roles. The members of the Commission who had been playing the role of "angels of justice and clemency" were now showing their true nature as demons of death. There was no need for concealment anymore. Members of the Commission repeatedly referred to the direct order of Khomeini to purge the prisons.

The guards had now taken to brutally beating and injuring the Mojahedin prisoners in solitary confinement. Whenever a guard opened the door to a cell, even at meal time, the prisoner had to introduce himself, saying he was a *Monafeqin* sympathizer. Then, he had to shout a series of slogans denouncing the Mojahedin and Masoud Rajavi. The slightest negligence or hesitation, or reluctance to say any of their slogans, would lead to a severe beating.

Wednesday, August 10 (19 Mordad)

On my way to the bathroom I found a pot, which I thought could come in handy. For example, we could use it for our meals or, in case of emergency, to relieve our bowels. I washed it with soap and took it to the cell. The other prisoners seemed nonchalant about my find, but *I* knew it would serve a purpose some day.

Everyone seemed to be in good spirits except one prisoner who had succumbed to despair. Roshan was saying that he had visited many beautiful places in the world, and had experienced the ups and downs of life and had no fear of dying. He became very emotional all of a sudden. Choking back his tears he continued: "I just feel sorry for these kids who know nothing about life except for pain and suffering." I couldn't help thinking about Soheil Daniali, Mohammad Reza Ali Reza Nia, Ahmad Gholami, and Masoud Eftekhari, who had all reached puberty in prison.

Thursday, August 11 (20 Mordad)

On Thursday afternoon we were busy sending Morse code to Siamak Toobaii in the adjacent room when suddenly the door to our room opened and Nasserian, accompanied by a few guards, walked into the cell. Nasserian asked each and every one of us what our charges were, how many times we had been tried, if we were ready to write a recantation letter, and if we would give an interview. He had drawn a line in his notebook to make two separate columns. In one column he wrote the name of the prisoner and in the second column his comments about each one of us. He was doing this openly and was not trying to conceal anything. At one point, he even left the notebook open right in the middle of the room for everyone to see.

He wrote "villain hanging" next to the name of Hossein Feizabadi and wrote "hanging" next to my name, too. Masoud, too, joined our group. Froth appeared at the corners of his mouth as he repeatedly threatened us, saying, "We'll make you drown in shit."[25]

The members of the Commission did not know the prisoners. Nasserian and Lashkari in Gohardasht and Majid Halwaie in Evin knew the prisoners and their records and were therefore responsible for categorizing and selecting the prisoners in order of priority for the court hearings. It was their duty to inform the members of the Commission about the "true" orientation of each prisoner. In fact, they were the intelligence antennas of the Commission, necessary because of their fear that the prisoners would take a different position in view of the situation.

Later in the night, when no sound could be heard from anywhere or anybody, I stood by the window. I could not see anything except the sky. I hummed some songs to myself, shedding tears in memory of the friends I had lost. I was brooding over the recantation letter that I had written. Had I done the right thing? I tried to take a bit of heart from historical figures. Joan of Arc, a simple peasant girl who led the French assaults on the British troops, helped me the most. She rose to prominence in French history because of her bravery. She was later arrested near Paris due to machinations and schemes

---

25 When a person is hanged from a rope, the residues in the stomach drain due to the shock received by the cords.

against her and then was turned over to the British troops. She was condemned to death for heresy and wearing men's clothing by the ecclesiastical courts. She signed an abjuration document under threat of immediate execution, and her death sentence was commuted to a life sentence. Soon afterward, the prison guards reported that she was still wearing trousers; therefore, her case was reexamined. She was burned at the stake in front of a church in the city of Rouen, in northern France, on May 30, 1431.

No one ever blamed Joan of Arc for signing the abjuration document. On the contrary, she became the heroine of the French nation, a symbol of resistance and a source of inspiration for future generations. Wasn't my condition similar to hers?

Friday, August 12 (21 Mordad)

After lunch, I was summoned to the court. The guards sat me down near the door. A hearing was in session. I got up and went to the bathroom, and on the way back I headed for the Corridor of Death and sat there. I had noticed that Nasserian asked the name of prisoners sitting near the chamber and took them for a hearing. I knew that going to court could be dangerous for someone who had already written a recantation letter. They would probably ask me to collaborate with them and give them information, and that would mean the end of the road.

Mohammad Farmani had already been tried. I called him by his father's name, "Shozeb," and he recognized me. I asked him how it had gone. He replied, "I defended the Organization and took back my recantation letter." He was of the opinion that they would execute everyone. So, why should we let them continue this game?

Nayyeri had asked Mohammad at court if he would give an interview. Mohammad had answered that he did not even approve of the recantation letter he had written. He considered himself a Mojahedin sympathizer and agreed with all positions taken by the PMOI. Nayyeri had pointed out that he had expressed a different opinion before, and Mohammad had responded, "I was wrong then, and I'm correcting myself now."

After that I saw Manouchehr (Ali Akbar) Bozorg Bashar. He had taken the same approach. Hessamoddin Savabi had also taken the same approach. His sister had been heroically martyred in 1981.

During Hitler's era, the mass slaughter of Jews and the disposal of the corpses in the crematory ovens was done by the operational forces, and the decision-makers merely signed the commands from long distance, without thinking about the consequences or knowing any of the victims. Here, however, the commanders had full knowledge of the situation of the victim and were acquainted with the victim and his family, and there was a sort of dialogue between them. In fact, a personal relationship was established between the prosecutors and the victims!

Moving back to the Corridor of Death was a great help for me. This corridor was the place for those who had already been tried. Prisoners were either taken to the gallows or back to their cells. So long as I was there, they thought that I had already been tried and was awaiting my fate. Even if they noticed me, I was running no risk. I could simply say that a guard had placed me there.

In the evening, we were lined up to go back to our cells. The guard said, "Those in the solitary ward raise your hands." A few did so, but I did not. I planned to claim that I had not heard the guard, if I got found out, knowing that at most I would be kicked and slapped a few times.

Those days, there were no statistics, and the guards and prison authorities did not have an accurate list of the prisoners in each wing. If I raised my hand, I would risk going back to solitary again. Nasserian was very sensitive to prisoners who were in solitary confinement, trying his best to send them to court, where there was nothing but death.

I was taken to a hall with closed, single cells, along with three other prisoners. Lashkari was standing in the hallway when we arrived, and he assigned me to Room 3. All of us in that room were newcomers, and the composition of the people in the room had just taken form. As soon as I got acquainted with the other inmates, I went to the window. I could see the prison grounds through the bent slats of the shutters. I had a good view of the frontage of the prison from where I was standing, but I could see only a small area.

I spotted Nayyeri's BMW parked in front of the building. Nayyeri was standing beside his car, and his chauffeur was selecting potted flowers for him. It was unbelievable. Just a few hours earlier, this same man had been instrumental in destroying the dearest of all flowers. Now he was selecting potted flowers in peace and serenity, to take home with him.

Josef Mengele, known as the "Angel of Death" at the Auschwitz concentration camp, after having performed the most horrific medical experiments on captive children—experiments that led to their deaths—would read bedtime stories to his own children and kiss them good night. I could never understand that kind of duality in a person. Nevertheless, I could now see an example before my very eyes.

After supper, we talked about what we had experienced in the past few days and analyzed the processes we had gone through. We knew well that each dinner together might be our "Last Supper" and each goodbye a last farewell. We were talking about our memories when a guard announced that those who wanted to buy cigarettes should get ready to pay. Thinking that this might be our last purchase and we would not need money anymore, we used up all our money. We decided to smoke a single cigarette among five people. We rationed the cigarettes and smoked each one with the group to stock the rest for those who were in solitary. From that day on, each time we went for a hearing, we would put several packets of cigarettes in our pockets to distribute to the inmates in solitary.

We were smoking when suddenly, the content of my last will and testament—which so far had eluded me—appeared in front of my eyes. I composed it immediately, hoping it would survive me. It read:

> Dearest Grandmother, dearest Mother and Father,
> When I was born, I cried but everyone else was happy and smiling. Now that I am departing this life, I am laughing with all my heart. I hope you, too, will laugh along with me. I wish you joy and happiness. Say hello to everyone for me. I love you and everyone from the bottom of my heart.

I felt it was brief but not overly emotional and explicit. It expressed everything I wanted to say. However, at times, "silence speaks louder than words." I had decided to depart this life happily and I wanted to share this happiness with everyone.

Saturday, August 13 (22 Mordad)

On Saturday morning I was called to the court. I decided to move down to the Corridor of Death as I had done the day before. I thought I would be safer there. Excusing myself to go to the bathroom, I quickly found my way there. A few minutes later, I saw Nasserian searching for prey. I tried to hide myself from him. I could feel my muscles tightening, my heart beating faster, and my temples throbbing painfully because of this stress. I did manage to evade Nasserian, but at the cost of putting one of my friends in peril: Ibrahim Akbari

Sefat was selected to be executed. In a few days, he would have completed his prison sentence. He was from an extremely poor family in the northern region of the country.

"DS" was one of the prisoners in solitary confinement. He asked for a cigarette. I said, "Quiet! I've got some!" and gave him a cigarette, but I didn't have matches to light it. So he called the guard again and again, asking for matches. It brought to mind a poem, "His Unlit Cigarette," by Nazim Hikmet who spent seventeen years in prison for his political activity with the Communist Party.[26] Morteza Mollah Abdalhosseini had once recited it to me:

> He might die tonight
> The breast of his jacket burnt by a gunshot
> He strode to meet death tonight
> He asked:
> Do you have a cigarette?
> I said: yes
> Matches?
> I said: no
> Maybe a bullet will light it up. He took the cigarette and went by...
> He could be flat on his back by now
> An unlit cigarette between his lips and a wound in his chest...

In the afternoon, I noticed that inmates who had been with me in Annex 17 had been summoned for the hearings. I had almost forgotten about the three Kermanshahis. Seeing my friends there did not ring a bell either. Nasserian called a prisoner's name, but he did not respond. Then I heard *my* name. I did not respond either. I thought: *They're not giving away goodies. If they come closer and call my name, then I'll respond. Otherwise, I'll say that I was asleep.* What I did not realize at that time was that the prisoner really *was* asleep. If he had been awake and had responded, he definitely would have been executed. Normally, if they called someone and got no response, they would search for the person in the wings. It was a matter of luck if they failed to recognize the prisoner on the spot because, if they did, you had to justify yourself.

An agent from the Intelligence service carrying a docket approached Dariush Hanifehpour and asked him why he wanted to flee the country.

"To continue my studies."

---

26 Nazim Hikmet (1902–63) was a renowned Turkish poet, playwright, novelist, and screenwriter.

The agent slapped him across the face. "Villain! Why are you lying to me? What's this?" He then read a few charges against Dariush from his file.

Nasserian happily approached the two men and slapped Dariush on the back. "Your visa has been issued." Then he shoved him toward the court.

"I've been expecting this moment for a long time, you miserable thing," Dariush said, sneering. "But what will you get out of it?"

Nasserian was flabbergasted. Sadly, I did not get a chance to have a final word with Dariush.

A few minutes later, Mojtaba Akhgar was taken to court, but soon afterward he was escorted to one of the annexes. They were trying to persuade him to write a recantation letter. Mojtaba said calmly, "I'm illiterate. You write whatever you want, and I'll sign it." Flogged with a cable during the interrogations, his feet had been severely damaged. He had been sent back and forth between the court and the interrogation room. They did not know what to do with him. He would accept something under torture, but would deny it in court. So he was sent back to the interrogation room again. This time, Nayyeri condemned Mojtaba to one hundred lashes for lying. Hamid Abbasi, Nasserian's assistant, volunteered to carry out the punishment.

Nasserian was worried that the floggings would not be administered properly and would be "wasted" as he put it. In their eyes, torture and mistreatment of the prisoners was a religious duty and, by performing this duty, they would gain proximity to God Almighty. I was still trembling when they dragged Mojtaba's limp body from the room and left him behind at my side.

I held his hand in my hands. "Mojtaba, it's me, Iraj."

He moaned in pain. "I know. What's up?"

I nearly exploded with laughter. Mojtaba always wanted to be up to date with the news. Here he was, in terrible shape, yet spirited and nimble.

"Be quiet, I'll tell you!" I focused all my attention on him.

It was evening when Kaveh Nassari was called for a hearing. He was sick and could hardly walk. One leg was semi-paralyzed as a result of sciatica, and he suffered from chronic epilepsy. At least once or twice a week he would have seizures. His teeth were badly damaged due to grinding. His family had paid a huge sum of money to bail him out for medical treatment. While he was out on sick leave, he had fallen to the floor in the grip of an epileptic convulsion. He had lost his memory as a result of head injury, and could not remember the past.

Upon his return to prison, the court administrator had been forced to explain to Kaveh why he was in the prison and what he was charged with.

They had sentenced him to five years, but after he had completed his prison term, they said there had been a mistake at the time of sentencing and he had to stay in prison for another five years.

Kaveh was taken to court and apparently the hearing went well. I was very happy to see him escape death. My happiness did not last long, however. After a short discussion, the "Amnesty Commission" decided to finish him off. They called him to court again and this time they asked Kaveh to work in the workshop, but he refused. As soon as he left the court, he had a seizure. He was lying on the ground limp and motionless when he was called for execution.

At this time, they called Zafar Jafari Afshar. He and Kaveh were both Mojahedin prisoners from Karaj, and both had been my cellmates. Zafar moved to lift Kaveh up. Kaveh was limp and exhausted. When Zafar was putting Kaveh on his back, I was ready to explode. Although at a distance from them, no one could witness that scene better than me. It was such a painful scene. I clenched my teeth in anger. Zafar walked away ever so proudly, carrying Kaveh on his back.

The guards would point to the prisoners they knew or against whom they had a grudge, boasting that they, themselves, would do the final "kicking in the chest." They would thus get a heavenly reward for killing the "Enemies of God." No barbaric act was off limits when performing their duties. One had to know these people, their upbringing and their cultural backgrounds, in order to understand their deeds. The fact is that they had grown up in a traditional and religiously backward environment.

In the evening, I saw Faramarz Jamshidi, with whom I had been cellmates since 1986, sitting close to the courtroom's door with a few sheets of paper scattered around him. I said, "Hey, Brother!" (Everyone called him Brother.) He lifted his head up and looked at me in surprise. There was a sparkle in his eyes. His blindfold was on his forehead. He adjusted his blindfold a few times. He couldn't contain his happiness. His face was covered with a big smile.

"I'd heard that you were executed. You can't imagine how happy I am to see you alive!"

Finally, I was led, with a group of prisoners, to the single-cell block and then straight to my old cell. There, my fellow cellmates gathered around me wondering how I had made it back safe and sound. Their attitude was quite strange. They informed me that the guards and the three Kermanshahi *tavabs* had been looking for me everywhere; they had come to the cell to fetch me, they had called my name in the courtroom hallway (that was the time I had not answered), they had even checked almost all the prisoners one by one. I don't remember where I was at that moment. I could have been hiding my face from Lashkari with my "long," with my head tucked between my legs. Or I could have gone to the toilets. Later I found out that they had even searched for me in the Marxists' wing. Maybe they had concluded that I had already been hanged. I suddenly realized why all the inmates from Annex 17 who had been tried that day had been hanged.

The three Kermanshahis who had been with us in Annex 17 had stood as witnesses in the court and had testified against each and every one of the prisoners housed in Annex 17. The only one from Annex 17 against whom they had testified but had survived was a man named Mehdi. The Kermanshahis had said that Mehdi had analyzed the *Forough-e Javidan* Operation news, saying the Mojahedin had reached the gates of Hamedan. In defending himself, Mehdi told the team that the Kermanshahis were liars. All he had done was to relay what was broadcast on television to the other inmates. He said, "I didn't know that relaying the television news was a crime. How could I have said such things? I saw the operation until its final stages on television?" Apparently, his argument had been accepted by the Commission and Mehdi was not executed.

Sunday, August 14, and Monday, August 15 (23 and 24 Mordad)

On Sunday, after breakfast, we kept watch in turns. We were on the lookout for the "Carriage of Death." We had to prepare ourselves for the slaughterhouse if and when we saw Nayyeri's car. We knew no execution would take place in his absence. But his car didn't appear. We could breathe easily again. On the other hand, the team's absence at Gohardasht meant they were busy killing in Evin.

What did I have to say for myself if the three Kermanshahis spotted me? I was proud that none of the prisoners had cooperated with the executioners. The regime could not understand this. During the past few days, I had seen on several occasions how Nasserian flew into a rage to express his frustration. Exhausted and worn out, he was humbled by the resistance of the prisoners. This degree of resistance and steadfastness was unprecedented.

Most cellmates from Karaj were executed; there were very few exceptions. Karaj prisoners had been under a lot of pressure and were under constant control of the Karaj Public Prosecutor. In court, too, they were in a much more difficult situation. As there were only a few Karaji prisoners, Naderi, the prosecutor, and Fateh, the intelligence agent, knew each of them. Moreover, Raisi, a prominent and active member of the Death Commission, also knew nearly everyone.

Raisi had been deputy prosecutor in Karaj prior to his appointment to the post of deputy prosecutor of the Islamic Judiciary Division in Tehran in 1984. Naderi and Fateh were the principal decision-makers regarding the Karaji prisoners, and their addition to the composition of the Commission demonstrates the depth of the catastrophe.

Thursday, August 16 (25 Mordad)

On Thursday, I felt I had reached the end of the road and had lost the opportunity to escape death. I remained on the alert, however, and I could see everything very well through the "long." At one point, Lashkari went out on an errand. Nasserian left the courtroom looking for prey. He was walking around carrying a notebook with a list that was updated daily, searching for victims to send to the slaughterhouse. Nasserian had not come back yet. Nayyeri loudly called for the next prisoner. He repeated: "Mr. Nasserian, next defendant please." Apparently, he was angry that there had been a delay in their proceedings. It seemed that the Commission was in a hurry and was hoping to finish off the trials as fast as possible and leave the premises. I had to go to court anyway, so it would be better to appear in court in the absence of Nasserian and Lashkari. I took my chances; I got up and walked into the room. When I removed my blindfold, Nayyeri thought that a guard had led me to the courtroom. For him the only thing that counted was to conduct a trial so that he and the other members of the Commission would be able to do their job. Nayyeri asked me, "How many times have you appeared in court?" I answered, "Once." I knew that I would complicate the matter if I admitted to more than that. They would then be more demanding. I thought to myself, if Nayyeri noticed that I had been there three times already, I would deny it, saying that, in fact, I had been interviewed only once. The second and third interviews had been for clearing up the misunderstandings, so that he would clearly explain his demand. Fortunately, nobody said anything. As it was not my turn to appear in court, my prison file was not in front of them, but I *could* see a file with my name on it on a desk in the corner of the room. Each detainee had a prison file containing information about the behavior of the prisoner during his incarceration. Every time you appeared in court, your dossier, your bill of indictment, and your prison file would be in front of the judge. In my prison file there was a signed document that proved I had not wished to vote in the third election of the Islamic *Majles* (Parliament). Once your trial dragged out, there was no chance to win the battle.

As they were not prepared for my case, they had nothing in hand to use against me.

"Have you written the recantation letter?" Nayyeri asked.

"Yes!" Then I added stupidly: "A few days ago you promised to grant me pardon if I wrote a text. I wrote the letter. I thought it'd be enough. I can't understand why my release has taken so long."

The members of the Commission smirked.

"Go!" said Nayyeri. "Write a text worthy of an interview."

I had not been in court more than one minute and had not answered yet, when suddenly Nasserian rushed into the room. He frothed at the mouth. I was frightened that everything would go wrong. Everyone turned his attention to him. I ignored Nasserian and his untimely presence. I pretended I was trying to wear the blindfold again before leaving the courtroom. Nasserian was unaware of what had taken place in the courtroom. He couldn't urge them to hold another hearing because he had been absent. He tapped on my back and shoulder. Then, addressing Nayyeri, he roared, "Haji, these villains have made our life hell! No one has accepted to cooperate with us!"

Immediately, my heart swelled with pride. I could see his frustration and distress. I felt light. I felt proud that my friends had made their life miserable.

I left the room and wrote another recantation letter. This time, however, I felt much less stressed. The letter's content did not differ too much from the ones I had previously composed. However, I elaborated on the main idea. I added a few lines explaining that during my stay in prison, I had always tried to observe the rules and had never participated in any kind of collective activity. I also mentioned that I was a reclusive person. I thought: *If Lashkari were to see this letter, you could knock him over with a feather*. There was not a single activity in which I had not participated, and of course I had paid a price for that. I had always had one of the responsibilities of the cell and/or the wing.

On my way out of the court, I noticed that Akbar Band Ali and a few others who had been, up to now, excluded from the execution process had been brought there too. They were sitting in the corridor. The testimony of the three Kermanshahis—that we had communicated with other prisoners by Morse code—had apparently convinced Lashkari that more people needed to be executed. My heart sank when I saw them. I had been right to worry about the presence of those three men in Annex 17. I was thinking to myself that honesty and integrity were not the only qualities we needed to resist and win the combat. We also needed maturity, experience, skills, knowledge, and insight.

I found myself next to Adel Nouri, who was in high spirits. "For the love of life," he said, "I tried my best to stay alive, but now I'm ready to embrace death peacefully. I'm so happy that I'm going to meet the martyrs."

I asked him to say hello to Mousa Khiabani for me. Mousa had been killed in a battle with the Revolutionary Guards in 1982. His body and those of his companions had been taken to Evin prison. To torture me psychologically, a guard had taken me to see the corpses. It was unbearable. I suffered many atrocities throughout my years in prison, but I will never forget that scene.

Saeed Attarian-Nezhad had agreed to write a recantation letter a few days before, but had changed his mind the night before, claiming that his death would be more fruitful than staying alive. (He seemed to believe that his death would bring people closer to one another.)

As usual, we had bread and cheese for lunch. At about 1:30 p.m. five prisoners were called in: Adel Nouri, Mohammad-Rafi Naghdi, Saeed Attarian-Nezhad, Ghanbar Nemati, and Gholam Reza Kiakajouri. My heart sank. This was our last meeting. It was close to 2:30 p.m. I noticed that the members of the Commission were leaving the premises. This meant no more hangings that day.

As soon as the commission left for Evin, those of us in the Corridor of Death were lined up and taken back to our cells in groups.

There were six of us still waiting in the hallway until six o'clock in the evening. The guards went back and forth. They could not give an answer to our inquiries. Probably they did not know what to do with us. They did not want to send us back to our cells.

August 16 turned out to be the last day of executions for the Mojahedin prisoners of Gohardasht. Evidently, the arrival of the month of Moharam, combined with Ayatollah Montazeri's protest,[27] had somehow had an effect. The death machine had run in Gohardasht on July 30 and 31, and then on August 2, 6, 9, 12, 13, and 16. Except for a few Mojahedin who were later martyred along with the Marxist prisoners in the last days of August, the Mojahedin prisoners of Gohardasht were, for the most part, executed during those eight days.

---

27 Montazeri was the only ayatollah who condemned the mass killings of political prisoners who were tried, sentenced, and imprisoned.

Wednesday, August 17,
and Thursday, August 18 (26 and 27 Mordad)

It was the month of Moharam, and the country was in mourning. Night after night, the guards and the nonpolitical prisoners would congregate in the yard and perform the mourning rituals, and recite religious poetry. We would watch them through the shutters of the windows. They even had flags and banners. They marched in procession, tapping their chests grieving for the innocence of Imam Hossein, flagellating themselves.

I later found out that on that day, some of my friends had been tried in court at Evin. The executions had only stopped at Gohardasht.

Friday, August 19 (28 Mordad)

On Friday after breakfast, we stood guard by the window. We did not know whether or not the death machine had ceased operating. Things were still on red alert. We were still either in solitary or closed cells, and were still provided with only the minimum of facilities.

Shortly before noon, the doors to our room suddenly swung open. Nasserian, along with a few other guards, walked in. There were about eight of them, and Nasserian looked exhausted and worn out. (Obviously, he was suffering from a lack of sleep because he yawned repeatedly.) He complained of a headache and asked one of the guards to fetch him some painkillers from the dispensary. He asked my name and then asked how many times I had been tried.

"Once."

"Where were you before being tried before the Commission?"

"Wing 2."

"Were you there at the time of Eid-e Qurban?"

I couldn't say no; otherwise, he would know that I had been in solitary confinement and it would be worse. "Yes, I was."

"Who was serving the drinks during the ceremony?"

I hesitated, swallowed my saliva, and mumbled, "I wasn't there at Qurban. I was there at Ghadir. No, I wasn't there at Ghadir, I was there at Qurban." I mixed up the two events, repeating the same thing with a stammer until he was totally confused.

"Even if they question you a hundred times, it's not enough! Villain! Your visa's been issued. Get out of here!"

"Would you please let me pack my things?"

He agreed.

I noted that the guards had remained silent and had not interfered. They left our room and moved on to other cells. I did not have much to take with me, but I used it as an excuse to say goodbye to my cellmates. I kissed everyone goodbye, thinking I would never see them again.

Outside the cell, I stood against the wall, thinking about my friends and their heroic resistance. Nasserian was making every effort to find out who had served the drinks during the Eid-e Ghadir ceremony, as well as who had organized the ceremony! Many dozens of prisoners from our wing had been executed, and yet no one had volunteered to give him any information. For a moment, I thought that maybe he had not recognized me. Without hesitation, I answered that I did not know why I was there. They had brought me there and told me to wait there. I deliberately used the word "brought" in order to make him think things had happened somewhat differently than they actually had.

"How many times have you been questioned?" asked Nasserian once again.

"Once."

"Even one hundred times would not be enough for villains like you." He pointed to the cell I had just left. "Throw him into the cell!" he said to the guards.

The guards opened the door and kicked me in. The other inmates immediately gathered around me, delighted by my return. Everyone kissed and hugged me. One friend had become so emotional that he *covered* me with kisses. They had not held out much hope that I would stay alive.

From Saturday, August 20, to Wednesday, August 24 (29 Mordad to 2 Shahrivar)

On the day of Ashura, the executioners of Gohardasht headed by Lashkari, together with the prisoners who worked in the workshop and the ones in jihad, commemorated Imam Hossein,[28] tapping their chests and weeping over his innocence all throughout the day. They were hoping to gain proximity to God Almighty. All the executioners were in black.

---

28 Hossein, who was martyred in Karbala by Yazid in 680, was the third Shi'ite imam and the grandson of Prophet Mohammad. "The martyrdom of Hossein gave Shi'ites the ethos of suffering and martyrdom." *The Oxford Dictionary of Islam*, p. 120.

Saturday, August 27 (5 Shahrivar)

There had been no executions in Gohardasht for eleven days. We were convinced that the court had adjourned for Friday (the Persian weekend). If the trials did not recommence on this day, we could speculate that there would be further developments.

Dead silence fell over the room. No one said a word. I had butterflies in my stomach. At 9 a.m. a few of our cellmates were summoned to the courtroom. Nasserian arrived at 9:15 a.m. Soon afterward, a guard called my name and told me to prepare myself for the court. It was about 10 a.m. and I was preparing myself for questioning when my cellmates returned. As it turned out, my court hearing was canceled too, and the guard did not come to fetch me.

Mohammad V. was one of the detainees who had been summoned that morning. He explained later that apparently there had been a mistake, that the hearing was meant for Marxist prisoners and not us. The criminals had returned with new instructions by Khomeini. It seemed that they had started the second round of their deadly game.

It is alleged that Mohammad Yazdi, Ahmad Pourzanjani (a close friend and deputy of Reyshahri, the then Intelligence Minister), and Javad Mansouri (one of the founders of the Islamic Revolutionary Guards Corps instrumental in suppressing and killing the opposition who later became a Foreign Minister Deputy) had had an audience with Khomeini. In that meeting, they had explained to Khomeini that the mass killing of the Mojahedin while sparing the lives of the Marxist prisoners had sparked a backlash from some clergy in Qom. They deemed that it was an opportune moment to also eliminate Marxists. Did Khomeini remember the promise he had made a decade before? He had stated the Marxists would have the right to express their opinions in the IRI. How was he going to justify his new decree?

Seemingly, the first group of Marxist prisoners taken for hearings were housed in Annex 20. They were either members of the Tudeh Party or the Majority wing of Feda'ian and they were all executed.[29] Dozens of prisoners of Wing 7, who were taken to the courtroom in the first few days, were also martyred. It was only after the Marxist detainees understood that executions were actually taking place and eventually accepted defeat that the execution machine stopped.

---

29 See Appendix B for entries on the Tudeh Party and Feda'ian (Majority).

In the evening, the guards went to all the cells, telling everyone to get ready for immediate transfer to another wing. None of us took the news as a bad omen. We were all acquainted with the phrase "take them to their wing" and had heard it several times in the past few days and we knew they meant "the netherworld," but this time their tone of voice was different.

It seems that we understood each other's language. It didn't take long for us to go from the single-cell block in the *Mellikesh* section to Annex 6. In fact, this was the first gathering of Mojahedin survivors.

Once again, I kissed everyone in the room. I think everybody else did the same thing. To me, those around me were lost jewels that had been recovered. I could not conceal my joy at finding this big and precious treasure.

Monday, August 29, to Sunday, September 4 (7 Shahrivar to 13 Shahrivar)

The Death Commission was busy killing in Evin prison on Monday, August 29, and Tuesday, August 30, before returning to Gohardasht on August 31. All prisoners who had survived the trial were now housed in Wing 8. The sounds of beating and flogging with cables could be heard every day. Apparently, those who refused to say the daily prayers received ten lashes at each prayer time.

It did not take long for the Marxist inmates to see that resistance was pointless. Adel, who escorted the victims to the gallows, led the daily prayers and the Marxists prisoners were forced to follow his lead. The Marxists who had escaped death were those who had grasped the gravity of the situation and had said they were Muslim and accepted the performance of prayers.

The trials of the Marxist prisoners were a reminder of the sorrowful scenes of the Inquisition and the medieval courts. The cardinals, or rather the inquisitors, prosecuted blasphemous and heretic beliefs in Inquisitorial courts all over Europe, demanding that the heretics and apostates kneel in front of them and vow that that they would be good Catholics and follow the Catholic Church and the Holy Apostles.

September 4 (13 Shahrivar)

September 4 was the last day of these systematic executions in Gohardasht. After this date, no executions took place on the basis of the decrees Khomeini had decreed in August. In the afternoon, the guards told us to pack our belongings and prepare ourselves for a new transfer. Soon afterward, we found ourselves in Wing 13. All the prisoners from Annex 14 and the solitary cells were gathered there too.

The inmates settled in the rooms quickly. About 130 of those in our new population were Mojahedin who had either been tried and somehow escaped execution or were being tried when the killings had suddenly stopped. In addition, there were about 70 prisoners from Wing 1 who had not been tried at all. Out of 700 Mojahedin prisoners, excluding the ones working in the work shop, only 200 had survived. In a period of seventeen days the regime had executed more than 450 Mojahedin prisoners.

It was now about a week into September. The storm had passed and the sea had calmed, and I was ready to set about learning the fate of my Marxist friends.

TRANSLATED FROM PERSIAN BY ALI HOJAT

Life-Bestowing Telephone Call

MEHDI ASLANI[30]

Iran is my motherland and Tehran is my hometown. Along with many other shattered wishes of mine, the dream of returning and seeing its blue skies once again may be buried with me in exile. I've left my ravaged youth and thousands of bittersweet memories in Tehran.

Old Tehran was known for its seven famous gates, its old plane trees dating back hundreds of years, the Museum of Crown Jewels, and its precious carpets. Nowadays Tehran is known for sites such as the notorious Evin and Gohardasht prisons, and Khavaran cemetery, embodying the injustice and atrocities of its Islamic fundamentalist rulers. The cold, dull, gray walls of those two prisons bear witness to the slaughter of thousands of young souls. There, the hopes of a nation withered away.

I was incarcerated in Ward 8 of Gohardasht prison in summer 1988 when the Great Massacre took place. I was serving my seven-year sentence on the charge of membership in the People's Feda'ian (adherents of the December 7 Declaration).[31] This was a split-off from the OIPFG, a Marxist organization that fought against the Pahlavi regime and earned popularity and respect because of the resistance and heroism of its members against SAVAK's[32] henchmen.

---

30 Mehdi Aslani, born in 1959, was raised in a popular neighborhood in the southwest of Tehran. The 1979 Revolution made him sensitive to political issues and induced him to support the Organization of Iranian People's Feda'i Guerrillas. Aslani was arrested in 1984 and was detained in Evin, Qezel Hesar, and Gohardasht prisons. He witnessed and survived the 1988 Great Massacre. He was released in February 1988 and managed to flee Iran in 1998. He settled in Germany as a political refugee. Since then, he has written and lectured extensively on prison life in the IRI and the 1988 Massacre. He co-published with Masoud Noghrekar *The Hemlock Forest* (2005), a collection of last wills and letters by executed prisoners. Aslani also published his prison memoirs, *The Crow and the Rose* (2009). His latest book is *The Last Breath of the Rose* (2016), a collection of 137 letters and artworks of men and women who did not survive the IRI's prisons.

31 See Appendix B, OIPFG.

32 The National Agency for Information and Security, Mohammad Reza Shah Pahlavi's secret police.

Ward 8, as well as Ward 7 and the sub-Ward 20 in Gohardasht, all over-looked the *Hosseiniyeh* (a Shi'ite place of worship) where the Death Row prisoners were hanged. During that bloody summer, the Islamic court hearings inside Gohardasht lasted only a few minutes, and the thousands of death sentences given out were implemented just as quickly.

The misfortune befallen upon me and all other left-leaning survivors of those three wards may be interpreted as a historical stroke of fortune, enabling us to record our observations and reveal the story of the Great Massacre, in order to prevent it from being buried in the archives of history.

> *"To taste seawater, just a mouthful, would be enough."*
>
> ALEKSANDR SOLZHENITSYN,
> *The Gulag Archipelago*

If I had known I was to recount the events I partially witnessed some thirty years ago, I would have fully absorbed all the instances and disregarded nothing. However, this was not the case, and so I apologize to all my deceased fellow inmates for failing to observe, remember, and register many details.

It was on July 18, 1988, that the leaders of the IRI unexpectedly accepted the terms of UN Security Council resolution 598, effectively putting an end to a devastating eight-year war with Iraq—a war that had left behind hundreds of thousands of dead and disabled on both sides as well as billions of dollars of material loss.

Soon afterward, a carefully calculated plan was effected in prisons throughout Iran, the outcome of which was the hanging of almost four thousand men and women.

July 18, 1988, can hardly be forgotten by the inmates of Gohardasht prison. At 2 p.m., over the loudspeakers, we heard: "Ayatollah Khamenei [then the President of the IRI] in a dispatch to Javier Pérez de Cuéllar, the UN secretary-general, has given the Islamic Republic's official approval of the resolution 598." There was complete silence accompanying the trembling voice of the newscaster of the state-run radio, Islamic Republic of Iran Broadcasting (IRIB). It was difficult to believe that the regime had finally accepted ceasefire with Iraq. Two days later, Ayatollah Khomeini in justifying the acceptance of the UN Security Council resolution likened it to "drinking a chalice of poison." In taking the responsibility for this historic decision he stated, "If I ever had some honor before God, I've lost it in this transaction."

Ayatollah Khomeini had, until a few days before, vowed to continue the war until total victory. Hearing his new positions made us prisoners so happy that we couldn't contain our joy. This multifaceted joy was mainly due to:

1. Our objections to a war called a "blessing" by Khomeini, as it was in reality a pretext for repression and the allocation of all resources to the war machine.
2. Khomeini's call for international uprisings against satanic powers was muffled. So was the charisma of a leader who had pledged to export the "Islamic Revolution" to the neighboring Karbala as the first step on the path to "liberate Jerusalem."

On Friday, July 29, 1988 (a bank holiday in Iran), the prison guards removed our television from the ward on the pretext of needing to repair it. Thus, we were deprived of our most important means of communication with the outside world. The information compiled later by surviving inmates of other wards indicates that this measure was carried out simultaneously in all prison wards. The loudspeakers were also switched off.

At that time, our basic means of communication with the outside world were:

- IRIB Television (starting at 7 a.m. and often signing off at 11 p.m.)
- the radio news broadcast twice a day at 8 a.m. and at 2 p.m.
- two morning dailies and two evening newspapers (all state owned)
- family visits every fifteen days
- five-line letters to and from immediate family members once a month.

In the days after the television sets were taken away, the morning and evening newspapers were not distributed, doors to the prison yard remained locked (we were normally permitted to go to the yard four hours a day), and our bimonthly visits with family members were canceled. In effect, all our communication channels with the outside world had been cut off.

All of these measures were imposed upon prisoners with no explanation. Nevertheless, we were held totally incommunicado for a whole month. During this period, the usual exchanges with the prison guards came to a halt, as they refused to answer our questions and observed an absolute silence, only opening the doors of the prison ward three times a day for our daily meals.

"The one who laughs has not heard the horrific news yet."

BERTOLT BRECHT

Although the cutting off of all communication channels posed a serious question for us all, a hidden joy could be traced in the face of each and every inmate. This fleeting joy, however, ended in the bloody execution of opponents and dissidents captured in the early 1980s and spared from execution up to that point. The mass killings of summer 1988 were different from all previous waves of executions because of the secretive manner in which they were carried out, thus making it an "Iranian-style Holocaust."

Ayatollah Khomeini's abrupt and unconditional acceptance of UN Security Council resolution 598 was deemed as an opportune moment by the People's Mojahedin Organization of Iran (PMOI)—the strongest opposition force at the time—to call for people to rise up and join forces with its armed wing, the Iranian National Liberation Army (NLA). The NLA was dispatched from its bases in Iraq with the mission to deal the final blow to the IRI. However, the PMOI's call to arms was not heeded by the people. On July 25, 1988, the NLA crossed the western border of the country and entered the frontier towns. In the ensuing three-day battle, *Sepah Pasdaran* (the Revolutionary Guards) who felt disgraced and humiliated for not delivering victory in the war against Iraq, vengefully and brutally crushed and killed hundreds of NLA militants, and captured others who were later transferred to Evin prison.

On July 27, 1988, Ayatollah Khomeini appointed a three-member commission to re-interrogate and re-try the political prisoners. This commission, entrusted with absolute power and later called by the prisoners the "Death Commission," consisted of a shari'a judge, Hojat al-Islam Nayyeri, a public prosecutor, Morteza Eshraghi, and a representative of the Ministry of Information, Mostafa Pourmohammadi. (It is noteworthy that seventeen years after the Great Massacre, Mostafa Pourmohammadi was appointed Interior Minister by President Mahmoud Ahmadinejad!)

The Commission started work on July 27, 1988, in Gohardasht prison and later in Evin, first re-questioning and re-trying the members and sympathizers of the PMOI and then the prisoners of Marxist persuasion.

On August 27, 1988, we the detainees of Ward 8 of Gohardasht heard some noise coming from Ward 7 upstairs. It seemed that the inmates were speedily being taken somewhere. Where? We did not have to wait long to find out what was going on. The next day, around noon, the same thing happened to us. The whole ward was ordered out, blindfolded in two rows. Soon afterward, we found ourselves in front of the warden's office. Seated on the floor, we had to wait hours before being called to the warden's office, one by one. There, the same clichéd questions were put to us. Muslim or Marxist? Do you say your prayers? Charge? Are you ready to condemn your group in front of other prisoners or in a video interview? Are you ready to repent and put in writing your repulsion for your group?

Davoud Lashkari, the director of Gohardasht, and Nasserian, the prison prosecutor, were the ones posing these questions. More than sixty out of eighty inmates from Ward 8 answered the questions in the negative. Seventeen of us were taken back to the ward and the rest were lined up blindfolded in the prison corridor. All of a sudden, four or five Revolutionary Guards with shaved heads, dressed in black from head to toe, swinging cable cords in hand, appeared in front of us. We knew none of them. They ordered us to get up and whipped us brutally all the way up to cells located at the furthest end of the hall upstairs. The cells were so small and we so many that the guards could not easily shut the doors. We could not make sense of what was going on. None of us could come up with any realistic analysis of the situation. A few hours later, the door opened and a guard holding a walkie-talkie in his hand yelled, "The first ten to the Commission!" The Commission? Which Commission? Before we could manage to react, the guard picked out the ten himself: "You, and you, and you."

I was among those who were picked. We ten had nothing in common except for the fact that we were all more heavily built than the others. Because I was the first to leave the cell, I was the first in line. None of us could guess what was in store for us. We were trying to figure out what the panel was all about and what it was up to. In this space of frozen time, we walked like robots turning left or right by the orders of the guards. At one of the left or right turns, I did the opposite of what the guard had ordered. Consequently, we were forced to line up anew, this time with me at the end and Jahanbakhsh Sarkhosh at the head. When we arrived, we were ordered to sit not too far from the *Hosseiniyeh*, in front of a room where the panel was stationed. The first person to be called out was Jahanbakhsh. He was a member of the People's Feda'ian (Minority), had served his sentence, and was to be released in a few months. While he was in the room, time dragged terribly, heavily weighing on us, breaking our nerves. When he left the room, the prison prosecutor told one of the guards, "Left. Take him to the left." Jahan was taken to the left of where we were sitting. Then Nasserian called out Mehrdad Neshati. Mehrdad was also a member of the People's Feda'ian

(Minority). He too was to be released in a few months. His mother was a Christian and his father a Muslim. When the Commission asked him, "Are you a Muslim or a Marxist? Do you say your prayers or not?" Mehrdad found recourse in his father's Christianity to escape the inquisition. The shari'a judge said, "Your mother is a Muslim and you have been raised in an Islamic family, so you're a Muslim too and have to say your prayers." Mehrdad did not succumb and refused to pray. The judge's verdict was: "Whip him until he accepts to say his prayers."

At that moment, no one understood what the shari'a judge meant. Many, including myself, thought that we could withstand fifty to one hundred lashes as punishment for not praying. But we were mistaken. There was a hidden message in that verdict: if the prisoner is steadfast in his decision not to say his prayers, he should be flogged until he drops dead.

They took Mehrdad neither to the left nor to the right. He was taken to a place where those who refused prayer were kept. They were to be given ten lashes on the soles of their feet at each call for prayer. It is significant that Muslims have to pray five times a day (at dawn, at noon, in the afternoon, at twilight, and at night); thus, anyone who had admitted to being a Muslim but refused to say his prayers had to bear fifty lashes a day until he gave in and attended to his prayers. The punitive flogging was given by guards who had no specialization in the trade and tried their best to give lashes with the utmost force. This was unlike the flogging given by experienced torturers whose aim was to extract information from prisoners. Such torturers would hit so skillfully that the sole of the foot would not crack, facilitating the continuation of the torture and depriving the prisoner of time-out to make rational decisions. On the contrary, in flagellation (also exercised as a punishment for "sexual sins," drinking alcohol, drug dealing, and so forth) there is no consideration other than delivering a certain number of blows with full force. It could be carried on until the convict lost consciousness, was maimed, or prostrated. At the time, it was unclear to Mehrdad and all others who refused to pray what price had to be paid.

After Mehrdad Neshati, Ali Akbar Elli-een was called out. Again Nasserian ordered, "Whip him until he says his prayers."

THE PHONE CALL THAT SAVED ME

It was finally my turn to go to the room. I was instructed to push up my blindfold. Sitting in front of where I was standing, at a large table, were the three main members of the Death Commission. It was Hojat al-Islam Nayyeri who started the interrogation.

"Are you a Muslim or a Marxist?"

Throughout my years of imprisonment, I always shunned ideological issues and usually answered questions with other questions or evaded them by giving ambiguous responses. I must admit that the period in which I was imprisoned permitted such maneuvers. Had I been arrested sometime between 1981 and 1984, I would have been immediately executed by the firing squad for having played such a game. Yet this time around, facing the Commission, there was no room for maneuver.

"I was born a Muslim, but philosophically speaking I consider myself neither a Muslim nor a Marxist."

"But you are charged with membership in a Marxist organization."

"I was attracted to the People's Feda'ian because they advocated equal rights and justice. I didn't care about their philosophy."

"It was damn wrong of you. Who said only Marxists talk of equal rights and advocate justice?"

The telephone rang. Nayyeri picked up the phone and respectfully started talking with someone unknown to me up to this date. After exchanging a few polite words, he hung up the phone, got up, and signaled with his hands to his colleagues to also get up and accompany him to where he had been summoned. Leaving the room, he turned toward Nasserian. "Take him away for now."

I was led out and taken to a large cell along with the other six waiting in front of the door. Apparently, I was the last person to appear before the panel on August 7, 1988, and after that the trials stopped in Gohardasht for two days. One of the unanswered questions of the Great Massacre is the reason for this interval and why no one was called for interrogation on days 8 and 9 of that bloody month. As there is no clue up to now, I can only guess that it was Ayatollah Montazeri's unexpected protest of this disgraceful criminal act that made the panel temporarily cease its work. (At the time, Ayatollah Montazeri was second to Ayatollah Khomeini and his heir apparent. The protest of such a high-ranking official could not have gone unheeded.)

Upon our arrival in the cell, sounds from outside immediately captured our attention. As the *Azan* (call for prayers) was heard from the loudspeakers, the guards began calling prisoners to do their ablutions and say their prayers. It wasn't difficult to realize that some were resisting and being beaten for not joining the worshippers. The prison guards didn't call out to us as if we were not there. As soon as the shouting and crying faded and silence prevailed, one of my fellow inmates initiated contact with the adjacent cell. All our eyes began following the incredible movements of artful fingers exchanging information using Morse code. Thirty years after that dreadful day, I still can't believe how fast those fingers tapped. What was relayed to us was horrendous: "Threat of death. Serious. Ideological defense equals death. Refusing to pray equals whip. Mojahedin almost all killed. Watch out."

A deadly silence reigned in the cell. Fourteen eyes popped out of their sockets. Our faces turned white as if there was no blood running in our veins. It was difficult to believe what we had heard. The new developments did not correspond to our analysis of the political situation. It simply didn't make sense. None of us felt like talking. Each of us became lost in his own thoughts. Suddenly we were all awakened by a sudden cry: someone was being whipped. We started counting the number of lashes. One. Two. Three... The deafening cries went deep into our souls.

"No, I will not pray. No way!"

And the whipping continued. Then we heard a different voice.

"Enough. It's enough. I'll say my prayers. Don't hit me anymore."

"Untie him!" we heard someone order.

The surprising thing was that nobody ever bothered us and we were left to our own devices. In the silence that followed the lashing, one of us said, "It's all a setup. Maybe the guards are making all this up to shatter our morale and break down our resistance." Yet deep in our hearts, we knew the tragedy was real.

We hardly slept a wink that night—listening to the walls, exchanging news, and analyzing facts. We tried to remember all the happenings, put the pieces of the puzzle together, and comprehend the sequence of events. The key question was what had happened since July 27 up until this inferno burning up thousands of political prisoners.

As mentioned earlier, we prisoners of Wards 7 and 8, because of our location, had seen things not seen by other prisoners. To give a few examples, for consecutive nights in the month of August we had seen refrigerated trucks parked near the *Hosseiniyeh* of Gohardasht. These trucks delivered meat to the prison kitchen, but this time around, instead of unloading meat, they were being *loaded* with something we could not determine. But what? We had also watched guards with masks on their faces wearing plastic boots, spraying something. What? Were the guards in masks and plastic boots spraying to get rid of the fetid stench of the dead bodies? Were the refrigerated trucks transporting the executed Mojahedin to their burial grounds? Was the *Hosseiniyeh* the execution site? With the call to prayer at dawn, the ordeal of the previous day repeated itself: howling, crying, shouting, and yielding. A while later, we heard by a Morse code message that a veteran prisoner had committed suicide with a broken glass jar that we used for drinking tea. In the afternoon, we were not permitted to go to the toilets, and in the evening, when the guards searched the cells and removed all the glass jars, there was no longer a shadow of doubt that the suicide news was true. That night we all stayed awake. Even though we were exhausted, we couldn't sleep and wanted to talk. I was the first to speak my mind. I had decided not to put up an ideological defense in front of the Death Commission—not to say I am a Muslim but won't pray. I didn't know refusing to pray was tantamount to being whipped to death, and fifty lashes of cable cord a day could not be tolerated for long.

> *"Nothing but a story, never to become repetitive."*
>
> HAFEZ

Finally, the determining moment came: around noon on Wednesday, August 9, all seven of us were taken out of our cell and brought to the administrative section. I was the first to enter the room. Upon removing the blindfold, Nayyeri asked my name, organizational affiliation, and charge:

"Mehdi Aslani. I was charged with supporting the People's Feda'ian, adherents of the Sixteenth of Azar Declaration."

"Muslim or Marxist?"

"Muslim."

"Do you say your prayers?"

"The truth is, Haj Agha, like many other Muslims I have never prayed in my life. And I guess my pretense to pray would even offend you, wouldn't it, Haj Agha?"

Then the Revolution prosecutor, Morteza Eshraghi, intervened and told Nasserian, the prison prosecutor, "Take him away. How dare he not say his prayers."

"Haj Agha, I have never prayed in my life. I don't even know *how* to pray."

"A Muslim must say his prayers. Take him out. Shave off his moustache and he will then pray."

As Nasserian grabbed my shirt pulling me outside, Nayyeri said, "First make him sign the form, then shave off his hair and moustache, and let him pray. If he doesn't, beat him up until he says his prayers."

Blindfolded, I was directed out of the room, and my moustache, a symbol of being a left-winger in my generation of Iranian revolutionaries, was humiliatingly shaved off. Then a handwritten affidavit was given to me, which I had to sign. The text consisted of several clauses, the most important of which was: "The undersigned is a Muslim and Shi'ite who has not observed his religious duties up to now. Hereby, he undertakes to perform all his religious duties, particularly the daily prayers."

I crossed out the second sentence, signed the affidavit, and handed it back to Nasserian. Noticing the alteration, he flared up and tore the paper and started kicking, punching, and shoving me into a cell already occupied by a few prisoners. They, too, had refused to pray.

After a couple of hours, Nasserian appeared again with bloodshot eyes and two guards at his sides, both with cable cords in hand. "Who's not praying?" he roared.

Some accepted to pray right away; others, including me, continued to say we didn't want to pray. Nasserian signaled to the guards, and they brutally whipped us all the way to the ward.

"I'll be back in a couple of hours to deal with you guys."

Nasserian left us, and we found ourselves in a ward full of left-leaning prisoners. It didn't take long to realize that we were all the survivors of the massacre in Gohardasht. In an atmosphere of consternation, grief, and confusion, with tearful eyes, each asked about his companion, comrade, and kin.

"Where's Ahmad?"

"Not among us."

"What about Dariush? Mahmoud? Homayoun?"

"They, too, are here no more. I mean, they're gone forever."

That is how I learned that the veteran prisoner who committed suicide with the broken glass jar was Jalil Shahbazi. Arrested before the all-out attack of the IRI on the opposition (1981–84), he had gone through the height of repression aimed at making prisoners repent and turning them into born-again Muslims. During that period, flagellation by cable cord, one of the harshest and most intolerable torture techniques, became common in the IRI's prisons. Jalil, aware of the excruciating effects of this torture, decided to kill himself instead of betraying his principles. After having received fifty lashes by cable cord at five calls for prayer, Jalil Shahbazi ripped open his stomach with a broken glass jar and pulled out his intestines.

That is how I figured out what Nasserian meant when he ordered the guard to take Jahan to the left. **Left** was the code name for the death chamber, the

Hosseiniyeh,[33] located on the left of the administrative section. The gallows awaited those who had failed the "death exam." So Jahan walked *himself* to the gallows after being interrogated by the Death Commission. He was probably carried to Khavaran and buried there in a mass grave. I wish I had known they were going to kill him, and I had the courage to get up and shout out, "Sir! Brother! Haj Agha! Murderer! Bastard! Take *me* to the left, not him." It was because of *me* that the line-up changed. He was placed first and I last. I should have gone before the Death Commission first, not him. This bitter nightmare I have not forgotten to this day. Alas! Jahan could have been the narrator of this account of the bloody summer of 1988 when death reigned in Gohardasht, Evin, and… If I have survived for one thing only, it is to recount this story.

> *"I prayed and was massacred because I was considered as a Qaramatian.*
> *I prayed and I was massacred because I was considered as a Heretic."*
>
> AHMAD SHAMLU

How many were executed during that bloody summer? *Why* were they executed? We were so tormented by those questions that we couldn't help but to promptly come up with some answers. As to the reason why the regime had slaughtered the Mojahedin, we were of the opinion that it was the regime's vengeful response to the armed incursion of the NLA into the border cities in western Iran. But there was no consensus among us about the mass execution of our left-leaning comrades.

Ayatollah Khomeini himself had ordered the executions. The justification wasn't the same for the Marxists and the Mojahedin. Whereas the Mojahedin and their sympathizers were charged with "war against God," the Marxists were charged with apostasy. The key question of Nayyeri for the members and sympathizers of Marxist groups, including myself, was, "Are you a Muslim or a Marxist?" Whoever responded "I'm a Marxist" went to the gallows. As to the Mojahedin, it sufficed to use the word Mojahed, and not *Monafeq* (hypocrite), to be sent to the death chamber. Moreover, the sympathizers of the PMOI had to condemn their leader, Masoud Rajavi, and call him a traitor. Refusing to do so was punished by death too. The re-interrogation of the Mojahedin took a whole month; however, the re-interrogation of the Marxist prisoners did not last more than a week as they were less numerous.

---

33 The *Hosseiniyeh* of Gohardasht was used for hanging political prisoners condemned to death by the Death Commission.

In retrospect, however, I classify all who perished or survived during that deadly summer into three main categories:

1. The Death Conscious: detainees who were conscious of the fact that to expose one's true political identity and ideological orientation before the Commission would mean death. As one who appeared twice before the Commission, I testify: Of all the Marxists in Gohardasht, only a few put up a stalwart defense of their ideological orientation and embraced death.

2. The Unconscious: detainees who were either totally unaware of the IRI's plan to purge prisoners or deluded by the Commission to believe that the re-interrogation had no objective other than a new displacement. Living for years in Gohardasht, having known many political prisoners intimately, and taking into consideration the course of events there, I am convinced that many of the executed had no clue as to the Commission's intention of purging all who remained steadfast in their conviction. I'm inclined to think that the vast majority of the detainees only realized the true objective of the Commission at the gallows.

3. The Survivors: mainly people who gave ambiguous or double-edged responses to the Commission. By declaring, "I'm a Muslim but won't say my prayers," one could bring about a punishment with a tragic end. The shari'a judge would order: "Whip him until he prays" and one would be lashed until either submission or death.

It must be emphasized that the abovementioned classification is only a schematic outline of the general trend observed in Gohardasht on the five crucial days between August 27 and September 1. It is worth mentioning that there are some exceptional cases that should not be overlooked.

While many aspects of that shocking extermination remain hidden by the powers of the IRI, the importance of discussing and researching the horrific events that occurred, in order to memorialize those who were lost and prevent similar atrocities in the future, continues to prevail.

TRANSLATED FROM PERSIAN BY ROXANA FARD

Awaiting Our Fate

NASSER KH.[34]

I was arrested on July 23 of the turbulent year of 1981, a few weeks after Ayatollah Beheshti, the head of the Supreme Court, and seventy other leaders of the Islamic Republic of Iran (IRI) were killed in a bomb blast. The bombing was purported to be a response to the crackdown on the peaceful demonstration of July 21 against the removal from office of Abolhassan Banisadr, the first president of the IRI. The day after my arrest was the presidential election that brought Mohammad Ali Rajai to power. I was taken to the headquarters of the Revolutionary Guards in Azimiyeh.

Azimiyeh is one of the upper-middle-class neighborhoods in the city of Karaj. It was a detention center where the preliminary interrogations took place. Prisoners were then taken to the Prosecutor's Bureau and, after a few hours of interrogation, were transferred to a place called Kanoon. Azimiyeh Headquarters did not have many solitary cells. Convicted felons and political prisoners were kept together. Only unruly and violent prisoners were kept in solitary confinement. Those days when the regime was out to eliminate all the opposition, some political activists were executed there.

I think it was July 29 when I was transferred to the Kanoon in Karaj, now the notorious Shahid Kajoui prison. Kanoon was a large site constructed in

---

34 Nasser Kh. was born in 1962 into a working-class family on the east side of Tehran. Gradually, he became active in the movement that brought about the downfall of the Shah in 1979. In the more or less open political atmosphere of 1980–82, he acquainted himself with an array of progressive and revolutionary groups. The utter repression that followed the abdication of President Abolhassan Banisadr entrapped Nasser Kh., too. He was apprehended on July 23, 1981, in a working-class neighborhood in Karaj, a city close to Tehran. He was taken to Qezel Hesar and Gohardasht prisons. His eight and a half years of imprisonment obliged him to be a meticulous witness of many crimes of the IRI in the 1980s and also the Great Massacre of 1988. He was released from prison at the beginning of 1989. It took him eleven years to escape from Iran. He managed to get asylum in Canada in 2001 through the UN office in Turkey. Nasser now resides in Toronto as a blue-collar worker.

the later years of the Shah's reign. Unemployed or homeless people were taken there for vocational training such as carpet weaving. There were workshops for some handicrafts and martial arts too.

Until September 22, 1981, I was incarcerated in the Kanoon. There, I was interrogated and tried within a month. The shari'a judge sentenced me to seven years of imprisonment. Afterward, a few weeks following the assassination of Mohammad Ali Rajai by the People's Mojahedin Organization of Iran (PMOI), I was transferred to Qezel Hesar prison. On that day too, Mojahedin had bombed a governmental site. With each spectacular operation of the Mojahedin, we were transferred from one ward to another. We were moved again and again. We witnessed many kinds of cruelty, torture, and executions on a daily basis, sometimes even group executions. We saw the ins and outs of the operation of the Islamic prison system, designed to make prisoners repent and very often succeeding at its purpose. We saw that and much more between 1981 and 1984.

GOHARDASHT

By the end of 1985, Qezel Hesar prison had been evacuated and all the political prisoners had been transferred either to Gohardasht prison or Evin prison. It was said that the prison officials wanted to transfer all the Iraqi prisoners of war, as well as convicted felons, to Gohardasht. We were transferred to Gohardasht in winter 1986. Upon arrival, all the transferred prisoners were given a seven-page form. We were seated on the floor of a big hall and permitted to push our blindfolds up a little to fill out the forms. Then we were divided into several groups and put in solitary confinement. After a couple of days, we were taken from the solitary cells to the main wards. I was placed in Ward 5.

The main wards were in one of the three-story buildings of Gohardasht, and each ward was on a separate landing. Each of the main wards had a wing for minors, a communal room, several cells, and toilets and showers. Each minor wing included two rooms, a storeroom, a bathroom, and a toilet. Each cell was originally designed to hold between eight and ten prisoners, and each ward contained between eighty and a hundred prisoners. Our ward was in the last building opposite the Gohardasht wall, and adjacent to the *Hosseiniyeh* on the left. Ward 7 was on the upper floor, and Ward 8 was on the lower floor. There were no prisoners on the ground floor; it was empty.

Prisoners organized themselves into *senfi-ha*. The duty of each *senfi* (guild) was to manage the internal affairs of each ward including maintaining orderly routines, housekeeping, hygiene, distribution of food and newspapers, and so forth. Each *senfi* basically represented the supporters of one political party. If there were only a few people from a political group, the prisoners would join a *senfi* they felt close to. Sometimes there would be supporters of diverse ideologies in the same *senfi*. In Ward 5, the Mojahedin were the vast majority and had their own *senfi*. There were nine or ten people in ours. We were known as the leftist *senfi*. This included the supporters of Peykar, Aqaliyat, Razmandegan... and also people like me without any particular political affiliation. The *senfi* of each group acted independently. In some *senfis*, it was arranged for the prisoner to pay a certain sum to the treasury after each visit with his family. Some members had calculated precisely how much each person had to pay.

One of the leaders of the Arman-e Mostaz'afin group was in Ward 5 too. Mojahedin prisoners had to introduce themselves as *Monafeq* (hypocrite), the name chosen for them by the regime. Only three people among all the Mojahedin in our ward said they were Mojahedin. Basically, the Mojahedin who had come from Evin prison had a higher rank. All in all, Mojahedin inmates avoided using the word "Mojahed." The most common words for introducing their political identity was "sympathizer of the Organization" or "*Monafeq*." The leftists, however, were not afraid of revealing their political identity. They easily said they supported Aqaliyat, or Peykar, and so on, as the regime had not given names to the leftist organizations.

At that time, there were no *tavabs* (penitents) in any of the rooms in our ward. Of course, once in a while they sent penitent infiltrators. With experience, we had learned to identify them quite rapidly.

One of the duties of the *tavab* was to prepare detailed reports about the inmates. This ploy had gotten many prisoners into trouble and created many problems. We had been hurt so much that we had become sensitive to such people and could easily identify even complete strangers. Mehr Ali Teimouri and a couple of others whom I don't want to name here were "exported *tavabs*." Sometimes they were sent to the cells of newly arrested prisoners. And sometimes they played the role of a provincial prisoner who had just been transferred to Tehran only to face the death penalty. This was so that they could get close to the prisoners and get them to talk, as many newly arrested prisoners were seeking someone to talk to. It's at such moments that the "exported *tavab*" appeared on the scene, gathered information from the inmates, and brought suffering to the prisoner.

Anyhow, at that time there were no *tavabs* in Ward 5. As the guys said, "our ward had been liberated." I mean everything was in our own hands. There was a person in charge of each of the chores including distribution of newspapers and daily food, also cleaning and medical care. We were responsible for the discipline in the ward too, and we had a chief. I think the *zir-e hasht* (ward control desk) was not aware of the internal division of chores, but all the inmates were aware of who was the *mass'oul-e band* (the person in charge of the ward). Each *senfi* had a person in this capacity who would meet daily and discuss issues. They gave us the summation of their discussions and then the inmates voted. I think it was a nice process. Nobody was permitted to impose his opinion and there was a ballot for each issue. We had a very good time. We made our own decisions. As the saying goes, "the ball was in our hands." This situation was totally different from what reigned in prisons from June 1981 to fall 1985 and is considered to be one of the better times of incarceration in the IRI detention facilities.

We lived through several important events in Gohardasht. We organized a strike that would never have been possible in Qezel Hesar prison. When the guards brought food into the ward, we protested that the food was not sufficient. We pushed the food out and refused the meals for several days. And once when they brought the food to the communal room, nobody touched it. The guards came and asked, "Why didn't you eat your meal?" We said, "It's not enough for us." We protested against the quality and quantity of the food with three- or four-hour strikes. The courage to mount such protests was achieved little by little.

ILLUSION OR APPREHENSION

The prison atmosphere between 1985 and 1987 was misleading. Few people could see through their wheeling and dealing. We had a hunch that they were making some arrangements for the steadfast political prisoners. The Great Massacre of 1988 proved that our fear was not groundless. For example, Solitary Cell 3 in Qezel Hesar prison was a real hell for the prisoners at the time. The prisoners who were transferred from Evin or other prisons to Qezel Hesar were immediately taken to Solitary Cell 3. There was an interrogator called Zoori who was from the Zoorabad neighborhood, one of the slums in the vicinity of greater Tehran. He crushed the prisoners. (In the events related to the 2009 controversial presidential elections that brought Mahmoud Ahmadinejad to power, the IRI media reported that prison authorities had submerged the head of Hashemi Rafsanjani's chief of staff in the toilet to force a confession that Rafsanjani—then chairman of both the Assembly of Experts and the powerful Expediency Council—was undermining Ahmadinejad.) They used exactly the same technique of torture in 1981. It was even more savage than what was described after Ahmadinejad's reelection. In 1981, they would tear out the hair of the prisoners and throw it in the toilet and then say, "Eat it!"

In summer 1982, there was a very heavy atmosphere in prisons. Lajevardi, chief prosecutor and warden of Evin prison, obliged some of the Marxist detainees to say the daily prayers. I was in Qezel Hesar, Unit 3, Ward 1. It was midday. The inmates were going from the yard to the central dayroom in groups. Near the fences, Haj Davoud Rahmani, the head of Qezel Hesar, and Lajevardi were standing and talking very loudly. The inmates were sitting in rows in the dayroom ready for the prayers. The room was full. The authorities had obliged everyone to pray. I was passing by when I heard Haj Davoud saying to Lajevardi, "Look Haji," and then he recited a verse from the Quran:

When Allah's succor and the triumph cometh
And thou seest mankind entering the religion of Allah in troops,
Then hymn the praises of thy Lord, and seek forgiveness of Him. Lo!
He is ever ready to show mercy.[35]

Lajevardi answered, "You don't know them yet!" implying that the prayers were not authentic. I'll never forget this. I said to myself, "Lajevardi is an experienced man, but Haj Davoud is a common man." Haj Davoud was really an ordinary and uneducated person. Later, when the inmates abandoned the praying strategy, Haj Davoud said, "You should always be under pressure. You're like a spring; the more we press against you, the more you squeeze up." Everyone in the ward remembered this speech.

I was in contact with many detainees between 1982 and 1985. I had no particular political affiliation and maybe that's why I could easily communicate with many people. Additionally, at the time, I was trying to educate myself as much as possible. Ever since I had developed a leftist leaning and

---

35 Surah al-Nasr (victory) (110), verses 1, 3 (Picthal translation). "Surah: usually translated as 'chapter.' The Quran is divided into 114 surahs, arranged by descending length rather than chronological order." *The Oxford Dictionary of Islam.*

no longer considered myself to be religious, I began asking many questions from a comrade who is fortunately still alive. He had experienced imprisonment both under the Shah and the IRI. He was older and quite knowledgeable. He answered my questions clearly and carefully, and as I trusted him I could ask all sorts of questions. He was and still is one in a million. One of his guidelines was: "Now that your worldview has changed, I suggest that you don't reveal it to them. A Muslim who turns his back on Islam will have to deal with God Almighty! Stick with your daily life. Never declare the change in your ideology to the prison guards and the interrogators." It was also he who said, "Don't be tricked by this situation. This will not last long. We will have a phase similar to that of 1981 ahead of us. I can't say when, how bad, or how widespread it'll be, but our previous experience shows that it's impossible for the regime to leave us alone." Of course, he was not the only person to think this way. The radical prisoners, who had a good in-depth knowledge about the essence and fundamental characteristics of the regime and knew people like Lajevardi, were not optimistic about the future.

Now that I'm writing these words, I can see that skepticism was not limited to the radicals. The words of Lajevardi and his likes would suffice to illustrate the point. He had said over and over: "We won't let you become heroes in here," or "Do you see these walls? They are getting your life out of you. These walls will come to life. But you're doomed to death." Haj Davoud was always saying, "Don't worry! God willing, you'll be released! But horizontally! I mean your *dead body* will leave this place."

I remember another clear example. In 1986, there was a Revolutionary Guard called Adel. He was from Karaj. When he came into the ward, he liked to talk to everyone. If someone went to get something from him or give him the list of items we needed from the dispensary, he would not let him go. He would rattle on. No one said anything; we just listened to him. From time to time he would spill the beans and give us some useful information. In spite of the fact that he was a simpleton, Adel had a hand in all sorts of crimes. He was always preaching to us. Many a time he said at the end of his speech, "Look, this is an ultimatum!" We wondered what he meant by "ultimatum." We later came to discover that once or twice a month there were briefing sessions for the prison guards in which specific instructions were given about how to deal with the prisoners. Of course, none of the guards told us anything about it, but by repeating that sentence with its dangerous implications Adel was unknowingly giving us a message.

LAYING THE GROUNDWORK

From autumn 1987, the regime treated the political prisoners in a more calculated and careful manner. I remember one autumn afternoon we were sent out for *havakhori* (getting fresh air in the yard) and the prison guards went to the cells for a thorough search and, as usual, many of our belongings were stolen. We returned to the ward after they had finished their job. Then they instructed everyone to wear their blindfolds and leave the ward. We came out of the ward in groups of ten. The prisoners who were taken out did not come back to the ward immediately. They didn't want the prisoners who were still in the ward to know what questions they had asked. Almost everyone in the ward had gone when, together with a few others, it was my turn. In the past they would take us one by one or in groups of two, but this time we were all taken together. They always gave us a form to fill in; the form was either brief or lengthy, according to the occasion. But this time the form was even more detailed than usual. The questions were different. It was too detailed. They even asked if we were Muslim or apostate.

Afterwards, they started a new classification. It was mid-January 1987 when they separated the Mojahedin and religious prisoners from the leftists. They separated the detainees according to their prison term. The leftist prisoners who had been sentenced to less than ten years were transferred to Wards 7 and 8. (I was taken to Ward 8.) This new wing was made up of various leftist tendencies. Each political current organized its own *senfi*. The rooms of the ward were distributed as follows: Tudeh and Aksariyat near the entrance door; then the inmates known as the Sixteenth of Azar supporters; then the Aqaliyat; and then adherents of the "Third Tendency" (*Khat-e 3*) and people who had no particular political affiliation.[36] Of course, the Aksariyat and Tudeh Party didn't really interact with the others and kept to themselves. But the other groups communicated with each other and exchanged information.

News, when it came, was first broken to the members of one *senfi* and then spread quickly around the ward. Each person somehow passed on the news haphazardly to the other *senfis* depending on his own personal contacts. Thus, the news was spread by word of mouth until it reached everyone in the ward. Sometimes the news didn't go further than one *senfi*. Such news usually arrived either after the visits or when someone was taken to the dispensary or for a brief interrogation.

---

36 See Appendix B for political tendencies and parties.

The detainees actively read books and newspapers. The ward's library provided us with the newspapers. If a 150-page book arrived at the ward, it was divided into five parts. In fact, we took the book apart and passed it around. We read it around the clock. If someone's turn was at midnight, he would stay up to read the book. Then two nights before returning the book, we fastened the pages of the book again. We had become experts in bookbinding. We returned the books neat and tidy. We had even copied some of the books and the handwritten copies were passed around from one person to another.

This period continued until the month of Ramadan 1988. That year the regime treated the leftist prisoners very differently. They didn't give us *sahari* (the meal eaten before the dawn prayers during Ramadan). But at midday the door to the ward swung open and our lunch was sent in. This was very surprising for many of us. Through all the years of imprisonment, and no matter which ward I was in, food was sent into the ward at dawn during the month of Ramadan and there were no meals before *iftar* (the meal eaten after sunset, to break the day's fast, during Ramadan). There had been many clashes over this issue. When I was in Ward 5, the leftist prisoners and a large majority of the Mojahedin had clashed with the prison management. We would say, "We don't fast. You must give our meals at lunchtime. It's hot. The meal that you distribute at dawn goes bad by lunchtime and we'll get sick." We even sent back the food.

The question was: "What are they up to?" Most of the Tudeh and Aksariyat prisoners, and even some inmates from revolutionary currents, interpreted the situation this way: the regime has finally recognized the leftists. Most of the radical leftists were of a different opinion, though. They had learned through experience that no matter what the warden did, there must be a strategic reason or logic intended to further their power behind it. I believe that the interpretation of the Tudeh Party and Aksariyat was due to the illusions they had about the regime. Although some of the Aksariyat prisoners chanted antigovernment slogans, most of them were still in their old cocoon. In any case, that strange Ramadan went by and, in July, the regime accepted UN Security Council resolution 598 calling for a ceasefire with Iraq.

A while before Ayatollah Khomeini's acceptance of the peace with Iraq, the Iraqi army had launched several shocking attacks and was advancing. The regime announced on prime-time news on radio and television that "the combatants of Islam are fighting mightily and have now taken new positions." Whenever we heard "have now taken new positions," we understood that the "combatants of Islam" had been forced to withdraw. Those inmates who had some military knowledge or acute political instincts analyzed the wordings and sentence structures pointing out that this or that sentence spoke for the dire situation on the various war fronts. After the acceptance of the ceasefire, one of the issues discussed in the wards was, of course, the question of what policy would be adopted regarding the political prisoners. Some believed there might be less pressure and better conditions. Some said peace with Iraq would lead to our release from prison. But the majority of the prisoners feared the worst. The television news attracted all the inmates. We all gathered around the television especially for the news headlines. I can say ninety-five percent of the inmates watched the news on television. We also listened to the two o'clock news on the radio.

CEASEFIRE AND THE CONSEQUENCES THEREOF

After the acceptance of UN Security Council resolution 598, we heard on the radio and television that the Mojahedin had invaded Eslamshahr, a city in western Iran. Soon after the Mojahedin's attack on July 29, *pasdar* Nemati, a twenty-six or twenty-seven-year-old man came to our ward and removed the television. The broadcasting of radio programs also stopped. Before that, all we could hear on the radio were military marches. I remember very well that one of the broadcasters repeated several times: "Farhadians rise to your feet, Bistoon is in danger!"[37] When we heard this we said to ourselves it must be a grave situation. They must be talking about Bistoon because the Iraqis are approaching the city of Kermanshah.

After the television was removed from the ward, all of our communication channels with the outside world were cut off. We were shut out of the yard, the dispensary, newspapers, and so on. No one entered the ward any more, and no one went out. None but the person who brought bread for us. Once a day either a *basiji* or a *pasdar* opened the door to the ward, came inside, counted the loaves of bread in the doorway, distributed the bread, and left. The *pasdars* who brought the meals to the ward didn't answer any questions. And if they ever answered, they either gave a short noncommittal response or said something nonsensical.

If I'm not mistaken, it was in mid-August that I was called together with some detainees whose political affiliation had not been pinned down during the interrogations, or who were there on several charges. There was Siavash

---

37 Bistoon, a historic mountain site in Kermanshah, the history of which goes back to the Achaemenid and Sassanid empires.

Soltani and Faramarz Zamanzadeh. I don't remember the name of anyone else. My charge was incomprehensible. I was charged with collaboration with *all* political parties. What a ridiculous charge! They called us, and we all put on our blindfolds and left the ward. I guess we were four people.

"I'm from Karaj," I told the *pasdar* of our ward. "This group that you've called is not from Karaj—maybe you're dealing with those from Evin!"

"You're from Karaj?"

"Yes."

He gripped my hand and took me to the Karaj Intelligence Bureau located in another ward. This was a ward *exclusive* to the Karaj Intelligence Bureau, and no one was allowed to step in, not even the *pasdars* of Gohardasht prison. Only people from the Prosecutor's Bureau and the Karaj Intelligence Bureau could go there. All the interrogations and solitary confinements of Karaj were dealt with by the Karaj Intelligence Bureau. The *Pasdaran* (Revolutionary Guards) stopped in front of the Karaj Intelligence Bureau, knocked at the door and said, "He's your convict." Someone opened the door, gripped me by the collar, and shoved me into the room. It was Nasser, the interrogator of the Karaj Intelligence Bureau. I had already seen him several times. This time, however, his attitude was totally different. He asked my name and then, all of a sudden, started beating me. He kicked and punched me in the stomach, slapped me across the face, and hit any part of my body he could get his hands on. He hit me very hard. I was shocked. They usually beat us up so savagely for a *reason*—most of the time when we had done something that did not suit their taste or because we had staged a protest, or the like. But we had been behaving in the ward and nothing particular had happened. Such treatment for no reason was astonishing. As he was beating me up, he swore at me too. He screamed, "You bloody *Monafeq*." Under his beatings, I realized this time around that something had happened. There had to be a reason why he was calling me a *Monafeq*. His attitude was a warning and a wake-up call for me. He called me "*Monafeq*" repeatedly.

All of a sudden I retorted: "What are you talking about? You have already looked into my file several times. Why do you call me a *Monafeq*?"

I don't know how long he beat me. I was pushed and shoved from one side of the room to the other. Finally, he stopped beating me; he sat me on a chair and gave me a form to fill in.

"What's this?"

"Shut up and fill in the form!"

They were asking for my name and other particulars. I filled in the form in the same manner I usually filled in forms. He hovered above my head reading my answers.

"What's this nonsense?"

"It's not nonsense. I've been writing these things for seven years."

He started beating me up again, then suddenly asked, "Are you a *Monafeq*?"

"No."

"Whose supporter were you?"

"I have never supported any political party."

"Are you a Muslim? Do you say your prayers?"

"I'm a Muslim, but I don't say my prayers."

He started beating me again. "What kind of a Muslim are you if you don't say your prayers?"

"I'm a Muslim like many other people you see in the streets. I'm a Muslim, but I don't say my prayers."

He hit me relentlessly. I was blindfolded. There was no one else in the room. He endlessly repeated that I was a *Monafeq*. But I didn't give in. It was only then, under the beatings, that I understood the depth of the advice of my experienced friend who had said, "If a Muslim turns his back on Islam, he'll have to deal with God Almighty." Fortunately, I had hidden the change in my ideology from the warden consistently all through the years.

After he had given me a good beating, he called a *pasdar* and said, "Take him away." The *pasdar* dragged me out and shoved me into a cell. I sensed that I was in a solitary cell. I removed my blindfold. I couldn't hear a sound. It was not the first time I had been thrown into a solitary cell. There was absolute silence. I realized that there were prisoners in other cells but no one in the adjacent cells. I was alone for two days. Nobody bothered me until they ordered me to leave the cell. It was the same interrogator I'd had before who told the *pasdar* again to take me back to the ward. The interrogator didn't say anything else. When the *pasdar* was taking me back to the ward, the two o'clock news was being broadcast in the corridor for the guards. Ever since they had cut the radio in the ward, at two o'clock sharp six or seven inmates would lie down on the ground near the doorway and stick their ears to the floor to hear the news. Those who were able to hear something would later tell the others. I was totally unaware of the things that had happened during my absence. The guys gathered around me and we went straight to our own cell. Everybody asked me questions. "What happened? What did they do to you?"

They could see that I had no energy. I told them what had happened. Usually after an interrogation, one would keep things that were related to his personal file to himself and would only disclose general matters. We would only talk about our personal file to close friends or people we trusted. But my case was public and there was nothing private about it. I told them what had happened emphasizing that the behavior I had encountered was different this time and that I felt that we were in a special situation. I insisted on the importance of the three key points of the interrogator about God, Islam, and the accusation that I was a *Monafeq*. I said all the beatings I got were for these three questions. I tried to describe every minute of the interrogation in full so that the guys would know exactly what was going on. I had been in prison for seven years and was supposed to be released in August 1988, but now I was back where I had started. With this interrogation, I had gone back to square one. I told myself I wouldn't be released soon.

After talking to my cellmates, I washed my face, ate some food, and got some rest. I was drained of energy. Nevertheless, a couple of inmates came to ask their questions privately for a better understanding of the situation. I repeated the same things. I gave a blow-by-blow account of the interrogation a couple of times.

The other prisoners who had been taken away with me had returned to the ward the same day. Some of them had identified the interrogator as Nayyeri. One of the inmates was called Poupak. He was a member of Feda'ian (Minority) but was serving time in prison as a Mojahed. I remember quite well his response to my question about what they wanted. He said, "They told us they were the Amnesty Commission and had come to ask us some questions." They had asked him, "What are you planning to do once you are released from prison?" Questions like this. They had not asked him about God or Islam.

A few days after I had returned to the ward, at midday, an old *pasdar* who was sometimes accompanied by a convicted Afghan came to distribute bread. The old man bent to count the loaves of bread, and the Afghan used this opportunity to tell us something by gestures. The entrance door had two panels. The old man was in front of the left panel and the Afghan went toward the right panel so that the old man would not see him. Then he jabbed two of his right fingers like a knife in front of his throat, meaning that they were killing. We got the message immediately. That Afghan took a great risk by giving us the news. The prisoners who worked in the ward that day passed on the information. I was perplexed. I was certain that it was a special situation and something strange was happening. But what?

A few days later, toward the end of August, we were having a siesta after lunch when we heard some sounds from the ward downstairs, which was usually empty. We could hear through the trap doors. There used to be some toilets in the room, but they had been destroyed and replaced by tiles. It was this that allowed the noise into our cell. We found out that they had taken some people to the ward downstairs. The noise was the sound made by prisoners. It was possible to hear some people talking with each other, but it was unintelligible. Sometimes we could hear someone crying. Sometimes we heard a song. We even heard Lashkari's voice, but it was not clear what he was saying. We were all curious to know what was going on.

Two days later, early in the afternoon, they called Davoud Heidari who was known as a sympathizer of the Peykar Organization in prison. Davoud was from Nazarabad in Karaj. He put on his blindfold and left the ward. He never returned. We never knew what happened to Davoud until we left the ward.

It was probably August 25 or 26 when at about midday there was an overpowering stench in the ward. Obviously it came from outside. Where precisely? We couldn't tell. Everyone was trying to block off the smell by stuffing rags around the window frames. The inmates whose cell was opposite the Gohardasht wall with the *Hosseiniyeh* on their left reported that Lashkari, Nemati, and another *pasdar* were standing near the wall of *Hosseiniyeh*. We all went to the window and looked over. They were wearing masks on their faces. There was a jug of lemonade nearby. They looked exhausted. It looked as if they were gasping for breath. One of them was wearing a gas mask and the other two had covered their mouth and nose with a piece of cloth. I saw them holding insecticide sprayers in their hands.

We asked each other, "What the hell are they doing?" We were trying to understand the relation between the fetid stench, the sprayers, and their condition. But we could not say what was happening. We understood that all these events were closely linked. The fact that the prison's deputy secretary for military affairs was busy disinfecting like ordinary *pasdars* added an especially puzzling aspect to the events that had happened up to that moment. Though we were confused, we were luckier than the other wards to have seen this string of events, events that finally helped us solve the puzzle.

"WE'RE GONNA EXECUTE YOU"

In the afternoon of August 27, the guards called on the prisoners of our ward. They told us to put on our blindfolds and come out. Whenever they said "All prisoners out!" some inmates ran to the toilets. They knew they might not be allowed to go to the toilets for hours. We all left the ward blindfolded and sat in the corridor. I remember quite well when Davoud Lashkari called someone for questioning, he would strike the metal desk behind which he was sitting with a piece of wood or a whip singing quietly, "We're gonna execute you..." Then he would bang on the desk again and again as if he were humming a song. I personally heard him singing this song. I am sure many other prisoners queuing with me also heard it.

Then Lashkari questioned us one by one: "Charges? Do you believe in God? Are you a Muslim? Do you say your prayers?" As far as I remember, fourteen people from Ward 8 said that they were Muslims and that they said their prayers. He sent them back to the ward. This was just the preliminary program. He just wanted to see how many people would answer yes to separate us accordingly. He hummed his ominous song during the questioning: *We're gonna execute you...* Then it was my turn. This time it was clear. The questions were more or less the same as the questions asked by the interrogator of the Karaj Intelligence Bureau. I paused before I gave an answer. I wanted to think before answering. Finally, he pushed me out and said, "Get lost, you bloody communist!"

I was taken to the line of people who had answered "No." After the questioning was finished, they ordered us to get up. Then we were lined up. It was sunset by then. Many of the inmates felt an urge to go to the toilet. (There was always a sudden urge to go to the toilet when one was under pressure.) They took us to another ward. I don't know how many people we were, probably somewhere between twenty-five and thirty. They separated us. Some were put in one room and the rest, including some of my cellmates, were taken to another. What I remember from that instance is that some of the inmates said there were signs written on some doors: "Determined" and "Undetermined." I myself didn't see these writings. "Determined" pertained to people who had gone on trial, and "Undetermined" included people like me who didn't even know there was going to *be* a trial. We were thrown into a room which was next to the "Determined" room.

As we were being taken there, we noticed a large group of prisoners passing by, going toward the *Hosseiniyeh*. We could hear the call for prayers and people praying. After the prayers, the congregation returned. We tried to get a glimpse of them coming back. We could see only their feet from under the door. At last, some inmates identified a couple of people, including Mehrdad Neshati. Mehrdad was one of the staunchest and most resistant men of our ward. Among the group who had gone to the *Hosseiniyeh*, there were people known for their steadfastness and endurance. They were people who would not easily accept being forced to pray. Their steadfastness was proverbial among all. Seeing them in the line of worshippers was baffling. We asked ourselves how it was possible that such people were saying the daily prayers. One of those worshippers was the dear comrade who had an important role in the shaping of my thoughts. It was difficult for me to grasp this complicated and astonishing situation. I knew him very well. I knew he would not give in so easily, especially after all these years.

We were all waiting to find out our fate. My cellmates knocked at the door and said we needed to go to the toilets. A *pasdar* opened the door and asked, "Who says his prayers?" No one replied. He locked the door and left. After a few minutes, we knocked again asking to go to the toilets. "We haven't gone to the toilets for hours." He said, "Okay," then locked the door and left. After a few minutes, he came back and said, "You can go to the toilets!" We weren't used to this ward and didn't know we had to put on blindfolds to go to the toilets. Some of us went toward the toilets without blindfolds. I had a strong urge to go to the toilet and was the first one to run out of the cell—without a blindfold. All of a sudden, because some of us had forgotten to put on our blindfold, the *pasdar* said, "You're not wearing blindfolds?" And then several *pasdars* attacked us. I just remember a sharp pain radiating in my rib cage: one of the *pasdars* had punched me just under the ribs. It was such a severe blow that I was knocked out. How long was I unconscious? I don't know.

I remember I had not fully regained consciousness when I realized I was back in the cell. Some cellmates slapped me to wake me up. They said, "Nasser! Nasser! Wake up!" Little by little, I gained consciousness. I sat up. After a few moments, I noticed that I was not the only one who had been beaten. We were analyzing the situation when they came and said, "Put on your blindfolds and go to the toilets." This was strange too. The situation was becoming more and more unusual. That night some of the inmates communicated with the adjacent cell by Morse code. I was so weak that I could not move. I just sat there close by. The message we got by Morse was: "They have executed a hundred people so far. This is a religious trial. They ask about God, the Prophet, and Islam. A 'yes' or 'no' can determine life or death." We were astounded by the news. Speechless. The puzzle had been solved. A few simple yet difficult questions and answers would seal our fate: life or death. We had found the variable in the equation.

We were in that room for two terrible days. It was as if everything had come to a standstill. There was no come and go. The door to the cell was opened and closed at certain hours for the meals and the toilets, but nobody had anything to do with us. It was as if even the *pasdars* had forgotten about us.

Some people had not come to believe the news yet. Some of the inmates were of the opinion that we should not spread the news that a hundred people had been executed because it would "dampen our morale." But the majority had realized the truth and they spread the news. In one of the toilet rounds, one of the inmates found a written message: "The situation is grave. It's a matter of life and death. Religious Courts are being held. God and the Prophet are of great importance in the questionings." (I don't remember the exact sentences but this was the gist of the message.)

Very early in the morning, on August 30, I heard a horrible noise. It was as if they had dropped a big container of food from a great height. We were all woken up in terror. What were they aiming at? Did they want to frighten us? Dampen our morale? *Everything* was unusual.

RELIGIOUS COURT

On September 1, the *pasdars* came at around nine or ten o'clock in the morning to fetch us. They told us to put on our blindfolds. We were shepherded along the corridors of Gohardasht for a while and then taken to a room on the ground floor. I don't know which ward it was. The lights were off. We could not see anything from under the blindfolds. Then they told us to sit down. Here we were allowed to push up our blindfolds and whisper to each other. I looked around; it looked like one of the minor cells on the ground floor in Gohardasht. There were people from other cells as well. There and then I realized that our lives depended on the answers we gave to their questions.

They kept us in that room for about an hour. Then they told us to put on the blindfolds again and get moving. Again we were shepherded in the corridors where we remained for a while before being taken to a room. Everyone was directed to the far side of the room. Haj Davoud Lashkari and a bulky *pasdar* (I think he was called Faraj) started the questioning. Lashkari asked, "Do you believe in God? Are you a Muslim? Do you say your prayers?" They asked each and every one of us these three questions. As we had found out what was going on, all of us except for two people answered "Yes" to the first two questions. Only two people said that they didn't believe in God, were not Muslims, and didn't say their prayers. All of a sudden, Faraj shoved back a couple of detainees and said to Lashkari, "Haji, they've found out what's it all about. There's no need to question them. Let's take them away." We heard this remark, but Lashkari ignored him and continued with his job. After everyone had answered the questions, he ordered the two people who had given a negative response to go to another corner of the room. Then he faced us and said, "We'll take you back to the ward. But from now on, if you don't say your prayers and don't observe the religious rules, you'll have the harshest punishment. Keep this in mind! Go to your ward and say your prayers!" Nobody protested. There was nothing but silence. Absolute silence.

We were sent back to our old wards, where our belongings were. Listless, drained, exhausted, and crushed, we entered the ward. But the ward was not empty. There we saw some prisoners who had been taken back before us. At that moment, I sensed that we were the last group to have undergone an inquisition. Halfway through the ward I realized many of my friends had been killed. I started asking my new cellmates if they knew where so-and-so was. They would say, "He was shot. He was executed." I asked for news about many people, but the answer was always the same. I realized that when they had removed the televisions from the wards and cut our communication with the outside world, they had executed Khomeini's fatwa. They had started with the massacre of the Mojahedin in July. In August, they slaughtered the left-ists. A few of us could not control ourselves anymore and began sobbing. We couldn't take it anymore. We could not assess the full extent of the disaster, yet we were terrified by its depth.

Our ward, Ward 8 of Gohardasht, was the sum total of the leftist prisoners of Gohardasht. That means all the leftist survivors of the massacre were put together in one place. We wept uncontrollably. We thought of those who had gone and ourselves who had somehow survived. We lived their departure and our own survival. The inmates who had returned to the ward before us had better self-control. Or maybe they were stronger than us. They brought us water, rubbed our shoulders, consoled us, and nursed us. I always say to myself what a beautiful thing they did in those deadly moments. How strong they were! How quickly they had gained control of the situation and undertaken the responsibility of taking care of us!

We had survived thanks to the sacrifice of some prisoners who had given us vital information. People had risked their lives here and there to gather information and transfer it to the others. Later, some inmates recounted that even the Mojahedin prisoners had risked their lives to inform others. For instance, in some wards where only a few people had survived, the remaining prisoners had hung their red "longs" out of the window as a warning signal, hoping to alert the others, making them wonder why the longs were hanging from the windows. We were very lucky because the executions had stopped for two days and nobody had come to fetch us. Keeping in mind all the data, we were able to interpret the Morse code messages rapidly and make decisions that were appropriate to the situation. For this reason, Ward 8 had the lowest number of executions—only five people.

The next day, a man about twenty-eight years old who was either a *talaba* (seminary student) or a *Saqat al-Islam* (lowest-level cleric in Shi'ite Islam) was sent so that we would perform prayers in congregation behind an imam. A large number of *pasdars* were mobilized in the *Hosseiniyeh* to see who was praying and who was not. We bowed and prostrated pretending to be praying. We had heard that people who had not agreed to pray were flogged for each of the compulsory daily prayers (that is, five times a day).

The inmates were now friendlier to each other. We had set aside old differences and disputes. We lived together like close friends. The relationships were excellent. One day, Lashkari and Nasserian came to the ward together and told us to gather in the middle of the ward. Then they called several people and took them away. This was repeated for several days. Mostly it was Nasserian who came. Eventually, he didn't call anyone's name, he just looked and pointed: "You! You! You! Get moving!" And he took them away. It was not clear what the criteria were, but we realized that he was picking stout and burly inmates. After a while, we just sent the big and strong ones to the toilets, hid them, or would sit in a way so that they would not stand out. Some of them returned but others never came back. I don't know what happened to them. I didn't know any of those prisoners.

The *pasdars*' duty was to force the prisoners to pray. Praying had become a real comedy, a reason to laugh, and laughter boosted our morale. I remember quite well that during the congregation, some of the inmates who stood in the back rows wrestled with each other or pulled pranks. The imam led the prayers in the front row, and some of us bowed and prostrated. Such was the atmosphere. They had to break it.

Once, in the dead of night, we were raided by hollering *pasdars*. They ordered us to put on our blindfolds and go out. As we were getting out of bed, they kept threatening us. Their behavior reminded us of earlier dark days, and scenes of violence appeared before our eyes. We were taken to the corridor of the building opposite Ward 8. They kept us standing in the stairway three flights up. We were on our feet for three or four hours. At dawn, we were taken back to the ward. They tormented us physically and psychologically with such horrifying acts. For a while, we imagined that the executions had started again and this time it was our turn, especially when every once in a while they took some of the detainees and put them in solitary confinement or in segregation units for punishment. Every time the door swung open, we rushed to see who had come back and asked him many questions.

This situation endured until we were separated again and put in other wards. At first, we were transferred one by one. Then they told everyone to pack their belongings. Each time, they called some names and took some prisoners away. They continued in the same manner until the ward was completely empty. I think we were the last group of Ward 8 to be moved. It took a long time for them to call our names. In the meantime, we were busy making guesses and assumptions. During this process, we were no more afraid of death and execution. We believed ultimately that they would take us and shoot us like the others. They had killed all of our friends, and we were just like them. Life in prison had *prepared* us for death. We could not tell what would happen in another hour. Indeed, death had become a part of ordinary life.

As I said, in Ward 8 of Gohardasht, only five people were executed; among them, Siavash Akbarzadeh Shokoohi, a member of the Organization of Iranian People's Feda'ian (Majority). He was very young, maybe twenty-five or twenty-six. He went mad because of the ordeal he had gone through in prison. Before the executions, he would stand near the cell door and shout profanities to God, Mohammad, Marx, and Lenin. He had really lost his mind. He could not even clean up his own cell. When he came out of his cell, the other inmates cleaned it up rapidly. He was really mentally ill and needed other people's help for many things. The *pasdars* of the ward and the prison officers all knew about his condition. But they killed Siavash too. Who would answer for the execution of a person who was totally deranged? His death came as a terrible blow to me.

The events of 1988 were not really surprising. In fact, I had been expecting such a disaster. What I did *not* expect was its extent and dimensions. I could never have imagined such a large-scale massacre of prisoners who had been interrogated numerous times, tortured, and sentenced; people who were doing time in prison, and some of whom were even on the threshold of freedom. We could not believe that it was so easy to execute so many people.

TRANSLATED FROM PERSIAN BY SINA NAVAIE

A Defining Moment

MEHRDAD NESHATI MELIKIYANS[38]

I had been transferred from Ward 1, Section 1, of Qezel Hesar prison, to Gohardasht prison. Before then, I had spent some time in Tehran's Evin prison.

In Qezel Hesar, I was in close contact with my comrades from the Minority faction of the Feda'ian. Relations and communication among us, the Minority's sympathizers, were very good: organized, consistent, and naturally more trustworthy for me. Two of my comrades whom I had close contact with were Mohammad Ali Behkish and Jahan Sarkhosh. Mohammad Ali was

---

38 Mehrdad Neshati Melikiyans was born in 1960 in Tehran. His mother was from Azerbaijan and his father was Armenian. His father left Iran because of political reasons and took residency in the Armenian Soviet Socialist Republic when Mehrdad was only three years old. Mehrdad grew up in several underprivileged neighborhoods on the east side of Tehran and graduated in 1978 from one of the oldest schools of the capital, the Dar al-Fonun. He became interested in politics in high school during the trial of two revolutionary intellectuals, Keramat Daneshian and Khosro Golesorkhi, in 1974. The arrest of several of his relatives in that ordeal flamed his anti-establishment tendencies. Meanwhile, he became acquainted with the two important revolutionary organizations of the time, the Organization of Iranian People's Feda'i Guerrillas (OIPFG) and the People's Mojahedin Organization of Iran (PMOI). He took part in the 1979 Revolution and was involved in the insurrection of February 21, 1979. However, it was at the end of a 1979 trip across Iranian Kurdistan that he decided to join the OIPFG. He sided with the Minority faction after the main split in that organization and became active in organizing neighborhood committees. Mehrdad was detained along with his wife and their fifteen-day-old baby in October 1982, and he was taken to Evin prison. He was placed in solitary confinement for several months and sentenced to six years imprisonment. In 1983, he was transferred to Qezel Hesar prison. Because of defying the authorities, he stayed in solitary confinement until 1988. He was taken to the inquisition tribunals but was not condemned to death. He is one of the living witnesses of the Great Massacre. He was released in fall 1988, right after his prison term came to an end; however, he had to present himself at Evin prison every month and face regular interrogations. In 1990, he decided to leave Iran. He paid a smuggler to take him to Turkey. After forty days in Turkey, he left for Germany and requested political asylum at the airport. He has lived in Frankfurt ever since. He is still an active member of the OIPF (Minority).

trusted by all Minority's sympathizers as he was from a well-known family in the Feda'i movement and respected by all militants.

In Qezel Hesar, I also knew many people affiliated with other organizations, people that I trusted and could exchange information with whenever possible. Among them were the supporters of the Mojahedin (PMOI) with whom I had regular contact. The trust between us was a product of shared years of brutal detention in Evin and Qezel Hesar prisons.

In Gohardasht, we were divided into different wards. Jahan and I ended up in Ward 8. Mohammad Ali was the only Minority person who was in Ward 40 where the Tudeh Party sympathizers were detained. The PMOI sympathizers were moved to Wards 1 and 2, which contained larger cells, as there were more Mojahedin sympathizers than leftist prisoners. Ward 8 housed ninety-five leftist detainees with various organizational affiliations. These included members or sympathizers of the Tudeh Party, Peykar, Rah-e Kargar, Ranjbaran, Vahdat-e Komunisti, Feda'ian Minority faction, and Feda'ian Majority faction. Ward 7 was right above Ward 8. The ward below Ward 8 was usually not occupied, but once in a while nonpolitical prisoners were held there. The prison auditorium was just outside of our ward, and we could see past the auditorium building all the way to the street because we had bent the bars on our cell window.

We were able to remain somewhat connected to the outside world through radio, television, and some daily newspapers. Our access to radio and television was limited. We could only hear one state-owned news radio station when the guards decided to have it broadcast through the prison's central public announcement system. The guards also controlled the channel on the one television we had access to. However, the air ducts in the building were transformed into an unrestricted channel for conveying information as they carried voices and noises from ward to ward.

There were a few means of communication among the prisoners: writing on the wall, on the molding at the base of the wall, or exchanging information in the ward's public bathroom, exchanging notes during yard breaks, and passing letters between the cells. We used some of these methods to communicate with Mohammad Ali and other Minority sympathizers, in order to analyze the authenticity of the recent news and its practical significance and implications.

The prison had specific operating procedures that were enforced upon all prisoners. One was blindfolding prisoners every time they were taken out of the ward. Tilting your head back and trying to look below the blindfold was prohibited. A prisoner must either follow every order given by the guards or face punishment. Outside the ward, the guards were the law.

It is noteworthy that my father was Armenian, and for Muslim Iranians all ethnic Armenians are generally assumed to be Christian, as most are. While in prison, I consciously and deliberately used this religious identity in my favor. It should be noted that non-Muslims were not bound by all the rules and regulations imposed upon Muslims. Thus, Christians were excused from daily prayers and other Islamic practices and punishments.

LEADING UP TO THE MASSACRE

All contact with the outside world was cut off in late July. We had little access to news and information as all means of communication, such as radio, television, and newspapers, had been taken away from us, and even access to the prison yard and prison infirmary (a way to contact detainees in other wards) had been prohibited. Our only source of news was what we received through Morse code from other prisoners, specifically other sympathizers of the Minority. Most of the news that we received was regarding the Mojahedin's attack on the IRI's forces from their bases in Iraq (the operation called *Forough-e Javidan* (Eternal Light)). This news was communicated mostly by means of Morse code between the detainees.

Isolation from the outside world and prohibition of access to the prison yard and the infirmary clearly meant that something unusual was happening. Based on our limited knowledge of the situation, we had concluded that the IRI had been weakened, as it had not been able to win the war, and consequently would take more repressive measures to solidify its position in society. For that reason, the prison, as part of the larger society, would be the ground zero for whatever form the increased pressure would take. We, Minority sympathizers, were of the opinion that the regime lacked the ability to preserve itself due to loss of forces and successive failures in the war. We concluded that it was an opportune time for the opposition to rise. I think the PMOI's attack on the IRI's forces along Iran's western borders was based on a similar understanding.

We had a limited analysis and understanding of the situation. We anticipated that the regime would revert to the prison conditions of 1981–82, and in so doing some prisoners would be executed. But we never imagined so many would be killed so ruthlessly. We never imagined the IRI would aim to *eliminate* their problem, us prisoners, instead of solving it.

We had contact with the PMOI members and sympathizers until they imposed isolation on us. I lost all contact with them once we all were denied access to the prison yard and going out for fresh air. This development was somewhat expected and did not raise our suspicion. The reality was that we still could contact each other through Morse code. One way to send signals was to use the light through the window and hands' shadows. This method of communication required coordination with the other prisoners in our cell as well as the other party. It required the unanimous agreement of all cellmates since it was dangerous, as the light and the shadows could become visible to the guards. If caught, everyone in the cell would be punished.

After losing access to the prison yard, the Mojahedin set a signal for communication. Unfortunately, that was not accepted and heeded by everyone in our cell. I never had the chance to inquire about the kind of information they wanted to pass on. (I recently read that they had contacted others through different channels to warn about the impending executions. Alas, the news never made it to our ward!)

Based on our analysis, we expected increased pressure and needed to find a way to minimize its impact. The common belief among many prisoners was to resist and try to push back the regime's onslaught. We were determined not to let the prison officials easily attain their goals. We were planning to buy as much time as possible. At the time, the prisoners' morale was high, and we had taken an aggressive stance.

THE BEGINNING OF THE MASSACRE

During the last week of August and after about a month of isolation, some prisoners from different wards were summoned. As I recall, it was probably on August 25 that they took a couple of prisoners from our ward, Ward 8, for "Q&A" (questions and answers) along with two or three guys from Ward 7. On August 26, they took another batch of prisoners, again from different wards.

After exchanging information with the two wards, the only common characteristic which we could establish between those selected on August 25 was that they all had two allegations against them. For example, they could have been arrested at a PMOI demonstration in 1982, but were also accused of being a Feda'i sympathizer. (Some had changed their ideological and/or political affiliation in prison.)

The common characteristic that I could see between the prisoners from Wards 7 and 8, who were taken away on August 26, was that they were ten to fifteen years older than us and that they all had been arrested in 1982.

Those taken away on August 25 were kept away from us for a whole day. Upon their return, we inquired about what had happened. Our returning cell-mates had been told that the Q&A was to assess and to "properly" segregate the prisoners. They did not mention any hearing or interrogation.

We never got any information about what happened to those taken away on August 26, as they never returned. They were mostly Minority and Peykar sympathizers. I heard, sometime later, that all but two of them had been executed.

We had already been segregated, but at the time we concluded that the transfer of prisoners could be part of the segregation process. On the other hand, the events of the previous few days had been unusual and suspicious, and could indicate the beginning of the anticipated mounting pressure on the prisoners.

On August 28, some Ward 7 inmates were taken away. We heard only their footsteps. We tried to contact them but to no avail. Some were saying that they heard shouting through the air ducts: "Write your will! We are going to take care of you! You are finished." We waited for our turn. At around 11 or 12, the guards barged into our ward and forced everyone, who were in as they were (with pajamas and T-shirts), out of the cells. These were all new guards whom we had not seen before. They lined us up, single file, one behind the other, and gave us the blindfolds. They ordered us to put on our blindfolds and put our hand on the shoulder of the person in front of us. Then they moved us out of the ward to a hallway in a different part of the prison. There, they lined us up in two rows and ordered us to sit on the floor, facing the wall. From then on, only the guards' voices could be heard. One at a time, they would touch the prisoner's shoulder to get him up and walk him into a room off the same hallway.

Finally, my turn came, and they took me to the room. I knew the place. I recognized Davoud Lashkari's voice. He asked for my name while he was writing something on a piece of paper. I gave him my name and he checked it.

"Charge?"

"Feda'ian, Minority faction."

"Do you still support them?"

"I have lost contact with them. I don't know what they stand for. So I don't know what to support."

This was our prepared answer for such questions.

"Are you a Muslim?"

"No."

"Do you pray *namaz* [daily obligatory prayer]?"

"No."

"Are you willing to take part in an interview condemning Feda'ian?"

"No!"

"That is it. Get out!"

My interrogation was short, and without any given purpose I was blind-folded the whole time and, as far as I could tell, no one else was in the room other than the guard, who had brought me in, and Davoud Lashkari. After the interrogation, the guard took me back to my original place in the hallway. We ate our lunch right there, sitting on the floor of the hallway facing the wall. Meanwhile, by quietly whispering to one another, we found out that we had all been asked the same set of questions.

Three weeks earlier, during the isolation period, from our window we saw unusual movements of people and trucks in front of and around the auditorium. The trucks were equipped with containers used to transport meat. One day we smelled an unusual, foul odor. On that day, the truck had broken down and was stuck right below our window. Many people had surrounded the truck while some were trying to fix it. The guards gathered around a big man wearing a suit. That was Eshraghi. We didn't think much about it at the time, but we understood later that the containers were used to transfer the corpses of the PMOI sympathizers, who had been executed. Our understanding was that some PMOI sympathizers had been arrested and taken to Gohardasht or Evin for interrogation. Given the recent round of the PMOI's armed confrontation with the regime, we expected that they would be executed following their interrogation.

As we passed by the prison dispensary, not much seemed familiar. I only knew that the auditorium was ahead of us. I had a feeling we were in Ward 2. As we got closer to the entrance, I heard screams and the sound of whips cracking. While we were passing through the door, the guards welcomed us with punches, kicks, cables, and whips. Blindfolded, we tried to protect ourselves in the mayhem. After they whipped us with wire whips, they split us and sent us into two different cells. We had been brutally beaten before under different circumstances, but none of us had ever experienced such a savage attack for no reason.

There were forty-five to fifty people in each cell. We took the blindfolds off. It was a tight space, but we managed to sit in clusters to discuss what had just happened. The clusters were based mainly on political affiliation. A few comrades, including Jahan Sarkhosh and myself, sat together. Everybody had his own take on the situation. The common conclusion after discussions within and between the clusters was that a new wave of repression was being unleashed. We anticipated solitary confinement and other intensified measures to force us to give in. Repression and return to early Islamic prison life were the extent of our thoughts. A mass execution had not crossed our minds yet.

Some writing on the molding, at the bottom of the wall, caught our attention. It was very small and in pencil. One had to lie down to read it. Some of the writing, for example, documented the dates and numbers of people who had been taken. The dates were recent (August), so it had to have been written by the PMOI sympathizers, the ward's most recent occupants.

Based on this information, we concluded that suppression of the Mojahedin had already begun. We had just been brought to the vacant ward where they had been housed. The key question, for which we had no answer, was: Where had they taken them?

After half an hour or so, at about 2 or 2:30 p.m., we heard a terrifying noise. It sounded like a whip cracking and metal hitting metal. We also heard a scary scream from the hallway. I had not heard such screams before. Clearly, they were beating someone to get something out of him. Among the noises, we heard, "Will you say prayers or not?"

All the noises died down abruptly. We were left wondering what was going on. We had nothing to do with prayers. True, this was the IRI's prison, but they had never forced leftists to pray. Our first interpretation of the situation, however wrong, was that they were beating Mojahedin sympathizers who had embraced Marxism while in prison. The idea that they would put such pressure on leftists never crossed our minds.

Thirty minutes into the discussion about the situation, Nasserian, "governor" of Gohardasht, entered the cell with two guards. He selected a few of us by pointing: "You, you... and you—come out." I don't remember how many there were, but Jahan Sarkhosh and I were among those chosen. As a routine, we put our blindfolds on to leave the cell. Jahan Sarkhosh was ahead of me and Mehdi Aslani was behind me. They took us down to an area that was unknown to me. We lined up, still blindfolded. The first person they took into the room was Jahan. After about two minutes, the guard who had taken Jahan in came back and whispered in my ear.

"Hey."

"What?"

"Do you know the one that just went in?"

I gave the logical answer. "No, I don't know him."

He went and came back again. "Don't you know who that was?"

"No, what is going on?"

"You see, this guy is very brave, a real man!"

"What are you saying?"

"He has a lot of courage and is fearless! May he live long!"

At that moment, the door opened and I heard a voice saying, "What is all this mockery? What are you talking about?" That is all I heard. Clearly, Jahan had stood up against them, but I didn't understand over what.

Jahan came out. They took him to the other side of the hallway. I didn't get to talk to him. I was next. The same guard took me to the door and delivered me to Nasserian.

"Come in," Nasserian said. "Take your blindfold off."

When I took the blindfold off, I saw a mullah and two other men sitting at the table right in front of me. One other person was behind them. He was writing something. The mullah was Nayyeri. The man next to Nayyeri was Eshraghi (as I learned later). Nasserian joined them at the table.

Nayyeri asked for my name, and I told him. He opened a file and looked at it. "Charge?"

"Minority (Feda'ian, Minority faction)."

"Years of sentence?"

"Five years plus reprimand for one year; total, six years."

Usually the sentences began from the date of the verdict. I had been interrogated for one year, which was counted as an extra reprimand year.

"Yes, I know. When does it end?" Nayyeri asked.

"It *should* end by October 7, 1988."

"Do you still approve of them?"

"What can I approve of? Is there anything left to approve or disapprove of?"

This was the usual clichéd answer for this type of question.

"Will you give an interview or not?"

"No."

"Do you say prayers or not?" Nayyeri asked, suddenly taking on a casual air. "We are from the prosecutor's office and are segregating the Muslim and non-Muslim prisoners."

"No, I don't."

"Aren't you a Muslim?"

The usual routine was to give indirect answers to such questions, so I didn't answer him. (I always carefully avoided ideological discussions with prison officials.)

"Weren't you born to Muslim parents?"

"No, my father is Christian."

Upon hearing that my father was a Christian, their attitude suddenly changed. I had used the fact that my father was Armenian many times in prison to reduce their pressure on me—all Armenians are assumed to be Christians—but I never claimed to be Christian. (Of course, Christianity is a religion and Armenian is an ethnicity. I am Armenian, as my father was. But I was an atheist then as I am now.)

"Are you married?" asked Nayyeri.

"Yes."

"With children?"

"Yes." My file indicated that my wife was a Muslim.

"How did you marry your wife?"

"We just registered our marriage with a notary."

"But then, how did you?"

"We went there, and he married us, and that was that."

"How is it possible?"

"Well, it must have been possible. We have a marriage certificate." I had this problem at my trial too. They insisted on nullifying the marriage.

"Then, you must have converted to Islam?"

"No. I was never asked. They never asked me whether I was a Muslim or a Christian. We signed the papers and left."

"Then it must be—"

"You see, my son, you *are* married!" Eshraghi interjected in a friendly tone, while Nayyeri remained in puzzled silence.

"Yes."

"Kids too?"

"Yes."

"Then if these are all true... we are here to identify and segregate Muslim and non-Muslim prisoners, and you will pray *namaz*," said Eshraghi, repeating what Nayyeri had said.

"No, Haj Agha, I won't. I don't even know how."

"You'll learn."

"What will I learn?"

"You'll learn to do it. Muslims must pray *namaz*."

"I told you my father is Armenian."

"In any case, we consider you a Muslim. You *are* one," insisted Eshraghi.

"I haven't performed *namaz* and I am not going to."

Eshraghi turned to Nasserian. "Haj Agha, get him out of here, he will pray his *namaz*."

I had put my blindfold on to leave the room when they put a sheet of paper in front of me and ordered me to sign.

"What am I signing?"

"Sign," Nasserian said firmly.

"Let me see what I am signing."

"No. Sign it!"

Some of the prisoners had seen what they signed, but I, still blindfolded, drew some lines on the page without seeing what was written on it. I didn't even attempt to put my real signature. Then, it was over. The same guard took me out and ordered me to stay on the side, by the door. After a couple of minutes, I heard Eshraghi's voice from the room: "Do you pray *namaz*?" A bit later, I heard Nayyeri saying, "Where are you going Haj Agha? Stay here!" to which Eshraghi responded, "I will return after hitting those guys."

I didn't know what was going on. I was contemplating whether he was going to whip us or something else. For us, or at least for me, up to that time, when stated by prison officials, "hitting" meant getting whipped. Prisoners had occasionally used the term to mean "execution," but not the officials. Even at that point, it didn't dawn on me that execution was in order for us. It couldn't be, it wasn't possible, as we had already been prosecuted and sentenced in a court. I understood what he meant later. It was a code for "let me see through the execution of the recent batch before more interrogation." The consent of these three people—Nayyeri, Eshraghi, and Nasserian—was required for the hearing to proceed. This was different from the proceedings during summer 1981 when the shari'a judge could make all the decisions by himself.

Once Eshraghi left, the hearing was put on hold. A guard took me back to the cell. Later on, I heard that those who were to be executed were taken to the auditorium, and the rest were moved back to the ward to be whipped or to face some other punishment. We went upstairs to the same holding cell before interrogation. Jalil was with us. He committed suicide the next day.

They threw me in a new cell at about 4 or 5 p.m. Those who were in the other cell with me and had been taken for hearing were transferred elsewhere. My analysis was still bounded by the idea that they were trying to break those of us who were known for not giving in, because they knew accepting to pray *namaz* would be too much for us.

I thought first they would force us to perform the *namaz* and, if successful, they might ask us for more, like information or even cooperation. As prisoners, we had specific "red lines" of our own, which we would do our best not to cross. They left me alone that night. What was going on? And why? I kept going over the day's events. First, they threw forty to fifty people in one cell and now I was there all by myself. Where were the others? The strange thing was that no matter how much I knocked on the door to go to the bathroom (there was no toilet in the cell), no one responded.

Other prisoners from Ward 8 were in the next cell, and I contacted them via Morse code. I described the situation in detail. I told them about the questions and the consequences. None of them knew what was going on, as none of them had been taken to the Death Commission for a hearing yet. I don't remember who was receiving my Morse code (probably a Rah-e Kargar sympathizer,) but I passed on all I knew and warned them to be alert. That was all I could do. They, in turn, passed on the information to the others. Some of those prisoners are still alive.

Nasserian came by after 8 or 9 a.m. He called my name and ordered me out. I went out without a blindfold. He asked me if I pray *namaz*.

"*Namaz*? Why? I am not a Muslim! My father is Armenian!" I answered loudly so those across the corridor could hear me. I had passed the information to the cell next door, but I wasn't sure if those across the corridor knew of it.

"No," Nasserian said. "You must pray *namaz*. Take him for punishment."

Nasserian's reaction was not one of anger or vindictiveness. It was more like he was just doing his job.

The first cell on my left was set aside for punishment. This was a smaller cell with a bunk bed. Five other guys, sitting either on the bed or on the floor, were there when the guards took me out for punishment. Those five people were Akbar Shalgouni from Rah-e Kargar, a young Minority sympathizer from Ward 7, and three sympathizers of the Tudeh Party. After exchanging introductory formalities, Akbar asked if I was aware of the executions.

"What!? Execution of whom, prisoners!?"

"They have executed some of the prisoners."

"What are you talking about? Who have they executed?"

"All the guys who had their hearing. We are forced now to either accept to pray *namaz* or—"

"Akbar, you cannot just say such things without confirmation by a reliable source."

"The Tudeh sympathizers," confirmed Akbar.

"Who has told you this?"

"Mohammad Ali Behkish."

This set me back, as I knew Mohammad Ali would not make such claims casually. I had total trust in him. "Are you sure?"

"Yes."

"And Mohammad Ali himself?"

"He was executed."

Taken aback by the news, I saw Jahan before my eyes and thought that he was gone too. I then remembered all those from Ward 7 who had been taken to an interrogation session after the segregation of prisoners. *Does this mean that they executed everyone?* I started thinking about the men I had contacted the day before. They didn't know what was going on. I had only passed on what I knew yesterday and, in the meantime, they might have already appeared in front of the Death Commission.

SURVIVING THE MASSACRE

After that shocking conversation, the only issue that preoccupied my mind was to inform others. But how? I wished I had known this one day earlier so that I could have informed them about the executions. Moreover, after five or six years in prison, some inmates had become closer to me than my own brother, not to mention those I had been affiliated with before being captured.

We followed the usual ritual. We sat in a cluster on the floor and started discussing what should be done and how we should react. "Any retreat should be accompanied with resistance" was the conventional rule, at least for the Minority sympathizers. So, if we had to retreat, we would do it in a way that would hinder their next attack. We knew that an easy acceptance of praying *namaz* would be followed by other requests (for example, turn into an informer or other forms of cooperation). They had done this before with those who had shown remorse and repented, known as *tavabs*. Based on this awareness, the consensus of the group, six of us, was not to accept their demand for praying *namaz* right away, but to buy some time and see what would follow.

After a few minutes, the door opened and Nasserian, who was carrying a folder, while being followed by a couple of guards, entered the cell. He acted as if he was just taking care of some administrative business. He looked around and ordered us to step aside. We all went to one side. He had not even finished asking, "Who won't pray *namaz*?" when the three Tudeh sympathizers said that they would perform *namaz*. That was a bit of a disappointment for the rest of us, but I didn't blame them and never asked them why they did so.

For me, their agreeing to go along with us was unexpected in the first place. Tudeh sympathizers did not usually accept such positions.

Akbar was the first one that they took to be whipped, followed by a young comrade. I was last. Ten lashes with a wire whip.

I could see the flogger below my blindfold. He was a big, tall, bald man wearing dark clothes. They laid me down. One person sat on my back and held my legs. With a loud voice, the flogger said, "God, I hit him for Your satisfaction." The sharp pain of the first strike on the sole of my feet went all the way up to my head. He was using a wire whip with stripped ends (bare metal) that would wrap around and hit the top of the feet as well. The pain on the top of the feet was worse than that of the soles. My feet had been whipped with wire whip before, but never like that. He flogged so hard as if he was trying to slice my feet into pieces. After the ten lashes, I was ordered to walk. (They forced us to walk after lashes to avoid blood coagulation, which could cause embolism and a heart attack.) While walking, I could see below the blindfold that we were not being watched.

"He flogs hard," I told Akbar as our paths crossed.

"We can take it for now."

"Yeah, at least ten more."

I passed Akbar and got to the young comrade.

"I cannot take it anymore," he said.

"Okay, just tell them you will pray *namaz*."

They took Akbar for ten more lashes. I knew what ten lashes meant. I couldn't expect everyone to take ten more. When the young comrade came back, he was asked about *namaz* and replied that he would do it. I don't know where they took him. After I finished my walk, my answer to the *namaz* question was negative. My feet were cut all over, skin and flesh, after the second round of ten lashes. Akbar and I were the only two who still refused. They took us back to the cell, cursing, belittling, and threatening us with death or more beatings along the way. One of the guards came to us with a manual hair clipper and started to cut our moustaches. It was an old, dull clipper. They were mocking us, saying things like, "You haven't shaved your moustache to look like Stalin. You think you are a real communist?" and "Let me cut a bit of his manhood."

"I need to use the bathroom," I suddenly said.

"Not possible," said one of the guards.

"I *need* to go to the bathroom," I said more aggressively. "Will you take me or should I shit right here?"

Realizing that I wasn't bluffing, he yielded.

In the bathroom, I came across a guard whom I knew. He had brought my son to me a few times.

"What are *you* doing here?" the guard asked.

"What I am doing here? They have brought me here. I have done nothing."

He looked at my wounded feet. "Listen, you have not heard this from me. But listen to them. Listen to whatever they say. Do whatever they want you to do. If you don't, they will execute you!"

What I had heard from Akbar now became a certainty. At that moment, any hope for Jahan and the others died in me. Before he left, the guard also told me that someone had committed suicide right there. He didn't say who, but he was talking about Jalil. (I would learn about his ordeal a few days later.) He had cut himself open with a broken glass jar. After his suicide, they collected all glass bottles and jars from the cells.

I told Akbar what I had heard. We started thinking about what we should do.

THE STRATEGY TO NOTIFY OTHERS

We were trying to find a way to inform others about the executions. But how? Morsing wouldn't work since the other cells were too far away. We concluded that they might take us back to our old cells as they had taken those who had consented to pray *namaz*. So, we decided to accede and pray *namaz*. It was time for the dusk *namaz*. Nasserian showed up again. We told him about our decision. He said, "very well," shut the door, and left. But nothing happened afterward. Nobody came to take us, to ask us anything, or to see if we were actually praying *namaz* or not. It felt like it was over for that afternoon. They were only interested in breaking us. To notify others of what was going on was the *only* reason that Akbar and I had agreed to pray *namaz*. They had robbed us of that opportunity by not taking us to our old wards.

The next day, they called me around noon. I was standing blindfolded in the corridor when they brought in someone else. I think his name was Azim. He was affiliated with the Majority faction of the Feda'ian. I knew him. He had been in the cell that I had contacted by Morse code. They took us downstairs to the same notorious corridor between two wards, in the administrative section where the hearings were held. This time it was all quiet. Nothing was going on; no movements either, nothing. They brought two more men to our cell. Then, they started calling names. Based on my recognition of the names and the knowledge that all their sentences were also about to end, I was certain this was related to the termination of our sentences. They would not let us talk to each other, not even a whisper. They took me to a room. An office chair was in the room. The guard sat me down and put a piece of paper in front of me. It was from the Prison Prosecutor's office. I couldn't figure out what was going on. One day they were executing us or whipping us for refusing to pray *namaz* and now, "your sentence is about to end"?

We had to answer the questions on this paper. They were the customary set of questions in written form: Name? Offense? Sentence? When does your sentence end? And, at the end, "Are you willing to condemn the organization you are affiliated with? Will you participate in an interview?"

Azim, the Majority sympathizer, and I were next to each other on the way back. I found the opportunity, for only a few seconds, to tell him, "Be aware, they are hitting the guys." I couldn't say anything else as the guard had come to our side again. Walking was painful, as my feet were severely injured. Azim couldn't miss noticing my troubled walk and that I had been whipped.

I heard later that he had told his cellmates, "I saw Mehrdad. He had a hard time walking." He had told them that I had said, "They are hitting the guys." There were inmates with multiple affiliations in that ward. There were a few Minority sympathizers among them too. But none of them had believed the news. One of them had said, "Mehrdad has always had a troubled walk." After all, "hitting" could be interpreted differently. Years later, I met a few of those guys in Europe and asked them what they were thinking at the time. They said, "We didn't think you meant execution." They knew me and knew that I would not make such assertions without a reason. They had gotten the message but couldn't believe executions were in order. They had heard me say, "I won't agree to *namaz*." Thus, they thought that I had been flogged for refusing to pray *namaz* and that the next day would be *their* turn.

It suddenly got noisy and the cell doors opened. (They could be opened only from outside.) All the inmates came out of the cells.

They took us to the ward's hall. It was quite clear that they had plans for us. They made us sit around the hall and started threatening us. There were a few guards holding whips and clubs. They were intimidating us to pray *namaz* but didn't beat us. A mock of a clergy started to lead the mass prayer. They lined us up behind him. The guards stood around to watch us. We kneeled when the clergy kneeled, we stood up when he stood up. We did this once or twice a day.

I think it was August 31, around 7 p.m., that they took us back to our old cells in Ward 8. They told us to gather all personal belongings, even for those who had not come back to the cell. It was obvious that they would *never* come back. After we gathered our stuff, they brought the survivors from Ward 7 to our ward downstairs. Dinner was served around 8 p.m.

The first thing that came to my mind was to inform the other wards of the news, but the situation had changed. It would not be an easy task. Our ward was no longer what it had been. New inmates had joined us. Some knew each other and some did not. The established relationships were lost, and this had caused mistrust in some. One had to be careful about which cell one ended up in. On the one hand, inmates who had been charged with the same political affiliation could not gather in one cell to give the officials any excuses. This was known and accepted by all inmates. On the other hand, one had to pick cellmates carefully. The makeup of the people inside every cell had to be a trade-off between those two concerns. There were more of the Minority sympathizers, so every cell ended up with two or three of us. In that terrifying environment, the guards would routinely enter the ward and threaten us. The guards wanted to make sure that we felt like we were being watched at all times. In this daunting situation, all I could think of was how to update those in the other wards. I knew they were anxious to hear the news. I could often see their shadow at the spot where we used to communicate. It was obvious to me that they wanted to know where we had been for the past two or three days.

I shared my thoughts with a few people in our ward that I trusted. I told them we were duty bound to inform others (Evin and *Mellikesh* prisoners) of what was going on. It would undoubtedly be the end of us if we were caught in the process, but we could save at least a hundred souls. One or two people could be sacrificed to this end. I shared my intention with the few inmates whom I trusted, and convinced them, but then one of the other men asked me not to do it.

"Why?" I asked.

"I will do it, Mehrdad. You are close to the end of your sentence and you may be released soon. I am stuck here for a long time. Let me do it."

"Fine, but I have to be there so that those at the other end will be assured of the validity of the information."

We had gotten so good at Morsing that we could tell who was tapping just by listening to the taps. We had three people on lookout. In our cell, such communications were made in the bathroom. Our ward had two entrances. At one end was the main entrance, which led to the vestibule, and at the other end was the door that led to the prison yard. Guards could have entered from either door at any time.

It was about 10 p.m. I asked one of the comrades affiliated with Rah-e Kargar to take position and be on the lookout. Two other guys helped to cover both entrances. I started to Morse. The comrade who had volunteered to Morse started passing on the information after I established contact. He was excellent in Morsing. It was important to be good at Morse code. In fact, only Mojahedin inmates who had spent many years at Gohardasht prison and we, the Minority, Morsed well. At any rate, in that very situation, not many people would dare to do it even if they knew how. Getting caught meant death. The frightening shadow of death definitely had its effect.

"Mehrdad, they do not believe it is you who is conveying the news," our comrade retorted after passing on the information.

I asked him to stand watch and started Morsing myself. "This is how we have decided to relay the information to you guys. I accept all responsibility for this. All the information you have received is accurate. Jahan, Mahmoud, and Mohammad Ali Behkish, plus others, have been executed. This is Mehrdad talking to you. I am responsible for this report."

Then I moved out of the bathroom again and went on watch. The Rah-e Kargar comrade went back to his position and continued to Morse. It is easy to talk about it now. But then... what the comrade did was truly something. It had, and still has, special meaning for me. Luckily, no one bothered us. Neither did the guards step in.

That night we reported all that we knew to the ward of *Mellikesh* people. I trusted them to pass it on to the Evin prisoners, especially since I had accepted responsibility for the validity of the reported news. I still regret that I didn't try to contact the Evin prisoners directly. I wish I had done it myself. Fortunately, I heard that they had gotten the information later, but I never forgave myself for not contacting them directly. The next day, I went to the Morse station, but nobody showed up. They had been taken to face the Death Commission.

Maybe if I had contacted them directly some of them would have made a different decision. I still feel that there might have been a few people who just didn't believe the turn of events. To this day, that bothers me, and I still feel like I have an unfulfilled obligation to them.

They had taken them. Fourteen men, most of them affiliated with Minority, were executed. Unlike those executed from our ward, these guys chose their faith as they knew execution was in order, but they still didn't give in. Those who survived were brought to our ward. Later on, the survivors from the Evin and *Mellikesh* prisoners were brought to our ward as well. Ward 8, the survivors' ward, was filled up beyond capacity with people who had different political and organizational affiliations.

POST-MASSACRE

The shadow of death was still lingering over everyone's head for about a week after the massacre had ended. A dead solitary mood had taken over a ward filled with people. Most had withdrawn and were reclusive. As people saw each other, the response to a simple "Hello" was "Shhhhh, don't say hello!" Even among those I had known for five or six years, some of whom I had known through their affiliation with the Minority organization.

"What is to be done?" was the question of the day. This was a unique group. Some of the guys from Ward 1, Section 1, of Qezel Hesar, who had been separated, were back together. For the next two or three weeks, we would try to change the mood and make our surroundings more bearable by joking around and pulling pranks. During this time, mass prayer was enforced at least once, and sometimes twice, a day. The mass prayer was led by a clergy who stuttered. We couldn't stop laughing when he sounded like a percolating coffee pot, "ghol, ghol, ghol, ghol" trying to say "Gholhovallah." These were quiet laughs as death could be the consequence if one were caught. On top of that, we would stand together during the mass prayers and pull pranks on each other. It got to the point that quite a few people would not dare to stand next to us. One of the guys used to say "long live the Organization of People's Feda'ian of Iran" as he was getting into prostrate position during the prayer.[39] That is how we made it through those days.

I was transferred to Evin prison after a few weeks. I spent about a month in solitary confinement at Evin before I was released. After walking through the prison gates, I had a tough time believing what had just happened to me. I wondered what might be happening to those still confined within the prison walls, which had cast the long shadow of death on everyone inside.

In hindsight, I find it unsettling that not much attention is given to the role of communication in prison during those days. Not many survivors, many of whom live abroad now, mention this in their memoirs. I am not uttering this because I was involved in it. I had accepted death from the beginning. I could never forget the bravery of my comrades who volunteered to take

---

39 Prostrate position involves putting the bare forehead, both palms, both knees, and the base of the toes of both feet on the place of prostration. The position symbolizes total submission during prayer.

such a risk in that daunting situation. Death would have been the inevitable consequence of getting caught while passing information at the time the regime was trying to veil the ongoing massacre. I cannot imagine what might have happened if we had not been able to pass on the information, or if no one had been there to receive it.

TRANSLATED FROM PERSIAN BY EBRAHIM NOURI

Chapter Three

THE MASSACRE
IN THE PROVINCES

Still an Enigma

FATEMEH JOKAR
INTERVIEWING MS. ZAHER[1]

FJ: When were you arrested and on what charges?

z: I was arrested in Mashhad, in 1985, for having ties with the Mojahedin Khalq Organization.

FJ: Did you notice anything in particular about the displacement of prisoners inside the Vakilabad prison in 1988? For example, did the guards separate prisoners who had long sentences from those who did not, or were leftists separated from the Mojahedin?

---

1 Fatemeh Jokar was born in 1960 in Quchan, in the province of Khorasan. She grew up in Mashhad, obtaining her diploma from Farah Pahlavi High School and continuing her higher education at the Mashhad School of Public Health (MSPH). After graduating from MSPH in 1980, she sought employment at the Ministry of Education as a health instructor. In 1981, Fatemeh married Saeed Bajani, a sympathizer of the People's Mojahedin Organization of Iran (PMOI). With the inception of widespread repression in June 1981, she and her husband abandoned their jobs, joined the resistance movement led by the PMOI against the IRA, and started an underground life. While pregnant, Fatemeh was arrested along with her husband. Both were subjected to severe torture and tried in a kangaroo court. Saeed Bajani was condemned to death and executed in April 1982, and Fatemeh was sentenced to thirty years of imprisonment. A month later, their daughter was born in jail. In 1985, Fatemeh and her daughter were released under the pretext of a "long furlough." She was forbidden to leave Mashhad. Furthermore, she had to report to the city prosecutor's office every week. Since she was prohibited from government employment, she had to earn her living by doing odd jobs. After a few years, she married an ex-political prisoner, a marriage that resulted in two daughters. In 2011, Fatemeh, her husband, and two of her daughters left Iran, and, after living in Turkey for two years, they resettled in Finland as political refugees. From the outset of her life in Europe, she has cooperated closely with Iran's Political Prisoners' Association in Exile. She has written articles in Persian-language journals and spoken on the prison machinery of the IRI in gatherings of exiled and immigrant Iranians. Fatemeh Jokar was one of the witnesses in the Iran Tribunal, an international people's court, which was founded in 2007 and concluded its findings in 2012.

z: No, we were not separated. I heard that there were some changes in the men's prison, but I was not aware of any separation of inmates on the women's side.

FJ: Did you ever hear that the regime had plans to murder the prisoners and not disclose their fate? Or that none of those who continued to remain steadfast on their positions would be released?

z: Everything happened so suddenly; no, we did not hear anything during that time.

FJ: Did you hear anything about the Mojahedin's operation before the Islamic Republic of Iran accepted UN Security Council resolution 598?

z: No, we heard nothing regarding the Mojahedin's operations before acceptance of resolution 598 by the IRI.

FJ: What was the reaction of prisoners to Ayatollah Khomeini's speech, in which Khomeini said that "making this decision [of accepting UN Security Council resolution 598] was more deadly than taking poison. I submitted myself to God's will and drank this chalice of poison."

z: It was unexpected, a shock for everyone. On the one hand, we were happy that the war was over. On the other hand, we did not know what would happen next. We were unsure what the future would hold.

FJ: It seems as though there were no premeditated plans for the execution of the women prisoners at the Vakilabad prison. I mean, even after the Mojahedin and their National Liberation Army crossed Iran's western borders, you continued to have access to newspapers and could watch the news on television. Did you have any visitation rights?

z: Yes, that's correct, it seems there was not a premeditated plan. We had the right to one visitation after the Mojahedin's operation; however, that right was revoked for about three months.

FJ: When and how did you hear about the *Forough-e Javidan* Operation—the so-called Mersad Operation, as the regime referred to it?

z: We heard about it watching the news on television, which we had access to at all times. We watched the interviews conducted with those who were arrested in the Mersad Operation, namely Saeed Shahsavandi and four or five others whose names I don't remember.

FJ: What was the reaction of the Mojahedin prisoners to these operations? Did they believe that the Mojahedin would succeed in defeating the regime's armed forces and would then go on to liberate city after city on the way to Tehran?

z: The Mojahedin members in prison were quite happy. I remember that a friend of mine visited her husband in the men's ward, and she was very happy when she returned. She said her husband had indicated that they would all be released shortly, that it would all be over soon! As we know, this was not the case, and sadly soon afterward, her husband was executed.

FJ: How was the general atmosphere inside the prison during the two days of bloody battle between the Mojahedin and the IRI's armed forces?

Z: Everyone was in a state of shock. No one knew what was happening. In the men's ward there was a hopeful spirit. In multiple instances, the names of prisoners were called and they were taken to the Information Ministry, most believing that they would soon return. We did not know what was to become of them. Two inmates were also taken from our ward: Shamsi Barari and Shirin Eslami. We did not know where they were being taken or what was to happen to them. The night they took Shamsi, she had a bad headache and had tightly fastened her scarf around her head. Shirin Eslami, the other prisoner, was a young woman who had a two-year-old child.

A few days later, one of our friends asked a prison guard, "Where did you take those two? Shamsi had a bad headache, where are they now?" The prison guard told her, "Worry about yourself, they won't be coming back."

When our friend told the rest of us of her conversation with the guard, everyone understood that we were not going to be freed and that perhaps Shamsi and Shirin had been executed. Silence and horror spread throughout the prison ward, and everyone kept busy with work or sleep. After the first two, ten more prisoners were taken. No one knew what happened to them; since Shamsi and Shirin had not returned, we thought these ten had the same fate. However, all ten of them returned and that brought a wave of happiness to the ward.

FJ: What was the leftist prisoners' assessment of the Mojahedin's attack and its consequences?

Z: Some of the leftist prisoners questioned the Mojahedin's move and were frustrated that they were being punished the same as the Mojahedin and questioned why their visitation rights had been revoked. Others were silent and were waiting to see what would happen.

FJ: Were you aware of the regime's propaganda, especially during Friday prayers, where they would say, "Armed Mojahedin must be executed," "Treacherous *Monafeq* (hypocrites) and mercenaries must be vanquished..."?

z: Yes, we were aware of the propaganda. We followed the news on television and would listen to the Friday prayer announcements. It was very painful and difficult for us to swallow what we were hearing.

FJ: Did a Death Commission come to Vakilabad prison? Did you know any of the Death Commission members and why they came to the prison?

z: I do not remember if a Death Commission ever came to our ward. The prisoners whose names were called were taken to the Information Ministry and were interrogated and tried there. Valipour was the prison prosecutor and had a role in identifying prisoners and providing the names of those to be summoned to the Information Ministry. Moghisseh was the prosecutor at that time. He or Valipour came to the prison and talked to the prisoners many times before the 1988 Massacre.

FJ: How many of the Mojahedin women were taken from your ward and never came back? What did you know of the situation of Mojahedin men in those days?

z: Two people were taken from our ward and never returned: Shamsi Barari and Shirin Eslami. We learned from the women who went to visit their husbands or brothers in the men's ward that at the height of the executions, groups of men were taken from the ward and never returned. I don't remember clearly if the visitation between men and women prisoners stopped or not. As far as I remember, it did not.

FJ: What did they do to the leftist women? Did you know that in the Evin and Gohardasht prisons they would whip women until they agreed to say prayers? How did they treat the women in Mashhad?

z: As we were all together, I did not see that sort of behavior with the leftist women in Mashhad. No whipping.

FJ: When did the prison, more specifically your ward, return to a normal state? When were visitation rights reinstated? Did you have access to the recreation yard?

z: It was around Aban (October) that they reinstated our visitations. We had the opportunity to go out to the recreation yard during my entire time in prison; it was never revoked. Our ward conditions gradually returned to normal over time. People from the Information Ministry began coming to our ward to interview prisoners for the possibility of parole. Some of the prisoners were taken to the Information Ministry and asked if they would be willing to give interviews, asking them to repent in order to be freed. Some accepted, but many did not.

FJ: How long after the massacre did you become aware of what had happened in the men's section? What specific information did you hear about the massacre?

Z: We became aware only after our visitations to the men's ward were reinstated. We became more aware of the extent of the massacre through our families too. Our information was not accurate; it is still not. We knew only the extent of what our families were telling us. Sometimes we would hear about it from the sisters or wives of male prisoners who had been executed.

According to the female prisoners who met their brothers or husbands in the men's ward, there were only fifteen Mojahedin men left in Ward 1. All other prisoners in Quarantine 4, individual cells, and Ward 2, were executed. After the executions, one day Valipour, the prison prosecutor, came to our ward and said, "We killed ninety people in one night." I'll never forget that statement.

FJ: Many thanks. I understand that talking about those difficult times is not easy. During the time that I was in the Vakilabad, the shadow of fear dominated the prison. I understand how painful it is to live in the shadow of an unknown destiny, worrying about what tomorrow will bring, and to be isolated from the outside world. I imagine it was even more painful during that time period and in light of that horrific massacre.

I wonder why the conditions in the women's ward in Mashhad prison in 1988 were noticeably different from those in other prisons, as I know the situation was much more dreadful and brutal in other women's prisons throughout Iran. While Evin and Gohardasht prisons were notoriously hard, none of the other prisons had conditions as lax as those in Mashhad. Why did they adopt a different strategy in Mashhad? When they revoked visitation rights, why were other rights, such as access to the recreation yard, newspapers, and television, still provided? Why did they not torture leftist women in Mashhad prison? These are only some minute unanswered questions among so many unanswered questions about this heinous crime.

TRANSLATED FROM PERSIAN BY ARAM NOZAD

Executions in the Provinces: Summer 1988

ASSAD SAIF[2]

The execution of political prisoners, which had started at the very outset of the post-revolution regime, reached its peak in summer 1988. There may have been many reasons for this Great Massacre, but the political prisoners were more or less certain that they would not be released and might perish in prison. The prisoners imagined death, but not as it actually occurred during that bloody summer. We should also keep in mind that a large number of leaders, cadres, and activists were kept as hostages in the prisons of the IRI.

In the history of modern Iran, Tehran has always played a central role in the country's social history and political development.

The acceptance of UN Security Council resolution 598, which was equivalent to the IRI ending the conflict with Iraq without achieving any of its intended objectives, was the immediate reason for the extermination of three generations of political prisoners. The wave of executions reached the provinces as well as Tehran with the utmost rage and violence. Family visits

---

2 Assad Saif was born in 1955 in Anzali, a city in Gilan Province. Upon finishing high school, he attended Tabriz University in Azerbaijan Province to study human geography. He was drawn into political activity at this highly politicized university, one of the epicenters of the radical student movement in 1970s Iran. After graduating, he took courses in the College of Education and thereafter started to teach in Tabriz schools. He joined the Tudeh Party of Iran in the wake of the 1979 Revolution. Saif was arrested in Tabriz during the crackdown that swept the country after June 1981. His incarceration didn't last long as he was released after a few months. However, after the IRI rounded up the members of the Tudeh Party in 1982, he decided to flee Iran with his wife. The Saifs crossed the border into the former Soviet Union and asked for asylum, which was granted to them. Disenchanted with the Soviet system, the Saifs left for West Germany in 1984. Exile made Assad Saif a prolific literary critic. His books include *Love in Iranian Fictions in Exile* (2008), *Humor in Iranian Fiction in Exile* (2017), *A Book for Books* (collected volume of book reviews, 2018), and *Homosexuality in the Literature of Exile* (2019). Assad Saif has been an active member of the Iranian Writers Association in Exile.

were disrupted, radio and television sets were removed, and newspapers were not delivered any longer.

The executions started in late July. Most of the prisoners, however, became aware of the situation a few weeks later. This time a new method was used, with the gallows replacing the bullets. In previous years, the prisoners would become aware of the number of executions and the depth of the catastrophe by counting single shots. This time, however, an effort had been made to begin the operation silently.

In the provinces, the prisoners had been asked almost the same questions as in the prisons of Tehran.

According to Khomeini's fatwa, all *Mortads* (apostates) and *Moharebs* (warriors against God) were sentenced to death. The execution of the Mojahedin was more widespread than that of the leftists. In many of the cities, almost all of the victims were Mojahedin. Looking at the list of victims, we notice that no leftist women were executed in the provinces and all the women who were executed there were Mojahedin.

The inquisition board, later known by the prisoners as the "Death Commission," was responsible for deciding who should be put to death.

Reza Saki, a detainee from Isfahan, stated:

A few months before the massacre, a committee made of a mullah and a couple of plainclothes officers from Tehran came to Dastgerd prison. They went to the wards and asked the prisoners questions about the prison conditions and their problems. They said their goal was to empty the prisons; they wanted to dispatch the lifers and the Death Row prisoners to the prisons of Tehran and to free the others.[3]

Ahmad Mousavi from Rasht stated:

The Death Commission behaved in a completely different manner in the Rasht central prison...[they] had already reviewed the files and made their selection before seeing the prisoners. After the interrogation, they would mark positive or negative in front of the names; positive meaning execution.[4]

---

3 Reza Saki, interviewed by Monireh Baradaran, available at www.bidaran.net, accessed October 12, 2019.
4 Ahmad Mousavi, interviewed by Monireh Baradaran, available at www.bidaran.net, accessed October 12, 2019.

Hadi Aminian from Hamedan stated:

> One evening Salimi, the shari'a judge, Raisi, the prosecutor, and Maleki, the prison warden, together with some prison guards, came to our ward and asked each and every one of the prisoners to express their opinion about their organization and *senfi* [literally, guild-related] demands... The next day they called in the prisoners one by one and this went on until early in the morning.[5]

Jahangir Esmailpour, from Adelabad prison in Shiraz, wrote:

> The three members of the Death Commission in Shiraz were Nurollah Eslami Nia, the prosecutor; Mossayebi, the shari'a judge; and a representative from the Intelligence Ministry.[6] First they took the oldtimers and then, in the second round, they even interrogated the repentants, some of whom were executed. Even some prisoners who were on furlough were called in and placed on Death Row.[7]

Mohammad Reza Matin from Tabriz prison has testified:

> In June of that year, if I'm not mistaken, they gave the prisoners some questionnaires to fill out. The questions were about the prisoner's standpoint, belief in Islam, and also the conditions under which they would be released. I mean, they asked: If you are released from prison, will you make a pledge not to take action against the Islamic Republic? Then they interviewed us one by one in person. Someone from the Intelligence Ministry was there who asked us ideological questions too, and we were obliged to answer. Afterwards, they sent us to the solitary cells.[8]

In the same spirit, another prisoner from Tabriz wrote:

---

5 Hadi Aminian, interviewed by Monireh Baradaran, available at www.bidaran.net, accessed October 12, 2019.
6 Jahangir Esmailpour, *Adelabad: Ranj-e Mandegar* (Sweden: Baran Publications, 2010), p. 120.
7 Esmailpour, p. 123.
8 Mohammad Reza Matin, interviewed by Monireh Baradaran, available at www.bidaran. net, accessed October 12, 2019.

[After individual interrogations] a Committee from Tehran was stationed at the Revolutionary Court to judge the extent of the prisoners'
commitment to the Mojahedin. For several days, they interrogated,
judged, and sent several prisoners to the gallows.[9]

With the attack of the Mojahedin into the border towns in the west of the
country,

> the prisoners of Ilam and Kermanshah were sent to Tehran. The reason
> for this was the proximity of these towns to the frontiers and the attacks
> of the Mojahedin in the area... All the prisoners who were transferred
> to Evin and Gohardasht in 1988 were executed during the massacre
> of the political prisoners in that summer.[10]

According to the interviews conducted by Amnesty International, further
transfers of prisoners were mentioned in the following locations: Borujerd to
Khorramabad, both in Lorestan province; Astara, Fouman, Anzali, Roudbar,
and Langaroud to Rasht, all in Gilan province; Ilam and Kermanshah to Tehran
or Karaj; Babol and Sari to Qaem-Shahr, and vice versa, all in Mazandaran
province; Orumiyeh in East Azerbaijan Province to Tabriz in West Azerbaijan
Province; and Zahedan in Sistan and Baluchestan Province to Ahvaz in
Khuzestan Province and Mashhad in Razavi Khorasan Province.[11]

In Hamedan, "even the windows facing the yard were welded."[12] The last
information from the outside world probably dated back to the broadcasting
of Friday prayers after the Eternal Light Operation in Tehran. Astounded,
the prisoners heard slogans that sounded completely new to them: "Armed
Monafeqin [hypocrites] must be executed. *Monafeq* prisoners must be executed." It was evident that the speaker was intentionally instigating such
slogans. Nonetheless, the prisoners did not foresee that death was looming.

---

9 As stated at www.bidaran.net/spip.php?article207 from the Ashiyan weblog, accessed
October 12, 2019.
10 Mohammad Reza Eskandari, interviewed by Monireh Baradaran, available at www.
bidaran.net, accessed October 12, 2019. Eskandari, a Mojahed prisoner, was incarcerated
in Ilam, Kermanshah, and Qom for five years before summer 1988. He was in charge of
a Mojahedin cell in Ilam after he was released.
11 Transfer of political prisoners was alluded to in interviews conducted by Amnesty
International, "Families kept in the Dark," *Blood-soaked secrets* (London: Amnesty
International).
12 Hadi Aminian, interviewed by Monireh Baradaran, available at www.bidaran.net,
accessed October 12, 2019.

During the course of new transfers, when prisoners were summoned with all their belongings, and afterwards during the repeated interrogations, most of the prisoners visualized freedom in their minds. In Zanjan prison, "it was believed that they would soon be transferred to the newly built prison due to the fact that the new prison building had been under construction for years."[13] Another prisoner from Rasht wrote:

> On July 29, at nine o'clock in the evening, Ramezan Keshavarz, the prison guard, known as Red Beard, came to Corridor 1 with a list in his hand announcing, "Those whose name I call, gather your belongings." A gunny sack full of books and magazines was given to them as a departing gift on behalf of the remaining prisoners... we all thought that they would be transferred to Lakan prison and enjoy better conditions.[14]

Mohammad Reza Ashoogh, a Mojahed prisoner from UNESCO prison[15] in Dezful, said:

> Toward the end of the war, they gathered all the political prisoners in one place. At that time, someone called Gharaati who was in charge of the Guidance [Section] in the prison summoned me several times... While preaching, he advised me to abandon my political leanings and accept some responsibilities in the prison... I assumed that his suggestion was on a personal basis and its acceptance would prove my own lack of identity. A few weeks later, they gathered all the political prisoners, including those who were in solitary cells, and some detainees from other provinces, such as Ahvaz, in one place and took them to a new ward with three rooms... they brought a television. They broadcast scenes of war and also the People's Mojahedin attacking Iran from the borderlines of Iraq... Rumor went around that Khomeini had sent a Clemency Commission to decide about the fate of the prisoners. We also heard that there had been a meeting in the prison's Administration Bureau that day. Later on, they took us to the Bureau in groups of

13 Rahmat Gholami, a prisoner belonging to the OIPF (Minority), interviewed by Monireh Baradaran, available at www.bidaran.net, accessed October 12, 2019.
14 Ahmad Mousavi, "Bidad," in Behrouz Sheyda (ed.), *Kabus-e Boland-e Tizdandan* (Sweden: Baran Publications, 2003), p. 39.
15 UNESCO prison is situated in Dezful. This site was a school constructed by UNESCO to help the children of that town during the reign of the Shah. It was turned into a prison after the 1979 Revolution.

eight, blindfolded and handcuffed. They removed the blindfolds for a short while during the interrogation. The questions were: Charges? Are you ready to fight against the Mojahedin? That's all... [If anyone protested] the plainclothesmen would immediately request to have the name of the prisoner on the list... we were between sixty-two and sixty-six people. In our group of eight, except for a teenage boy, everyone was sentenced to death.[16]

Ashoogh, who had been sentenced to death, managed to escape on his way to the gallows:

They came to the ward and announced, "Pack your things! We're taking you to Ahvaz prison..." I was sitting in the open-air area. I looked from beneath the blindfold... I could see the compound was filled with prisoners... We were taken to Karkheh Garrison... We were given a shroud and camphor, and we were instructed to take off our clothes and wear the shroud... The Interrogator sat me facing the wall and said write your last will and testament... The voices of women who were being executed could be heard... Then we got on a minibus... As soon as the minibus took off, some prisoners started protesting. I consulted with two oldtimers. I said I had loosened my handcuffs and was able to untie my wrists. I told them I wanted to run away.[17]

He estimated that between fifty and sixty people were executed on that day.[18]

In Mashhad prison, there were three series of executions. At least 178 men were killed, all Mojahedin.[19] In Zahedan prison "none of the non-sentenced

---

16 Mohammad Reza Ashoogh, interviewed by Monireh Baradaran, available at www. bidaran.net, accessed October 12, 2019. Regarding Dezful prison, Mohammad Ashoogh writes: "There were no court proceedings in the year 1988. Prison authorities canceled visits on Tuesday, August 6, 1988, and an 'amnesty commission' on behalf of Khomeini came to the prison to determine the fate of the prisoners."

17 Mohammad Reza Ashoogh, interviewed by Monireh Baradaran, available at www. bidaran.net, accessed October 12, 2019.

18 According to Ashoogh, "several dozen prisoners, including at least three women, were executed during the mass killings in Dezful. As far as he is aware, the victims were all imprisoned in connection with their support for the PMOI." *Blood-soaked secrets* (London: Amnesty International), p. 142.

19 *Blood-soaked secrets* (London: Amnesty International), p. 149; see also, Reza Fani Yazdi, interviewed by Monireh Baradaran, available at www.bidaran.net, accessed October 12, 2019. According to a UN report (E/CN.4/1989/25, February 6, 1989, p. 29), as early as July 28, fifty PMOI sympathizers were executed in Mashhad.

prisoners or those awaiting their trial returned. We didn't see them again. They had been executed."[20] In Hamedan about thirty-two people were killed: "some were hanged in public places together with the newly arrested people." Those, too, like the ones executed inside the prison, were all Mojahedin.[21] According to Mohammad Khoshzough, a member of the OIPF (Left Wing) and, later, Minority, the executions in Rasht began on July 30, 1988, and lasted until September 6:

> From men's Ward 2 of Rasht prison, 75 were executed. Of the 25 prisoners in the women's ward of Rasht, 16 were executed. From Ward 1, where we were, 96 prisoners were executed. There is no exact information about the number of executed prisoners in individual cells... However, up until the executions more than 30 people were living in individual cells.[22]

Detainees from other towns in Gilan Province were also executed in the same manner in the same prison. Between seventeen and thirty prisoners from Bandar-e Anzali prison were executed in Rasht. A group from Langarood was also executed there. One of the prisoners, Shahbaz Shahbazi, was taken to the gallows on a stretcher. According to Shayesteh Vatandoost, at least twenty-six women affiliated with the PMOI were executed in Nirouyeh Darya'i (Naval Forces) prison in Rasht.[23] According to Ahmad Mousavi, the OIPF (Minority) member and political prisoner, on July 30, in the men's ward of Rasht prison, one prisoner was summoned and never returned. Then, in the evening, a guard took away sixteen people. Shortly afterward, another guard collected ten people. This process continued over the following days until only 25 out of about 120 prisoners in the ward survived. In addition, Mousavi is of the opinion that dozens of men from other sections of the prison whom he did not know were also taken away at that time, including at least 10 prisoners who had been imprisoned for their support of leftist and other

---

20 Eyewitness account of Zahedan prison in Monireh Baradaran, available at www.bidaran.net, accessed October 12, 2019.

21 Hadi Aminian, interviewed by Monireh Baradaran, available at www.bidaran.net, accessed October 12, 2019. Amnesty International, also based on Aminian's testimony, writes: "several dozen prisoners, including at least two women, were executed during the mass killings in Hamedan." Amnesty International, *Blood-soaked secrets*, p. 145.

22 Mohammad Khoshzough, *Mala (Khaterat-e Zendan)* (Sweden: Arzan Publications, 2012), p. 438.

23 *Blood-soaked secrets* (London: Amnesty International), p. 153.

groups.[24] Thus, more than three hundred people were killed in just a few days' time.[25] According to Akbar Kazemi, who was in Lahijan's Malek-e Ashtar prison (1981–88) for his support of the PMOI, several dozen prisoners of both sexes were collected and never returned, including at least five leftists.[26]

In Ahvaz, the executions lasted three nights. All of the fifty-seven to sixty prisoners killed were Mojahedin. At the outset, they took some of the prisoners to Isfahan prison. On the return journey, they became aware of the tragedy. In Masjed Soleyman, too, seventeen to twenty Mojahedin were executed.[27] In Ahvaz, prisoners from Ahvaz and the outskirts, Mah Shahr, Howeizeh, and other towns were executed. According to Jassem Hardan, "During the execution ceremony, in addition to the Revolutionary Court authorities, Jazayeri the Imam Jom'eh [Friday prayer leader] of Ahvaz was also there making sure that the executions were performed correctly."[28]

After the *Forough-e Javidan* (Eternal Light) Operation in Ilam, "the prisoners who had been released were arrested again and taken back to prison for execution." These people had not taken part in the operations and were not willing to cooperate with the Mojahedin. A total of 102 people from Kermanshah and 17 people from Sonqor Koliai were executed.[29] In Shiraz, between 170 and 200 people were executed.[30] According to Jahangir Esmailpour, in August and early September, every day a group of 15 to 20 Mojahedin prisoners were summoned and the majority never came back. Moreover, Amnesty International obtained the testimony of a survivor who was held in the women's ward in Adelabad prison in Shiraz, estimating "that there were about 40 to 50 women in her prison before the mass killings and less

24 Ibid., pp. 153–4.
25 Mohammad Khoshzough, "Jenayat-e Azimi," in Sheyda (ed.), *Kabus*, pp. 190–1.
26 *Blood-soaked secrets* (London: Amnesty International), p. 148.
27 Manouchehr, interviewed by Monireh Baradaran, available at www.bidaran.net, accessed October 12, 2019.
28 Jassem Hardan, "Ta Koshtar," in Sheyda (ed.), *Kabus*, p. 61.
29 Mohammad Reza Eskandari, interviewed by Monireh Baradaran, available at www. bidaran.net, accessed October 12, 2019.
30 Jahangir Esmailpour, *Adelabad: Ranj-e Mandegar*. The statistics provided by Esmailpour, a member of the OIPF (Minority), vary considerably and must be treated with caution. He has given three different numbers on three different occasions. The other number of executed political prisoners he cited is "around 250" (2009) and "at least 250 to 300" (2018) men and women. See *Deadly Fatwa: Iran's 1988 Prison Massacre* (New Haven, Connecticut: Iran Human Rights Documentation Center, 2009), p. 37; see also *Blood-soaked secrets* (London: Amnesty International), p. 160.

than a dozen survived."[31] In Tabriz prison, the number of victims is estimated to be between sixty and seventy, all of whom were Mojahedin.[32] About twenty Mojahed prisoners from Orumiyeh, who had been incarcerated in Tabriz prison, were returned to Orumiyeh and executed. All these prisoners had been tried and sentenced. Only one leftist prisoner was executed in Tabriz.[33] Two additional Mojahedin prisoners in Shiraz, Mehdi Abdolrahimi, and Hamid Taheri also witnessed that their section ("She Ganeh") was put on lockdown on July 29. In the following days, over two dozen prisoners were collected and only a few returned.[34] In Kermanshah and Ilam, anyone who was arrested in the Eternal Light Operation was hanged in public.[35] Abrahamian states that no one was executed in Isfahan during the Great Massacre. It seems to us that he is referring to leftist prisoners and not the Mojahedin. According to Reza Saki, a member of the OIPF and an advocate of the 16 Azar Manifesto, 140 to 150 prisoners detained in Isfahan's Dastgerd prison and other detention facilities were executed.[36] As Mohammad Hoshi testified, "at least 200 former PMOI prisoners who had been released in earlier years were also re-arrested, forcibly disappeared after arrest and extrajudicially killed during this period."[37] In addition, Amnesty International writes that, "several men and women who had been imprisoned in connection with their support for leftist political organizations were also executed."[38] According to Saki, all the Mojahedin from Section 1, all but two from Section 2, and one leftist, a Feda'i (Minority) member, were executed. Another eyewitness reported that guards entered his ward every day between August and December 1988 and took up to ten prisoners, who then disappeared.[39] In Zanjan, more than two dozen people,

---

31 *Blood-soaked secrets* (London: Amnesty International), p. 161.

32 Eyewitness account of Tabriz prison, from the Ashiyan weblog, available at www. bidaran.net, accessed October 12, 2019.

33 Mohammad Reza Matin, interviewed by Monireh Baradaran, available at www.bidaran. net, accessed October 12, 2019. Matin, who had been transferred from Orumiyeh to Tabriz in 1986, was a supporter of the Tudeh Party; also see *Blood-soaked secrets* (London: Amnesty International), p. 163.

34 *Blood-soaked secrets* (London: Amnesty International), p. 164.

35 Tahereh Gholami, interviewed by Monireh Baradaran, available at www.bidaran.net, accessed October 12, 2019.

36 *Deadly Fatwa: Iran's 1988 Prison Massacre* (New Haven, Connecticut: Iran Human Rights Documentation Center, 2009), p. 42.

37 *Blood-soaked secrets* (London: Amnesty International), p. 144.

38 Ibid., p. 144.

39 *Deadly Fatwa: Iran's 1988 Prison Massacre* (New Haven, Connecticut: Iran Human Rights Documentation Center, 2009), p. 43.

all Mojahedin, may have been executed.[40] In Sari, about thirty-five political prisoners appear to have been killed. According to Amnesty International, an anonymous survivor reported that:

> … leftist prisoners were not targeted during this period, but there may have been one or two individuals among the disappeared who were imprisoned in connection with their support for the Organization of the Vanguard Fighters of the Oppressed (Arman-e Mostaz'afin).[41]

In Semnan, Assadollah Nabavi estimates that:

> several dozen prisoners, both men and women, were killed… and he knows of only two men other than himself who survived. He says that the real number may be much higher as the authorities also re-arrested and executed some former prisoners who had been released several years earlier during the July to September period. Assadollah Nabavi said that, as far as he knew, all of the execution victims were imprisoned in connection with their support for the PMOI.[42]

Regarding Zahedan, Abbas Torabi testifies that "he also learned about the execution of several dozen people in Zahedan who had been arrested several weeks or months before the mass prisoner killings."[43]

According to the UN Economic and Social Council, "On 8 January 1990, Mr. Abdolrahman Karimzadeh, spokesman for the Kurdistan Democratic Party, handed the Special Representative a list of 95 persons alleged to have been executed in prisons in Kurdistan in 1988."[44] As to Sanandaj, Azad Zamani and other survivors testified that:

> … a few hundred prisoners were executed during the mass killings of July–September 1988 in Kurdistan province. They included men, women and children as young as 16. Some of the victims were also

---

40 *Blood-soaked secrets* (London: Amnesty International), p. 166. Another source writes: "It is estimated that between thirty-five to forty (out of one hundred or so) prisoners were executed in Zanjan prison." *Deadly Fatwa: Iran's 1988 Prison Massacre* (New Haven, Connecticut: Iran Human Rights Documentation Center, 2009), p. 41.

41 *Blood-soaked secrets* (London: Amnesty International), p. 157; also see Appendix B (this volume).

42 Ibid., p. 159.

43 Ibid., p. 165.

44 UN report, E/CN.4/1990/24, February 12, 1990, p. 13.

elderly and in their 70s. According to Azad Zamani, the victims were predominantly imprisoned in connection with their real or perceived support for Kurdish opposition groups KDPI [Kurdish Democratic Party of Iran] and Kumeleh. However, among them were also some men and women who had been imprisoned in connection with their support for the PMOI and leftist groups.[45]

In mid-summer 1988, especially in early August, there were also executions in Arak, Varamin, Bakhtaran, Kangavar, and Eslamabad-e Gharb.[46] Unlike executions in previous years, the prisoners were hanged, not killed by firing squads. This was not an exception but rather the rule of the Great Massacre.

In Mashhad the prisoners were also sent to the gallows in batches of six. They apparently were hanged in the backyard of the detention center of the Ministry of Justice branch in Kouh-sangi Street.[47] In Rasht "the prisoners were executed by suspension hanging with rope. Later we heard that in the yard of the Naval Forces prison, a garage (oil-change service) was used for executing the prisoners."[48] There were even some repentants among the victims. Most victims had already been sentenced and were serving time. Among them were prisoners who had been sentenced to several years of imprisonment for possessing a Mojahedin newspaper or leaflet. Among the victims you could

---

45 *Blood-soaked secrets* (London: Amnesty International), p. 155.

46 It is not clear how many people were executed in these locations. According to Amnesty International, seven members of the PMOI were hanged in public in Bakhtaran on August 1, 1988, and another member of that organization was hanged in public in Ilam on August 3. Amnesty International Index: MDE 13/13/88, Distr: UA/SC, August 16, 1988, p. 1. According to the UN, about eighty members of the PMOI, mostly prisoners or former prisoners, were reportedly executed in early August 1988 in the towns of Arak, Varamin (and also Mashhad, Kermanshah, and in the prisons of Evin, Shiraz, and Malayer). According to a *Keyhan* article (August 3, 1988), ten members of the PMOI were hanged in public in Bakhtaran, western Iran, on August 1, 1988. According to the Islamic Republic News Agency information, reported by Reuters on August 4 and 5, 1988, a leading member of the PMOI was hanged in public in Ilam, western Iran, August 3, 1988, and two other members of that organization were hanged in Kangavar, western Iran, on August 4, 1988 (UN report, A/43/705, October 13, 1988, pp. 12, 15). A few months later, another UN report pointed out that alleged collaborators with the members of the PMOI were publicly executed in Kangavar, Bakhtaran, and Eslamabad-e Gharb. "According to the official account, 15 PMOI supporters were executed on about August 5, 1988. They included seven persons executed on August 1, 1988, in Bakhtaran and one person on August 3, 1988, in Ilam" (UN report, E/CN.4/1989/25, February 6, 1989, p. 29).

47 Reza Fani Yazdi, interviewed by Monireh Baradaran, available at www.bidaran.net, accessed October 12, 2019.

48 Ahmad Mousavi, "Bidad," p. 39.

find fourteen-year-old kids and sixty-year-old men and women. Most of the victims were teenage school kids who had reached adulthood in prison. A look at the list of executed prisoners reveals that the average age of the victims was about twenty-five. Other ranks of victims were university students, teachers, and civil servants.[49] Among the religious groups, in addition to the affiliates of the Mojahedin, the three "Babri" brothers affiliated with Arman-e Mostaz'afin were arrested in Anzali and executed in Rasht. It must be noted that contrary to the general policy of not killing by firing squads, the sound of machine guns was heard in Ahvaz, Hamedan, Shiraz, and Orumiyeh.[50]

In none of the prisons were the prisoners aware of the massacre until it had been going on for at least a few days. In Tabriz prison, when the prisoners returned from *havakhori* (getting fresh air), they saw "a black curtain covering the beds of a number of victims, and their belongings placed upon another bed alongside the message: This is the ill fate of the enemies of the Islamic Republic."[51]

The dimensions of this national catastrophe are still unclear. There was no report of the executions in the national media. The families of the prisoners were the first people who became aware of the massacre and they were the ones who informed families and friends inside and outside the country.

In most towns, all family visits were canceled for two months.[52] There were only a few exceptions, such as in Zahedan where there were no political prisoners at the time, or in Adelabad prison in Shiraz, where only the prisoners who had been separated from the other detainees and placed at the detention center were deprived of family visits.[53]

In those days the confused families waited anxiously in front of the prisons, unsure if their children were dead or alive. In Mashhad, the father of Bahram Parandeh, a Mojahedin supporter, went to the public prosecutor's office and

---

49 The list of victims is available on many websites, such as www.iran-archive.com. One could extract the age, profession, political affiliation, and place where the person was executed from this list, which is still not exhaustive.

50 Ghar-Neshin (Caveman), prisoner in Mah Shahr, Ahvaz, and Isfahan, interviewed by Monireh Baradaran, available at www.bidaran.net, accessed October 12, 2019; see also *Deadly Fatwa: Iran's 1988 Prison Massacre* (New Haven, Connecticut: Iran Human Rights Documentation Center, 2009), pp. 37, 44.

51 Gholam Reza Ardebili, interviewed by Monireh Baradaran, available at www.bidaran. net, accessed October 12, 2019.

52 Eyewitness from Zahedan prison, interviewed by Monireh Baradaran, available at www.bidaran.net, accessed October 12, 2019.

53 Jahangir Esmailpour, interviewed by Monireh Baradaran, available at www.bidaran. net, accessed October 12, 2019.

said, "If you don't say where Bahram is, I'll kill myself." Moghisseh, the shari'a judge, responded, "No problem! Kill yourself!" The father then jumped out the window of the public prosecutor's office and died.[54] Mohammad Reza Matin, imprisoned in Tabriz prison, stated:

> During the time when all visits had been canceled, my mother, together with the mother of another prisoner who was a supporter of one of the leftist groups, after going to the prison every day and getting no information, took some petrol with them one day. They doused themselves with petrol in front of the prison, saying if you don't let us visit our sons, we'll set ourselves on fire. The prison authorities felt compelled to let them visit us... The first thing she said was: My son, they've executed all of your friends in [all] the prisons of Iran.[55]

In Hamedan, "the families gathered in front of the city court every day until they were told... to get the belongings of their children. In Shiraz, when handing over the belongings of the victims, they warned the families that mourning ceremonies were forbidden."[56] In Mashhad "families waited anxiously for their loved ones in front of the prison doors, the public prosecutor's office, and the intelligence bureau for weeks and months."[57]

In Rasht, the prison warden called the names and

> ... asked the families to move forward. A piece of paper was given to them on which the date for delivering the victim's bag of belongings was written. All of a sudden, sobs were heard and the naked truth of the tragedy fell upon the families. After years of wandering from one prison to another, only a piece of paper remained in the hands of a bereaved mother, a distressed father, a mourning wife, and a restless child.[58]

---

54 Reza Fani Yazdi, interviewed by Monireh Baradaran, available at www.bidaran.net, accessed October 12, 2019.

55 Mohammad Reza Matin, interviewed by Monireh Baradaran, available at www.bidaran. net, accessed October 12, 2019.

56 Jahangir Esmailpour, interviewed by Monireh Baradaran, available at www.bidaran. net, accessed October 12, 2019.

57 Reza Fani Yazdi, interviewed by Monireh Baradaran, available at www.bidaran.net, accessed October 12, 2019.

58 Ahmad Mousavi, "Koshtar-e Zendanian-e Siasi dar Zendan-e Rasht dar Sal-e 1367," available at www.bidaran.net, accessed October 12, 2019.

The most common manner, which had become the norm over the past few years, was a telephone call from one prison official: "Come to this address... on this day..."

From what has been revealed so far, the corpses of the victims of summer 1988 were not delivered to their families. It is believed that they were buried in the deserts, in individual or mass graves. However, in some cases the families were informed of the burial sites. Amnesty International reports:

> In Ahvaz, the authorities told the families that they had buried the victims in a mass grave on a barren piece of land 3km east of Behesht Abad cemetery. The authorities poured concrete over the site immediately after the burial in an apparent effort to prevent families digging up the ground to identify and recover the bodies of their loved ones.[59]

Recently, Amnesty International has also reported that the families of political prisoners in Mashhad learned about three mass gravesites on the outskirts of Behesht Reza cemetery in August 1988, which have since been desecrated and destroyed.[60] The remains of some of the victims are believed to be buried there.[61] Jahangir Esmailpour has said that the victims in Shiraz were secretly buried at nighttime. He is of the opinion that some, including Javad Izadi, a member of the PMOI, were buried in Shiraz cemetery among the common graves.[62]

In Ahvaz, they did not "officially say anything about the burial spot. But the families know where their children have been buried: in the deserts."[63] In Orumiyeh they were buried in a part of the Baha'i cemetery known as Rezvan Garden. This part is separate from the other graves.[64]

Regarding Mashhad, Reza Fani Yazdi, a Tudeh prisoner, wrote: "Whoever we asked about had been executed... Nothing went back to normal after that. Visits resumed more or less, but not like in the past."[65] According to

---

59 *Blood-soaked secrets* (London: Amnesty International), p. 142.
60 Ibid., p. 152.
61 Ibid., p. 152.
62 Jahangir Esmailpour, interviewed by Monireh Baradaran, available at www.bidaran. net, accessed October 12, 2019.
63 Ghar-Neshin (Caveman), prisoner in Mah Shahr, Ahvaz, and Isfahan, in an interview with Monireh Baradaran, available at www.bidaran.net, accessed October 12, 2019.
64 Mohammad Reza Matin, interviewed by Monireh Baradaran, available at www.bidaran. net, accessed October 12, 2019.
65 Reza Fani Yazdi, interviewed by Monireh Baradaran, available at www.bidaran.net, accessed October 12, 2019.

Mohammad Reza Matin, in Tabriz prison, "During those days, there was less pressure than in the past. The number of repentants had decreased a lot. They didn't have anyone to watch us all the time anymore. We could even go for *havakhori*."[66]

After the executions came to an end, little by little the survivors were released on bail on the condition that they would not engage in political activities. Most of them were released in small groups after being paraded in Friday prayers. They left dark, narrow, and humid prison cells and stepped into another, greater prison called Iran.

TRANSLATED FROM PERSIAN BY HEDAYAT MAHDAVI

---

66 Mohammad Reza Matin, interviewed by Monireh Baradaran, available at www.bidaran. net, accessed October 12, 2019.

Chapter Four

THE MOTHERS OF KHAVARAN

Past and Present

NASSER MOHAJER

The suffering of the families of prisoners of conscience in Iran in the 1980s, and especially that of the families who were bereaved in the waves of massacres, the peak of which was the Great Massacre of 1988, is still an untold story. The support they rendered to their loved ones in the detention facilities of the Islamic Republic of Iran (IRI) was undoubtedly a source of inspiration to thousands of imprisoned women and men across the land. The families were a continual force of pressure on the IRI, the most reliable source of information about resistance in Islamic jails, and an active conduit in spreading the word about what happened during that bloody summer of 1988. Their continuous and courageous efforts to draw international attention to the plight of political prisoners in Iran was instrumental in exposing one of the most heinous crimes against humanity in the last quarter of the twentieth century. And it is only fair to say that the vanguard of this resistance and struggle was made up of women: the mothers, wives, daughters, and sisters of those who braved tyranny, aspiring for a better future for their country.

In spite of all this, there exists no substantive study on these women, or on their individual initiatives and collective actions for the release of their loved ones from one of the most cruel prison systems of our time. We know neither the personas nor the ideas of these women, who are in effect role models for a widespread pro-democracy movement in Iran.

This chapter introduces two of these women: Forough Lotfi Tajbakhsh (who passed away on February 10, 2019), one of the undisputed leaders of what is called the Movement of the Mothers of Khavaran; and Dr. Brigitte Behzadi, the spouse of Dr. Manouchehr Behzadi, who from East Germany carried out an unrelenting struggle to seek truth and justice after learning about her husband's execution in the Great Massacre of 1988. Regrettably, the agony, efforts, and struggles from abroad of the wives, daughters, and sisters of the executed prisoners, even though they played an active role in the international recognition of that historic atrocity, are not even known to many of the Iranians conscious of human rights.

The chapter ends with a history of the Movement of the Mothers of Khavaran, who may be likened to the *Madres de Plaza de Mayo* of Argentina.

Anoush Brought Me Back to Life[1]

SAID AFSHAR[2] INTERVIEWING FOROUGH LOTFI

Forough Lotfi (1930–2019) was one of the prominent figures in the movement of the Mothers of Khavaran.[3] She is revered across the political
spectrum because of her continuous struggle for seeking truth and justice. A small framed picture of her son was always hanging around her
neck. Her son, Anoushirvan Lotfi, was imprisoned both under the Shah
and the Islamic Republic of Iran. He was executed in 1988 and his grave
is in Khavaran. This interview was conducted in summer 2006 in Köln,
Germany.

FL: I would like to start by saluting the martyrs of the 1988 Massacre who
are buried in Khavaran and other mass gravesites. That place is so sacred
to me that for years I went there every Friday. But now we mothers are
not able to make it every week.

Do you want me to talk about Anoush's imprisonment in the Shah's
prisons?

---

1 The Persian version of this interview first appeared in *Baran* (the Persian quarterly
on culture, literature, history, and politics), 17–18, autumn 2007/winter 2008. We have
translated excerpts from this interview into English with the kind permission of Massood
Mafan (*Baran*) and Said Afshar.
2 Said Afshar, born in 1960, participated in the 1979 Revolution against the Shah's
dictatorship. Like many of his youth generation, he continued his political activism after
the 1979 Revolution and joined one of the revolutionary left-wing political organizations.
He was forced to flee Iran in 1984 after the widespread brutal crackdown by the IRI. He
has been living in Sweden since January 1985. In exile, he has continued his political
activism in different ways. He is one of the founders and managers/executives of the
independent and nonprofit Sweden-based Persian radio program *Hambastegi*, which
started its broadcasting in 1989.
3 See Nasser Mohajer, "The Mothers of Khavaran" (this volume).

SA: Yes.

FL: Well, he was imprisoned in 1971 in Qezel Qal'eh prison. That prison does not exist anymore. They arrested Anoush in the mountains, along with a number of his friends. He was not immediately tried and sentenced. He spent a year in prison... and was out for a year before they arrested him again. This time he was imprisoned for almost five years and was set free on January 21, 1979. I visited him more or less regularly during the time he was in the Shah's prison. There were difficulties then, too. Sometimes they would give us visitation times and sometimes not... Anoush was in Qasr prison for some time and later he was transferred to Evin.

SA: So why was Anoush freed soon before the 1979 Revolution?

FL: A number of mothers and I held a sit-in at the Ministry of Justice. We stayed there for two weeks until they set our kids free. They told us our children were *abad-shahi* (those condemned to prison indefinitely) and would never be set free. We asked, "What do you mean? We will stay here until you free our children." Then they told us, "If you don't go, we will throw you out of the window." Ms. Sanjari, God bless her soul, said, "Whatever you do, we're not moving from here." She was Khashayar Sanjari's mother, who had shared a safe house with my son.[4]

A bit later, Mr. Hedayat Matindaftari, Dr. Mossadegh's grandson and a prominent lawyer, came to the sit-in. He said, "I will also sit-in with you," and told the soldiers, "You are not allowed to set foot in here. This is the people's house and they have the right to sit-in here." Finally, they yielded to our demands and set our children free.

SA: How did you feel then?

FL: When I found out, I was very happy. There was an uproar in the hallway of the Ministry of Justice and the place soon became very crowded. You could hear rejoicing everywhere. All the mothers were ecstatic. We were told that the prisoners would be brought to the Ministry of Justice. In fact, they were carried on the shoulders of the masses that were on the street rallying for their freedom. Everyone was wearing a circle of flowers around their necks. At last, they were brought to the Ministry of Justice where we were sitting in. We all kissed each other and were very happy. We stayed there that night and the day after, and then we left for home.

---

4 The underground guerrillas in Iran in the 1970s lived in safe houses the locations of which nobody beyond the leadership of the group knew.

As we were getting close to our house, I noticed the street had been decorated with lights and flowers... On the street walls they had written slogans such as, "Hail to the parents who have given society such wonderful children," and other such sentiments. There was a feast and a celebration... I will never forget that joy... All the shopkeepers in our neighborhood knew us. Each one carried Anoush a few steps on their shoulders until we arrived home.

After he was freed, Anoushirvan and his friends in their Marxist political organization, the Organization of Iranian People's Feda'i Guerrillas (OIPFG) set up their headquarters at the Technical Department in the University of Tehran on Azar Sixteenth Street. I remember that [Ayatollah Khomeini] announced that Marxists had the right to freedom of speech, but unfortunately it didn't take long before the regime undermined their freedom and began attacking the youth again... One day a group of people raided the OIPFG headquarters and destroyed all the documents. Those of us who were there were also beaten. I remember, one day when I was visiting the headquarters along with some other mothers, a mob raided it and we were attacked with clubs as we were leaving. We shouted, "Why are you beating us?" They said, "You are the mothers of these communists..."

SA: Was Anoushirvan married at that time?

FL: A while before this period, Anoushirvan had married Mitra, a doctor. Their life together was very short. At that time, the war with Iraq had begun and some doctors, including Mitra, had left for the city of Khoramshahr [one of the frontlines of the war]. So Mitra was frequently moving between Tehran and Khoramshahr. One time, when she returned after three months, she was pregnant and Anoush was in hiding... I had no news from him. Mitra decided to live with me.

One day, when we went together to visit Ms. Targol—one of the mothers whose son, Houshang, had been killed by the Shah's regime—the house was under surveillance... Mitra was arrested by the Revolutionary Guards along with a group of visitors as they were leaving the house. A few days later, they were all set free except Mitra. She gave birth in prison.

SA: And all this time you hadn't received any news from Anoush?

FL: No news whatsoever. We didn't know that he had been arrested. We were under the impression that he was among a group of Feda'ian that left Iran in 1983. Whenever Mitra's mother went to visit her in prison,

I would go with her... First, we would go to Luna Park, which is next door to Evin prison, to get a visitor's identity card that we wore on our chest. I was not allowed to see Mitra, but her mother would inform me afterward that Mitra hadn't heard any news about Anoush either. Three years passed without any news from him.

One night the telephone rang and we were told that Anoush was alive and in Evin prison. This information came from the family of another political prisoner. Apparently, they had arrested him in 1985. I went to Evin a few times asking about Anoush, but they denied he was there and told me to check other prisons. I went to prisons in Isfahan, Mashhad, and Shiraz, but to no avail. Finally, I was called by the Revolutionary Guards asking if I was Anoush's mother. My heart sank. I replied, "Yes." The man passed the telephone to Anoush. Anoush's voice was very weak. I asked him where he was. He said, "I'm somewhere, still alive." He talked about ordinary things and asked about his sister and brothers and his wife. He said, "They say they will let you visit me." I asked, "What do you want me to bring you?" He said, "You have to ask them." That was all.

SA: When did you hear about Anoushirvan's execution?

FL: Iraq was bombing Tehran. In order to be safe, we had all left for my sister's villa in the north of Iran. I remember we were listening to the Toilers Radio.[5] They kept repeating: "Anoushirvan Lotfi's life is in danger. People, stand up and demonstrate!" They kept announcing that he had been sentenced to death. As soon as the bombing came to a halt, we went back to Tehran. When we got home, we saw that all the windows in the house were broken.

I have gathered that on Friday, May 26, 1987, they executed Anoush at five in the morning. I was cleaning up the house when Mohammad Partovi's mother came by. I realized that she was distressed. I asked, "What is it?" She said that newspapers were reporting that some OIPF Majority leaders had been executed. "God forbid!" I replied. Around two in the afternoon the doorbell rang. I opened the door and saw some of the mothers standing at the door, each with a rose in hand. I realized my Anoush was among the executed. They put their arms around me and we cried. I sat down and damned the murderers to hell. Then, I read the newspaper. They had written that three people had been executed. One,

---

5 Toilers Radio, a radio station based in Kabul, Afghanistan, was jointly run by the Tudeh Party and the OIPF from 1984 to 1990.

a person called Mohammad, remained unknown. The other two were Saiid Azarang and Anoushirvan Lotfi. The regime claimed they were terrorists, that they were giving arms to Iraq. I said, "Goddamn you! How could they give arms to Iraq from prison? What are they talking about?" That really burned me up inside and I wept. During the Shah's reign, Anoush and his friends were called saboteurs; now they were terrorists. Anoush had asked me not to wear black. He had asked me to wear white, which is the symbol of purity, and to put a red flower, the badge of the martyrs of freedom, on my dress.

SA: Had you talked about this issue when you visited him in prison?

FL: On my last visit, I saw tears in his eyes. I had never seen him so disturbed. I said, "Dear Anoush, you stood tall during the Shah's reign." He said, "I miss Mitra and Khatereh [his daughter]." I asked, "Didn't they let you see her?" He said, "No. A month ago, our friend Mahmood Zakipour was executed. Did you go to visit his family? What were they wearing?" I replied, "The same as everyone. They were in black." He said, "Mother, don't wear black for me." And, as I said, he insisted that I wear white. I said, "I hope you will be freed. You are resolute and strong."

When I went to visit the following Sunday, along with my son and brother-in-law, all the mothers held a red rose. I went in. An official there was passing around a collection plate to collect money from the visitors to give to their loved ones behind bars. I told the official I wanted to visit my son. He said, "He doesn't have visitation time." I asked, "Why?" He said, "Anoushirvan is dead. He is in the ground." I said, "I hope you die!" and smashed the collection plate. The shattered pieces flew into his face. The other mothers pulled me outside. Then the official touched my shoulder from behind and asked who I wanted to talk to. "Not with you, beast!" I told him. He said, "Haven't you read the newspaper?" I said, "No! I came to visit my son and you tell me you killed him! Why? What have all the people like Anoush done? They didn't struggle to depose the Shah for you to come and do what you're doing!" He said, "Such things don't concern me. There are other people responsible for these matters. You have to go ask *them*." I said, "I'm not leaving here until you give me Anoush's bag while it is still warm and smells like him and holds his clothes." He said, "You have to go to Evin prison."

When I came out, the mothers threw their flowers at my feet. An official there said, "Why are you making a scene?" Revolutionary Guards were called to harass and threaten me. The mothers yelled out, "Why are you doing this? This is a grieving mother! She came to visit her son and you told her that her son is dead."

My son and my brother-in-law then insisted that we go home, but I said I wanted to pick up Anoush's bag, and we went to Evin. A man sitting in front of the entrance said, "His belongings are in different wards." I said, "No, he was only in Ward 1." He said, "First we have to gather his things." I said, "He didn't have a truckful of things! He had a bag with four shirts in it! You have to give it to me today!" He said, "You're pressuring us. We can find where it is by next week." I said, "That's impossible!" I was getting loud and people who were leaving from their visitation came into the room. I said, "They killed my son and they don't want to give me his belongings!" The people began agitating along with me.

Then the guards called me and put a cream-colored bag in front of me. The bag contained two shirts and Anoush's medication. "Where is his will?" I asked. They said, "He didn't have one." I said, "It's impossible, especially for Anoush. He wasn't afraid of anything." The guard took out a piece of paper and tore off the top of it. Anoush had written, "Give my watch and my wedding ring to my wife. My mother has my permission to spend all the money I have on my child and the organization [OIPF (Majority)]. They had crossed out the word 'organization'." I said, "Why did you cross this out?" He said, "He did it himself." I said, "That's not possible—you did it!" He said, "Okay, either you take this, or I'll tear it up right now." I took it and left the room. It was in Anoush's own handwriting. I didn't want to lose his last will and testament. Then we went home.

SA: Did they ever give you the top part of the will that they had torn up?

FL: No. It was evident that he had written much more than that, but they never gave it to me. Only the three lines...

All our friends came by the house. They had placards with slogans on them and brought flowers. It was a big crowd. Many people, especially the mothers, came everyday for seven days. On the third day I went to Evin again and asked where Anoush was buried. I knew about Khavaran, where they had buried atheist prisoners, but I had never been there... An official told me, "We've buried him in a cemetery." Another one said, "No! We threw them in a ravine for the wolves to eat." I said, "Okay, we'll find him ourselves." The mothers gave me the address of Khavaran and we went there. I found an area covered with fresh earth. I asked the caretaker and the people working in the nearby Baha'i cemetery about it. They said, "One Friday morning they brought three corpses.

Someone had seen that one of them was wearing a checkered beige shirt." Earlier I had heard that that was what Anoush had on the last day he was seen in prison. People working in the Baha'i cemetery had also seen an ambulance come by and throw two or three bodies into a hole. My brother-in-law and my son asked me if I wanted to see his face. I said, "No, I just want to mark the place."

On another day we went there with a small shovel. It was three or four in the morning. I started shoveling. They had not buried the bodies very deep. His hand, along with parts of his shirt, was exposed. I knew it was him; I had bought the shirt for him myself. I said, "That's him!" and fainted.

SA: How did you find the strength to do such a thing?

FL: I just found an extraordinary power deep inside of me. I didn't know what I was doing. I had scratched the earth so much that all my nails were bleeding. After that, we went out to the car where we had already put the shovels. We noticed a patrol car approaching. They asked who we were and what we were doing there. My brother said, "We read in the newspaper that they had executed Anoushirvan Lotfi, so we came here." They said, "You are gravediggers! You came to dig and find his grave?" My brother said, "No, we weren't doing anything. His mother just wanted to feel the soil." They asked, "How did you know he was here?" My brother said we had gotten an indication from some official that he may be here. They threw us out. That's how we found out where Anoush was.

Later we heard that the Zarshenass and Zakipour families had also found their children in Khavaran. Then came the fortieth day [when Iranians hold a ceremony for their dead] of Anoush's death and we went to Khavaran and put flowers on his grave. Suddenly my sister cried out and pointed to a hand protruding from the ground. The graves were so shallow that an animal might have tried to unearth them... The mothers were crying and people were brushing the dirt away and someone with a camera took a picture. I saw the corpses of several young people. There was a young man shot in the forehead. Then, a patrol car came. We hid the camera. I believe these were the first series of photos that were taken of this site that reached the hands of those who needed them, even though such photos were also taken later by others.

From then on, each September 1 we would go to Khavaran to venerate our loved ones with *halva* [a special pastry served at internment and other ceremonial commemorations of the dead] and fill the site with flowers to make it a beautiful garden. Of course, the authorities would come and bother us, break car windows, beat us, and kick us out. After a few years, this harassment stopped, but in 2005 they began harassing us again. Time and again, they took our cameras and confiscated our cell phones and demanded to know why we were there.

SA: When the authorities announced that they wanted to rebuild Khavaran, what was your reaction?

FL: They wanted to destroy all the evidence of the executions and massacres so that no proof would be left. When the Special Representative of the UN Human Rights Commission, Reynaldo Galindo Pohl, came to Iran in the 1980s, we held a gathering in front of the UN office in Tehran to let him know of our plight, but we were assailed and chased away by the security forces. By that time, they had bulldozed Khavaran and made it look like a farm plot so that they could tell people like Galindo Pohl that no such burial ground existed. Later, they paved it over. Two to three years ago, an official who called himself Hassani came to Khavaran and told us that they wanted to rebuild the site and wanted a list of those who were buried there. He claimed they wanted to turn Khavaran into a formal cemetery. We, the bereaved families, decided to go to Behesht Zahra to find out for ourselves. The man in charge said, "We want to make Khavaran like Behesht Zahra for you." We said, "First, make a list of all the people who are buried in those canals, then build the place." He said, "Canals?" I said, "Yes, there are two canals on the left side and two canals on the right side." He said, "I never knew that there were canals there." I said, "Then, we will not allow it. Even if we have to burn ourselves alive in Khavaran, we won't let you."

SA: You, the mothers and wives of the martyrs of the 1980s, have struggled for years along with your children...

FL: In my opinion, the mothers, struggling along with their children, have achieved many things. They wanted to take Khavaran away from us, but we resisted and they had to retreat. But, well, we didn't succeed in expanding the movement as we wanted. The mothers have grown old; they are weak now and cannot be as active as they once were. The young people are busy with their schoolwork. The government stops the spread of any kind of protest from its very inception. There are many such reasons for both our successes and our failures.

SA: Do the mothers and the rest of the families of political prisoners keep in touch?

FL: Yes, there has always been a warm relationship among us. Since the Shah's time we have seen each other regularly. We talk to each other. We sing songs and celebrate anniversaries...

SA: Did you ever wish that Anoush would cooperate with the government or repent so that he might stay alive?

FL: Never, not at all. I am proud of Anoush. He loved his organization, the OIPF, and I loved *him*. I love all his friends' mothers. I will stay with them until my death. I would never have asked Anoush to repent in order to stay alive. Never. I'm proud of him. Anoush belongs to the people of Iran, not to me. He was my child, but he did not belong to me...

SA: Tell us about the people's reaction to these events.

FL: Those who are pro-Shah say it was our fault that the Shah's regime was overthrown and replaced with the Islamic regime. I remind them of the dictatorship under the Shah... and they ask me if it is better now. My answer is no, most things have become worse. But now people are more aware and they are interested in hearing me talk about the 1980s. I talk about all those who were executed. I have the courage to say that I have felt these realities with all my being... Of course, they have arrested me for a few days sometimes. They ask how we mothers came to know each other. I tell them it is because of *you*. You arrested our children and killed them. Only then did we mothers meet and become friends and comrades. Now I love them more than my own family.

SA: As a mother of one of the political prisoners executed in the 1980s, what would be your message?

FL: As a mother of a martyr, and on behalf of all the bereaved mothers, I say the following: stay united so we can do something positive for our country. After all the massacres and suffering, we should be united and active so that we can build a free and flourishing Iran. The middle and lower classes don't live comfortable lives... I was told that when Anoush was being taken for execution, he said that we must all be united, we are all killed by the same henchmen, and we are all of the same blood... When we are all struggling for the good of our people, we should not let differences and divisions about unimportant issues destroy our unity, our love, our struggle.

TRANSLATED FROM PERSIAN BY YASMIN JAYHOUN

A Note on Two Letters

NASSER MOHAJER

On December 12, 1988, Dr. Brigitte Behzadi, the spouse of Dr. Manouchehr Behzadi—who was executed in the Great Massacre of 1988—submitted a letter (written on December 10, 1988) to the editorial board of the East German weekly *Die Weltbühne*, expressing her anger and grief about this atrocity. The letter was not published, and the journal did not bother to inform its readers about the protagonists or the chronicle of this crime—the news of which had appeared on December 1 of that year in *Neues Deutschland*, the central organ of the Socialist Unity Party of what was then called the German Democratic Republic. After the political editor of *Neues Deutschland* declined to publish her (or any other) comment on the wave of executions in Iran, Dr. Behzadi stated her disappointment in her cover letter to the editor in chief of *Die Weltbühne*, Helmut Reinhardt:

> We are sad and furious that the comrades of the Tudeh Party, even now, won't get any appreciation, after the German Democratic Republic managed to avoid any public solidarity with the prisoners over the past six years. A whole communist leadership has been slaughtered, and there is nothing but silence here.

A couple of weeks after this complaint, on December 27, 1988, *Die Weltbühne* published an article by Stefan Parvis Töpelmann (see Chapter Five), the son of Dr. Ahmad Danesh, another victim of the Great Massacre. This article contains parts of a letter Dr. Danesh wrote to Ayatollah Montazeri on May 6, 1987.[6] In all probability, this further encouraged Dr. Behzadi to write a letter

---

6 The entire letter of Dr. Danesh to Ayatollah Montazeri appeared in *Nameh Mardom*, the central organ of the Tudeh Party of Iran (no. 211, June 14, 1988). The following is a summarized excerpt of the very last page of the four-page letter: "On April 27, at dawn, several armed young men attacked my house. After they created fear and intimidation

to the UN Commission on Human Rights in January 1989, appealing for an investigation into the Great Massacre in Iran. Though this letter, like many other petitions, did not lead to immediate action, Dr. Behzadi continued her efforts to expose the crime. Neither did it stop her from writing to the leading East German journals, especially to the editorial board of *Die Weltbühne*. On December 22, 1989, she wrote to them:

> I am starting to grasp the true reasons for the silence of the press concerning the events in Iran: it was about leaving undisturbed the transactions of arms deals... Now, I have to assume that these people who stood up for freedom, social justice and democracy in their country have been murdered with weapons from the GDR, and that the GDR and its elites even profited economically from this inhumane policy.

However, Helmut Reinhardt, the editor in chief of *Die Weltbühne*, responded, "You should, with all your bitterness, keep in mind that we all, including you, did not know anything about the dirty arms deals at the time."[7] This unpublished correspondence took place a month before the Special Representative of the UN Commission on Human Rights, Reynaldo Galindo Pohl, left for Iran. (The two unpublished letters by Dr. Behzadi have been translated from German and are included in the pages that follow.)

---

for my wife and two daughters and messed up the house, they blindfolded me and took me away. I was beaten up many times in prison for being falsely accused of touching my blindfold, even when I was asleep. I was denied any contact with anyone outside or my family. I had no visitation for over a year and a half. My phone contact was discontinued, and my family had no news of me for several months. Then, I was allowed to call my family for only a few minutes, blindfolded and under the supervision of a guard, every fortnight or sometimes every month. I received the worst political and honor defamation and spent two and a half years in solitary confinement or even worse conditions." Translated by Human Rights & Democracy. A project of the Abdorrahman Boroumand Center. "Memorial: Omid, a Memorial in Defense of Human Rights in Iran," available at www.iranrights. org/memorial/story/-7285/ahmad-danesh-shariat-panahi, accessed October 20, 2019.
7 For more details on East Germany's media coverage of Iran, including GDR–Iran relations between 1980 and 1989, see Edgar Klüsener, *How Did East Germany's Media Represent Iran between 1949 and 1989?*, PhD dissertation, University of Manchester (2014); see especially pp. 182–218.

Human Rights in Iran[8]

BRIGITTE BEHZADI

After nearly six years in prison under inhumane conditions, the victims of this torture have now been slaughtered in a bloodbath unprecedented in today's world. We are not talking about the history of fascism here, but of recent news from Iran, dated November 29, 1988.

Since February 1983, after a wave of imprisonments, thousands of political prisoners have been waiting for official charges, a fair trial, and the possibility to defend themselves. These people, who had nearly been forgotten behind high walls, mostly belonged to leftist, progressive groups and parties, among them progressive clergymen.

Beginning about November 25, 1988, relatives of a large number of prisoners received a short notification to come to the prison and collect the belongings of the executed. This is how they were informed of the death of their loved ones. We have no concrete information. Formal trials, promised earlier, never took place; court verdicts were not disclosed. No relative had been informed prior to the execution. The relatives were not able to bury the executed; they were not even informed where the corpses were interred. In the meantime, some loosely and carelessly buried corpses have been found on the outskirts of Tehran.

One of those murdered, Manouchehr Behzadi, lived in the German Democratic Republic from 1956 to 1979, having fled the Shah's regime in Iran. He had many friends here; he was interested in this country, its history and culture. He respected and especially appreciated the genuine fight of the German communists against fascism. During 25 years of exile, he never gave up hope of returning to Iran. How often he enthusiastically spoke to us about his homeland! When the revolution started in 1979, he didn't hesitate for one moment to [go back to Iran and] get involved, by whatever means

---

8 From the private archive of Dr. Brigitte Behzadi.

he had at his disposal. As editor in chief of *Nameh Mardom*, the organ of the communist Tudeh Party, he took on a responsible and difficult assignment. Soon, the newspaper increased its circulation. It was an important voice in the diversity of opinions regarding the debates about the revolution. It should be emphasized that the newspaper was legal, though time and again there were interruptions due to censorship.

After his imprisonment, we initially believed he would be quickly released. Later, we supposed that a due process ought to bring about an acquittal. Nothing of that sort happened. Our contact was extremely limited. We exchanged a small number of very short, strictly censored letters. Years went by. Sometimes we heard bitter rumors about the tightening of prison conditions or the execution of particular comrades. In July 1988, an entire group of prisoners were executed. We received a letter, written in August [1988]. After that, nothing at all. We were in an awful state of fear for his life, and for those of his friends and comrades. And then his brother got a call to come fetch his belongings, because he was dead.

We, his wife and his daughters, are full of grief, but also full of anger at the unscrupulous murderers who acted on behalf of a fascist regime. The Day of Human Rights goes by unnoticed in the current buzz surrounding the distribution of business contracts with Iran, without a public condemnation of this regime. We are deeply disappointed and disturbed by this international silence, as well as by the silence maintained by the brother parties which added up to the burden of these prison walls. Under a dark cloak of silence, people were murdered because of their political opposition to a dictatorial regime. It is not enough to commemorate the victims of the past; we also have to raise our voice against cruel torture and mass murder in the present.

The international public has to know about these inhumane atrocities in order to protest against them. Every voice counts! Perhaps lives can yet be saved.

Berlin, December 10, 1988

TRANSLATED FROM GERMAN BY LALE BEHZADI

To the UN Human Rights Commission

BRIGITTE BEHZADI

As someone who is distressed by the appalling crimes against humanity in Iran, I am turning to you with a request to shed light upon these crimes.

My husband, Dr. Manouchehr Behzadi, born in 1927, had to leave his homeland in 1955. He was politically persecuted by the Shah's regime because of his membership and political activity in the Tudeh Party of Iran, which was outlawed in 1949.

I met my future husband in 1965 in the German Democratic Republic, where he was in exile... We got married and had two daughters, Lale and Asita. Throughout the years of his exile, his greatest wish was to return to Iran. As an intellectual, and by his prolific writings, he contributed to the many political debates which ultimately led to the awakening of the Iranian people and the overthrow of the Shah's regime in 1979.

In 1979, we returned to Iran as a family. My husband became the editor in chief of the newspaper *Nameh Mardom* (The People). This newspaper, the organ of the Tudeh Party, was registered at the Ministry of Information and Guidance of the Islamic Republic of Iran, and as such my husband was recognized as editor in chief of the newspaper. Although *Nameh Mardom* was under the control of the Ministry of Information, and was occasionally not allowed to be published, it was regarded as a legal newspaper. Nevertheless, the government did nothing to stop extreme groups who attacked the newspaper building, occupied the editorial offices, and destroyed the archives [time and again]. My husband demanded a full investigation, which was never done. I realized that the government would not protect its citizens and respect their very basic rights. After a few similar and unsettling events, I and my two daughters left the country in 1982. My husband remained in Iran and, along with his comrades and colleagues, continued to publish the legal newspaper of the legal Tudeh Party, all the while complying with censorship regulations.

In February 1983, a sudden wave of arrests took off that to this day has never been explained. My husband, together with his colleagues from the editorial board and many of his comrades and friends, was arrested and imprisoned. We all believed that there would be a fair trial and that they all would be acquitted. But things turned out differently.

The families and friends of the prisoners were not informed about the charges. Their requests for information were rejected. My husband was once allowed to call his 80-year-old mother. After that, there was only silence again.

Eventually, I received a letter from him in which he asked me for a divorce so that my life would not be destroyed. This request, along with his grateful and affectionate memories of our life together, seemed to me to be a sign of utter hopelessness. Apparently, he no longer expected justice to be served, but instead believed he faced an undefined period of time in confinement.

After his brother got permission to visit him, he called and told me that my husband had some problems with his teeth, and therefore they had pulled them all out. To me, there was only one explanation: he had been beaten up and lost his teeth. In order to spare my feelings, his brother did not share any more details from his prison visits. He got permission to visit irregularly, sometimes twice a month, sometimes every few months; sometimes the visits were canceled on short notice.

During the visits, they were separated by a glass partition and could talk only via intercom (under supervision, of course). My brother-in-law is hearing impaired, so the contact was difficult. I never learned anything about the prison conditions, housing, nutrition, work, and so forth. The ten-minute visits were the most likely chance for my husband to get news about his family. We therefore tried to give him positive accounts of our situation. I forced myself to finish my PhD thesis and thus tried to demonstrate to him that I was strong and capable. I wrote to my brother-in-law about the upbringing of our children, about school, and about how we spent our holidays. He forwarded some of the details to my husband.

In the meantime, my husband was allowed to write letters from Evin prison. They too arrived sporadically; sometimes six months went by without a letter. The letters had to be written on special prison forms. These forms had seven lines on the front for my husband, and seven lines on the back for us. We were strictly ordered to write in Farsi only. During the five and a half years of his imprisonment, I received twenty-five letters from my husband.

The last one was dated August 1, 1988. It arrived in September 1988. In this letter, he congratulated my daughter Asita on her fourteenth birthday. (She had last seen him when she was seven years old.) There was no hint of a change in circumstance, no parting words. Throughout this time, his family in Tehran received no information about a hearing or court ruling.

On November 29, 1988, I got a phone call from my brother-in-law in Tehran: he had been asked to come to the prison. There, they gave him some of my husband's clothes and other personal belongings. They told him that my husband, Manouchehr Behzadi, was dead.

I could not believe or accept this message; therefore, on December 2, 1988, I went to the Embassy of the Islamic Republic of Iran in Berlin and requested information regarding the following points:

- the indictment against my husband
- conduct of the case, including his defense
- the verdict (content and justification)
- how the verdict was implemented (day and manner of execution)
- location of the gravesite.

To this day, four weeks after my inquiry, the embassy of the IRI has not responded to my query because the Ministry of Foreign Affairs had nothing to say. My relatives in Tehran were not given the corpse for burial, and they were not given any information about the grave's location.

My husband's fate is not a singular instance. Others have gone through the same sequence of events: imprisonment without legal procedure; evidence of torture and solitary confinement; and the absence of basic rights with regard to due process, court rulings, humane prison conditions, regular family contact, and so forth, till the unknown date of death in summer or fall 1988. Our friend, Amir Nikayin, suffered the same fate as my husband. He shared a house with us in Tehran, and his wife and children are equally shocked, bitter, and devastated. The same is true for another close friend of ours, Dr. Ahmad Danesh, whose daughters were friends with our daughters and studied in the same school. It probably applies to thousands of people.

I ask you as the United Nations Commission on Humans Rights to take up these homicidal crimes in Iran, to find out the truth and hold those responsible accountable, in order to prevent further crimes against humanity in Iran.

January 1989

TRANSLATED FROM GERMAN BY LALE BEHZADI

The Mothers of Khavaran:
A Unique Movement

NASSER MOHAJER[9]

WHO ARE THE MOTHERS OF KHAVARAN?

The "Mothers of Khavaran" is a term commonly used for bereaved Iranian women who turned to civic activism after the repressive forces of the Islamic Republic of Iran executed their sons, daughters, husbands, brothers, and sisters. The Mothers of Khavaran particularly refers to empowered women whose left-leaning sons, husbands, or fathers were killed in the Great Massacre of 1988. The children, husbands, and fathers of these women were mostly buried[10] at a location adjacent to Khavaran Road on the route connecting Tehran to Semnan–Mashhad.

ROAD MAP TO ANNIHILATION

The disillusionment of Iranian society's modern classes and strata with the Shi'ite fundamentalists, who seized the state apparatus right after the 1979 Revolution, rendered a strong momentum to the anti-theocracy

---

9 I express my sincere appreciation to Jafar Behkish for his meticulous presentation of details of the early stages of the Movement of the Mothers of Khavaran. I am also indebted to him for his careful reading of this study and invaluable suggestions. It goes without saying that all the shortcomings and probable flaws of this chapter fall on my shoulders only.

10 Khavaran Road is the main artery of the Khavaran district. "It starts from Khorasan Square and after joining Ahang Highway, it turns into the Khavaran Highway. Khavaran is a populated district with many narrow streets. After Khavaran Highway crosses Afsarieh Square (Basij Mostaz'afin Square), its name changes to Imam Reza Highway." *Atlas-e Kamel-e Tehran*, 2006, p. 182.

and pro-democracy political groups.[11] Hence, sometime in spring 1981, Ayatollah Khomeini authorized his forces of repression to devise a road map to annihilate the adamant opponents of his Islamic fundamentalist rule. Following Ayatollah Khomeini's directive, the forces of repression (the Ministry of Intelligence, Revolutionary Guards, Kommittehs, *Basiji* Militias, and so forth) planned the "final attack." Their step-by-step plan was to first eliminate the "actually hostile groups" (e.g., the Democratic Party of Iranian Kurdistan, Kumeleh, Peykar, Organization of Iranian People's Feda'i Guerrillas—independent faction) and then exterminate the "potentially hostile groups" (e.g., the People's Mojahedin Organization of Iran, People's Feda'i Guerrillas—Majority faction, Razmandegan, Arman-e Mostaz'afin, Rah-e Kargar).[12] To this end, they had to provide an exclusive cemetery for thousands and thousands of "pagans," "apostates," and "infidels" who had to be annihilated.[13]

The rundown of the consultative session on June 3, 1981, called by Prime Minister Mohammad Ali Rajai, and attended by a number of his ministers, as well as Tehran's mayor and a few experts on urban planning, was as follows:

> A third of the meeting time was allocated (on where) to build a separate cemetery for the infidels. One of the proposed sites was south of Farahabad garrison where the cemetery for Jews and Armenians had been located. At the end, the mayor was assigned [with the task] to promptly designate a site for the cemetery, wherever he deems appropriate.[14]

There was a religious justification behind the selection of this barren land (130 by 120 meters) in Khatounabad, on Khorasan Road, 14 kilometers from

---

11 "Modern classes and strata" refers to classes and social forces (i.e., blue- and white-collar workers, university students, lawyers, secular intellectuals, doctors, engineers, artists, and so forth) that emerge and develop with capitalism and industrialization. It is noteworthy that the social bases of Ayatollah Khomeini consisted of the following: traditional merchants; bazaar employees; clergy, seminarians, and all who work in religious institutions; the peasants or uprooted peasants driven from their land living in shanty towns and poverty belts around big cities; traditional craftsmen; and salesmen.

12 See Appendix B.

13 *Kar*, Organization of Iranian People's Feda'i Guerrillas – Minority, 112, June 3, 1981, disclosure of a document concerning the suppression of political organizations and groups.

14 Ibid., special edition 4, vol. 3, June 29, 1981.

Tehran, which is said to have been a cemetery years ago.[15] This area became a cemetery for non-Muslims after the construction of Beheshtieh Jewish cemetery in 1936,[16] followed by the establishment of an Armenian cemetery and later by an Indian cemetery (where a number of Indian soldiers of the British Army killed in the First and Second World Wars were buried).[17] As such, the authorities and functionaries of the Islamic Republic of Iran (IRI) concluded that all who did not belong to the community of Muslims, and were considered to be "infidels," would have to be interred in "pagan lands" or "damned lands."

"CEMETERY OF THE DAMNED"

We do not exactly know the identity of the first dissidents buried in this barren land, but we do know that the establishment of this cemetery was an impetus for the "final attack," which began right after the crackdown on the peaceful demonstration of hundreds of thousands of Tehran residents on June 20, 1981. That was when Abolhassan Banisadr was deposed from the presidency of the IRI.[18] We also know that a number of dissidents, who were executed at dusk on June 20, were buried in Khavaran. The prison officials

---

15 "Before the 1920s, there were four or five public cemeteries in: ...Seyyid Malek Khatoun and Emamzadeh Golzard (southeast of Khorasan Road)..." Jafar Shahri, *Social History of Tehran in the 13th Century* (Tehran: Resa Cultural Institution, 1990), 2nd edition, vol. 1, p. 443.

16 One of the most outstanding Iranian Jewish architects, Jahangir Banaian, writes: "The fourth cemetery on Khorasan Road was situated between the Muslim and Baha'i cemeteries. [The 'Muslim cemetery' is Mesgarabad cemetery, which was founded in 1944 and closed in 1964. *Ettela'at*, August 1, 1964]. The land of this cemetery was purchased in 1932, and its central building was designed by a Jewish architect named Bedanski who had deserted from the armed forces during World War II... Three years before the Iranian Revolution of 1979, the government exerted pressure on the Jewish society of Tehran and forbid them to bury their dead in this cemetery." Jahangir Banaian, *Iranian Jews in Contemporary History: Oral History of the Iranian Jews*, 1st edition (California: Center for Iranian Jewish Oral History, 1996), p. 235.

17 "In Memory of the Indian Soldiers in Iran," BBC Persian, October 27, 2005.

18 "In July 1981, 15 members of the Peykar Organization were arrested in an underground printing house in Tehran and were tried and executed within two days. In fact, Khavaran cemetery was inaugurated with the burial of these prisoners. The corpses of none of the fifteen were given to their families. They were buried in shallow graves, unwashed, still having on the bloody clothes in which they were executed... On each grave, there was a pink piece of cardboard with the identification of the grave written in pencil, for example: Row 60, number 15, executed on July 12th 1981..." Arash Okhovat, asar.name/1980/01/ezzat-arash-okhovat.htm, accessed October 4, 2019. Editor's note: The date July 12 is not correct—it was July 22 (according to *Peykar*, 116, August 31, 1981, p. 5).

handed over the corpses to their families, who later buried them in Tehran's major cemetery, Behesht Zahra. However, the corpses were stolen in the middle of the night and taken to Khavaran, now called the "Cemetery of the Damned" by the officials of the IRI. Even though they were apprehended and tortured long before that date,[19] these well-known opponents of the IRI were falsely accused of being "the perpetrators of the June 20 confrontation."[20]

The official report of the "Behesht Zahra Foundation" of Tehran's municipality to "the Honorable Prosecutor of Tehran" delineates the will of the paramount leaders of the IRI to separate the pious from the infidel and bury the infidel in the "damned land." The plan was ratified in that very session of Prime Minister Rajai with his ministers on June 3, 1981:

> Hence, as stipulated per correspondences no 0/1310/30 dated June 27 1981 (6/4/60 Iranian year), and no 30/1319 dated June 30 1981 (9/4/60), [of which] the copies are attached, the ordinance issued, that the bodies of the individuals Manouchehr Oveisi, Alireza Rahmani, Qassem Golshan, Mohsen Fazel, Saeed Soltanpour and Taqi Shahram, buried on July 28, 1980, must be exhumed and be reburied in the infidel cemetery, which would be established on the order of [his Excellency] the new mayor. Therefore, to carry this out, it is requested to issue a written order to comply with the ordinances.[21]

It is noteworthy that before Taqi Shahram's exhumation, his gravestone was repeatedly broken and destroyed, as he was perceived as a traitor to Islam.[22]

EXECUTIONS, COVERT BURIALS, DETERMINED FAMILIES

After the crackdown of June 20, 1981, the IRI's policy of catch, arrest, and kill kicked into high gear. The Revolutionary Guards went after the former

---

19 Mahnaz Matin and Nasser Mohajer, "And They Furrowed Such a Boundless Cemetery," *Arash*, 77–78, 2001, p. 32.

20 Matin and Mohajer, p. 32.

21 The letter is signed by Ahmad Birjani, director of Behesht Zahra Foundation. For the original letter in Persian see *At War with Humanity* (People's Mojahedin Organization of Iran, 1982), p. 160.

22 Taqi Shahram (1947–80) was a veteran of the People's Mojahedin Organization of Iran who led that organization in 1974 to adopt Marxism–Leninism. After the downfall of the Shah in February 1979, Shahram was arrested and imprisoned by the Revolutionary Guards, underwent cruel treatment, and was condemned to death in a kangaroo court and executed by firing squad on July 24, 1980.

political prisoners of the Shah's regime to eliminate all "potential danger." In the space of a year, thousands of young women and men were accused of being sympathizers of this or that opposition group or for possessing "subversive leaflets and periodicals" or carrying knives and sharp objects, and were subsequently executed, most often without due process. The bodies of the executed were not often given to their families, but instead were buried covertly. They would bury the dead Mojahedin and sympathizers of other Islamist opposition groups in the Behesht Zahra cemetery, and most of the leftist prisoners in Khavaran. The prison officials did not even deem it necessary to inform the families of the executed about the burial place of their loved ones:

> To obtain some news [about their loved ones], the families would gather at the prison's gate. These gatherings... had transformed into a focal point [for the families] to recount [their] information, angst, and desolation. Mostly women; mothers, sisters, and wives... they would gather at six o'clock in the morning at the previous location of Luna Park, or at the prisons of Qasr and Gohardasht... they'd exchange direful news of the executions. Some were sobbing. As yet, no [official] outlet was set up to look into the appeals by the families. The only information that would sporadically come out of prisons was [prisoners'] handwritten personal wills which were handed to families. That was a strange feeling. Pain, anxiety, trepidation, and more trepidation. Having achieved anything, at noon, like a defeated army, they would be heading home to restart anew the next day; a new beginning with no end in sight.[23]

This is how the families of the prisoners became acquainted with one another. A feeling of trust and reliance developed during these trying times, and their common pain made them empathize with and help one another. They would assist and support families who were having a hard time making ends meet, as the breadwinners of the families were in prison or had been executed. Gradually a bond was formed that could not be easily broken.

---

23 The speech, on the anniversary of the 1988 executions, given by Mihan Rusta in Köln and Stockholm in September 2002 was organized by the Association of Iranian Political Prisoners in exile. This unpublished paper addresses the effects of torture and execution on the families of political prisoners.

On November 23, 1981, Yadollah Sepehr, who was executed in Evin prison for being a Baha'i, was buried in Khavaran.[24] This paved the way for burying eight other executed Baha'i members of the Second National Assembly on December 27, 1981, and seven members of the Tehran Assembly on January 3, 1982.[25] After closing down and then destroying the Golestan Javid Baha'i cemetery in Tehran early in 1982, the northwest section of Khavaran was allotted to the Baha'is who were either exterminated by order of the IRI officials or died of natural causes.[26]

In 1983, the repressive forces of the IRI attacked those political organizations and groups who were designated as "potentially hostile."[27] Although the wave of executions had slowed down, it did not stop. The bodies of the executed leftist political prisoners were still taken to Khavaran. It was a cemetery like no other; a wasteland with no water so that nothing would grow, and no gravestones so that no graves could be discerned. In spite of this, the families would place flowers or plants here and there and would irrigate the land occasionally:

> They would put symbolic gravestones in certain places. It is said that two or three families had erected gravestones as they had somehow found out where their executed loved ones had been buried. In addition to these gravestones, at times, some flowers and trees could be seen which would eventually die due to lack of water.[28]

---

24 Mahmehr Golestaneh, *Flights and Memories* (Texas: Supreme Co., 1992), p. 93.

25 The members of the second national Baha'i assembly were as follows: Jinus Mahmoudi (Ne'mat), Mehdi Amin, Dr. Ghodratollah Rohani, Dr. Cyrus Roshani, Kamran Samimi, Jalal Azizi, Dr. Ezatollah Foruhi Borujani, and Dr. Mahmoud Majzoub. The members of the Tehran assembly were: Shiva Assadollahzadeh, Shidrokh Amir Kia Bagha, Kourosh Talai, Eskandar Azizi, Fathollah Ferdowsi, and Ata'u'llah Bavari. Golestaneh, *Flights and Memories*, pp. 94–108.

26 "This inhumane action took place in Tehran during Mr. Rafsanjani's presidency. Golestan Javid Baha'is cemetery which was located on the actual Farhangsara-ye Khavaran, was excavated and all the bodies of the Baha'is which were buried there from 1935 until 1981, were exhumed and taken to an unknown place. The Baha'is appeals demanding justice went nowhere and the Iranian government allowed itself to exhume many bodies which had been buried for less than ten years, although according to Islamic Sharia, one is only allowed to exhume a body after thirty years of burial. The former Baha'i cemetery was alongside the Jewish cemetery, but only the Baha'i portion was excavated." "Sarvha va Sarvaghdan," January 23, 2009, available at https://news.persian-bahai.org/story/75, accessed November 6, 2019.

27 "Preface," in *Kar*, Organization of Iranian People's Feda'i Guerrillas – Minority, 112, June 3, 1981.

28 "Khavaran Cemetery: The Unknown Tombs of the Executed," BBC Persian, September 1, 2005.

Throughout this period, families would gather and go to prisons with one another, the General Auditors Agency, Ayatollah Mortazavi's office, the High Judiciary Council, Red Cross offices, and the United Nations bureau in Tehran to ensure that their loved ones would not be deprived of the most basic of rights. Jafar Behkish attests:

> Due to lawlessness and backwardness of the judicial system in [the Islamic Republic of] Iran, Prisoners are not entitled to any rights, and in contrast to countries with modern judiciary systems, there are no attorneys. A prisoner is not kept at a specific location, nor is the time of the arrest specified or lawful. The prisoners are not made aware of the charges against them, nor are they permitted to defend themselves.[29]

Behkish continues:

> Thus, many of these duties were undertaken by the families themselves. Families had to visit the prison in person to obtain information about their [relatives'] cases. A family had to resort to a thousand of ploys and endeavors to uphold the basic rights of prisoners: proper food and clothing, as well as adequate space. The essence of the struggle of the families of "prisoners of conscience" were much more different from the activities for which their loved ones were captured. These struggles were for the release of prisoners, or their entitlement to rights that are recognized for the incarcerated in the domestic laws and/ or the international conventions. Hence, they are within the general framework of struggles for human rights, and epitomize a shining light in the history of such struggles.[30]

A turning point in this struggle was in August 1987, when the political prisoners in Gohardasht launched a hunger strike "protesting torture and poor sanitary conditions."[31] Many of the prisoners' families, who were concerned about the conditions of their loved ones, launched a campaign in solidarity with the hunger strike and shed light on their plight. "They visited the

---

29 Jafar Behkish, "A Glance at the Struggle of Political Prisoners in the 1980s," available at Bidaran.com, accessed October 8, 2019.
30 Ibid.
31 Ibid.

authorities and appealed for the review of the prisoners' demands..."[32] A month later, when Javier Pérez de Cuéllar, then secretary-general of the United Nations, visited Iran, 300 members of the political prisoners' families tried to present their case to him. However, the IRI's security forces led by the Revolutionary Guards not only closed the street to the United Nations' bureau, but also harassed and intimidated the families and did not permit them to see the secretary-general.[33]

In April 1988, three months before the great massacre, some eighty members of the political prisoners' families wrote a letter to United Nations Commission on Human Rights which read:

It has been years that our loved ones have been the prisoners of the Islamic republic regime. We, the families of political prisoners, have voiced our protestation again and again, verbally or in writing and through frequent visits. We have remonstrated against the unlawful and inhumane measures of judiciary and its associated organs, and it is not conceivable that the government authorities have not heard our protestations, lamentations, appeals and outcries for justice. Nor [is it conceivable that the authorities] are not aware of the way in which our loved ones have been treated in the prisons of the Islamic Republic of Iran. One clear example of the authorities' unlawful acts is to hold the prisoners in captivity past the end of their sentences. Presently, hundreds of prisoners who completed their sentences months or years ago, remain imprisoned and subject to torture, harassment, food deprivation, humiliation, and... solely because they refuse to submit to staged interviews or because they still adhere to their beliefs. The authorities' response has been limited to recounting this medieval phrase: 'these prisoners are like garbanzo beans, until they are well done and soft, they can't be taken out of the pot.' And since the Supreme Judicial Council sanctions these injustices, and no action is taken to thwart such inhumane practices, the number of prisoners who have served their sentences and are still in prison, is constantly on the rise. Once again, we voice our aversion and inquietude with regard to the inhumane practices of the authorities and those running the prisons of the Islamic Republic of Iran... We demand unconditional release of

---

32 Ibid.
33 Ibid.

all political prisoners especially those who have already served their sentences.[34]

The families of political prisoners had reason to be apprehensive. The escalation of social tensions, which was accompanied by the assertive attitude of the masses, worrisome rumors about prisoners and their possible execution,[35] international diplomatic maneuverings, the worsening situation of IRI armed forces in the face of the Iraqi Army, and the increasing number of military operations by Mojahedin Khalq (PMOI) along Iran–Iraq borders, was a notable development.[36] The summary executions on June 26, 1988, of Anoushirvan Lotfi, a leading member of the Feda'ian Organization (Majority), Hojat Mohammadpour, a member of the Union of Iranian Communists, and Hojatollah Ma'boudi, a member of Mojahedin Khalq—and their secret burial in a mass grave in Khavaran[37]—followed by the killing on July 20 of two

---

34 Ibid.

35 *Kar*, Organization of Iranian People's Feda'i Guerrillas – Majority, 49, March 20, 1988, "According to the news leaking out of the dungeons of the regime, around 70 political prisoners are in danger of being executed and their lives are in real danger. In order to create an atmosphere of terror and anxiety in prisons, Khomeini's guards subjected a group of the most resistant prisoners to a re-trial and their sentences were to be reviewed in unjust religious courts. The political prisoners who had served a number of years in prison were tortured again and pressured to do television interviews, denounce their political activities, and condemn their ideals and political beliefs. A number of combatant political prisoners, who had been incarcerated for years without being charged, were kept in the dark and felt the hangman's noose tightening around their necks every minute. The terrible prison conditions—lack of hygiene, medicine and food—showed the inhumanity of the Islamic Republic. According to the whim of the jailers, some family visits were canceled and postponed indefinitely. In an interview on January 7, 1988, Moghtadaie, Speaker of the High Judiciary Council, announced that 'the political prisoners, who did not repent and were not affected by imprisonment, would not be set free.' Only if the prisoners wrote a 'renunciation' form which was provided by the Ministry of Intelligence, did they have a slight chance at freedom. In the same interview, Moghtadaie shamelessly told the families of the political prisoners: 'Instead of writing letters and meeting authorities, you should try to convince your children to change and repent and try to gain the trust of the guards'."

36 "Why did the Islamic Republic Accept the Ceasefire?" Special Issue of *Aghazi-No*, Paris, August/September 1988.

37 Forough Tajbakhsh (Mother Lotfi) revealed that Mohammadi and Saiid Azarang were executed along with Anoushirvan Lotfi on May 27, 1988. However, *Kar* (Majority) 53, June 22, 1988, quoted Amnesty International's report (August 18, 1988) which named Hojat Mohammadpour and Hojatollah Ma'boudi the two individuals who were executed along with Lotfi (Iraj Mesdaghi, *Neither Life nor Death*, vol. 3, Alfabet Maxima, Kista, Sweden, 1983, p. 102). On the other hand, Feda'ian Khalq Organization (Majority), Tudeh Party, and Efat Mahbaz confirmed that Saiid Azarang was executed on July 20 in *Kar* (Majority), 54, July/August 1988. *Tudeh Martyrs* (Germany: Tudeh Party Publications, 2002), 1st edition, pp. 83–4; and in Efat Mahbaz, *Do Not Forget Me* (Sweden: Baran Publications, 2008), p. 342.

prominent cadres, Saiid Azarang and Kiumars Zarshenas, of the Tudeh Party, and Faramarz Sufi of Feda'ian (Majority), Rahim Hatefi of the Communist Party of Iran, and three other imprisoned activists, were preludes to the Great Massacre.[38]

CEASEFIRE

The acceptance of UN Security Council resolution 598 by the IRI on July 17, 1988, and the ceasefire between Iran and Iraq, took a heavy toll on political prisoners across Iran. Evidence strongly suggests that the IRI had planned an all-out purge of political prisoners months before the ceasefire.[39] Moreover, in the face of anticipated mounting pressure from the population for basic cultural, political, and social rights that were curtailed under the exigencies of war, certain concessions were unavoidable, including the amelioration of the condition of political prisoners and the release of those who had served their sentences. Furthermore, a direct consequence of accepting the UN Security Council resolution was the de facto recognition of the international community and its conventions, including standards of human rights and external scrutiny of prison conditions. All this was probably a factor leading Ayatollah Khomeini and his confidantes to consider the "cleansing of prisons as an urgent matter and a precautionary step in confronting the new political circumstances."[40] In the speech given by Ayatollah Khomeini on July 21, he likened the acceptance of the UN Security Council resolution to drinking from a chalice of poison.

SHAM PROMISES AND DECEITFUL WORDS

Four days after Ayatollah Khomeini's speech and eight days after the acceptance of UN Security Council resolution 598, on July 25, international

---

38 *Communist Party of Iran*, 46 and 47, November/December 1988, announced Rahim Hatefi's execution on July 19.

The central committee of the Feda'ian Khalq Organization (Majority) wrote on July 21, 1988, "The unjust courts of the regime have admitted the execution of 55 courageous children of our country who were in the dungeons of the Islamic Republic. The lives of your children are in danger. Khomeini's criminal regime wants to kill all the political prisoners secretly."

39 See Chapter One, "The Great Massacre," and, in Chapter Two, "This Is a Warning: We Plan to Kill You" in this volume.

40 Ibid.

news agencies reported the armed incursion of the Iraqi-based Mojahedin Khalq forces into the western regions of Iran. Their National Liberation Army (NLA) was to exploit the chaotic circumstances and the deteriorating conditions of what they characterized as the "disheartened army" to overthrow the "Khomeini regime." For three days the political atmosphere of the country remained in the shadow of this military adventure. After three days of combat, the Mojahedin forces were crushed by the combined armed forces of the IRI; 1,263 Mojahedin militants were killed, and a substantial number of NLA combatants were captured by the IRI armed forces.

The ensuing propaganda against the "armed *Monafeqin*" (hypocrites) and the "treacherous mercenaries" tormented the families of the political prisoners more than ever. Suddenly everyone knew that the government was planning a reprisal—vengeance on the *Monafeqin* and the die-hard "enemies of the Islamic Republic." The collective action of the families was expected. They went to Luna Park, to prison gates, and later assembled for a sit-in in front of the Islamic Parliament. When the Revolutionary Guards forced them to leave, on August 17, they went to the Ministry of Justice. Here is a brief description of their collective action:

> On this day, after several hours of a sit-in protest and demands, to which judicial authorities paid no attention, the families appealed to other families of political prisoners to join them the next day to continue their sit-in protest. On Thursday, August 18, at 8 a.m., this remarkable sit-in began with the massive presence of some 600 people... The courageous and persistent endeavors of the anguished families, who tried all day to enter the offices and bureaus of the colossal Islamic Ministry of injustice and press the officials to respond to their demands, was stifled and dispensed with by the end of working hours, and the families had to end their sit-in at 11 p.m. only to resume it on Saturday, August 20. At 8 a.m. on Saturday, August 27, once again the space in front of the Ministry of Justice and its vicinity was packed with the concerned families of prisoners who were demanding visitations with their dear-ones in captivity. A group of families representing the protesters in the sit-in entered the Ministry, and after an hour of negotiations, eventually, Borujerdi, Member of High Council of Justice, appeared in front of the protestors addressing them that in a week or two, visitation of the prisoners at Gohardasht prison would be resumed, but visiting

Evin's prisoners is not yet permitted. Upon receiving this news, the families ended their three-day sit-in.[41]

We have since realized that the plan was to liquidate prisoners in Gohardasht in two weeks and then do the same in Evin, but the families were entirely unaware of what was being concocted and were apprehensive about the fate of their loved ones, especially those incarcerated in Evin. Hence, a few days after the sit-in, a group of them went to the Prime Minister's office. Again, the authorities sent them home with sham promises and deceitful words. The authorities even assured some of the families that their loved ones soon would be released in a "general amnesty."[42] To those families who were under the impression that visitations were canceled because their loved ones were on strike, the authorities would say: "Don't be scared, they are not on strike. We have taken care of things in such a way that they can never go on strike again!"[43] Visitations had been canceled,

Nonetheless, they were taking money and clothes from the families. It was revealed later that some of the prisoners, under whose names money and clothes had been received, were amongst those executed. (It is difficult to fully grasp the emotional seesaw that the families experienced. First, there were false hopes cultivated by the authorities when they were taking money from the families, and then the tremendous blow and shock the bereaved families had to undergo once they were informed about the execution of their loved ones.)[44] The families of leftist prisoners were also told in the Prime Minister's office that if their son or daughter "is not a Mojahed, you should not be worried." The IRI officials were spreading such lies right at the time when they had completed the execution of Mojahedin and were preparing themselves for the execution of the left-leaning men.[45]

---

41 *Rah-e Kargar*, 55, September/October 1988.
42 *Kar* (Majority), 61, February 20, 1989, p. 11.
43 Ibid.
44 Mihan Rusta (from a confidential source). Mihan Rusta is a feminist and human rights activist who fled Iran with her one-year-old son in 1982, after her husband, Reza Ismati, was arrested. Ismati was executed in the Great Massacre of 1988. Rusta works with the Iranian Women's Studies Foundation and was on the editorial board of the Bidaran website (www.bidaran.net), which endeavors to shed light on the IRI's crimes against dissidents and prisoners of conscience.
45 Ibid.

The families would do whatever they could to find out the fate of their children, spouses, mothers, and fathers. They wrote petitions, collected signatures, and went to the General Inspection Office.[46] They also wrote an open letter to the then secretary-general of the United Nations, Peréz de Cuéllar, and pleaded,

> leverage your influence and credibility in international assemblies and in the Security Council to save the lives of thousands of political prisoners who because of their beliefs have been locked up in the medieval dungeons of Iran, from north to south and from east to west. Since July 28, 1988, concurrent with the mass executions in prisons, prosecutors of the Islamic Republic have suspended all visitations and any sort of contact or communication between prisoners and their families. Mr. Secretary-General, we plead with you to oblige the Islamic Republic regime to immediately:
>
> 1. Stop the execution of the prisoners.
> 2. Reinstate visitations and communications between the prisoners and their families as well as the outside world.
> 3. Free the prisoners who have served their sentences and are still in prison only because of their refusal to participate in staged press conferences and interviews.[47]

The families did not stop there. Some even went to the abodes of Ayatollah Khomeini, Ayatollah Montazeri, and Ayatollah Mar'ashi Najafi.[48] All this

---

46 Accordingly, "on August 18 and 20, 1988, a copy of a protest statement signed by 730 members of the families was sent to the International Committee for Defense of Political Prisoners (connected to United Nations in Iran)." *Rah-e Kargar*, 55, September/October 1988, p. 22.

47 *Nameh Mardom, Tudeh Party*, 221, August 30, 1988. According to this weekly journal, the open letter written to the secretary-general of the UN "was sent by a huge number of the families of political prisoners who were imprisoned in Evin, cell numbers 1, 2, 3 and 4 (upstairs and downstairs), cell 3/5 Jahad, halls 6, 5, and 1, in Gohardasht prison cells 1 to 12, and prisons in Rasht, Isfahan, Hamedan, Tabriz, Khoramabad, Shiraz..."

48 *Islamic Revolution Journal* (in exile), 185, September 1988, wrote: "They have executed a great number of prisoners in Tehran and other cities. The reason given by the executioners was that prisoners in Evin prison had revolted...! The families of the prisoners went to Ayatollah Mar'ashi in Qom. He calls Montazeri and asks him to interfere and prevent the executions. Montazeri calls the Prosecutor General and hears from him that this is the command of Imam [Khomeini] to finish them off."

paved the way for Ayatollah Montazeri's intervention and his three protest letters to Ayatollah Khomeini and members of his designated commission of the inquisition tribunals.[49] For months to come, the contents of these letters were concealed from the public eye, and people did not realize that Ayatollah Khomeini—immediately after "drinking from the chalice of poison"—covertly commanded the massacre of "the counter-revolutionaries, especially the hypocrites (Mojahedin.)"[50]

"YOUR IMPRISONED RELATIVE HAS BEEN EXECUTED"

From the news leaking out of the prisons, some Persian periodicals and Iranian political organizations in exile concluded that a catastrophe was in the making. *Kar*, the monthly publication of the Feda'ian Khalq Organization (Minority), reported the following in its August issue:

> During the past month, the henchmen of the Islamic Republic have launched a new wave of mass executions in prisons. On July 20, seven political prisoners were handed over to a firing squad. Death sentences of dozens have been confirmed by the unjust courts of the regime. All visitations of the political prisoners by their families have been canceled until September, and the henchmen, in response to the families' protestations, shamelessly and hideously declared that: "We are busy cleansing the prisons."[51]

The headline of the August 1, 1988, issue of *Nameh Mardom*, Central Organ of the Tudeh Party, read: "What do they mean by cleansing?" It went on:

> The Islamic Republic prison guards' assertions to the families who insist upon seeing their loved ones insinuate a bloodbath. They said "right now it's not possible, we are cleaning house..." Here and there, the news of a bloody disaster taking place in the prisons leaks out... Mousavi Ardebili's Friday prayer speech on August 5 adds to the suspicion. "... Today, the judicial system is under the pressure of

---

49 See Appendix A, "Theocracy Memos."
50 The term "anti-revolutionaries, especially the hypocrites (Mojahedin)" is taken from Ayatollah Khomeini's message to Ayatollah Montazeri on August 6, 1988. *The Memoirs of Ayatollah Montazeri* (Union of Iranian Editors in Europe, 2001).
51 *Kar* (Minority), 224, August 1988, p. 30.

public opinion. People are asking the courts: Why are the hypocrites (Mojahedin) being taken to court; why aren't they being executed?" It is obvious that what Mousavi Ardebili means—but dares not to say—is that they are arbitrarily executing not only the Mojahedin but also those steadfast political prisoners who continue to oppose the regime... The head of the country's judiciary, by resorting to lies about the pressure of the "general public" and "public opinion," is in fact preparing the ground for the arbitrary executions and deaths under torture, which have secretly taken place but not yet been made public. The looming danger that hangs over the fate of those whose lives are at great risk has placed the families of political prisoners into great anguish and anxiety."[52]

Based on the above facts and analysis, the Tudeh Party warned: "The campaign to save the lives of our political prisoners must be considered as one of the most important battlegrounds against the regime of *velayat-e faqih*."[53]

The September edition of the *Enghelabe Eslami* (in exile) revealed: "According to the information we have received on August 17 and 18 [1988] Khomeini's barbaric regime has... executed a large group of [people]."[54] The October edition of the same journal reported that "the number of the executed exceeds 2,500 people."[55] It was only by the end of November and beginning of December that the dimensions of this national tragedy became apparent to the families. Mother Riahi remembers:

> One day I'd go to Evin, another day to Qezel Hesar. They would tell us "There are no visits." Then, in November, we all went to Evin. They asked for our phone numbers. We said, "We have already given them to you." The same day, they informed us that they had executed our kids. All the seventeen Kommittehs of Tehran were handing over belongings of our dear ones. Such an inferno it was.[56]

---

52 *Nameh Mardom*, Tudeh Party, 221, August 23, 1988.
53 Ibid.
54 *Enghelabe Eslami* (in exile), 184, August 29 to September 11, 1988.
55 Ibid., 187, October 10 to 23, 1988. In this edition, for the first time it is disclosed that Ayatollah Montazeri has written a letter of protest to Ayatollah Khomeini. Excerpts of the Ayatollah Montazeri's letter accompanies the news.
56 Mother Riahi video interview, 2007.

Ms. Saberi also attests:

> On November 19, 1988, I received two bags with my husband's personal belongings from my father-in-law... I saw how the parents were devastated. I smelled death. I felt the depth of the calamity... and heard the breaking of hearts.[57]

Fariba Kaviani writes:

> No! No! I did not want to believe the truth. I was not officially informed yet. I had to wait. I was fighting with myself every day and was drowning in doubt and uncertainty. Finally, it was my turn. They called my sister-in-law from Evin and told her that a male member of the family should go to the prison at three o'clock on December 5. When I heard this, I packed immediately and left for Tehran along with my son. Now it was my turn.[58]

Jafar Behkish confirms: "The families were not informed until November. It was only then that the names of a large number of executed prisoners were released to their families..."[59] How? Rah-e Kargar Organization reports:

> The criminal regime of the Islamic Republic, who has executed thousands of steadfast political prisoners in the past four months, has of late employed a new way to announce the execution of altruistic children to their parents... First, they go to the executed prisoner's family home and ask to speak with a male member of the family. Then, they give him the address of a Kommitteh... and emphasize that he should take the prisoner's identity card with him without being accompanied by any female family member. At the aforementioned Kommitteh, the authorities utter, "Your imprisoned relative has been executed and you should not make a fuss about it. You don't have the right to hold a memorial in a mosque or make any public announcement about his/her demise." Then, they ask him to sign a statement containing the abovementioned remarks. Concerning the burial site of the executed Mojahedin sympathizers, they would say that the grave is in Behesht Zahra and that they would be given the grave's location later. The

---

57 *Enghelabe Eslami* (in exile), August 29–September 11, 1988.
58 See https://news.gooya.com/politics/archives/035495.php, accessed October 8, 2019.
59 Jafar Behkish, "A Glance at the Struggle of Political Prisoners in the 1980s," available at Bidaran.com, accessed October 8, 2019.

belongings of the prisoners, which were packed tidily, with the clothes even ironed, are given to them together with a couple of bars of soap.[60]

It must be mentioned that many mothers, wives, and daughters of the executed prisoners defied the order of the authorities and went to the Kommitteh, alone or accompanied by relatives, to face up to the authorities. Scores of them confronted the Kommitteh officials in an assertive or even aggressive manner. They let their feelings go, cursing the authorities and venting frustrations. Moreover, they did not deprive themselves of the right to hold memorial services for their loved ones:

> From dawn to dusk we would visit the families who had lost one or more of their loved ones in this calamity. Startled and bewildered, we would go from one house to another. In those gloomy days of November, it is said that hardly did any flowers remain in the flower shops.[61]

EXPATRIATE AND EXILED IRANIANS TAKE ACTION

Soon after becoming aware of the reality of the massacre, the mothers and other close relatives of the executed contacted the people they knew abroad. Upon being informed, the expatriate and exiled Iranians contacted the media, Amnesty International, human rights organizations, and the political parties in Europe and North America. From then on, protest actions against the IRI took off through hunger strikes, sit-ins, rallies, and marches. The Iranian exiles and émigrés began to spread the news of the massacre around the world.[62]

---

60 *Rah-e Kargar*, 57, December 1988, p. 27.

61 Jafar Behkish, "A Glance at the Struggle of Political Prisoners in the 1980s," available at Bidaran.com, accessed October 8, 2019.

62 From December 26 to 29, Mojahedin Khalq sympathizers went on a hunger strike in twelve different countries. Sympathizers of Organization of People's Feda'ian (Minority) and Rah-e Karger Organization went on a hunger strike in Frankfurt, Germany. *Enghelabe Eslami* (in exile), 191, December 1988.

   Also, twenty different committees for the defense of political prisoners and democratic associations joined ranks in a large gathering in Bonn, Germany, on December 10 (Human Rights Day) denouncing "the recent tragic execution of political prisoners in Iran... and demanding that an international committee be sent to Iran to inspect prisons and report about the mass graves." *Kar* (Majority), 59, December 22, 1988, p. 12.

   A letter of the Iranian Writers' Association (in exile) to the United Nations secretary-general and the director general of UNESCO (September 1988, Paris) read as follows: "The Islamic Republic's fruit of 'peace' to our people is this mass execution... The Iranian Writer's Association (in exile) calls on all democratic forces and all broadcasting media in France and around the world to help the cause of the Iranian political prisoners."

Thus, the wall of silence around the massacre, which had been erected by the IRI, cracked.

A HAND STICKING OUT OF THE GROUND

The worldwide dissemination of the news gave a new impetus to the collective action of the bereaved families in Iran. In small groups, mothers and wives and daughters went to Evin, Qezel Hesar, the Ministry of Justice, and other authorities demanding the exact date of the death of their loved ones, the exact justification for their execution, their burial site, their last will and testament, and their sack of belongings. But to no avail. The officials were either uninformed or, if informed, would not say a word.

The discovery of a mass grave near a Baha'i mortuary next to a canal at the end of the burial section of prisoners executed before the summer of 1988, and later the discovery of a mass grave in the southwest section of the Khavaran cemetery, solved the mystery. The families found out that a large number of leftist political prisoners executed during the Great Massacre were buried in Khavaran. They also found out that the victims were buried in this barren land sometime between July 7 and August 5, 1988.[63] Forough Tajbakhsh (Mother Lotfi) describes the discovery of one of these mass graves as follows:

> It was Anoush's fortieth day of mourning. We took some flowers to Khavaran and laid them there. All of a sudden, my sister cried out, "What's this hand doing here?" We turned around, looked, and saw a hand sticking out of the ground.[64]

SOFT SOIL: HOW MANY HAVE BEEN KILLED?

The next step in the struggle of the bereaved families was to compile a list of the political prisoners who were executed in July and August 1988. Due to the hard work and collective endeavors of the Center to Support the Political Prisoners in Iran (inside the country), which had close ties with bereaved families—and most of its advocates and activists were the wives, sons, daughters, fathers, and mothers of the Tudeh Party and the Feda'ian Organization (Majority)—a list of the victims of the 1988 Massacre was compiled sometime in late September to early October 1988 and published outside

63 Jafar Behkish in conversation with the author of this article, May 2009.
64 In Chapter Four, see "Anoush Brought Me Back to Life: Interview with Forough Lotfi."

the country at that time. The list contained the names of 1,345 victims of the Great Massacre. *Bang-e Raha'i* (Cry for Freedom), the organ of the Center to Support the Political Prisoners in Iran (inside the country), emphasized in its preface that the list named only "some of the thousands" of victims of "that barbaric massacre."[65] It comprised more names than the list published by the Feda'ian Organization (Majority) in January 1989. It is noteworthy that although the Mojahedin Khalq was the first political organization to publish a clear-cut number of executed prisoners in the summer of 1988, claiming 12,000 executions, their claim was not supported and substantiated by an actual list of names and political affiliations. Moreover, their inflated list revealed that they had little concrete information about what went on inside prisons throughout Iran.[66] Paradoxically, the Communist Party of Iran, which until October 1988 was in a haze with regard to the unfolding events, published a list in November that was accurate but consisted of only the few members and sympathizers of their party.[67] They stated: "In the recent wave of executions of political prisoners, we have received as of now news of the execution of 30 of our members and sympathizers."

Rah-e Kargar also published a short list of thirty-eight victims with their names and political affiliations: "Since the end of war with Iraq, a bloodbath has taken place in prisons. We know only the names of a few of the executed..."[68]

The list of *Rah-e Kargar* became more comprehensive in November and the number of names reached the hundreds. The Organization of People's Feda'i (Minority), which was the first organization to report the "new wave of executions of the political prisoners," announced in September: "In the past months, hundreds of political prisoners have been executed." In January, a list compiled by the Feda'ian (Minority) was published that comprised twenty-seven names. They stated the following:

> We still do not know the exact number of the executed prisoners. However, the information that has reached us from different prisons indicates that almost in all detention centers the majority of prison-ers have [been killed]. In some wards all political prisoners have been

---

65 *Bang-e Raha'i*, 8 and 9, August/September 1989.
66 Masoud Rajavi mentioned the number 12,000 in an interview with Radio Mojahed on December 1.
67 "A New Wave of Torture and Execution," Bulletin of the Central Committee of the Communist Party of Iran, September 25, 1988.
68 *Rah-e Kargar*, 55, October 1988, p. 2.

massacred. To this date the number of the executed has been estimated at a few thousand...[69]

The Tudeh Party, too, stipulated that,

> As many of the executed political prisoners are not identified and the regime does not disclose the names of its victims, we must wait till the resistance and struggle of the people forces the ruling criminals to retreat and families be allowed to visit their loved ones. It is only then that we can find out which prisoners are not in their cells anymore.[70]

From September 6, 1988, the Tudeh Party started to publish the names of the "murdered comrades." In spite of all these efforts, authorities did not retreat, and no name or number was revealed. It was in October and only after the revelation of Ayatollah Montazeri's protest letters to Khomeini by *Enghelabe Eslami* (in exile) that it became known that in fact and indisputably, "thousands of prisoners were executed..."[71]

THRASHED FAMILIES MAINTAIN THEIR QUEST

As of November 1988, the bereaved families started to go to Khavaran every Friday morning. The security forces stationed nearby would inspect the cars and the families. They insulted and intimidated the families, even in the cemetery. They destroyed any markings or motifs that the families had made in memory of their loved ones. They threw away the flowers the families had brought, and they chased after the old and grieving women to force them to leave Khavaran. The families did not give up. On December 26, 1988, they gathered in front of the Ministry of Justice. They tried to see Hassan Habibi, the Minister of Justice, to give him their petition. Despite the presence of a few foreign journalists, the guards blocked their way and tried to disperse them by beating and attacking them. The letter that never reached the Minister read as follows:

> ... in recent months, dreadful actions have taken place in the prisons of our country. Thousands of political prisoners who were already tried

---

69 *Kar* (Minority), 229, December 1988, p. 5.
70 *Nameh Mardom*, Tudeh Party, 223, September 6, 1988, p. 7.
71 *Tudeh Martyrs* (1982–1988), a Publication of Tudeh Party of Iran, Berlin, 2002, p. 487.

and were serving their sentences, and others who had finished serving their sentences, were executed. This has caused great bewilderment and sorrow in the public opinion both in Iran and throughout the world. The public seeks a proper answer. We require an appropriate explanation concerning these executions. We, mothers, fathers, and relatives of the victims, ask why our noble children were so ruthlessly massacred. In light of the prevailing conditions in the prisons, the allegations that they were somehow linked to the military operations of this or that group at the borders of the country is totally false... Our children faced some of the most difficult situations: 10-minute visitations every 15 days, by telephone and behind a glass partition, and being deprived of any sort of communication with the outside world in the past seven years, are proof of our claim. We inquire:

- If these actions were legal, why would the executions be kept secret from the public?
- If these actions were legitimate, why would they not be declared openly? Why should visitations, which are the natural right of any prisoner, be canceled?
- Why were our children killed in groups by firing squads in enclosures not even open to many in responsible positions?
- Why do the authorities oppose the inspection of prisons by a non-partisan international commission as well as negotiation with the prisoners and their family members?
- Which article of the constitution permits the authorities to conduct trials behind closed doors, whether in the past or at present? Specifically, why does a prisoner not even have the right to defend himself or herself?
- Which court has issued the death decrees of our loved ones, for what accusation, and when?
- Which law has permitted issuing the decree of mass executions? And we have many more questions, big and small...[72]

Soon after their gathering in front of the Ministry of Justice and petitioning the Minister Hassan Habibi, the families undertook the preparation of a program on the first day of the Persian New Year (March 21, 1989). The

---

72 Jafar Behkish in conversation with the author of this article, May 2009.

impressive memorial of Norouz 1989 was not only the manifestation of love and respect of the families toward their children, spouses, and parents, but also the assertion of their solid connection to the burial sites of their loved ones. That memorial motivated them to start planning and organizing for the anniversary of the Great Massacre in Khavaran.

The period August 26 through September 5 was announced as "Days of Memorial for the Martyrs of Iran's National Calamity of 1988":

> On Friday, August 31, the Center to Support the Political Prisoners in Iran (inside the country) invites "all noble and venerable human beings across the land, and all the progressive organizations and forces of Iran, to commemorate the anniversary of our martyrs... and pay their respect to... imprisoned revolutionaries for the cause of peace, liberty, and independence.[73]

On August 31, 1989, the grieving families headed to the cemetery with bouquets of flowers to observe the first anniversary of the loss of their dear ones. They encountered armed Revolutionary Guards near Khatounabad who stopped "suspicious vehicles," searched people inside the cars, and made an effort to send them back home. Nevertheless, a good number managed to make it to the cemetery and join those who had been there since dawn. However, as the authorities were determined to nip this attempt in the bud, the armed guards attacked the mourners before the flowers were spread across the cemetery. This brutality did not only occur in Khavaran. The Revolutionary Guards were also at work in Behesht Zahra and other cemeteries throughout Iran that day, especially where the Mojahedin were interred.

Hence, the commemoration of the victims of summer 1988 was much more than an anniversary. That commemoration was the beginning of a movement against forgetting and for seeking justice. The moving forces of this movement were a number of mothers, spouses, children, and sisters of the leftist prisoners who had lost their lives in summer 1988. The following demands were the epigraph of the movement:

- the date and justification of the victims' retrial
- the execution date of every prisoner
- handover of the last will and testament of the prisoners to their families
- the exact place of their burial.

---

73 *Bang-e Raha'i*, 8 and 9, August/September 1989.

The movement soon learned that it should not expect any answers to its basic demands, and that anything related to the Great Massacre of 1988 was a state secret.[74] But they did not give up. The release of the survivors of the Great Massacre, especially from the Evin and Gohardasht slaughterhouses at the end of the 1990s, supplied the movement with ample evidence and substantial details of what had happened in prisons during that bitter summer.

The flight of many of these former political prisoners from Iran, their asylum in Europe and North America, and their firsthand testimonies and narratives about the Great Massacre also enabled the Iranian exiles and immigrants to inform the world about those atrocities. These efforts resulted in the official visit of the UN Human Rights Commission's special envoy to Iran. He met with some of the relatives of the victims before his visit to Iran. Mihan Rusta testifies:

> A three-member committee of the families of the executed prisoners of 1988 (the Provisional Committee of Women Against Execution in Iran) went from Berlin to Geneva to meet with Galindo Pohl. In that meeting we gave him the address as well as the pictures of Khavaran cemetery. He announced to this committee, of which I was a member, the date and the place to meet the families and asked us to inform the families of the prisoners in any possible way. I announced that information in an interview with the BBC when I went back to Berlin.[75]

The families who were informed of Galindo Pohl's visit by relatives and friends abroad took measures to prepare the documents that would be delivered to the special envoy at the right time. The IRI security services were watching every move of the Mothers of Khavaran. They threatened some families and arrested a few others without any warrant, while the intelligence forces blocked the road to the cemetery.[76] All this had no effect on the Mothers' resolve to meet with the UN special envoy. When Galindo Pohl arrived in Iran, the Mothers of Khavaran came to meet him from every corner of Tehran:

> One of the Mothers who was paralyzed in one leg and sitting in a wheelchair had all the documents in a bag hanging from her neck.

---

74 Nasser Mohajer, "The Great Massacre" (2009), *Negah*, 23, p. 310, available at www.negah1.com/negah/negah23/jeld23.pdf, accessed October 29, 2019.
75 Mihan Rusta, in an interview with Nasser Mohajer, May 2010.
76 Mina Entezari in a private conversation with the author.

She was placed in front of the entrance so that she would be able to give them to Galindo Pohl. The State authorities took Galindo Pohl in from a side door and the poor woman was trampled over and over...[77]

Another ploy of the government was "to gather all the families whose sons were assassinated by the Mojahedin and let them meet Galindo Pohl to protest the violation of human rights by that organization."[78] At the same time, the families were surrounded by the repentant prisoners, who were shouting the slogan, "We are political prisoners and we are still alive!"[79]

The demonstration of the families had consequences. The regime had taken pictures of them and confiscated the letters they had written to the Human Rights Commissioner.[80]

FLOWER GARDEN OF KHAVARAN

The reality and recognition of a cemetery known as Khavaran provided the families of the leftist victims of the Great Massacre with significant evidence of the crime. From the time of its discovery, the families not only protected the graves of their loved ones and became the custodians of the most important proof of the crime of the theocratic rule in Iran, but also resisted the obscurantist Islamists. This fact was no secret to the IRI authorities. They knew very well that they had to destroy this most important evidence of their crime in any way possible. Mother Riahi, who lost three children in the National Calamity of 1988, remembers:

> They cut the water supply [to the cemetery] a thousand times. They did not let us take any water. There was a washroom; they destroyed it. There was a sunshield; they destroyed it. The Armenians and Baha'is planted trees around it (many) thousand times and they [the authorities] uprooted them and threw them away. The guards would say that "they are infidels and should not have any accommodations [resources]..." Those who were in prison as well as their parents, who were outside, were tortured. They would arrest us and/or our children and take us to the Kommittehs situated in Shah Abdolazim. They would

---

77 Mother Riahi video interview.
78 Nasser Mohajer, "According to the UN Special Envoy," *Aghazi-No*, 8, Fall 1991, p. 14.
79 Mohajer, "According to the UN Special Envoy," p. 14.
80 Mihan Rusta (from a confidential source).

keep us one day and one night and then let us go hungry and thirsty. In so much as they did this, we said: "Baba, just detain us, stop this drag and drop routines..." One day, on the anniversary of the execution of the guys, they deployed (their people) from Evin and brought in female guards to search us. They lined us up... They told us that men and women should stand in separate lines. They identified all of us one by one. Then, they said that Chehrazi family ought to stay there. We were there from 6 a.m. till 4 p.m. on a sizzling mid-summer day. We, the Mothers, got together. Some fifty, sixty of us had been going to the Ministry of Justice, hoping that someone would listen to our pleas. They would not even respond to us. When we went to the *Majles* [the Parliament], they let us in... Each and every office we stepped into, there sat a Mullah who would tell us: "Your children are murderers." Whenever we went for a visit, they harassed and tormented us on one pretext or another. One day, we went straight to the Leader's abode. Khomeini was still alive. We were let in. They said, "Tell your children if they do not cooperate, their release will be impossible."[81]

The Mothers suffered humiliation, endured harassment, and tolerated pain— but did not succumb. According to Forough (Mother) Lotfi, "Every year on August 31, we make Halva sweets and inundate Khavaran with flowers. Surely, they used to come and harass us. Smash the cars' windshields, and beat up the Mothers, and kicked them out of the cemetery."[82]

As such, Khavaran turned into the Flower Garden of Khavaran, a thorn in the eyes of the IRI.

"RECONSTRUCTION" OF KHAVARAN

In June 2005, the state authorities told the Mothers that they had planned the "reconstruction" of Khavaran, that they wanted to turn it into an ordinary cemetery.[83] Like many of the families, Farzaneh Raji was tormented by this news. Her brother, Farshid Raji, had been buried in Khavaran on October 9, 1981, exactly seventeen days after he had been arrested:

---

81 Mother Riahi video interview.
82 In Chapter Four, see "Anoush Brought Me Back to Life: Interview with Forough Lotfi."
83 Interview of Amir Mossadegh Katouzian with Parvaneh Milani (sister of Rahim Milani who was executed in 1981), Radio Farda, March 18, 2006.

I asked myself: what caused you this distress? I wasn't anxious about his disentombment or the disappearance of his grave. What makes me anxious is him disappearing, his memory vanishing, his name being erased from history. And I know if they want to do this, he is not able to do anything about it. So it falls on me to keep his name alive... I am saying: don't erase the names of our loved ones from the pages of history, even if there is not enough space to have gravestones for all of them. Forget about the gravestones! Just inscribe the names of those executed, those in the struggle who are now buried in this cemetery, on a tablet next to the entrance of the cemetery or above every trench in which dozens of our loved ones lie. Then, transform the cemetery into a garden of flowers where their children can play, where their sisters, brothers, mothers, fathers, and spouses can walk and smell the flowers in memory of their dear ones. That is, if the motivation is humane, if not, then we prefer to keep the cemetery the way it is.[84]

It was more or less in this spirit that, on Thursday, August 25, 2005, the families of those buried in the cemetery issued a statement that read:

We, the families of those executed and buried in the flower garden of Khavaran, declare that our children were neither buried in regular graves nor in such a way that is common and would make identification of the individual possible. Many of our loved ones are buried in mass graves. We also declare that, in case there is a need to reconstruct the flower garden of Khavaran, it is necessary that the names, the date, and justification of execution and the burial place of each of these loved ones be ascertained. Then, the families of the victims will take measures for the reconstruction of the cemetery.[85]

INTERNATIONAL RECOGNITION FOR THE MOTHERS OF KHAVARAN

Despite persistent efforts by the families, the IRI continues to deny access to any information about where the executed prisoners were buried and is

---

84 Farzaneh Raji, "Do Not Erase Our Children's Name from the Pages of History" (August 30, 2005), http://www.shabakeh.de/archives/individual/000444.html, accessed October 12, 2019.
85 Open letter to the public about the government's plot for "reconstruction" of the flower garden of Khavaran.

taking action to systematically demolish evidence of the massacre. A joint report by Amnesty International and Justice for Iran, released in April 2018, details the destruction of many of the mass graves by the government.[86] These plots of land that were a place of healing and remembrance for the families of the victims of the massacre are now being converted into roads and trash sites in an effort to conceal some of the last remaining forensic evidence of this heinous crime. Since 2003, at least seven suspected gravesites have been destroyed, including the Golestan Javid cemetery in Khavaran, and the evidence suggests that the destruction is ongoing.[87] In January 2009, the government demolished the graveyard in Khavaran and covered it with new grass and trees. To this day, nobody knows whether the bodies of the executed were removed during the demolition.[88] However, the demolition has failed to fulfill the objective of destroying the evidence of the massacre and disheartening the families who continue to call for the remembrance of their loved ones.

The Mothers of Khavaran have continued to resist the extermination of their children's legacy by persisting in their fight for truth and justice. The families continue to press the government to reveal how and why their loved ones were executed and why the government refuses to acknowledge or assume responsibility for their deaths. Though the government continues to disregard the movement and denies the families access to information, the movement has been successful in garnering some international attention to this horrifying crime. The Mothers of Khavaran have won international recognition for their efforts from various groups. In 2013, they received the Gwangju Special Award for Human Rights.[89] The prize was given to Parvaneh Milani on behalf of the Mothers of Khavaran.[90]

By fighting for the recognition of past injustice, the Mothers of Khavaran not only hope to gain more information, shed light on this unprecedented crime in Iran's modern history, and prevent similar atrocities from occurring in the future, but also hold the IRI accountable for its crimes against humanity.

---

86 Amnesty International, "Iranian Authorities Bulldozing Mass Grave Sites to Destroy New Evidence," April 30, 2018.
87 Ibid.
88 Mansoureh Behkish, "Mothers of Khavaran," November 29, 2015. May 18 Memorial Foundation, Republic of Korea, *Gwangiu Seogu Naebangro*, 152.
89 *Who Really They Are?* [*sic*] (The Laureates of Gwangju Prize for Human Rights Award), May 18 Memorial Foundation, Republic of Korea, 2015, pp. 211–34.
90 Ibid., pp. 211–34.

Chapter Five

SONS AND DAUGHTERS OF THE PERISHED SPEAK OUT

Home

SAMAD KIANI[1]

Up until the age of five I had no sense of "home." Home, for me, was a number of large rooms with tens of "aunties,"[2] a steel-frame bed for me and my mom, and a wall on the other side of which my dad and "uncles" lived; a dad whom I met occasionally in the visiting corridors. I kept asking my mom to tell me the story of our home, and she would say, "We'll be free and we'll get out of here. We'll build a house; our house has curtains and a television." Dreaming of our "home," I would slowly fall asleep. The bed on which my mom and I used to sleep was on the first floor. Farther down was the bed for Narges and her mom. I knew they had executed Narges's father. At the time, I didn't know what execution was; I just knew that it meant somebody's father was not on the other side of the wall. Just like Reza's dad, Mehdi's, Saeedeh's, Faezeh's, Hanif's, Zeinab's, Salman's, Ehsan's, Amineh's, and the fathers of many other kids of my age.

As far as I remember, Soosan was a beautiful lady, with black eyes and curly hair. I remember many things about Soosan. She often read us stories, like the story of the sheep and the wolf; and I remember her with a cast on her hand and I remember that she had punched her fist through the window opening to the courtyard, after which she had screamed and fallen down. But Soosan was beautiful, just like many of the aunties. Just like auntie Mojgan, Roxana, and Elham. They were kind and beautiful, unlike "the sisters." The sisters had frowning faces and wore chadors. They had thick eyebrows and faces striped with a pale mustache. Sister Mehri, sister Zohreh, sister Nazari... I loathed the sisters then and I still do. I found "the brothers" frightening;

---

1 Samad Kiani is a social activist. His political commitment is to struggle for a new socialist republic in Iran.
2 Young kids in the prison called female inmates "aunties" and male prisoners "uncles." They called female prison guards "sisters" and male prison guards "brothers," as these terms were in the lexicon of the IRI prisons in the 1980s.

brother Yasaghi and brother Hossain; grouchy with frowning faces and short beards, dark green outfits, holding small rifles.

We used to play games, the girls and boys. In our games we would have visitors, and they would bring us canned fruit, and we would take a temporary leave from prison. Sometimes, during the game, one would say, "By the way, kids, I will be free soon!" For a long time, we didn't know the word "courtyard" and would call any outdoor space "outdoor time."

The narrow space in the huge green gate of the Mashhad prison opens. To go to my mom, I have to bend; my aunt is on this side of the gate. I am crying and saying, "Auntie! You come to mom too." They take me back outside. Now I am crying louder and asking for my mom to come outside. It is just like my mom's last temporary release: Mom had to leave and I wanted to stay in the village with my aunt. I told my mom, "Go, I will shut my eyes, count to twenty, and you leave, so I won't see you." Mom left and my aunt cried even more than I did.

I am returning from the visiting hall; my dad is holding me. Uncle Gholamhossein kisses me and gives me some chocolate. He is wearing a yellow jumpsuit and has glasses on. Years later, I would hear my dad say that Gholamhossein had also been executed. Since then, any man with glasses and a yellow outfit reminds me of the name Gholamhossein. I remember uncle Siamak too. He used to draw. His book of drawings is still with my dad.

Uncle Abbas, Mohammad Ali. I remember vividly when I heard that they too had been executed.

I get sick too often. I get injections all the time. During the visiting time, Mom tells my aunt, "Take him out. The air in this place is too polluted and he is constantly getting sick." On the bus, I am crying nonstop and some passengers get fed up and tell my aunt, "Please make him be quiet." My aunt breaks into tears and says, "This kid's parents are not here, they are in prison." The passenger sitting next to us looks at me, and everyone in the bus, including me, is silent. The passenger sitting next to us reaches into his pocket and takes out a handful of pistachios and gives them to me.

I despise classes. My mom and aunties must sit and listen to Haj Agha. I like to get out and play. Some aunties are not good; they resemble the sisters, and no one likes them. They pray too much and they have Khomeini's picture hanging over their beds. They attend many classes and take everyone with them.

It's nighttime and we are sleeping. No lights! The curfew is on! Suddenly, we hear the ward's loudspeakers. All aunties go and stand behind the rooms' iron bars. They read a few names, among them my mother's. We are being released; everyone is kissing and congratulating us. Two aunties, who are sisters—one of them is being released and the other is not. The one who is being released is crying and she suddenly passes out. The next day, I give my clothes to the other prisoners' kids. I give Reza the car that I got from my cousins for my birthday. I like my car a lot, but I like Reza even more. I know Reza's father was executed, and Reza has to remain in prison. As we are leaving, my mother starts crying.

Outside the prison, our relative's car is waiting for us. I am going to my uncle's home, and it will be a few months later when I finally realize what "home" means.

TRANSLATED FROM PERSIAN BY MARYAM JAZAYERI

Thirty Years

SAIID ISMATI[3]

It is weird, but somehow you get used to it. Somehow you don't. Sometimes you're sad; sometimes angry. You get used to living with these feelings. Yet you never forget. You never forget. You don't forget how as a child walking home, you always imagined your father sitting there waiting for you. Somehow he has managed to escape. Somehow he isn't dead. When the doorbell rings, you see him standing there.

But then you get older and reality gets you. The reality is that my father was imprisoned when I was just a month old, in 1981, and spent the rest of his life in prison. A life which ended in 1988.

Thirty years.

I didn't feel exceptional in my situation. Unfortunately, there were many children like me, children who were missing a part of their lives. But what was really missing wasn't clear to the seven-year-old that I was when my mother told me my father had been executed. I remember that I crawled under the couch. I stayed there for some time. I don't remember how long, but it seemed to me that it was the only safe place in the world.

As a child I thought my father was fighting a battle with a sword in his hand. That's how kids think. They want to have heroes. Fighting with a sword, like a knight in shining armor. I liked this image. I still do, and won't let them take this away from me. They can't have *everything*. I won't give them that power. They have already taken so much. But they can't take our dreams. That's what I learned from my father. Though he couldn't teach me how to shave, I have become pretty good at that. I also learned to play soccer,

---

3 Saiid Ismati was born in Tehran in 1981. With the intensification of repression in 1982, his mother had to flee Iran taking Saiid along with her through Turkish Kurdistan. Since then, he has been living in Berlin and working as a pedagogue, especially on the topics of racism and democratic decision-making processes. In 2019, he obtained a bachelor's degree from the Alice Salomon University of Applied Sciences in Berlin.

football, and even to box. All on my own! It is easy to learn these things. But there are things that aren't so easy to learn, like to have an opinion, to stand up for your ideals, to do the right thing.

They can't take everything away from you. They? Who are *they*? Who is it that I hate so much? The hangmen? The officials? The snitches who gave them the names? Nobody? There has to be someone! When there is a victim, there must always be a villain. But not always is there justice. And what I want is justice. I want to see the murderers brought to justice. I want them to pay for their crimes. I want them to realize what they have done. And I know they are still out there. I know it. They have not disappeared. But who are they? They are not only a few people. It is a whole system I want to see torn down.

Thirty years and I haven't given up hope. I don't want justice just for myself. I demand justice for *all*. For all the mothers, fathers, sons, daughters, brothers, and sisters of the persecuted, imprisoned, executed, exiled! For each and every one who has suffered injustice. The murderers thought they could take all those lives and leave nothing behind. But they have created heroes. Heroes who are stronger than death.

This has nothing to do with justice, yet it's a good feeling to know you have your personal hero who doesn't bend. Maybe it would have been enough to have an ordinary father, someone who cared about the little things in life. But no, that has nothing to do with my dreams. To care for little things? No. Heroes care about the big things in life. For the real big things. That's the way heroes are.

Thirty years. Twenty years. And you get used to it. When you finally understand what they were fighting for, things start to make sense. No, they didn't die in vain. No, their death is not meaningless. Never. No hero's death is ever meaningless. They have changed our lives forever: the way we think, the way we behave, the way we live. You can't stop heroes. Somehow they always fight on. In many different ways. Silently maybe, and in silence, but they are always there. That's the destiny of a hero. The destiny of a knight in shining armor.

> Thirty years. Thirty years. Thirty years.
> Trying to be calm, for thirty years.
> Sensing the loss, for thirty years.
> Sad, for thirty years.
> Proud, for thirty years.
> I'm proud of my knight.
> The name of my knight is Reza Ismati.

Open Letter to
My Father's Hangmen[4]

LALE BEHZADI[5]

To this day, there exists no official record of my father's death. Nor is there a grave that we could visit. His mortal remains probably lie in one of the mass graves of the Khavaran cemetery around Tehran. In a one-liner dating back to 1991, the Foreign Ministry of Iran confirmed the "passing of the mentioned person" to the German embassy in Tehran.

Manouchehr Behzadi was a member of the communist Tudeh Party of Iran and chief editor of their weekly journal, *Nameh Mardom*. In the wake of his flight from the Shah's regime, he had lived twenty-four years in exile—most of the time in the German Democratic Republic—before he returned to Iran after the 1979 Revolution. I remember my father being a very educated, wise man who taught us to ask questions, inform ourselves, and not to accept injustice of any kind.

After our arrival in Tehran, I especially noticed how vibrant and zealous he was, how much he had missed Iran and its people, and how jubilant he was at the prospect of being able to shape and construct his country yet again. I

---

4 This letter was first published in *Zeit Online* on September 5, 2008 (updated on September 9, 2009).
5 Lale Behzadi is a German-Iranian professor of Arabic literature at the University of Bamberg in Germany. She was nineteen years old when her father was executed in Iran. Together with her younger sister, Asita Behzadi, a psychologist at a major clinic in Germany, she recently gave an interview to Amnesty International Germany ("The Dead Will Not Rest") to draw attention to the fact that thirty years after the massacre, not only does the abovementioned silence of the Iranian authorities still prevail, but the Iranian government also has started to destroy evidence of the mass graves by bulldozing, road construction, and mass rubbish dumping. See www.amnesty.de/informieren/amnesty-journal/iran-die-toten-geben-keine-ruhe; and www.amnesty.org/en/latest/news/2018/04/iran-new-evidence-reveals-deliberate-desecration-and-destruction-of-multiple-mass-gravesites, both accessed October 21, 2019.

know about a lot of things that happened in Iran after 1979 from my mother, my father's friends, the many eyewitnesses, and the few written studies about that period. But I also experienced how the initial enthusiasm and assumed liberties turned into depression and the restriction of basic human rights, spanning from the types of attire women were allowed to wear to curtailing freedom of press and assembly.

When the detention of left opposition members intensified, my mother went back to Berlin with us kids in summer 1982. In February 1983, my father was arrested with many other Tudeh Party members and put into solitary confinement in Evin prison, which was already infamous from the time of the Shah. After unimaginable tortures—which, among others, consisted of whipping and hanging with crossed arms behind the back for hours—some of the prisoners appeared in a staged conference in May 1983, shown on Iranian television. Men who were obviously marked by abuse were sitting at a round table. Manouchehr Behzadi was among them and over their heads were banners with typical slogans against the USA and the Soviet Union. The prisoners praised the Islamic Republic of Iran and damned their own "deviation from the right path."

We obtained twenty-five letters in five and a half years. They consisted of a preprinted seven-line form. On the back we had seven lines to respond. My father, according to his brother, was in bad condition. He had reportedly lost all his teeth and needed medical treatment due to other torture-induced injuries. He always wrote the same identical sentences: I'm well, how are you? I hope that everything is fine at school, at work, and so forth. Apart from a few of my uncle's visits, there was no other contact, no official information or explanatory statements by the Iranian authorities. Some of the few survivors report that—depending on which faction of the Islamic Republic's contested leadership had the upper hand—the conditions of detention deteriorated or improved in unpredictable ways.

In spring and summer 1988, measures were taken in several prisons that, in hindsight, must be assessed as preparing the ground for the executions. Contact with relatives was severed. Prisoners were classified according to party or group affiliation and were partly called in for interrogation. Suddenly there was no talk of espionage anymore. Instead, interrogation commissions asked questions about the prisoner's faith and practice of prayer. The interrogations were reminiscent of the inquisition tribunals, in which one could hardly give a "correct" response as the aim was to demonstrate apostasy.

The executions took place in the course of a few weeks and demanded great logistical efforts. In Evin prison, five or six prisoners were hanged every 30 minutes—often accomplished with the use of cranes that were specifically transported to the spot in order to accelerate the number of executions. When this method became too time-consuming (because Islamic hanging does not kill through breaking the neck but by suffocation) they switched to shooting, which, due to the possibility of the gunshots revealing what was happening, had previously been avoided. Corpses were then transported by trucks and helicopters from the prisons to the mass graves.

This can clearly be termed a purge. Human rights organizations assume that between 2,800 and 5,000 people were murdered in summer and fall 1988, but the estimated number of undetected cases are much higher.

In fall 1988, the ban on visitations was lifted. At the prison gate, families received some of their relatives' belongings and were informed about the death of their loved ones. Moreover, under the threat of punishment, absolute silence was imposed on the family members and the prohibition of obsequies was equally inflicted upon them.

It is remarkable that, in spite of this crime against humanity, to this day, the Islamic Republic has been able to deny the wave of assassinations and conceal it from the Iranian people and world community. Requests to the Iranian embassy in Berlin in 1990, for instance, were either responded to evasively or not responded to at all. Entire generations of dissident intellectuals were wiped out in these meticulously conducted executions, which is unprecedented in the recent history of Iran.

Some of the people responsible for this massacre are known. Besides Khomeini, who at that time decreed a fatwa against the "enemies of the revolution," they also include members of the current government apparatus. Evidence is hard to obtain as, to date, there is still no independent judiciary in Iran. Iranian human rights groups and journalists in exile are unremittingly working on gathering evidence and wresting these crimes from oblivion.

We will continue to ask for the whereabouts of my father's grave and the circumstances of his death. Manouchehr Behzadi is one among thousands who were imprisoned under the most deplorable conditions and, in the end, slain. We are complicit in these crimes if we remain silent.

PS: This testimony was published in 2009. Since then, my family has not stopped asking questions and will continue to do so.

TRANSLATED FROM GERMAN BY KAVEH YAZDANI

Testifying: A Journey
into the Past Ahead of Us

CHOWRA MAKAREMI[6]

A few years ago, when I was in the process of publishing a book on the massacre of political prisoners in Iran during the 1980s, I had a dream that stayed in my mind for a long time. I was in the presence of a tiny little girl, who was sitting on a table, dangling her legs. She had short, curly hair and I could see how much of a baby she still was. It was me, at the age of four or five, when I was living in Iran with my grandparents. My mother was then held in prison, and my father had had to escape to Europe after a long period spent in hiding. Beside the table where the curly-haired girl was sitting, a television was on. The news broadcast showed a cleric driving a bulldozer in the ruins of the Persepolis archeological site, which was a few kilometers far from our hometown, Shiraz. It was Hojat al-Islam Sadeq Khalkhali, an infamous hardliner appointed as chief justice in the revolutionary courts, where he sent maybe up to a thousand prisoners to

6 Chowra Makaremi is an anthropologist. Her work explores, through different media (i.e., literature, ethnography, and cinema), questions of borders, invisibility, violence, and memory. She has been a research fellow at the French National Centre for Scientific Research since 2011 and teaches at the EHESS Graduate Institute in Paris. She has been a visiting fellow at the Institute of Advanced Studies in Princeton and Columbia universities (US), Javaharlal Nehru University in New Delhi (India), McGill University (Canada), and a writer in residence at the Documentary School of Lussas (France).

She has published a number of articles on migration control in Europe, the government of borders, as well as legal and ordinary forms of violence in western democracies.

In 2011, she published *Aziz's Notebook: At the Heart of the Iranian Revolution* (Paris: Gallimard, 2011) based on the memoirs of her grandfather, Aziz Zarei. Since 2018, she has been the director of a research program funded by the European Research Council on "Violence, State Formation and Memory Politics: An Off-site Ethnography of Post-revolution Iran."

execution, and *personally* carried out some of those sentences.[7] Shortly after the revolution, Khalkhali called for the destruction of the Persepolis citadel, as the unwanted trace of a non-Islamic past. He made a spectacle by driving the engine to bulldoze the site. His fervor, however, did not pay and the citadel remained untouched.[8] The little girl was casually commenting on the television news to me. She was talking about Khalkhali and about other members of the government, who they were, what they did: all names and events I do not remember anymore. She was speaking in a clear and smooth Persian—a language that has lost its fluidity for me since I left Iran for France, at the age of six.

TESTIMONIES

In summer 1986, my grandmother managed to obtain visas for my older brother and me, and brought us to France, where my father was granted political asylum. My mother was still in prison in Shiraz, where she was held since her arrest on June 15, 1981. In December 1988, after a few months of silence and anxiety, my father told us that our mother had died. We were living in a small city in the center of France. In the next weeks, I remember our nanny was buying the national and local press every day.

And the first thing my father did when he came back home was to go through them: he had written to many newspapers to denounce the massacre of the prisoners.

The newspaper clips have been stored in a blue cupboard with glass shelves—the "Museum"—which contains the objects, the clothes, the pictures of my mother, her prison belongings, and the writings that relate to her (articles, tributes, and lists of executed prisoners). The cupboard smells of old clothes, lavender, and something a little acrid—maybe what a friend, a former prisoner, was referring to when she said about a shirt, "It still smells of prison."

The newspapers have gone yellow with the years. One is a two-column article published in *Le Monde*, the major national daily newspaper, dated Wednesday, December 21, 1988. Under the headline "Testimony," the title reads "Death of an Iranian, by Hassan Makaremi":

---

7 Ayatollah Sadeq Khalkhali, *Memoirs* (Tehran: Sayeh Publications, 1990), pp. 356–8.
8 For the mausoleum of the Shah, which was destroyed. See Elaine Sciolino, *Persian Mirrors* (New York: Touchstone, 2000), p. 168.

Today I can testify as one among the thousands of Iranian families that have lost beloved ones during the wave of executions of political prisoners, because my two children and I are safe in France.

I want to testify the following: my wife Fatemeh Zarei—a former candidate of the Mojahedin Khalq at the legislative elections in Shiraz—has been condemned to ten years of prison for having printed and distributed tracts against the Islamic Republic (see *Le Monde*, July 7, 1981).

During her eight years of detention in different prisons in Iran, she has been forbidden visits several times. In 1987, the prison authorities announced Fatemeh would be released in March 1989... However, after Iran accepted UN Resolution 598, all the political prisoners were forbidden visits. While I was making arrangements for her hospitalization in France in anticipation of her forthcoming release (Fatemeh suffered from spine problems and from serious vitamin deficiencies), we learned that she had been executed...

The same text was published on the front page of the regional newspaper *Le Populaire du Centre* dated Thursday, December 22, 1988, under the title "Executions in Iran: the '*J'accuse*' of a refugee."[9]

The weekly newspaper *Le Monde Libertaire* dated Thursday, December 29, 1988, published an article titled "Iran: The destiny of a woman." It begins as follows:

A night in December. A quiet house in the suburb of a provincial town in France. A room furnished in oriental style, spare furniture, some carpets. A man is taking care of two children, an eleven-year-old boy and an eight-year-old girl. He serves them dinner, brings the plates to the kitchen, and wishes them good night. Once they are asleep, Hassan says in a whisper: "They don't know yet..."

---

9 In January 1898, the French author Émile Zola published an open letter, in the newspaper *L'Aurore*, to the president of the French Republic. In this letter, which appeared on the front page under the headline "J'Accuse...!" (I accuse), Zola accused French officials of a "ghastly miscarriage of justice" in connection to the Dreyfus Affair (a political scandal that divided the Third French Republic from 1894 to 1906). Zola's accusations of injustice and anti-Semitism have turned "J'accuse" into an expression used to denounce abuses of power and authority.

The article features a large-scale picture of my mother (she is smiling and seems caught in the middle of a conversation, with her fingers pointing at someone), subtitled "Fatemeh Zarei, the year of her arrest."

The last newspaper clip is an edition of the *Populaire du Centre* daily dated Thursday, February 2, 1989. An insert framed in black is published beside the obituary section:

> In December 1988, my wife Fatemeh Zarei has been executed after eight years of detention in political prison, while she was a few months from completing her prison term. In her memory, we will gather on Saturday 4th of February, 1989, from 3 to 6 pm at the 93 R** street, 87000 Limoges. Hassan Makerami.

I remember that day: I told my father I would rather not take part in the gathering, and go to my Saturday gymnastics class instead, which is what I did.

A few years after that, as I was turning fourteen, my father told my brother and I that a meeting commemorating Iranian political prisoners was going to be held in Paris, and the organizers want some prisoners' children to attend the event: Would we like to participate? We said yes, partly because we were excited to go to Paris.

On the day of the commemoration, the organizers asked us if we were willing to testify publicly, and I accepted. The meeting was held in an auditorium. Behind the stage, a small corridor led to two rooms furnished with dressing-room mirrors and tables. I sat in one of them, with some sheets of paper and a pen. It was around five o'clock in the afternoon, and I had no idea what to say because I hardly thought about these issues at the time. I remember I kept writing at the table until a few minutes before my turn came, around eight o'clock in the evening. The auditorium was full of faces in the dark as I stood reading my testimony:

> Good evening,
>
> I am here to talk to you about my mother, Fatemeh Zarei, who was executed in 1988 as an opponent of the Islamic regime, while the family was informed she would be released shortly.
>
> She was arrested when I was six months old and my visits to prison were soon restricted to a phone handset behind a glass window, because children of more than four years old were judged dangerous and could not have physical contact with the prisoners anymore. Then,

I came to join my father in France, where I learned about my mother's death when I was eight. I thus have only sparse images of her.

However, I know what is essential to know. I have been taught that one should not forget out of weakness; instead, one should blow on the ambers to light again the fire of memories, of the actions she had brought to us, the lessons she gave us. There are few people who truly illustrate selflessness, and although I am aware that my judgment is hardly objective, I consider my mother to have been one of them. She knew, with little gestures in everyday life, how to spread her love around her, just like the sun rays warm up those who come close to them. But most importantly, she knew how to give, not to be given back in return, no, she gave her love, and she gave her life with a last lesson full of courage and will. Yes, she was a sun; like a star which continues to shine long after its extinction.

In Iran, there are boys who go from door to door with their donkey loaded with salt, which they try to exchange for stale bread. After my mother was arrested, one of them knocked at the door, asking for her, and started crying when he learned the news. He was saying in the middle of his tears that when Ms. Zarei opened the door on him, she gave him bread but did not ask for salt [in return]. My father used to tell me this small anecdote when I was a child, and this is the way I describe my mother to those who ask me, because these stories illustrate better than any beautiful speech who Fatemeh Zarei was.

I would also like to respond to the comments of narrow-minded people who are scandalized to see a woman, who is responsible for two children, getting involved in politics at the expense of her life. Well, my mother gave us the most beautiful proof of her love, beyond material comfort, by fighting for the future of her children and that of others, so that dictatorship does not devastate our lives like it has devastated so many other lives. This is something few parents have done, but those who did it offered their children the beautiful example of courage and generosity I have the chance to have, which helps me to put things in perspective, to understand better, and most of all to face difficult moments.

Before concluding, I would like to pay tribute to other stars: my aunt Fataneh and her husband, both executed a few months after my birth.

Here we are, all the stars are in the sky like every night, and it never feels like one is missing. Do you know why? I think these stars will never go out.

Ten years after I wrote this note, I came to learn more about my mother and the years she spent in prison through a notebook her father left behind at his death. In this handwritten testimony, my grandfather, Aziz Zarei, had consigned the events and feelings that marked the dark years of his life, from his two daughters' arrests to their executions. It began with these words:

Bismillah-al-Rahman-alRahim [In the name of God the Compassionate],

MY SORROW WEIGHS heavily on my heart and I know there is no escape from this endless pain. To keep myself occupied and to calm my mind, I decided to bring the adored beings who are no more, Fatemeh and Fataneh, back to life in a notebook intended for my beloved grandchildren. They know nothing of this story, or are unaware of its details, particularly the flesh of Fatemeh's flesh.

To start with, I must say I am not qualified to set down on paper all my memories and observations regarding what happened to us, to my children and me, during this fateful period of the revolution. Only on rare occasions in my life have I picked up a pencil and a sheet of paper, so what should I say now that I am a man of seventy, with trembling hands, bloodshot eyes, a broken heart, and a life that was swept away by the wind, the pernicious effects of this revolution?

But what can I do as I am in conflict with myself? My inner voice has taken everything from me and shouts, "Write down what you saw, what you heard, and what you endured." My inner voice shouts, "At least tell them your innocent Fataneh was eight months pregnant when they executed her." It shouts, "At least write that Fatemeh, sweet and righteous like the Prophet's daughter, whose name she bears,[10] was finally executed after seven years and six months in prison, where she suffered the most modern and the most savage forms of torture. And they did not return her body."

If there are mistakes in the manner in which I set down these memories, at least the essence will be understood. Of course, Fatemeh's children want to know who their mother was and why she was executed.

---

10 Fatemeh, daughter of the Prophet Mohammad, is an example of virtue for women.

As I did not read Persian at the time, and even less the handwriting of a trembling, seventy-something-year-old man, I asked my aunt to read the testimony to me and I recorded it. The story was difficult to bear, but at the same time, I was fascinated by its simplicity and its strength as the reader entered with Aziz into a world of absurd, collective violence. The testimony evoked a time when the frontiers of normality had disappeared, and reality suddenly took the texture of a nightmare. My grandfather was writing from this permanent state of astonishment and asphyxia that had been his everyday life during this decade, with the simple, stubborn, honest will to tell what he had seen: what he still couldn't believe, what in some ways no one of us can fully believe, had happened.

My grandfather recalled his days in front of Evin prison in Tehran looking for my mother, who had suddenly disappeared from the prisons of Shiraz in May 1984. There in Evin's admission office located at the parking lot of Luna Park, a funfair attraction park nearby Evin, a prison guard at the front desk advised him to stop looking for his daughter. She had been transferred to the infamous "Ward 3000,"[11] he told my grandfather, adding tersely that two of his own sons who had been detained there never came out. In the parking lot, the prison's minibuses drove the prisoners' families to Evin to visit their children. On the wall outside of the office the lists of the executed were displayed and a crowd of mothers and fathers were wailing.

Though a testimony is personal in so many ways—it is the story of a family, which is mine—it gives rise to questions that are political: How could such an apparatus of repression, and the ideology that it relied on, take shape in such short time—a dozen months between the revolution and the first backlashes? How could people not be aware of what was happening around the prisons, at the checkpoints, and in Luna Park?

A number of memoirs written by former political prisoners depict in detail the atmosphere and realities of repression in the early 1980s in Iran. These books have been published in exile since 1994. In addition to these memoirs, the Internet is a reservoir of more stories and testaments in different formats. These memoirs cannot be found in bookstores and libraries in Iran, but the reality they talk about is now easily at reach for most Iranians, if they wish so.

My grandfather wrote his testimony in a quite different atmosphere. The old man was alone. Since summer 1988, Aziz did not have any news

---

11 The Revolutionary Guards' secret detention center.

from his daughter, and the gates of the Adelabad prison in Shiraz had remained closed without explanations. When the news of the executions was displayed to the spouses and parents in early December, they were asked to sign an agreement stating they would remain silent about it. Aziz was writing in his house, and outside no one knew, and he couldn't tell. He was leaning back on the wall, sitting on the floor as I saw him doing so many times in my childhood, this time not with the Quran or a mini radio set receiving the BBC, but with his large notebook and a pen; and people on television or in the queues in the stores in town were talking about everything else but this. He was writing in a deafening silence and he knew that his writing would remain behind the closed gates of the house he hardly left by then. He had no idea that one day he would be published, outside of Iran, in a language he didn't know. He couldn't imagine that by that day, many other witnesses would have talked and written about his burdensome secret.

Silence and isolation was not new to him, however. He was living with it for almost a decade. I remember that during the restrictions of the war with Iraq, my grandfather used to queue for hours to buy chocolate powder to put in my milk. (I was a fussy eater.) Once home, he often reported what he had heard in the queue how people were supporting Imam Khomeini, how they were cursing the Mojahedin, how this sentence or the other he heard sounded cruelly ironical to those like him who knew things they couldn't talk about. His writing holds trace of this isolation and suffering; it has the bareness and strength of a voice that tries to rise over silence.

Memoirs may be written years after the events, and the life that goes on has remolded—softened or hardened—our feelings, faded or sharpened our memories. We write them at the light of our life, by its force and current, where we are, what we have lost, what we have gained, and what we have become. My grandfather was sick with an incurable cancer at the time he wrote. His memories do not flow on the currents of life; they are chained to death. He is talking from the edge of death: his death, the death of his children. His narration bears his endless love for his daughters. He writes, as he says, to "bring the adored beings that are no more back to life." Yet, there is an immutable roughness accompanying this gentle softness, as if frozen in the terror of what he bears witness of.

A critical translation of my grandfather's memoirs was published in French in 2011. It took me six years to translate the notebook. Toward the very end of this process, I had the dream that I reported earlier.

KNOWING AND FORGETTING

The interest I developed during the past years for what happened in my country through a microhistory of the 1980s led me to meet one of the finest historians of this period, Nasser Mohajer. As the chief editor of the journal *Noghteh*, it happened that Nasser Mohajer had published, among other testimonies about the 1988 Massacre, the one I gave at the commemoration meeting held in 1994—one of the first testimonies given by children of executed prisoners as he remembered. He asked me, within the project of this book, to look back, almost twenty-five years afterwards, at the small piece of testimony I wrote in memory of my mother.

When I look back at it today, the first thing that strikes me is invisible to the reader, as it was then to the audience: it is the gap between my fierce, strong position standing by the side of my mother, both as a militant and a mother, and the emotional detachment that I felt toward her at that age. At the time I gave that testimony, I was very far removed from the concerns I am talking about here: I hardly ever thought of my mother, ever dreamt of her, or even remembered her. Iran was absent from my life. My interests were elsewhere. I hardly remembered anything from my childhood then. I had lost the names, the people in prison and government, the places, and the rumors—all things that the little girl in my dream was reminding me of in Persian. In recent years, I have tried to reconstruct this knowledge through the testimony of my grandfather, through readings, archival research, interviews, and through questions to my father and other family members. In the midst of this process, the dream, however, warned me about a truth: the things I wanted to find out about, I once knew directly; the scenes that my grandfather recalls, I once lived *with* him.

What surprises me is that as these memories faded away, and I lost intimacy with the language I used to speak, the names and places associated with my mother and prison, at that very moment, I produced a clear, flowing "testimony." I have been able to talk about my mother and back her engagement and make sense of it in a way that is out of reach for me today.

Our lives as children of the disappeared are marked at different ages by different forms of knowledge of what happened. Ambiguously enough, it is when I knew the least and remembered the least that I had something to testify. I bore witness that my mother's fate and her absence in our lives not only had no negative impact, but also gave us a sense of her struggle and her love. However, what my speech did not reiterate, what it seems I am the only one to see in it, is how much of detachment from her and from the suffering caused by her absence I must have had in order to produce this combative discourse. It is the detachment, the forgetting, the coldness in relation to my deprivation that opened the door for this truth to emerge—a truth that in some ways did not belong only to me as a testimony.

TESTIFYING... OF WHAT?

But when I was asked by Nasser Mohajer to testify once again some years later, armed with a new, wider knowledge, then things got unexpectedly harder. Questions rose: What am I being asked to testify about? What does this uneasy display of an "I" bring to the events and the questions that are discussed in this book? What is it that I feel I have to say when I accept to testify, not really understanding why I should talk—I who saw nothing, I who was a child, I who remember nothing? How far I am from the flowing, casual mood that brought me to Paris in 1994 and dictated my words at the time! The time of "truth speaking" and "meaningful speeches" that touched the heart of the audience. The time of denial and silence in my inner world.

It seems to me that these difficulties are linked to the fact that testifying confronts us, the children, with three kinds of difficulties. The first is that we could not witness what happened. We were too young to remember what we saw as firsthand witnesses, and even if we remember some details, these memories are floating in the impressionist, inaccurate world of our preconscious minds. The children who were born in prison wards, those who were kept in the Kommitteh and Sepah interrogation centers with their mothers: What can they say about it today? Our testimonies are locked in the world of the immaterial and the invisible: feelings, impressions, emotions, and psychological effects. We are not eyewitnesses but in a certain way *heart-witnesses*. This is linked to the second difficulty: witnesses must overcome issues of modesty and reveal so much about themselves; otherwise, their testimony remains constrained and lacks sincerity. Keeping the world of our emotions and feelings under tight control dries up the narration and shrinks it to a juxtaposition of facts, crimes, and human rights abuses that pile up on the long lists of abuses around the world and do not really reach beyond a circle of human rights advocates and activists. Witnesses usually manage to balance the demands of dignity and issues of modesty through producing a narrative as accurate and precise as possible concerning what happened (the facts, the places, the people), yet in an openly personal way. The difficulty of modesty, which is holding together a sense of dignity and the disclosure of the intimate, is somehow sharper when one cannot rely on objective facts, when the testimony belongs almost exclusively to the immaterial and the subjective. And so our position is more fragile. Not only more fragile but also overly determined.

The third difficulty is the place assigned to the daughters and sons and testimonies they are to give. On the one hand, the young children, the defenseless beings robbed of their parents, are the closest possible persons to being pure victims, who did nothing to deserve their fate and had no defense against it. Did political prisoners deserve their fate? Of course not. Did they have a responsibility in the political culture of violence and martyrdom, in the disparity between the games of power politics and its assessment within political groups, which altogether contributed to the organization of state violence in the post-revolution era? I believe so. Beyond this, the political parties to which they belonged have been assailed, insulted, and demonized relentlessly in the Iranian state media, which served to mitigate, if not legitimize, practices of imprisonment and execution.[12] In contrast, the children were victims without nuances: in the complex reality of political violence, our innocence was absolute. I sometimes feel that, almost at a symbolic level, this innocence carries forever the intensity of the violence exerted on our parents.

On the other hand, children are treated with a kind of respect that does not have much to do with their own value or character. It feels like the public projects the respect it has for the executed parents onto their children as if, by being their children, we share our parents' greater fate and moral strength. On the other hand, this respect is looked at, or denounced, with envy by those who consider political activism to be essentially a game of fame and social recognition. In any case, victimization and heroization are two sides of the same coin: they both change the children into surfaces of projection.

I remember when General [Augusto] Pinochet, the former dictator of Chile, was arrested in London in 1998. The news broadcast showed former Chilean prisoners and opponents in exile chanting slogans in front of the court. They chanted, "With the bones of Pinochet we will make a rattle to

---

12 To mention this responsibility is not to fall into the game of comparison and causal explanations that has been nurturing denial and the legitimation of state violence for decades not only by Iranian officials, but also within society. On the contrary, I see this point as a needed rupture in the veil of silence that has surrounded the events and caused much political, cultural, and psychological harm to the social body. (I thank Shokoufeh Sakhi for bringing my attention to this necessary clarification.)

cheer up the children of our dead comrades." I remember it well, because I asked myself: But how old are the children of the dead comrades *today*? They should be in their late twenties—too old to play with rattles. In the eyes of their parents' comrades, they have been fixed in their infancy and childhood—in the victimization on behalf of which the Chileans were seeking justice in front of the London court. In the same way, many of us children ask how to divest ourselves from the assigned place of heroic victims, frozen in a childhood that ended for us a long time ago, and speak from a place that fits our evolving, living subjectivities: as young adults who were sometimes raised far from their home countries and have adopted a foreign culture, a diasporic condition.

The three kinds of difficulties I have experienced (the impossibility to witness what had happened, the issue of intimacy and modesty, the place assigned to the children of the executed and disappeared) may explain why many children remain silent and refuse to step into the ambiguous position of the witness. But these difficulties are all intermingled in one reality that is worth talking about: how the relationship between prisoners and their families, and specifically their children, were a point of application of power and a method of repression. Through my grandfather and many other family members' testimonies, I am convinced that children were not the only "casualties" in a violence that targeted their parents. In a more cruel and systematic fashion, the organic relation between parents and children—the need for parents to protect their children and not be humiliated in front of them, the torture of seeing their children in distress because they needed their parents, missed them, feared for them—all the veins of motherhood and fatherhood were used for harassing, punishing, and breaking down the prisoners. The psychological torture exerted through guilt, fear, and the pain of separation reached far beyond cables and torture beds, and their effects are long lasting in time. The prison system in Iran was a system that tortured children on a large scale: it deprived newborn babies from the milk of their mothers; it made infants watch their parents being tortured; it detained babies in hallways and corridors outside the wards where their mothers were detained, or in overcrowded wards; and it executed pregnant women in the eighth month of their pregnancy, as it did with my aunt. What has to be said is that prison and mass execution do not only break or suppress the targeted individuals, but they also affect a circle of relatives. They impact the lives of parents, spouses, sisters and brothers, and the trajectories of the children. They create black holes of silence within families and tear people apart through guilt and too-long-contained anger. What the children can talk about is this long-term effect of violence against the executed and the disappeared on the lives of the survivors. Our most private life was turned into a battlefield. This is what we can bear witness to; this is why our testimonies are loaded with challenges of decency and modesty; but this is also why they are necessary, no matter how much we loathe the roles of victims or hero substitutes.

A description of repression is not complete until one has mentioned its psychological and moral effects, the ways in which it was successful by rooting itself in the intimate lives of the families, and orchestrating from there another form of self-imposed silence. In showing the everyday reality of this process, my grandfather's testimony helped me understand how repression works. But it also showed how resistance works. The work of transmission undertaken by families who keep the picture of their loved ones on their wall, talk about the food, the music, the books they used to like: all these give the children the means to reconstruct a past that has faded away or has been erased by the tricks of their minds. These memories do not dwell in the hermetic, closed world of our souls, but instead they are carried, outside, by people who have seen and lived this period; they are transmitted through objects such as a piece of clothing, a doll, or a picture kept in a family "Museum," through the same old stories repeated again and again by grandmothers, and notebooks written by grandfathers.

FORGET AND FORGIVE

Decades have passed now, and we the families are asked to forget and forgive. The issue of forgiveness is not the matter of this writing. But as far as forgetting is concerned, my feeling is that we do not need to be asked to forget. We already have forgotten so much—not because we wanted it as an act of appeasement, but because we have erected screens in order to protect ourselves from the unbearable memories. I have forgotten everything that the five-year-old child of my dream knew: names, acts, discourses on Iranian television of the 1980s. I have forgotten the face of my mother. I have forgotten every single minute that I spent with her during the years she was in jail. I remember well the other people that were around me at the time, I have clear memories of my childhood, but I don't have any glimpse of a visit in prison with my mother. I have forgotten her smell, her voice. I have lost the most precious thing I had: the memories of the time I spent with her, what she told me, the way she hugged me, how she smiled. This forgetting is hard to forgive.

My Father, Ahmad Danesh[13]

STEFAN PARVIS TÖPELMANN

Dear *Die Weltbühne*, for weeks now, news agency reports on the execution of political prisoners and opposition members in Iran have been broadcast around the world on an almost daily basis. Among those who have recently been executed was my father, Dr. Ahmad Danesh. He was a member of the Central Committee of the Tudeh Party... His fate reflects the fate of numerous political prisoners in Iran...

Up to the very moment that I'm writing this letter to *Die Weltbühne*, official representatives in Tehran have avoided confirming any executions. Some have even denied [the recent wave of] killings altogether. However, we know that relatives of my father living in Tehran, as well as relatives of other political prisoners, were orally informed about the executions and asked to collect the personal belongings of the executed...

My father was born in Iran on January 5, 1930. He started to become active during the reign of the Shah and was involved in improving the living conditions of his home country. At that time, he was already persecuted due to his political convictions and therefore [left Iran and] lived in exile for 20 years. During that period, he became a urologist and surgeon before returning to Iran in 1972, although his life was under threat in the Shah's dictatorship. He became known for being the first to successfully perform a kidney transplant in Iran, in 1978... [After the revolution] Ahmad Danesh was active in the advancement of Iranian society, but only in strict accordance with the provisions of the laws of the Islamic Republic of Iran. In early 1980, he officially ran for a seat in the first parliamentary elections of his hometown of Semnan in the Islamic Republic of Iran.

As a doctor, his aim in life was to help soothe the medical and social malaise in his home country. Up until his arrest in 1983, once every week

---

13 *Die Weltbühne*, December 27, 1988, extracts.

or two, he regularly looked after and medically supervised the inhabitants of his hometown free of charge. He even personally paid for the operations that he conducted... After he was arrested on May 27, 1983, his relatives did not know what had happened to him for more than a quarter of a year. Not a single accusation against him surfaced. He himself was not aware of violating any laws of the land. Hence, he did not make any "confession"... [In prison] all his teeth had been knocked out... On April 6, he wrote a personal letter to Ayatollah Montazeri... in which he delineated the conditions of political prisoners in Iran, including his own situation.[14] It was perhaps the first time that such a distressing and detailed testimony about the destiny of political prisoners in Iran had reached the public. The letter went as follows:

> I have endured so much pain and physical torture... I have experienced so much indifference and, even worse, so much hostility... I am now in prison for five years... In prison, I have granted people all possible medical aid. Due to this work, the majority of the public prosecutors and personnel of Evin prison know me personally. Regarding my record, not a single culpable behavior can be found that justifies an interrogation... Countless children, juveniles, female and male geriatrics of different political orientations and groups with diverse political opinions, among which were many of my comrades, have to suffer this pain... Here the defamation and tarnishing of prisoners is the order of the day... I was often beaten without any reason or justification. I often witnessed how other prisoners were beaten and offended. And yet, I didn't even have the most basic and natural right to look my torturer in the face...
>
> While time and again, I heard and read in the constitution of the Islamic Republic that torture is illegal, I was tormented myself and witnessed over and over the merciless mistreatment of other people. I heard how people were crawling on the floor because they were not able to move otherwise after being tortured... It was the entire human race, it was humanity itself that was so much prostrated, helplessly and humiliatingly creeping on the floor. I have seen people who have vomited as a result of their unbearable pain and wounds of torture. They lost so much body fluid till the skin dried out and death could

14 The date is not accurate. This letter was written in Evin prison, Tehran, on May 6, 1987. It was first published in *Nameh Mardom*, the central organ of the Tudeh Party of Iran, 211, vol. 5, June 14, 1988.

occur at any moment. In order to save their lives—although they rather wanted to die—for the most part they had to be treated with infusions. I have seen people whose urine almost exclusively consisted of blood and who—due to the disabilities of their kidneys—had to be attached to "iron kidneys." [He is referring to hemodialysis]... I would not even wish my worst enemies to endure what I have suffered.

Finally, after two and a half years of confinement under harsh conditions, one morning I was taken to a room by some prison staff—as always, blindfolded. For the first time, I was allowed to take off my blindfold. A young cleric was sitting behind a desk and began to ask me questions from a file at hand. I responded to his questions. In doing so, I thought that this session was the continuation of previous interrogations for the completion of my dossier, as the same questions were asked as during previous interrogations. One of these questions was whether I have maintained my convictions. Even formally there was no indication that the session could have been a court hearing. The cleric and I were the only persons present during that session. He interviewed me and at the same time he kept the minutes. If this session was my trial, indeed, he was the chairman [judge], public prosecutor, jury, as well as my defense lawyer—all in one person. The session... only lasted a few minutes. Nonetheless, I was very glad that it ended rather quickly and that I was allowed to go back into my cell as it was the only place in which I felt safe.

After this letter became public, any contact between my father and the outside world was severed... Following numerous protests, which were also addressed to the Iranian ambassador to the Federal Republic of Germany, the ambassador felt compelled to comment on the fate of Dr. Ahmad Danesh:

> The death penalty is only imposed by the judges when the person in question is guilty of murder or committed a treason that endangered the security of the country in times of war. I am currently not able to assess if what Mr. Danesh is being accused of goes that far.

At the same time, he voiced his general condemnation of my father because of his political convictions and affiliation with the Tudeh Party. He justified this statement by quoting so-called confessions of other leading members of the Tudeh Party, even though it is provable that these were extorted through unspeakably ferocious torture... When the execution of my father became known, security forces monitored the houses and apartments of his relatives living in Tehran to prevent mourning ceremonies and expressions of condolences. Nevertheless, hundreds of people turned up to show their sympathy. Among them, there were persons that his relatives had never seen before; former patients and people who, despite the danger, wanted to express their gratitude and esteem for the work of Dr. Danesh.

TRANSLATED FROM GERMAN BY KAVEH YAZDANI

Chapter Six

A CALL FOR JUSTICE

The Iran Tribunal:
Justice in the Making

SHOKOUFEH SAKHI

I will begin with a cursory history of the Campaign for the Iran Tribunal, briefly touching on the reasons for its emergence and its objectives, as well as the procedures and the outcome of the Iran Tribunal. In the second part, I will discuss the ambiguities and complexities involved with the notion of justice and people's tribunals.[1]

A SHORT HISTORY OF THE IRAN PEOPLE'S TRIBUNAL

In 1988, for the first time, a diverse group of leftist Iranian intellectuals and political organizations in the diaspora attempted to set up a tribunal to condemn the Islamic Republic of Iran (IRI) for the massacre of thousands of prisoners, first between 1981 and 1983 and again in summer 1988. Though there was no shortage of willpower and motivation among the participants, this initiation soon dissipated due to political strife, lack of experience, and absence of a clear and common understanding of the objectives which are the necessary structure for such an undertaking.

In 2007, a new initiative with similar objectives took form which, after two years, surfaced into the public sphere. This new initiative, the Iran Tribunal Campaign (ITC), continued finding its form, evolving, defining and redefining its significance and position within the larger movement for the next five years until the formation of the actual Tribunal itself. The

---

1 This article is an expanded and updated version of a conference paper I presented at "Truth and Justice: Problematizing Truth Commissions and Transitional Justice: Guatemala, Kenya and Iran," held at OISE, University of Toronto, Canada, on November 29, 2012. A month before the conference, on October 26, 2012, I testified at the Iran People's Tribunal in The Hague, Netherlands.

Russell Tribunal of 1965–67 and the International Criminal Tribunals were its models.

The ITC introduced itself as a "Campaign" and "a social movement... initiated by a group of individuals composed of the families of the victims..., former political prisoners, the survivors of mass executions in the 1980s, political and labor activists, women's rights activists, lawyers, students, children's rights activists, writers, artists and human right activists."[2] It is noteworthy that, after the failure of the first attempt at creating a Tribunal, there was a conscious effort to bring people together as individuals and not as representatives of different political formations, nongovernmental organizations, and other organizations. The hope had been to prevent the Campaign from falling prey to the common fate of subordination of its cause and demands to a grander political objective.

THE OBJECTIVES OF THE IRAN TRIBUNAL'S CAMPAIGN

Knowing that, like any people's tribunal, the ITC and its findings did not, and could not, have a binding legal power within the structure of the international justice system, the Campaign and the movement it represented took pride in acting as a court of the people, a tribunal of conscience. It did not represent any state power, nor could it compel the perpetrators responsible for crimes against the people of Iran to be brought to justice. The truth is, neither the international legal institutions nor international powers have the will (or the interest) to hold the Iranian regime accountable for what it has done and is still doing to its own people. This was captured in the "Closing Submission" by the prosecutor of the Iran Tribunal, Sir Geoffrey Nice:

> The people of Iran may be said to have been let down by the international community and its lawyers and this Tribunal reflects the determination of victims of, and witnesses to, what happened to create a record of evidence that can enjoy some authority and that can be measured against the law in order to identify what laws were broken by the Iranian Republic in the 1980s.[3]

---

2 *Iran Tribunal – International People's Tribunal: Findings of the Truth Commission*, p. II. See www.peacepalacelibrary.nl/ebooks/files/380702266.pdf, accessed October 21, 2019.
3 See www.irantribunal.com/index.php/en/sessions/court/359-sir-geoffrey-nice-closing-submission, accessed October 21, 2019.

The objective of the Campaign was to investigate the mass executions and massacre of political prisoners in the 1980s, and to hold the IRI accountable for its crimes against humanity in a *court of the people* and *according to international laws*, neither restricted by nor obligated to the interests of a state and/or legal institutions. Therefore, throughout its course it acted on and maintained a level of autonomy. It hoped to raise the awareness of the people in Iran, the international community, and civil societies by exposing the horrific magnitude of this human tragedy, with the intention of preventing any further such atrocities.

THE PROCESSES AND OUTCOMES OF THE IRAN TRIBUNAL

The Iran Tribunal went through two stages: the Truth Commission (TC) and the People's Court. A panel of international legal and political experts, academics, and reporters[4] led the TC from June 18 to 22, 2012, in London, in Amnesty International's Human Rights Action Center.[5] During these five days, seventy-five witnesses appeared before the TC either in person or through Skype. Moreover, the Campaign supplied the TC with background evidence, names, details of thousands of executed and disappeared prisoners, and further written testimonies, all of which, along with the findings of the TC, were published in July 2012 and submitted to the Tribunal.[6]

The People's Court, or the Tribunal, was held on October 25–27, 2012, in the Peace Palace, The Hague, Netherlands. It was presided over by six international judges,[7] and a seven-member team of prosecutors[8] represented the people against the IRI. During the three-day course of the Tribunal, the jury listened to the testimony of eighteen witnesses, which included experts,

---

4 The members of the Commission were Maurice Copithorne (chairman), Eric David, Daniel Turp, Anne Burley, William Schabas, and Louise Asmal. See www.irantribunal. com/index.php/en/sessions/truth-commission/334-jury, accessed October 21, 2019.
5 See www.irantribunal.com/index.php/sessions/truth-commission/334-truth-commission-members, accessed October 21, 2019.
6 See *Iran Tribunal – International People's Tribunal: Findings of the Truth Commission*. Available at www.peacepalacelibrary.nl/ebooks/files/380702266.pdf, accessed October 21, 2019.
7 Judge Johann Kriegler (the president), Patricia Sellers, Makau Mutua, Margaret Ratner Kunstler, Michael Mansfield, and John Dugard. See www.irantribunal.com/index.php/en/sessions/court/332-jury, accessed October 21, 2019.
8 Payam Akhavan, Sir Geoffrey Nice, John Cooper, Mojdeh Shahriari, Kaveh Shahrooz, Nancy Hormachea, and Gissou Nia. See www.irantribunal.com/index.php/en/sessions/court/407-tribunal-members-2, accessed October 21, 2019.

family members of executed prisoners, and former prisoners themselves. At this stage, I gave testimony in the capacity of a political prisoner during 1982–1990.

The mandate of the Tribunal as outlined by Payam Akhavan, acting as the chief prosecutor, was to consider: "the State responsibility of the Islamic Republic of Iran and not [just] the responsibility of individual perpetrators." The Tribunal, then, aimed to determine:

a) Whether the alleged violation of human rights had occurred;
b) Whether these violations constituted crimes against humanity; and,
c) Whether, as a matter of international law, the Islamic Republic of Iran had breached its international human rights obligations toward its citizens.[9]

Knowing that this was a complex process, the tribunal initially set itself the task of creating a space for justice and accountability. The objective of the tribunal was to establish the truth about the use of widespread, systemic and systematic torture and executions of Iranian citizens, and the massive violations of basic human rights committed by the IRI. After three months of careful deliberation, presented in a fifty-two-page document, in February 5, 2013, the jury released its verdict. It states:

> We hereby unanimously adjudge and declare:
> ### THE VERDICT
> (I) The Islamic Republic of Iran has committed crimes against humanity in the 1980–1989 periods against its own citizens in violation of applicable international laws;
> (II) The Islamic Republic of Iran bears absolute responsibility for the gross violations of human rights against its citizens under the International Covenant of Civil and Political Rights; and,
> (III) Customary International law holds the Islamic Republic of Iran fully accountable for its systematic and widespread commission of crimes against humanity in Iran in the 1980–1989 period.[10]

---

9 *Prosecutor vs. The Islamic Republic of Iran: Judgment*, Article 28, p. 9, available at www.irantribunal.com/images/PDF/Iran%20Tribunal%20Judgment.pdf, accessed October 21, 2019.
10 Ibid., Article 170, p. 52.

A CRITICAL ACCOUNT OF THE NOTION OF JUSTICE AND PEOPLE'S TRIBUNAL

Unlike the original Truth and Reconciliation Commission (TRC) in South Africa, TJRC in Kenya, the Historical Clarification Commission in Guatemala, or the TRC in Canada as a component of the Indian Residential Schools Settlement Agreement, the Iran People's Tribunal is (a) an aftermath to neither the reign of an oppressive political system nor a specific conflict, and (b) not established within, working for, or supported by a new national political system and judicial apparatus. Nor, for that matter, is it supported by any international political power or judicial apparatus. All these, one could argue, would render our tribunal impotent—if one were looking for immediate results—but also could contribute to its autonomy.

It is obvious, since I participated in the campaign and gave testimony, that I was of the hopeful group and believed this campaign could be fruitful, not only for Iranians but for the larger community of suffering humanity. Yet, regardless of my hopefulness, one of the salient factors which can determine success or failure, and in general the quality of such a campaign, is the notion of justice.

Up to now I have emphasized the advantages of it being a grassroots movement, which allowed the ITC relative freedom from any formal power influences. It accomplished its goal to create an undeniable body of evidence, a space for the prisoners and relatives of the executed to surface and have their voice—a voice that was broadcast live into Iran through satellite television and the Internet—and not only to save a chunk of Iranian history from being erased, but also to project it back onto the national and international scene. And since then, the question of the 1988 Massacre has gained more attention among the politically aware, concerned, and conscientious individuals. However, *justice* is not something to be achieved either through a people's tribunal with moral and political authority or a formal court with judicial power. These are only steps in the long and convoluted process of establishing justice. Further steps require a *critical* understanding of the notion of justice in theory and practice.

The guiding principle in defining justice for the campaign behind the Iran Tribunal has been summarized in the motto: "No to forgetting and no to forgiving." This motto was formed among the Iranian opposition and a broader "justice-seeking movement,"[11] in contradistinction to the motto: "Remember but forgive." The latter has been mostly championed by Iranian officials known as "reformists," those who wanted and hoped to create some changes within the framework of the regime of the IRI. It is noteworthy that, due to the 2009 election and installment of Ahmadinejad as the president, a large number of the "reformists" were pushed out of the circle of power and forced to join the diaspora. Finding themselves among the opposition in the diaspora, they encountered the presence of a strong justice-seeking movement and realized that the crimes committed in the 1980s have not been forgotten. In this context, their motto "Remember but forgive" corresponds to their own pragmatic needs, instead of recognition of their accountability to the people and the country by taking responsibility for their direct and/or indirect hand in the first decade of suppression and atrocities.[12]

NO TO FORGETTING

It is of utmost importance to find a way of crossing the generational abyss in the areas of social and political movements and power struggles within the boundaries of a nation. By raising the issue of accountability for the crimes of the past, in a way, the general population has to *remember* and *reflect* on two things: first, the existence of particular sociopolitical movements and their suppression in its own history, and, second, to analyze and evaluate itself, the present generation, in relation to this history. Achieving such a feat is indispensable to the process of transcending the prevalent injustice and replacing it with a substantial, that is, in my view an *ethical* justice, a justice which goes beyond legal responsibility. Here of course, I am not arguing for making life easier, or healing the old wounds and remedying the troubled conscience of a people; I am arguing for making the public stronger by

---

11 See Nasser Mohajer's "The Mothers of Khavaran" (this volume), and Shokoufeh Sakhi's "Ethical-Political Praxis: Social Justice and the Resistance Subject in Iran," in *Iran's Struggles for Social Justice*, Peyman Vahabzadeh (ed.), (London: Palgrave, 2017).
12 It is apropos to bring Sir Geoffrey Nice's reference to Albert Speer, Hitler's architect's self-questioning "For heaven's sake, how could I?" and for stating "There is no reason to believe that the perpetrators in Iran have even approached his level of understanding..." ("Closing Submissions of Professor Sir Geoffrey Nice, QC," available at www.irantribunal. com/index.php/en/sessions/court/359-sir-geoffrey-nice-closing-submission, accessed October 21, 2019). I would only expand the category of the "perpetrators" to include the hopeful "reformers" as well.

stopping the process of forgetting and taking responsibility toward the past and the future.

One argument for transitional justice, and the rationale behind every TRC and People's Tribunal, is that seeking justice for an uninvestigated and unaccounted-for crime of the past brings closure for the survivors of the crime. It starts a healing process for the general society. Of course, giving recognition to the crimes of the past and the suffering of the present, and stopping the denial and dismissal of the pain of the survivors, are steps in the right direction. But these steps do not do justice to the past suffering or to future well-being.[13] I would like to go one step further in the understanding of what justice could and should be, especially in situations of mass atrocities.

Giving public recognition and therefore, releasing the survivors from their enclosed private and solitary space, and holding the perpetrators publicly accountable, may give some version of closure to the survivors, but it *does not do justice to the past suffering.* As it is a crime of the past, the suffering of the past can *never* be removed either with punishment or with clemency. In fact, no amount, nor any method, of justice is capable of relieving the suffering endured. The dead will never rise again. The lived experience of having lost a child, a loved one, never leaves one's body. Even healed wounds are still wounds that have been closed. The event of being wounded has happened. Justice cannot be reduced to an equalizing legal act, a tit for tat; nor can the crimes of the past be "restored" through a judgment. Justice also belongs to the ethical domain. *It is a response to the past but for the future. Justice is always the gate between the past and the future.*

In this sense the meaning and scope of not forgetting, of remembering, goes beyond giving recognition to the past suffering and providing closure to the survivors. It involves the *whole* society, *not* just those categorized as victims and victimizers.

In a country like Iran, or in more extreme cases, like Germany during the Second World War or Rwanda in 1994, one can say that one part of the population lined up against the other, regardless of whether the people stood against each other actively or passively. What matters is that these historical events have provided the circumstances within which the new generations will live and forge their identities. That perspective highlights the significance

---

13 There are many criticisms of the notion and practice of transitional justice and TRCs; that, for example, they are used to letting the perpetrators of a crime go unpunished in favor of holding up the stability of the prevailing political system. This discussion, however, falls outside the scope of the present article.

of *actively* "not forgetting" as an attempt to develop a historical memory and historical continuity, connecting the past experiences of sociopolitical struggles and personal survivals to its heirs. It is the future generations who inherit the visible and invisible effects of the crimes of the past and the responsibility to uphold justice. But what about the issue of "forgiving"?

NO TO FORGIVING

The idea of "forgiving," I believe, can be considered the Iranian version of the amnesty and clemency aspect of some practices of "transitional justice." Forgiveness is considered by its defenders to be a road back to a "normal life," a "starting out," a "new beginning." The idea of forgiving is given as an alternative to seeking revenge and punishment, as the way to reconciliation.

Under this general idea of forgiving and the goal of reconciliation of a nation divided (sometimes into many conflicting parts) lies the fear of an ever-repeating cycle of violence and revenge, and the desire for peace and "normalcy." But its opponents argue that it can also give rise to its opposite, to the fear of granting impunity to the perpetrators and thus maintaining the power imbalance. No doubt there is a dilemma regarding the possibility of retribution and reparation for physical and psychological damage as well as the loss of loved ones.

Who has the right and power to forgive? What is to forgive? What is the act of forgiving? And what does forgiveness mean in any case? The same way that a punishment can never restore the injustice of the past, forgiveness cannot erase the responsibility for taking part in that injustice. Justice and injustice are both very political and very personal, the same as the demands for forgetting/remembering and forgiving.

Here, I would like to give an example: I come from an extended family whose members occupied a wide range of the political spectrum, from pro-Shah (the monarchy ruling Iran prior to the 1979 Revolution) to pro-Khomeini and the Islamic Republic, to Marxist–Leninist. And we were no exception to the rule and not immune to the consequences. Many families had lost one member who defended the establishment, and another for being against it. When I was released from prison in 1990, those of my relatives who were actively supporting the regime during the early 1980s were there welcoming me home, being solicitous in their over-attentiveness without mentioning anything about the past. I could see that they had left the camp of the regime. I could see their struggle in creating a new identity and life for themselves. Time had passed and eased the harshness. Nonetheless, there was always something separating these sections of my family, as with all sections of the larger society. I tell this because, for people with experiences like mine, the need for reconciliation, for gaining an ability to live beside each other without the fear of betrayal or revenge, is very palpable. Yet, it is not only foolish to think that it could be achieved by giving amnesty, or by putting to death or imprisoning the culprits. It is also that "forgiving" or "punishing" in themselves can be, and have been, actually damaging to a *real process of creating a just and ethically responsible society in the future*. What is needed is to fight against the desire to *go back* to "normalcy," as if going back is ever possible. Such a desire often results in denial and leaving the new generation vulnerable to repeating history. Such a desire tends to shut the gate between the past and future, to miscarry a *justice in the making*. Rather, the ability to live beside one another without the fear of revenge or betrayal is gained through a conscious act of *being* responsible-for-the-other.[14]

Responsibility-for-the-other is, I think, the key concept.

One of the witnesses in the Iran Tribunal at The Hague, Mehdi Me'marpouri, was a prisoner who started pretending to be a convert in the prison, a slippery slope which ended up with his participation in executions: putting his hand on the hand, his finger on the finger, of a member of the firing squad who pulled the trigger, killing other prisoners.[15] He was there and testified in the Tribunal of his own volition; he took the responsibility to come forward, though all of us can imagine how difficult it was for him. He gave his account *without* expecting forgiveness, without asking for *anything*. There is no forgiveness; there is nothing to give—amnesty, forgiveness, normalcy—but just allowing the space for the taking of responsibility, and the courage to respond to the suffering caused.

Reconciliation is not the result of the good-hearted act of the victims or survivors of violence toward the guilty party; rather, it is achieved when the responsible party takes responsibility for his or her oppressive act, when he or she acknowledges and responds ethically to the pain and suffering he or she has caused. As one starts such a process, as a society starts such processes,

14 I am borrowing from and working through Levinasian critical phenomenology of ethical relations and his ethics-of-the-other.

15 See "*Mehdi Me'marpouri, dadgah Iran Tribunal, Laheh*" ["Mehdi Me'marpouri, Iran Tribunal, The Hague"] (2012), available at www.youtube.com/watch?v=Nc4okbjE_jU, accessed October 21, 2019.

of looking into its past injustices, then, I believe and hope, it may lay the foundation for a more just future.

The campaign of the Iran People's Tribunal, the Tribunal's procedures, findings, and judgment, are testimony to a collective resistance against condemnation to oblivion, a testimony to our persistent responsibility to the past and for the future, recording our experiences, having and passing that experience on to the next generation and to our global neighbors.

I would like to end this discussion with a quotation from one of the Iran Tribunal's prosecutors, Sir Geoffrey Nice, who led the prosecution of Slobodan Milošević[16] in The Hague:

> These two informal tribunals [Japanese 'Comfort Women' and the Iran Tribunal] were both very effective in settling some of the unresolved unhappiness of victims, yet they are little-known to the public at large. But their judgments may—along with the judgment of Russell's Vietnam Tribunal—come to be the only available evidence-based verdicts about criminal atrocities that powerful nations have sought to hide and keep from any judicial assessment. They may prove invaluable for the settling of historical uncertainties in the future.[17]

---

16 Milošević served as president of Serbia from 1989 to 1997 and the Federal Republic of Yugoslavia from 1997 to 2000.

17 Geoffrey Nice, "Japanese 'Comfort Women' and the Iran Tribunal," in *Justice For All* (London: Scala, 2017), p. 126.

The Movement for Seeking Justice in Iran: Which Strategy?

MOJDEH ARASI[18] AND HOMAYOON IVANI[19]

INTRODUCTION

Torture and subjugation of prisoners of conscience and political opponents of authoritarian regimes have had, and will have, different consequences in every country. Some of the more significant common issues may be addressed by answering questions like:

- How to deal with the authorities, the torturers, and the perpetrators of the crimes?
- How will justice be established?
- What will be the long-term political, cultural, social, and economic consequences of brutal politics in society?

---

18 Born in 1962, Mojdeh Arasi became politically active in her youth. She was arrested in 1982 in connection with the Organization of Iranian People's Feda'i Guerrillas (Minority) and was imprisoned in various detention centers of the IRI. She survived the Great Massacre of 1988 and became active in the workers' movement after her release in 1990. In 1996, she managed to escape from Iran and has been living in Germany ever since. Arasi obtained her Master's degree in teaching German-language and Spanish studies from Leipzig University in Germany. She is one of the founders of the *Prison's Dialogue* journal (1997–) and also a contributor to the theoretical journal *In Defense of Marxism*.
19 Homayoon Ivani was born in 1962 and joined the Organization of Iranian People's Feda'i Guerrillas (Minority) in his youth. In 1982, he was arrested in connection with that organization and was incarcerated in various detention centers of the IRI. After his release from prison in 1989, he worked for a computer company translating and compiling books and articles about computer science, as well as social and political subjects, in Iran. He escaped from Iran in 1997 and has been living in Germany ever since. He obtained his master's degree in computer science, communication, and media studies from Leipzig University in Germany. He is one of the founding members of the *Prison's Dialogue* journal. In addition, he is a contributor to the theoretical journal *In Defense of Marxism*.

Surely, there are different answers to these questions.

One response would lie in the international campaign known as the "fight against impunity."[20] This is a struggle that has started in multiple countries and, in spite of its ups and downs, has continued for many years. Various approaches have also been tried in countries such as Argentina, Chile, Uruguay, Paraguay, Guatemala, South Africa, Rwanda, and Sierra Leone. In Iran, heterogeneous and, at times, divergent, movements have shaped the "fight against impunity."

There is an ongoing debate among the activists and opposition with regard to what is known as the "movement for seeking justice." On top of that, the ruling Islamic Republic of Iran (IRI) actively disseminates a variety of distorted narratives by its official and unofficial agents (its state-owned broadcasting network, social media, Internet trolls, and so forth) in order to distort the debate, or at least to prevent development of a unified and persistent movement.

CURRENT SCOPE IN IRAN'S MOVEMENT FOR SEEKING JUSTICE

Characterizing, explaining, and categorizing every single point of view on justice and seeking justice is beyond the scope of this work. As with all political and social issues, each of the provided interpretations and solutions are formulated from the perspective of certain political-class interests. As is seen on the rulers' side, there is often an alignment between the interests of the rulers and those of other stakeholders such as the military, as in Pinochet's Chile, Franco's Spain, and Iran's Islamic Republic, despite attempts to mask the class and political motives with deceptively rational discourse.

Schematically, and without going into detail, the analysis and resulting viewpoints regarding the repression of recent decades in Iran, especially the 1980s, can be classified into four major categories. The goal of this categorization is to authenticate neither the narratives nor the narrators, but rather to introduce the characteristics and the tendencies of the oppressors and the oppressed in Iran. For example, the first category discussed below characterizes the distorted presentation of facts and false historical interpretation of events by the IRI. However, a reader unfamiliar with the details of the

---

20 See www.icj.org/wp-content/uploads/2015/12/Universal-Fight-against-impunity-PG-no7-comp-Publications-Practitioners-guide-series-2015-ENG.pdf, accessed October 22, 2019.

historical events of that period in Iran may be trapped in the false and distorted narratives provided by the IRI's intelligence and propaganda apparatus. At first sight, he or she may not easily discover lies or distortions in the writings or interviews of the Iranian government's propaganda.

The First Stance: The Oppressor Portrayed as Victim

This stance is taken by the IRI's military-security organization, the Islamic Revolutionary Guards Corp (IRGC), the Ministry of Intelligence, the torturers and former interrogators, and all those who represent the government of the IRI nationally and internationally, and who attempt to characterize the IRI as the "victim" of "terrorists" and "international enemies." It legitimizes suppression of all political opposition and dissidents as "self-defense" by its repressive forces. One such example is the "Tasnim News Agency,"[21] which is part of the Revolutionary Guards Corps' propaganda apparatus. The agency released a series of interviews on its website titled "The 80s; a Decade, a Century," which were published in interview format. The Revolutionary Guards' website summed up the opposition to one group only: the People's Mojahedin Organization of Iran (PMOI). They characterize the PMOI as being similar to the Islamic State of Iraq and the Levant (ISIL, aka ISIS/DAESH), who were responsible for killing 17,000 pro-government people.[22] The interviewees were "security figures" or "prison guards of the Islamic Republic"; high-ranking Islamic judiciary officials such as those who were directly involved in sentencing[23] and/or executing prisoners; a personal guard of the current Supreme Leader (Khamenei);[24] the head of the notorious Evin prison in the 1980s; the first spokesman for the Revolutionary Guards;[25] and the representative of the Islamic Republic Prosecutor's Office who was also the former head of the prisons.[26] With such narratives, repeating the self-serving scenario for an upside-down presentation of historical events is predictable.[27]

---

21 See https://en.wikipedia.org/wiki/Tasnim_News_Agency, accessed October 22, 2019.
22 See www.tasnimnews.com/fa/news/1396/04/10/1450109, accessed October 22, 2019.
23 Interview with Hojat al-Islam Razini, available at www.tasnimnews.com/fa/news/1396/04/11/1438610, accessed October 22, 2019.
24 See www.tasnimnews.com/fa/news/1396/04/17/1448257, accessed October 21, 2019.
25 Interview with Yousef Foroutan, available at www.tasnimnews.com/fa/news/1396/04/26/1450032, accessed October 21, 2019.
26 Interview with Seyyid Morteza Bakhtiari, available at www.tasnimnews.com/fa/news/1396/05/02/1465191, accessed October 21, 2019.
27 See http://dialogt.de/pad_goftar-8, accessed October 21, 2019.

In addition, disagreements among the heads of state are dealt with in such a way as to protect the image of the regime and the original narrative of the Great Massacre. For almost three decades after the Great Massacre, the regime denied the mass executions and consistently portrayed unity in leadership, although Ayatollah Montazeri's demotion and house arrest due to his objections to the executions had leaked long before. Then, in 2017, hard evidence in the form of audiotapes from 1988 surfaced, in which Montazeri criticized the delegation responsible for implementing prisoner executions in Tehran and its vicinity. The release of this evidence was condemned by the "Assembly of Experts for the Leadership," one of the main organs of the IRI, which blamed "criminal America" as the agent provocateur.[28]

Another noteworthy point is that, in exchanges with internationally recognized human rights institutions, progressive authorities, or renowned intellectuals in places such as the United States, Canada, and Europe, the agents of the IRI present themselves as "the victims of terrorism" of the 1980s massacres in Iran. The repeated claim of the "murder of 17,000 people by the 'hypocrites' (PMOI)" is an example of their attempt to confuse foreign observers, or even the new generation of Iranian youth, and to conceal the modality of the political suppression and extermination of prisoners of conscience in the 1980s. In addition, the Islamic regime strives to isolate Iranian dissidents and opposition forces in the international arena. Their most common propaganda target are the "anti-imperialist" groups and activists who, due to their lack of in-depth knowledge of the situation in the Middle East, and particularly Iran, assess the quarrels between the IRI and the West (mainly with the US) as an "anti-imperialist struggle" and are gradually lured into a quagmire of defending the hardline, right-wing rulers of Iran and overlooking their political suppression, medieval tortures, and executions.[29]

The Second Stance: Erasing the Past

The second stance is represented by a colorful array of political activists who have been driven out of the state apparatus in recent years and have joined either the ranks of the monarchist opposition abroad (Reza Pahlavi's circles) and/or the anti-left "liberal" and neoliberal groupings. Although

---

28 See https://fararu.com/fa/news/287309, accessed October 21, 2019.
29 See http://english.khamenei.ir/news/2160/MEK-When-terrorists-are-armed-funded-and-respected, accessed October 21, 2019.

their narratives of the IRI massacre in the 1980s differ somewhat from one another's, they provide similar interpretations of the events. The common theme among them is "the condemnation of the Islamic Republic, and in the same vein the condemnation of the political opponents."[30]

The monarchists defend an *ancien régime* whose record of repression and execution of political opponents was one of the worst in the 1980s and which was internationally condemned as having no respect for freedom of thought, speech, or assembly. They take a relativist approach, claiming that the Pahlavi regime respected individual freedoms and did not murder as many people as the IRI. Furthermore, they claim that communists, leftists, and progressive intellectuals deserved what they got, since they did not give any support to the positive socio-economic developments and the measures Mohammad Reza Shah took for the modernization of Iran. Thus, their condemnation of the crimes of the current regime is just a means to camouflage the many crimes of the Pahlavi regime.[31]

"Neoliberals" do not have one representative organization in Iran. Some fall into a very heterogeneous category known as the "religious nationalists," who either were part of the ruling IRI apparatus or had supported it during the IRI's early years. This group has its own reasons for muddying the truth. The truth is that the struggle against the suppression of fundamental rights, and to defend democracy and basic freedoms, especially in the first decade of the IRI's rule, was carried out by an anti-dictatorial, anti-fundamentalist movement the heart of which was the political left. By affirming these struggles, liberals and neoliberals would have to question their own existential principle: a deep-rooted, stereotypical anti-left propaganda. What role did neoliberals play while the left was fighting censorship, suppression, and social and political restrictions imposed by the IRI? Very little or none. For this reason, they are better off presenting their historical narrative of the struggle for freedom, as well as the defense of political prisoners, in a way that lessens political damage to themselves (by avoiding identification as accessories to, or participants in, torture or massacres).[32]

30 See http://isdmovement.com/2013/11/111013.Akbar-Ganji-Scientific-explanation-of-massacare.htm; also see https://youtu.be/nDEs3NIN3e4; both accessed October 21, 2019.
31 See http://padafandeir.blogspot.com/2011/12/blog-post_15.html, accessed October 21, 2019.
32 See www.dw.com/fa-ir/a-17413073, accessed October 21, 2019.

The Third Stance: Lobbying Professionally

The third stance is held by the PMOI, which opposed the Pahlavi regime and is now opposing the IRI.[33] The PMOI has tried all available means to seize political power in Iran and is now relying on the US and its allies in the Middle East to topple the IRI.[34] But lobbying the adversaries of the IRI is not exclusive to the Mojahedin. An array of ex-leftists (among them, some ex-supporters of the former Soviet Union) and also ethnic organizations with leftist backgrounds are following this path. Many Iranian non-governmental organizations (NGOs)[35] abroad, too, formed on an ad-hoc basis, receive relatively substantial funds from foundations and affiliated organizations associated with various European, American, Israeli, or Arab states to oppose the IRI's human rights record. Incidentally, the presence of these foreign government-funded Iranian human rights organizations abroad casts a shadow of doubt on the genuine, independent movement that has been fighting against the IRI and its systematic violation of human rights from day one. For instance, the request made by some NGOs to the "Organization of Islamic Cooperation" (led by Saudi Arabia and its allies) in 2012 to investigate the 1988 Massacre in Iran resulted in political disgrace and exposure of their infightings.[36] Nonetheless, it demonstrated that actions financed by other countries, regardless of their intentions, would have no political credibility.

The Fourth Stance: Outlook for Total Liberation

The fourth stance is maintained by a range of surviving political prisoners, relatives of the executed, some political activists, political prisoners' rights activists, intellectuals, and artists. This social force links the movement for seeking justice with the prospect of the emancipation of the entire society; hence, it starts at a significant distance from the popular and mainstream discourse on justice: namely, the punishment of criminals and torturers as

---

33 See http://irantribunal.com/index.php/en; also see http://dialogt.info/wp-content/uploads/2016/05/Dialog_11_Chalesh_ha.pdf; both accessed October 21, 2019.
34 See https://news.mojahedin.org/news/184327, accessed October 21, 2019.
35 See http://dialogt.info/wp-content/uploads/2016/05/Dialog_11_Chalesh_ha.pdf, accessed October 21, 2019. See, for example, p. 92 for a list of NGOs relying on financial support from the US government.
36 See "Who Are the Friends of People? by Mahmoud Khalili," available at http://dialogt.info/wp-content/uploads/2016/05/Dialog_11_Chalesh_ha.pdf, accessed October 21, 2019.

the ultimate goal. The rest of this discussion is dedicated to examining and providing an understanding of the range of ideas in this movement, which is often ignored by the mainstream media. The following sections are structured to present different perspectives in this regard. Such discourse is not unique to Iran; yet, we hope to present the reader with an understanding of the current Iranian experience and perspective.[37]

FREEDOM AND JUSTICE: THE CONJOINED TWINS

A document titled "The Movement for Seeking Justice with an Outlook for Total Emancipation" was published in December 2012 by a group of the IRI's surviving political prisoners, relatives of the executed, political activists, political prisoners' rights activists, intellectuals, and artists. This document represented the consensus of individuals who had either directly, or through one of their relatives, been tormented or harmed by the IRI. The 71-page document was the charter that presented to the public a condensed exposition of the discourse posed by the left-wing groups and surviving political prisoners up to that time. After publishing the original document, the sources related to the discussed topics were published in two books by *Prison's Dialogues* in issue numbers 11 (265 pages, 17 articles) and 12 (165 pages, 7 articles) under the title of "The Movement for Seeking Justice and Challenges Ahead."[38]

The key point for the survivors of the massacres, who published this document, is the inseparable link between holistic social emancipation as well as the prosecution and punishment of so-called political criminals. In its first introductory statement, the document formulates this issue:

> Tell me the course of justice you seek today and I will tell you the mode of justice that will rule your society tomorrow.

The approach taken is based on an assessment of the experiences of other countries considering qualitative and quantitative compromises between the opposition and the state, in order to inflict "less pain" during the "transition period." Our undertaking revealed that the agreements reached by oppositions

---

37 See http://dialogt.info/wp-content/uploads/2016/02/CheshmAndaz_Reahaiebakhsh_ 2012125.pdf, accessed October 21, 2019. The article is partially based on the article titled "Movement for Seeking Justice, Challenges Ahead," by Mojgan Arassi, 2014.

38 *Prison Dialogues,* 11, January 2013; and 12, May 2013. See www.dialogt.net/fileadmin/ user_upload/CheshmAndaz_Reahaiebakhsh_2012125.pdf and www.dialogt.net// fileadmin/user_upload/Dialog_11_Chalesh_ha.pdf; both accessed October 21, 2019.

through negotiations, usually from a position of weakness against the still-powerful rulers, could not and/or would not answer the key demands of the oppressed. Experience has shown that such opt-outs have led to immunity for, or empty promises by, the oppressors. Although such compromises made in the "transition period" might be perceived as "less painful" for the society, they have not brought about enduring peace and true reconciliation of the antagonistic social forces to the survivors or to those who had lost family members, and thus did not reduce their pain.

In addition, such common denominators used in the transition to democracy reduce the fundamental challenges of seeking justice to a mere legal debate, while the aforementioned 2012 document, written from a historical, social, and class perspective, reminds us that "if justice is coming," then its political, social, economic, and legal consequences must be clearly defined. From the perspective of the authors of the document, the dilemma does not cease to exist in the immediate aftermath of the transfer of political power and the transition to a "new society"; nor does it stop at the breakdown of former dictatorships. The process of seeking justice should continue to address the psychosocial as well as the cultural and individual aspects of the society. On the one hand, it should provide a clear plan to critique and refine the society and its culture from the oppressors' and torturers' values, and on the other hand, it should strengthen the support for human values and solidarity with the oppressed.

Holistic Approach

The holistic approach is reminiscent of Friedrich Hegel's famous statement in his introduction to the *Phenomenology of Spirit* manifesting the will and approach of the authors of the document of the movement they advocate: *The truth is the whole.*[39]

With this approach, the writers of the document introduce the Movement for Seeking Justice, like other social and class movements, with a certain systematic approach that *the whole truth about the suppression and execution of political prisoners in Iran is not achieved without complete disclosure of the truth*. For this reason, the writers of the document make a call for a widespread movement for justice, not only in the sphere of prison and direct political repression, but also in all social and class domains. They are of the opinion

39 G.W.F. Hegel, "Preface," in *Phenomenology of Spirit*, available at www.marxists.org/reference/archive/hegel/works/ph/phprefac.htm, accessed October 21, 2019.

that the movement for seeking justice is part of a global movement that is in the process of liberating the social classes from the domination of capital and capitalism; hence, this movement must be considered as a continuous and long-term struggle.

The movement for seeking justice is linked to other ongoing movements and as such, it neither begins nor ends with a demonstration or any other political act. Iranian human rights activists have learned from the experience of similar movements in other countries that justice cannot be accomplished easily or quickly. The authors of the document believe that the movement for seeking justice is to be understood and planned as a long-term struggle, a struggle that should try to be inclusive, facilitate the participation of several generations, and go far beyond the experience of one generation in order to assure the protection of democracy and the prevention of human calamities. One of the first and most momentous consequences of this approach is its emphasis on distancing itself from simplistic and conservative methods that seek to depoliticize the movement and separate it from other social rights activities in Iran.

Seeking Justice: A Class Perspective

Contrary to the dominant discourses on human rights, the document begins the debate on seeking justice from historical, social, and class perspectives:

> Seeking justice has class characteristics. The attempt to clarify the roots of the catastrophic massacres of recent decades in Iran, especially the extensive and nationwide massacres of political prisoners in the 1980s, is an attempt to expose how the roots of class interests is secured in killing tens of thousands.[40]

From the standpoint of the authors of the document, the brutality of the IRI and similar repressive regimes is not the cause of "violence," but instead the effect and expression of an order that cannot rule without repression. In this view, political prisoners who were tortured or executed are not considered "victims of violence," but rather fighters in the class struggle who were systematically executed by the security forces of the ruling classes in order to protract and protect the production and reproduction of the particular form

---

40 See http://dialogt.info/wp-content/uploads/2016/02/CheshmAndaz_Reahaiebakhsh_2012125.pdf, p. 10, accessed October 21, 2019.

of capitalism that is predominant in the IRI. The inherent tenets of the Shi'ite sect of Islam, the deep-rooted racism and cultural chauvinism prevailing in Iranian society, and the hierarchical clerical institutions are complementary factors that provide a populist justification for oppression by a new ruling class. Consequently, the document does not stop at revealing the class roots of repression, but instead attempts to depict the way in which this complex system works and the cancerous oppression and violence that is its modus operandi.

With this very first step, the authors of the document take a position against the defacing of political prisoners, reducing their role in the transition process and minimizing their political demands. Political or regime change does not solve the problem of imprisonment and torture in a durable manner. The radical transformation of the system is required to stop the vicious circle of violence, imprisonment, and torture. A tenacious human rights activist cannot ignore either the connections between the mechanisms of violence, imprisonment, torture, and execution, or the requirements of the prevailing socio-economic and political system that survives on repression. Regarding imprisonment, repression, and seeking justice, the futile "humanist" view does not discern the differences between the justice sought by dominant classes (regardless of who is in power) and that sought by the downtrodden, oppressed classes. The document emphasizes the differences between the justice sought by the ruling classes and the one sought by the oppressed classes.

At the same time, from our perspective, the movement for seeking justice is not a movement for seizing political power, as justice cannot be realized solely by overthrowing the IRI or even by abolishing private property. Seeking justice is a process that deepens over the course of its history and through the class struggle between the oppressors and the oppressed.

Seeking Justice: A Historical and Social Perspective

By distancing themselves from the idea of human consciousness as a spontaneous process, the authors of the document introduce a new perspective for a durable and enlightening course in the movement for seeking justice. The distinct historical and cultural memory of each individual takes form in a particular social congregate. At the same time, we are reminded that oblivion is the flip side of awareness. This argument considers the process of "recalling or neglecting." Thus, the answer to the question of *oblivion or awareness* depicts the will of individuals in any given society, as well as the balance of class forces. Consequently, depicting the connection between oblivion and awareness in recalling historical events—in this case, the suppression, torture, and execution of political prisoners in Iran—has a strong connection with class and/or social-group interests and the way in which each group aspires to reflect on the events; hence, the pedagogy of the oppressed, informing them of the multifaceted history of oppression and strengthening social solidarity with the downtrodden needs to be on the agenda for the movement, before and after the downfall of the IRI.

Confronting the ruling culture and transforming its social values is part of a colossal social effort, which requires the participation of all social groups in a public dialogue reckoning with the past.

Seeking Justice: A Political Perspective

One of the highlights of the document is its refutation of all illusions about the cruel nature of the IRI. This document emphasizes the necessity of over-throwing the IRI, in its entirety, as a precondition and a key demand of the movement for seeking and achieving justice in Iran. For persistent seekers of justice, the movement needs to broaden its scope and activities in order to be able to cope with post-IRI challenges in Iran. It is by such continual efforts that seeking justice becomes a meaningful objective reality that prepares the ground for the fair trials of perpetrators of atrocities against the Iranian people. The document clearly states:

> Therefore, for the left, socialist, and communist forces, holding dem-onstrations and other "consciousness-raising" activities, and continual collection of evidence of crimes committed by the regime as well as registering and archiving them to be presented at people's courts, are a continuous necessity. However, justice, especially the legal aspect of it, will materialize only after the revolutionary overthrow of the Islamic Republic of Iran.[41]

Seeking Justice: A Financial Perspective

The document affirms the lack of consensus among signatories regarding the financial aspects of seeking justice. Due to humanitarian, social, political, and

---

41 Ibid., p. 21.

cultural considerations, there has not been sufficient discussion regarding how to financially penalize the kleptocrats and agents of suppression, of both the Pahlavi and IRI regimes. For this reason, the authors of the document have recognized the right of the victims to demand allocation of reparation funds toward physical and psychological rehabilitation of the victims and/or their families. The more important issue for advocates of reparation is that, with such a supportive measure, the entire society both bears collective responsibility for such heinous deeds and declares support for the victims and/or their surviving families.

The experience of Nazi Germany showed the importance of this aspect, with its demand for financial reparation from the Nazis, much of whose wealth had been gained through pillaging the assets of the Jews and others. Dismantling the Nazi state apparatus was necessary in order to wrest back these assets, since the Nazis claimed ownership through inheritance and other legal maneuvers, and would not have returned any of it to the rightful owners.

In the case of Iran, since February 1979, many individuals working with the ruling regime have accumulated enormous, illegitimate wealth through confiscation, extortion, and embezzlement from public and private institutions and individuals of means. This can be seen as the IRI's payback to its torturers and security forces.[42]

The advocates of financial reparation envision the formation of a community-controlled public institution, upon the fall of the IRI, financed by confiscating the assets and fortunes that have been accumulated by officials of the state. The mission of this public institution would be to support the cultural, social, and individual restitution of victims. As mentioned above, the financial resources from reparations could partly be used at the discretion of the victims to compensate the victims and/or their family members. Compensating the victims is not the only end. The main purpose of financial reparation is not to compensate individuals and/or families for harm, but rather to create institutions that would strengthen the social and cultural defenses of the society against the roots of a politics of cruelty and violence.

There exists a contrary view among the authors of the document, opposing financial compensation to individuals for harm and injuries. These authors are of the opinion that such compensation to individuals is in a sense tantamount

---

42 See, for example, "L'économie politique de la République islamique d'Iran," *Revue internationale des études du développement* 2017/1 (229).

to marginalizing and, ultimately, excluding the survivors and the aggrieved families from political engagement, instead of encouraging political engagement and continual participation in the movement for seeking justice.

Seeking Justice: A Legal Perspective

The legal approach toward seeking justice includes holding accountable not only those who were agents of imprisonment, torture, and execution of prisoners of conscience, not only those who issued the orders, but also the political establishment that ordered and legitimized these atrocities. Thus, the ringleaders of the theocracy are accountable too. The objective is not only to examine, analyze, negate, and refute the IRI judicial system and its extrajudicial crimes, but also to put on trial the perpetrators of those crimes. From this perspective, any "form of justice in transition" that does not envision condemning the IRI, in its entirety, is inappropriate, inadequate, and not conducive for the institutionalization of democratic norms.

As mentioned in an earlier section (the "first stance"), prison guards, torturers, prosecutors, and organizers of the massacre disseminate false narratives based on "alternative facts" to craft a distorted account of a crime against humanity on the basis of which the perpetrators become victims. Yet, independent of the distorted false accounts and "alternative facts," the principle of the "presumption of innocence," along with perpetrators' denial of their role in tortures and executions, would make the pursuit of truth and justice a complex, prolonged, arduous, and at times impossible task. The core of the discourse, from a legal perspective, is that although the capacity of the existing legal system should not be overemphasized, the little legal leeway it does offer should by no means be disregarded; one must not fail to remember that no legal system is a set of eternal and unchanging commands. Consequently, the oppressed should lay the groundwork for an arduous and enduring struggle to foster ideas and legal standards that correspond to such complex cases.

In this regard, it may be helpful to examine the concept of "victim." Until now, in the human rights lexicon, there has been little distinction made between victims of a natural disaster (such as an earthquake) and victims of imprisonment or torture. From this perspective, all such people are categorized as "victims" and are subject to a form of trauma. The end result of this approach is the depoliticization and facelessness of survivors of massacres. In other words, a "victim" is in no position to play an active role in the process of seeking justice, as he or she is not qualified and needs to be "helped"! Although new formations need to come into being to represent victims who cannot come out in person and give their testimony in public, and new legal procedures are needed in order to represent victims, putting victims of political imprisonment and torture on a par with victims of natural disasters paves the way for the acceptance of the view that the "victims" of political imprisonment and/or torture, or the survivors of massacres, are not in a position to act in a fully independent capacity or to play an active role in the ongoing struggle for justice. In effect, their role is reduced to that of witness. Extreme interpretations of this approach may lead to reducing the role of survivors to mere *rapporteurs* of the events, the manifestation of which has already been seen in many commemorations of the Great Massacre of 1988 where ex-political prisoners have been asked only to *chronicle* their experiences. With regard to compensation for survivors as well, the survivors and families are advised to stay home and let the experts (lawyers, prosecutors, judges, or bureaucratic lobbyists) advocate for them. The authors of the document believe that active social monitoring, together with the presence of large groups of suppressed people, is needed to prevent the bureaucratization of the long litigation process.

Seeking Justice: An Individual and Psychosocial Perspective

The authors of the document focus on the individual and social consequences of violence inflicted on prisoners of conscience. Acute injuries are the known outcome of planned and systemic violence. This is the social trauma that manifests itself at the individual level. The purpose of state violence is to spread fear and a sense of impotence among people and to impose silence and conformity on the society. Therefore, raising consciousness, which is part and parcel of the process of seeking justice, is considered an essential step in reconstructing the damaged identity of self and society. In fact, seeking justice is defined as "overdue self-defense":

> Defending against state-sponsored violence is the unconditional right of members of any society. Self-defending on the face of any encroachment, aggression, and suppression is an alienable right of each individual. Those who stand for their rights, foster a more positive understanding of themselves. Therefore, people who stand up for their own rights have a better understanding of their capability and

identity, and are better positioned to transfer that understanding to future generations.[43]

Seeking Justice: A Basic Human Rights Perspective

The document recognizes the problematic nature of seeking justice, from an emancipatory viewpoint, with a perspective that walks us through the generalities to the concrete. At the core of the document is the demand for the "rights of each individual" as it differentiates itself from any *neoliberal views*. As a common standard of expectation for all peoples and all nations, the document quotes from the third paragraph of the preamble of the Universal Declaration of Human Rights, proclaimed by the United Nations General Assembly in Paris on December 10, 1948 (General Assembly resolution 217 A): "Whereas it is essential, if man is not to be compelled to have recourse, as a last resort, to rebellion against tyranny and oppression, that human rights should be protected by the rule of law."[44]

It is the human right of each individual to follow up on crimes and to seek justice, even if oppressive governments, and the "new world order," call people to silence and demand obedience to their outdated laws. Therefore, the signatories of the document consider it their right to speak for themselves, advocate for their demands, and not recognize, without their formal approval, any entity as their representative.

CONCLUSION

In this work, we have tried to present the reader with an assessment of the movement for seeking justice in Iran by drawing a schematic illustration of the ongoing discussions. As the titles of previous sections and the ongoing debate among a subset of the left-wing political prisoners and the survivors of the 1988 Great Massacre of Iran demonstrates, our intent is not to reduce seeking justice to legal pursuits, financial reparations, and so forth; rather, it recognizes radical political, social, and economic transformation of the society as a precondition for success of the movement for seeking justice.

---

43 See http://dialogt.info/wp-content/uploads/2016/02/CheshmAndaz_Reahaiebakhsh_2012125.pdf, pp. 54–6, accessed October 21, 2019.
44 "The Universal Declaration of Human Rights," available at www.un.org/en/universal-declaration-human-rights/index.html, accessed October 21, 2019.

The authors of the document have refrained from discussing interim or transitional demands, and have focused on the strategic objectives which they call "emancipatory perspective." With regards to a plan of action, the authors of the document have written:

> The publication of the present document reveals the serious shortcomings and limitations of the revolutionary left movement, including our own. Expressing our long-term, strategic demands in this document poses further questions that need concrete and practical responses for the plan of action to free all political prisoners. This is a challenge we consciously accept... The key points to all the issues deliberated in the present document emphasize the interconnectivity of various social, political, and economic components that coalesce in the movement for seeking justice. Freedom from such a hideous history of repression, imprisonment, torture, and execution of prisoners of conscience without an all-embracing emancipation from all the fetters of the politics of cruelty that make us conform to the existing ruling regime is only a deception, one which aims at pacifying all genuine movements against oppression and exploitation.[45]

The main axes of these long-term demands in various fields are as follows:

- With regard to the present historical, social, and class context, the document calls for connecting the movement for seeking justice to the global movement to liberate society from the domination of capital and capitalism. For this reason, this is a long-term movement with inevitable ups and downs.

  As to the massacres and the politics of cruelty by the IRI, the whole society should sincerely accept its responsibility and consider this pain as a shared pain from the wound inflicted by the IRI.

  The historical task of the movement is to raise consciousness about the false value system and to shed light on the true face of the rulers, the role of the state, the regime's repressive forces, as well as the top echelons of the technocrats and the bureaucrats working for the regime. In the historical-social perspective, another part of

---

45 See http://dialogt.info/wp-content/uploads/2016/02/CheshmAndaz_Reahaiebakhsh_2012125.pdf, p. 59, accessed October 21, 2019.

our mission is to fight against the ruling culture and their attempt to distort history.[46]

- In the domain of politics, the document emphasizes the interdependence of the national and international aspects of the struggle to advance the politics of an active opposition to the IRI that is necessarily in solidarity with the struggle of other peoples in the Middle East and the world over. Although the document was written in 2012, many of the problems in the Middle East and the world still persist.

In a region with an abundance of reactionary and oppressive governments, who are busy exceeding each other in exploiting people and violating human rights and international law, only a left-wing alternative which (a) insists on the complete separation of church and state, (b) demands the abolition of censorship, (c) guarantees political and social freedoms, (d) focuses on the interests of the people of the region against imperialist domination, (e) advocates for peace and disarmament in the Middle East, and (f) insists on a period of rapid economic, political, and cultural development to liberate the people of the Middle East from the vestiges of Middle Ages can provide hope for a viable, progressive alternative. Insisting on the presence of an independent, active, powerful left-wing opposition front is a necessity.[47]

In such a context, the document accentuates the necessity of overthrowing the IRI. However, as mentioned before, with regard to the "financial perspective," the debate is still open since no general consensus has been reached in the opposition to the IRI regarding how to financially penalize its rulers as well as its repressive forces and their associates who accumulated their wealth through pillage and embezzlement.

- On the legal front, various types of international tribunals, courts of justice (within the legal framework of different states), the (Bertrand) Russell Tribunal, and People's Courts have been studied in order to map out the legal path forward; however, the document emphasizes the need for further research regarding legal approaches.
- The authors of the document also envision a long road ahead with regard to restoring the psychological well-being of individuals, including ex-political prisoners, and of society at large. For the

---

46 Ibid., p. 63.
47 Ibid., p. 65.

Iranian society, after decades of repression, suffocation, and tremendous social and economic pressures, the transition to a healthy society requires long-term planning, the first step of which is the downfall of the IRI and a structural change in socio-economic relations. The document specifies the empowerment of society, and in particular that of political prisoners and survivors of prison massacres, as one of the most important agenda items for the movement to seek justice.

All in all, as indicated in the outset, the document does not reduce the movement for seeking justice to a legal debate or a discussion of human rights in a sterile and static fashion. It makes a connection between its demands and a broader movement for social change. Although the authors of the document neither specify any medium-term task nor detail a practical plan of action for the ongoing movement, we think their ideas and approaches are nonetheless worthy of attention and serious deliberation in the context of the predominant pragmatist and/or reductive interpretations of "transitional justice" in many countries.

TRANSLATED FROM PERSIAN
BY CYRUS BAHRAMIAN AND ALI DARVAZEHGHARI

Never Again

JAFAR BEHKISH[48]

[The ICC seeks to affirm] that the most serious crimes of concern to the international community as a whole must not go unpunished and that their effective prosecution must be ensured by taking measures at the national level and by enhancing international cooperation...

ROME STATUTE OF THE INTERNATIONAL CRIMINAL COURT

INTRODUCTION[49]

From February 1979, at least fifteen thousand[50] political and social activists,

---

48 Jafar Behkish was born in 1959 in Mashhad, Iran. He is a principal engineer in the field of environmental engineering. He completed his master of engineering degree at Imperial College London. He resided in Iran until April 2002, when he emigrated to Canada as a professional with his wife and son. He was a political activist from 1976 until 1989. Beginning in 1984, because five of his siblings and two brothers-in-law were, between 1981 and 1988, assassinated, killed under torture, summarily executed, or disappeared, he became involved in the movement of the families of victims of human rights violations in Iran. His late mother and his sisters are well-known activists in the Mothers of Khavaran movement. Jafar was arrested three times in the 1980s, tortured, and kept in prison for about eighteen months without any trial or conviction. From 1988 to September 2008, the time of his last trip to Iran, he was summoned many times for his active participation in the justice-seeking movement and his writings on human rights in Iran.

49 This work would not have been possible without the support and help of my wife, Leili, and my son, Nima. I am greatly indebted to Azam Kiakejouri and Nasser Mohajer for their comments and assistance throughout my work. I am also very grateful to Rhoda Howard-Hassmann, Parastou Forouhar, and Reza Afshari who read all or part of the drafts and shared their thoughts and comments with me, and to Bethany Osborne for her help.

I dedicate this work to the Mothers and Families of Khavaran, especially to the memory of Omol Banin Jalali Mohajer and Ali Asghar Behkish, my parents, who lost six of their children in the atrocities of the 1980s, and to my mother-in-law, Najiyeh Peyvandi, who lost her son in the Great Massacre of 1988.

50 BBC, "Executed in a Decade: More Than Fifteen Thousand" (2013), available at www.bbc.com/persian/iran/2013/09/130912_25_anniversary_political_prisoners_nm, accessed October 21, 2019.

ethnic and religious minorities, and nonbelievers were systematically executed, killed while being tortured, disappeared, or were assassinated by
the Islamic Republic of Iran (IRI).[51] Executions without due process began
right after the downfall of the Shah. In the first wave of executions, officials
of the Shah's regime were the primary targets. In the same period, the IRI
executed dozens of ethnic-minority dissidents (Kurds, Turkmen, and Arabs)
and religious minorities (Baha'is) across the country.[52] Furthermore, from
June 1981 to the end of 1982, thousands of political opponents, many of
them teenagers, were summarily executed, killed under torture,[53] or disappeared.[54] In summer 1988, under the direct order of Ayatollah Khomeini,
the then Supreme Leader of the IRI, more than four thousand political
prisoners disappeared and were secretly executed because of their political
affiliation or beliefs.[55]

The suppression of opposition groups did not cease after the Great
Massacre of 1988; the security forces inside and outside of Iran carried
out hundreds of assassinations. The IRI ceased its assassination campaign
in EU countries for about two decades after arrest warrants were issued
for the Minister of Intelligence and few months before the release of

---

The People's Mojahedin Organization of Iran claims that a hundred thousand were
executed or killed in the 1980s; however, according to some independent sources and
former political prisoners, this is a highly exaggerated figure; Iraj Mesdaghi, *Neither Life nor
Death: The Descent of Sunrise*, vol. 1; Mehdi Aslani, *The Crow and The Red Rose: Memoirs
of Prison*, 2nd edition (Germany: Arash Books and Magazines, 2009).

51 Ervand Abrahamian, *Tortured Confessions: Prisons and Public Recantations in Modern
Iran* (Berkeley, California: University of California Press, 1999), pp. 209–28; Kaveh
Shahrooz, "With Revolutionary Rage and Rancor: A Preliminary Report on the 1988
Massacre of Iran's Political Prisoners," *Harvard Law School Human Rights Journal*, 20
(2007); Iran Human Rights Documentation Center, "A Faith Denied: The Prosecution
of Baha'is in Iran" (2006), available at www.iranhrdc.org, accessed October 22, 2019;
Reza Afshari, *Human Rights in Iran: The Abuse of Cultural Relativism* (2001), pp. 104–18.
52 Iran Human Rights Documentation Center, "A Faith Denied."
53 Ervand Abrahamian, *Tortured Confessions: Prisons and Public Recantations in Modern
Iran* (Berkeley, California: University of California Press, 1999), p. 131.
54 UN report, "Situation of Human Rights in the Islamic Republic of Iran" (August 2017),
p. 8, available at https://documents-dds-ny.un.org/doc/UNDOC/GEN/N17/256/24/
PDF/N1725624.pdf?OpenElement, accessed October 22, 2019.
55 Hossein Ali Montazeri, *Memoirs* (2000), pp. 345–51; Ervand Abrahamian,
Tortured Confessions: Prisons and Public Recantations in Modern Iran (Berkeley,
California: University of California Press, 1999), p. 209; Kaveh Shahrooz, "With
Revolutionary Rage and Rancor: *A Preliminary Report on the 1988 Massacre of Iran's
Political Prisoners*," *Harvard Law School Human Rights Journal*, 20 (2007); *Deadly
Fatwa: Iran's 1988 Prison Massacre* (New Haven, Connecticut: Iran Human Rights
Documentation Center, 2009).

the verdict of the Mykonos trial (discussed later).[56] Similarly, it appears that the assassinations inside Iran halted temporarily after IRI officials acknowledged that high-ranking officers of the Ministry of Intelligence were responsible for the abductions and extrajudicial killings in autumn 1998 (also discussed later).

The IRI never stopped suppressing peaceful protests. The suppression of the student uprising of 1999 for substantial reforms,[57] the massive rallies against the result of the disputed presidential election of June 2009,[58] and the uprisings of January 2018 in eighty cities for better life conditions and radical changes[59] were important hallmarks in the political landscape and in relations between different sectors of the population and the IRI. As a result, a growing section of society began questioning the legitimacy of the IRI. This could pave the road for a strengthened justice-seeking movement in Iran.

This discussion critically reviews how different stakeholders tried to shape and preserve the collective memory of these atrocities and sought justice. Considering the political landscape, the main objective is to understand and find an answer to four fundamental questions:

- How did resistance to the suppression develop?
- How was the discourse on facing the atrocities shaped?
- How did the movement for truth and justice help the efforts for democracy and the pursuit of human rights?
- Why has the justice-seeking movement not grown as it should have considering the extent of the atrocities in Iran?

Before engaging in this discussion, it is necessary to clarify several points. First, I do not believe that justice seeking and shaping collective memory is a

---

56 For more on the Mykonos trial, see Abbas Khodagholi, Hamid Nowzari, and Mehran Payandeh, *The Criminal System: Documents of the Mykonos Trial* (Essen, Germany: Nima GmbH Verlag, 1999).

57 Ali Akbar Mahdi, "The Student Movement in the Islamic Republic of Iran," *Journal of Iranian Research and Analysis*, 15, 2 (1999), available at https://go.owu.edu/~aamahdi/students.htm, accessed October 22, 2019.

58 *A Year Later: Suppression Continues in Iran* (New Haven, Connecticut: Iran Human Rights Documentation Center, 2010).

59 Marwa Eltagouri, "Tens of Thousands of People Have Protested in Iran. Here's Why," *Washington Post* (2018), available at www.washingtonpost.com/news/worldviews/wp/2018/01/03/tens-of-thousands-of-people-protested-in-iran-this-week-heres-why/?noredirect=on&utm_term=.92d43d9cd37c, accessed October 22, 2019.

nonpolitical phenomenon.[60] On the contrary, there are many forces at work (for example, political camps) that have a significant impact on the politics of truth and justice.[61]

Second, although all opposition groups were treated very harshly by the IRI, discrimination against members and supporters of leftist groups (consisting of nonbelievers and agnostics) and the People's Mojahedin Organization of Iran (PMOI) in the 1980s, based on their conscience, far exceeded the discrimination experienced by other opposition groups. Specifically, I concur with Reza Afshari who argues that the 1988 Massacre was mostly a brutal violation of freedom of thought, conscience, and religion.[62]

Third, it is evident that Iran is not in a transitional period to a democratic regime, but I use the concepts and theoretical framework of transitional justice when I address the discourse among Iranians regarding the way in which we face the atrocities that were, and are, carried out by the IRI. However, the situation in Iran is rather complicated. Despite brutal suppression since the 1979 Revolution, many Iranians, even some opposition groups, believe that the Islamic reformists, who won the presidential elections of 1997, 2001, 2013, and 2017 with their so-called moderate allies, and who had the upper hand in all branches of power in the first decade of the IRI[63] and are mostly responsible for the atrocities of the 1980s, are the only realistic alternative for a peaceful transition to a less suppressive regime or even democracy. How is it possible to reconcile those who were the victims of the atrocities in the 1980s with the Islamic reformists? Is it morally and politically justifiable to ignore the criminal acts of the Islamic reformists because it might damage the current struggle for democracy? I employ the transitional-justice theoretical framework with caution to address these complicated issues.

Fourth, although the atrocities affected the entire nation, the victims' families suffered most; therefore, it is safe to say that they will be at the center of any effort to pursue truth and justice.[64]

---

60 For such a position see Mohammad Reza Moini, "Seeking Justice is a Campaign for Today" (2008), available at www.bidaran.net/spip.php?article167, accessed October 22, 2019.

61 "Introduction," in *The Politics of Memory: Transitional Justice in Democratizing Societies* (Alexandra Barahona De Brito *et al.*, eds.), 2001, pp. 1–39.

62 Reza Afshari, *Human Rights in Iran: The Abuse of Cultural Relativism* (2001), pp. 104–18.

63 Mustafa Tajzadeh, "The Analogy Between the Behavior of 'Authoritarians' and 'Mojahedin Khalq'," *Cheshmandaz-e Iran*, 29 (2004–2005), available at www.meisami. net/no-29/119.htm, accessed October 22, 2019.

64 Daniel Rothenberg, "Let Justice Judge: An Interview with Judge Baltasar Garzon and Analysis of His Idea," *Harvard Law School Human Rights Journal*, 24 (2002), pp. 951–3.

Finally, all oppressive regimes have their own official narrative justifying their politics of cruelty. All other voices, including those of political dissidents and victims, are silenced. They want the general population to forget about the atrocities. It has been argued that many state agents act under circumstances that do not permit them to make the right choice.[65] However, Hannah Arendt argues that human beings can tell right from wrong even when their own judgment is the only guide and when that judgment happens to be completely at odds with the unanimous opinion of all those around them.[66] For example, Ayatollah Montazeri, the deputy leader from 1985 to 1989, who, although he complied with the secrecy of the crime—the most important aspect of the 1988 Massacre—behind the scenes strongly opposed Ayatollah Khomeini's fatwa for the massacre.[67] Later, he was dismissed from his post.

It would be misleading to claim that all the survivors and victims' families are actively looking for justice and truth. On the contrary, most of them are silent. The brutal suppression produced an atmosphere of fear among Iranian citizens, including the victims' families. In addition, a significant portion of the urban population depends on, and is tied to, the state-controlled economy and wants to avoid confrontation with the government.[68] There are some survivors and victims' families who are active and vocal despite adverse circumstances. They want to know who is responsible for the deaths of their loved ones and the details of what happened.

At this point, it is important to mention that since February 1979, the IRI has implemented a systematic policy of discrimination and oppression against ethnic and religious minorities, women, as well as social and labor activists; however, in the sections which follow, the author's investigation focuses on the "most serious crimes" carried out by the IRI after the 1979 Revolution.

---

65 For example, see Lotfollah Meisami's interview with Ali Reza Alavitabar, a key member of the Islamic reformists, *Cheshmandaz-e Iran*, 19 (2004), available at www.meisami.net/ch19/34-47.htm, accessed October 22, 2019.

66 Hannah Arendt (1906–1975), a philosopher and political theorist, argues that citizens should be held responsible for their actions. Even when they follow orders, they have the choice to reject being involved in crimes and wrongdoings despite the adverse situation. See Hannah Arendt, *Eichmann in Jerusalem: A Report on the Banality of Evil* (2006), pp. 294–5.

67 *Deadly Fatwa: Iran's 1988 Prison Massacre* (New Haven, Connecticut: Iran Human Rights Documentation Center, 2009).

68 Iran is a country wherein more than seventy percent of the economy is directly controlled by the state; therefore, the weak private sector must be very careful to avoid any confrontations with the state. For example, in 1998, a private company was ordered to fire a very well-educated Baha'i engineer to avoid being blacklisted by the government (personal communication with the company owner).

SUPPRESSION AND RESISTANCE: VICTIMS' FAMILIES MOVEMENT

The 1979 Revolution was against the Shah's dictatorship and his Western supporters. But under clerical leadership, it became a means to reinstate the clerics' privileges. Although university students and graduates, progressive and educated workers, sections of the modern middle class,[69] intellectuals, as well as religious[70] and ethnic minorities[71] participated in the revolution to different degrees, they became the main targets of suppression in the IRI era. In the eyes of the clerics and followers of Khomeini, the victory of the Islamic revolution was completed when the IRI suppressed mostly educated and modern opposition groups as well as independent institutions of the Iranian civil society.[72]

In June 1981, only thirty months after the 1979 Revolution, the systematic and systemic suppression of all opposition and independent civil society began. Hundreds of thousands were arrested, tortured, summarily executed, killed in shootouts, expelled from their workplaces or schools, forced into hiding inside the country or in exile, or disappeared. Although the primary target were the activists, the main intention was to terrorize society at large. Ironically, the suppression led to the efforts initiated by victims' families[73] to defend human rights and seek truth and justice.

The focus of this section is on the personal, cultural, political, and social dynamics of collective actions made by the victims' families to fight for the lives of political prisoners, improve prison conditions, seek truth and justice,

---

69 From 1920 to 1978, the population of the modern middle class increased dramatically. They mostly lived in new urban neighborhoods and were disconnected from the traditional sectors and clerics. See Mohammad R. Farzanegan, Pooya Ala'edini, Khayyam Azizimehr, "Middle Class in Iran: Oil Rents, Modernization, and Political Development" 7, 9 (2017), available at www.econstor.eu/bitstream/10419/174352/1/56-2017_farzanegan.pdf, accessed October 22, 2019.

70 Iran Human Rights Documentation Center, "A Faith Denied: The Prosecution of Baha'is in Iran" (2006), available at www.iranhrdc.org, accessed October 22, 2019.

71 The enmity of the IRI with ethnic minorities is very complicated. Most of the ethnic minorities are of Sunni creed, except the Azeri people, who are Shi'ite, speak languages other than Farsi, have suffered discrimination, and are located in the border regions of the country (causing the IRI to be very concerned about their loyalty to a Shi'ite state).

72 See Lotfollah Meisami's interview with Saeed Hajjarian, deputy minister of intelligence 1984–88, advisor to President Khatami and member of the Tehran city council, assassinated in 1999 by a person connected to hardliners, *Cheshmandaz-e Iran*, 31, available at www.meisami.net/no-31/No-031-04.htm, accessed October 22, 2019.

73 See Chapter Four, "The Mothers of Khavaran."

and combat social amnesia, denials, and cover-ups. The central questions of this section are: Why have the attempts made by the victims' families, as the core of any movement for truth and justice, not developed into a strong social movement[74] like similar movements in other countries such as *Madres de Plaza de Mayo* in Argentina? What are the achievements of the movement?

The families used every means to save the lives and protect the rights of the detainees: complaining to the prison guards and authorities;[75] going individually or collectively to different government offices to ask for investigations or file complaints;[76] writing letters to high-ranking officials of the IRI; writing letters to international institutions and personalities, including the UN secretary-general,[77] or gathering in front of the UN offices in Tehran;[78] and even giving money to corrupt officials.[79]

The number of political prisoners beyond June 1981[80] is estimated to have been around thirty thousand[81] in all prisons around the country.[82] About half of them were in Tehran and its two major suburban prisons.[83] Evin prison, located in the northern part of the city, housed around 8,500 prisoners. When so many prisoners, most of them members and supporters of the PMOI, were being kept in one location, why did no significant collective resistance by the families against the state's brutalities take place? This question is critical

---

74 The author cautiously considered justice-seeking efforts as a movement, arguing that the Mothers of Khavaran are at the center of such a movement in Iran and also the Iranians in diaspora.

75 For example, in Chapter Four, see "Anoush Brought Me Back to Life: Interview with Forough Lotfi." Mother Lotfi was one of the well-known Mothers of Khavaran.

76 For example, see *Rah-e Kargar* 55 (October 1988), available at www.iran-archive.com/sites/default/files/sanad/rahe_kargar--rahekargar_055.pdf, accessed October 22, 2019.

77 An open letter to Javier Pérez de Cuéllar, the then secretary-general of the United Nations, is an example of such letters. See *Nameh Mardom* 177 (October 20, 1987), available at https://drive.google.com/file/d/120EfTbQXwCAyXA08NI-YWc_2gPA3iqB_/view, accessed October 22, 2019.

78 OIPFG, "Big Rally of the Families of Political Prisoners in Tehran," *Aksariyat Journal*, 73 (March 1990), available at www.iran-archive.com/sites/default/files/sanad/fadaiian_aksariiat-73.pdf, accessed October 22, 2019.

79 Nasser Mohajer (ed.), "*Aya O Hanooz Zendeh ast? In Ketab Zendan*" ["Is She Still Alive?" in *The Book of Prison*], 2001, pp. 426–7.

80 In May 1981, two months before the mass arrests and killings, 1,180 Mojahedin were detained around the country. Ervand Abrahamian, *Radical Islam: Iranian Mojahedin* (New Haven & London: Yale University Press, 1989), p. 213.

81 The total number that passed through the prisons seems to be much higher.

82 Iraj Mesdaghi, *Neither Life nor Death: The Descent of Sunrise* (2nd ed., 2006), p. 371.

83 There were 7,500 political prisoners in Evin prison, 6,000 in Qezel Hesar prison, and 1,000 in Gohardasht prison. Mesdaghi, *Neither Life nor Death* (2nd ed.), p. 371.

when considering that, on April 27, 1981, fifty-three days before the start of the mass arrests and killings, PMOI mobilized tens of thousands of supporters, many of them mothers of its members and sympathizers, in Tehran for a rally named "Mothers' Rally."[84]

Apart from the suppression policy of the IRI to prevent any collective resistance by using any means, including harassment, detention, purge from the work place, conviction, and even execution of some of the families, there are some internal dynamics which also minimize the participation of the families of the Mojahedin in the truth-and-justice-seeking movement. First, after June 20, 1981, the PMOI put all its effort and capabilities into enhancing its armed struggle against the IRI, with the hope of overthrowing the government in a short period of time.[85] Therefore, the most politically active families that wanted to do something collectively to help their relatives were mobilized to help with the armed struggle.[86] Second, contrary to many left-leaning political prisoners, in most cases the Mojahedin prisoners were not in favor of encouraging their families to engage in peaceful political actions for improving prison conditions or saving the lives of prisoners, instead encouraging them to help the PMOI in its armed campaign.[87] Third, most of the families of the Mojahedin prisoners either came from the traditional middle class with lower levels of education or the poor population who had very little experience with collective action.[88] Therefore, it was much more difficult for them to independently organize themselves for collective action to defend the rights of the political prisoners and participate in the efforts for truth and justice.

As a result, the engine of the movement for better prison conditions, human rights of the prisoners, and for truth and justice were the families of

---

84 Saeed Shahsavandi, "Step by Step Toward Catastrophe: Both Sides Did Incorrect Calculations" (2011), available at www.bbc.com/persian/iran/2011/06/110625_l78_3okhordad60_shahsavandi2, accessed October 22, 2019.

85 Author's observation and communication with two active Mojahedin families.

86 Author's personal communication with two supporters of the PMOI who were in prison from 1981 to 1988; also see Iraj Mesdaghi, "Mother Emami and Her Armful of Love" (2007), available at www.irajmesdaghi.com/maghaleh-98.html, accessed October 22, 2019; and also see "Mojahedin's Families in a Heroic Struggle Against Inhuman Regime of Khomeini" (1983), available at www.ketabfarsi.club/ketabfarsi/ketabkhaneh/nashriat/nash0044/0142.pdf, accessed October 22, 2019.

87 The same policy is still in place, and the PMOI tries to mobilize the families to participate in their narrow political agenda, instead of helping strengthen an independent movement for truth and justice in Iran.

88 Ervand Abrahamian, *Iranian Mojahedin* (1989), pp. 224–42; and Shahrnush Parsipur, *Khaterat Zendan* [*Prison Memoirs*] (Stockholm, Sweden: Baran, 1998).

the leftist prisoners, the executed and disappeared, who were mostly from the modern and secular middle class[89] with higher-education levels and, in some cases, with political and social experience for collective action in other movements,[90] or as part of the movement of victims' families from the previous regime.[91]

In addition, there were deep divisions between the families of the prisoners who supported the PMOI and those who supported leftist groups and even between the families of leftist prisoners based on their loved one's political affiliation. There were several reasons for these divisions. First, if it was physically possible, for example, in Tehran,[92] prisoners were divided based on their political affiliations, religious beliefs, prison sentence, and the level of resistance in the prison. The authorities arranged visits in a way to minimize any communication between prisoners from different wards either directly or through their families.

Second, in most cases victims' families built relationships with each other while they stood waiting in front of prisons. After a prisoner was released or executed, there was little reason for the families to return to the prisons, and so there was a strong possibility that the relationships between the families of the released or executed prisoners and the families of those who were still in prison would be discontinued.

Third, political divisions between the prisoners had a negative impact on family relationships. Prisoners who belonged to the same political group had close relationships inside prisons. They encouraged their families to strengthen their relationships with each other outside prison. In many cases, the families distinguished between themselves based on the political affiliation of their imprisoned or executed relatives. In addition, some of the relatives, especially young members of the victims' families, had a strong tendency to affiliate to a political group, and political rifts acted against the unity of the families. These divisions between the families significantly weakened their efforts.

After the 1988 Massacre, the IRI gradually released the survivors, and, by the end of 1989, the number of political prisoners was significantly reduced. The families of the Mojahedin victims went to Behesht Zahra cemetery with

---

89 Abrahamian, *Radical Islam*, pp. 224–42.
90 Nasser Mohajer, "Mothers of Khavaran," in *The Essential Needs of the Iranian Women*, Golnaz Amin (ed.) (Cambridge, MA: Iranian Women's Studies Foundation, 2008), pp. 117–30.
91 Mohajer, "Mothers of Khavaran," pp. 117–30.
92 In smaller cities, all prisoners were kept in the same wards.

the assumption that their loved ones had been buried there.[93] At the same time, having discovered new mass graves, the families of the leftist victims went to Khavaran cemetery. The massacre sealed the complete separation of an already weak relationship between the families of the leftist and Mojahedin victims.

Although few families of the Mojahedin victims were involved in family activities before 1988,[94] this study did not find reports about their participation in the justice-seeking movement before and after the 1988 Massacre; there were only a few reports about several arrests related to the annual commemoration ceremony in Khavaran cemetery.[95] According to Iraj Mesdaghi, who was in custody from 1981 to 1991 and after his release developed relationships with the families of executed Mojahedin, they went to Behesht Zahra cemetery every Tuesday afternoon, and they also held commemoration services for the victims in their residences under the cover of religious events to avoid reactions on the part of security forces. It is not known to what extent the pressure exerted by the security forces caused families to only hold informal commemorations.

Furthermore, while some of the families of the Mojahedin victims assumed for a long time that their loved ones were buried in Behesht Zahra, as was the case for those Mojahedin who were executed before the 1988 Massacre, no formal or informal memorials, such as those held in Khavaran cemetery, were held for the victims in Behesht Zahra.

There is no research available on the social status, social and political activities, education, and/or age of victims' families and their collective actions. However, the author's observations confirm that most active members of the Mothers of Khavaran belonged to the modern middle class and that many of them were involved in the activities of the families of the political prisoners and those executed during the Pahlavi era. The commemoration services that were held by these families in their residences and at Khavaran were

---

93 The author did not find any reliable evidence to show that Mojahedin victims of the 1988 Massacre were buried in Behesht Zahra cemetery.

94 Personal communication with Iraj Mesdaghi and one other member of the Mojahedin families.

95 For example; Ali Saremi, aged 63 years, a former political prisoner, who was arrested in September 2007 after speaking at a commemoration ceremony of the 1988 Prison Massacre in Khavaran Cemetery, was executed without warning on 28 December 2010 in Evin prison. He was accused of being a member of the PMOI which he strongly denied.

Amnesty International, "Man Executed; Seven Still at Risk of Execution" (2011), available at www.amnesty.org/download/Documents/32000/mde130022011en.pdf, accessed October 22, 2019.

mostly nonreligious. The families of the leftist prisoners acted with relative independence from the leftist political groups.

POLITICS OF THE BODIES

Just after the victory of the Islamic Revolution, graphic photos of the executed bodies of the *ancien régime*'s officials were published in national newspapers and broadcast on state television.[96] Except for a few intellectuals, nobody criticized the kangaroo revolutionary courts or publication of the graphic photos. In less than thirty months, after June 20, 1981, the photos of young girls were published in the state newspapers and media (at that time all independent media were banned), and the families of the disappeared were asked to go to the Evin prison to identify the unknown executed.[97]

After June 20, 1981, the bodies of Muslim victims were buried in religious cemeteries (there was no secular cemetery in Iran) in unmarked single or mass graves, and the bodies of nonbeliever victims were buried outside formal cemeteries in mass or single graves.[98] In Tehran, most nonbeliever victims and some dissidents killed in shootouts were buried in a piece of land southeast of the city in mass and single graves.[99] The regime named it "Cemetery of the Dammed," but the victims' families named it Khavaran.[100]

From examining current photos of plot 93 of Behesht Zahra cemetery[101] and Khavaran cemetery in Tehran, it is evident that the families were not allowed to put gravestones on the known graves in Khavaran cemetery and plot 93 of Behesht Zahra cemetery, and they were not allowed to put any signs showing who may be buried in the mass graves there. They were not

---

96 For example, see *Kayhan* newspaper, 27 Bahman 1357 (February 16, 1979).
97 Iraj Mesdaghi, "From June 20, 1981, to June 20, 2009" (2009), available at http://pezhvakeiran.com/maghaleh-11971.html, accessed October 22, 2019.
98 Sometimes, in small cities, the bodies of the nonbelievers were returned to the families. The families were not allowed to bury them in the official cemetery of the city; therefore, they had no choice but to bury them in their yards. See Masoud Noghrekar, *History Never Forgets Any Genocide*; also see "Prison Newsletter" (2009), available at www.akhbar-rooz.com/article.jsp?essayId=19379, accessed October 22, 2019.
99 See Nasser Mohajer, "The Mothers of Khavaran" (this volume); also see Jafar Behkish, "Khavaran Cemetery (Part 1)" (2010), available at http://jbehkish.blogspot.ca/2010/05/khavaran-cemetery-important-sign-of.html), accessed October 22, 2019.
100 Mohajer, "The Mothers of Khavaran" (this volume).
101 Behesht Zahra cemetery is the largest Muslim cemetery in Tehran. Behesht Zahra Organization oversees other cemeteries in Tehran. The main database of the deceased in Tehran is kept by the Behesht Zahra Organization.

allowed to plant trees and flowers. Plots 93 in Behesht Zahra and Khavaran cemetery are deserted and have remained so since the 1980s.

There is a confrontation over the victims' bodies. The IRI authorities buried the victims' bodies without any respectful ritual. The regime was of the opinion that the victims did not deserve peace and respect, even after death—that the public should know it is the fate of those who work against the IRI. Khavaran cemetery and other similar cemeteries serve such a purpose in Islamic Iran. The bodies of the enemies of the state are isolated.[102] In the formal database of the dead, there is no trace of those buried in Khavaran cemetery or even formal cemeteries. In the eyes of the officials, they do not exist.

Khavaran cemetery is not only a well-known symbol for the systematic human rights violations and atrocities in Iran; it is also a good example of the politics of bodies in the IRI era. The government buried the bodies in mass graves or unknown and unmarked graves in Khavaran to emphasize its opinion that the victims do not deserve any respect. But the families challenged this policy effectively. In the 1980s, when pressure on the families was very high, many families went to Khavaran each Friday morning.

On the first anniversary of the 1988 Massacre, the families of the victims, in collaboration with the Center to Support the Political Prisoners in Iran (inside the country), decided to hold a public commemoration in Khavaran cemetery on the first day of September 1989.[103] It was a very courageous action considering that any public commemoration for the victims was not allowed and was severely punished.[104]

Throughout the 1980s and most of the 1990s, the families were alone in Khavaran. Many families were arrested and detained for days or weeks in order to prevent the gatherings in Khavaran and the commemorations.[105] The perseverance of the families challenged the body politics of the IRI. Speaking on her arrest, Mother Riahi, who lost three sons in the 1980s

---

102 More than seventeen executed Baha'is are buried in Khavaran cemetery. In addition, deceased Baha'is are buried in several plots in the same area. See Mohajer, "The Mothers of Khavaran" (this volume).

103 Ibid.

104 Radio Hambastegi telephone interview with Mother Sharifi, a retired high school teacher and well-known member of the Mothers of Khavaran, about gathering in Khavaran cemetery for the victims of the 1988 Massacre, September 2008, available at http://radiohambastegi.se/sounds/sound.php?name=madar-sharifi.mp3&selectid=206, accessed October 22, 2019.

105 Maryam Hoseinkhah, "Unfinished Story – Mothers and Families of Khavaran: Three-Decade Search for Truth and Justice," interview with Manoto TV, September 20, 2015.

atrocities, recalled her answer to the interrogators who asked her to stop holding collective commemoration services and stop going to Khavaran cemetery with others:

> He said, "We're not telling you not to hold a memorial and we're not saying don't go to the gravesite. But why do you have to go there *together*? Why in groups?" I said, "You grouped us together. Eight years of going to prison to visit our kids got us acquainted. It's one year now since you've killed our kids. Acquainted, yes, indeed."[106]

The formal policy of the IRI against the families of the victims was to isolate them by arresting, harassing, and preventing them from going to Khavaran cemetery. The policy was somewhat successful in the early 1990s. During that period mostly families were going to Khavaran cemetery. After the 1997 presidential election, the gathering in Khavaran and the annual public commemorations became an important event inside Iran. Iranians in the diaspora also started to hold commemorations simultaneously in different cities in EU countries and North America. Subsequently, since 2004, the police and security forces have violently prevented the anniversary commemoration in Khavaran.[107] When these suppressive measures did not work as planned in June 2005, the authorities informed the families in Khavaran that they were going to "rebuild" the Khavaran cemetery.[108] Some of the families and Mothers of Khavaran issued a statement on August 27, 2005:

> If it is necessary to build a Khavaran flower garden, first the dates, the names, and the burial location of each of our loved ones should be announced. After that, the families of the victims would take care of the construction.[109]

---

106 Jafar Behkish, "Victims' Families: Searching for Truth and Justice" (2018), available at http://jbehkish.blogspot.ca/2018/03/victims-families-searching-for-truth.html, accessed October 26, 2019.

107 Mansoureh Behkish, "Khavaran and Continuation of Human Rights Violations" (2007), available at www.bidaran.net/spip.php?article131, accessed October 26, 2019.

108 Jafar Behkish, "Victims' Families: Searching for Truth and Justice" (2018), available at http://jbehkish.blogspot.ca/2018/03/victims-families-searching-for-truth.html, accessed October 26, 2019.

109 Ibid.

The Mothers of Khavaran were very active in successfully protesting the attempted destruction at that time.[110] But the gatherings in Khavaran cemetery became larger and larger; therefore, on December 25, 2008, the government sent bulldozers to Khavaran and demolished the graveyard, removed some topsoil, added new soil, and planted trees on individual and mass graves.[111] Nobody knows if they removed the remains of the victims. The destruction of Khavaran resulted in protests and led to condemnations from political, social, and human rights activists in Iran and international human rights advocacy organizations such as Amnesty International; the latter wrote in its statement:

> Amnesty International calls on the Iranian authorities to immediately stop the destruction of hundreds of individual and mass unmarked graves in Khavaran, south Tehran, to ensure that the site is preserved and to initiate a forensic investigation at the site as part of a long-overdue, thorough, independent and impartial investigation into the mass executions which began in 1988 and which are often referred to in Iran as the "prison massacres."[112]

POLITICS OF HUMAN RIGHTS AND JUSTICE-SEEKING MOVEMENTS

Other countries' experiences show that the movement for truth and justice is an essential component of the larger human rights movement.[113] But in Iran, after the 1979 Revolution and until 1999, there was no well-established and organized human rights movement. Before the 1979 Revolution, the grassroots collective actions for the defense of human rights were mostly limited to actions taken by the victims' families, student movements inside and outside Iran, and a handful of intellectuals and lawyers for the defense of political prisoners.[114]

---

110 Ibid.

111 See http://news.gooya.com/politics/archives/2009/02/083443print.php, accessed October 26, 2019.

112 Amnesty International, "Iran: Preserve the Khavaran Gravesite for Investigation into Mass Killings" (2009), available at www.amnesty.org/download/Documents/48000/mde130062009eng.pdf, accessed October 26, 2019.

113 Fernando J. Bosco, "Emotions that Build Networks: Geographies of Human Rights Movements in Argentina and Beyond" (2007), *Tijdschrift voor economische en sociale geografie*, 98, pp. 545, 550.

114 Nasser Mohajer, interview with Ali Shahandeh, member of the board of directors of the Iran Bar Association and Iranian jurist from 1979 to 1982, in *The Inescapable Escape* (2008), vol. 1, p. 84.

Several months after the 1979 Revolution, the IRI attacked the Iranian Jurist Association, Bar Association, and other lawyers' progressive organizations and personalities to eliminate any resistance against the Islamic judiciary system and retribution law.[115] Therefore, on June 20, 1981, when the systematic and widespread atrocities against dissidents started, there was no professional organization or grassroots human rights advocacy organization to stand beside the victims' families to save the lives of the prisoners and defend their rights.

In the late 1990s, when a new generation of human rights defenders emerged inside Iran, or some lawyers from the previous generation became active again, most kept themselves far from the issues of the IRI atrocities of the 1980s. Apart from ideological and political obstacles, the IRI made the risk of defending the victims of the 1980s atrocities so grave as to prevent activists from engaging in such activities.[116] Consequently, the emerging human rights movement developed ties with the Islamic reformists of the IRI, which allowed some space for their activities. In addition, the reformist camp and their affiliates in the human rights movement tried very hard to divide the justice-seeking movement into two periods: before and after 1997 and, later, before and after the Green movement.[117] This also weakened the justice-seeking movement in Iran.

Some of the victims' families were also active in other social movements, such as the women's movement. It was expected that the active presence of victims' families in other movements would facilitate a better understanding among other activists about the issues and demands of the victims' families. But in reality, most of the victims' families remained silent because they were afraid to be isolated by those who had close ties with Islamic reformists.[118]

Although there was no change in the policy toward the families of the victims of the 1980s massacres and toward the Mothers of Khavaran, the defeat of the Green movement and Islamic reformists made them more in

---

115 Mohajer, *The Inescapable Escape*, pp. 104–8.
116 Mansoureh Behkish, note on social media regarding her attempts to secure from Ms. Ebadi legal help for the families of the victims of the 1980s atrocities. Ms. Ebadi refused to even meet with her.
117 Although they never implicitly stated this policy, the content of their website shows that they have no respect or sympathy for the activities of the families, including those of the Mothers of Khavaran, of the victims of the 1980s atrocities.
118 Personal communication with six women's rights activists inside and outside Iran. As of 2018, all are in exile.

favor of radical change in Iran.[119] In recent years, a new generation of human rights defenders, especially in exile, have been radicalized and more open to support all victims and their families without discrimination.[120] Therefore, since February 1979, because of the discriminatory approach of many human rights activists toward the victims of the 1980s atrocities and their families, the IRI has been able to pursue its policy of isolation and denial with much less resistance. As a result, in most cases, the Mothers of Khavaran could only rely on its own initiatives and resources.

THE JUSTICE-SEEKING MOVEMENT IN IRAN SINCE 2000

The situation changed gradually after the presidential election of 1997. The re-emergence of resistance to dictatorship inside Iran led to a change in attitude of some social and political activists toward the massacres of the 1980s. The new environment provided more space for the victims' families to speak out about the massacres. They began to interact with the media whenever possible by writing articles or giving interviews about the atrocities and the ways in which the government had tried to stop the memorial services in Khavaran cemetery. Some contacted presidents Khatami, Ahmadinejad, and Rouhani, during each president's time in office, asking them to recognize their basic rights.[121] Their requests were as follows:

1. The names, dates of execution, and the burial location of the victims should be announced.
2. The burial of others on top of the mass graves of the victims should be prevented.
3. The restrictions on families to put signs and plant trees on the burial location of the victims should be removed.

---

119 A statement for peaceful regime change in Iran, signed by fifteen prominent Iranians including three members of the Defenders of Human Rights Center: Shirin Ebadi, Mohammad Seifzadeh, and Narges Mohammadi. Available at www.iranhumanrights. org/2018/02/15-prominent-iranians-call-for-a-referendum-on-the-islamic-republic, accessed October 26, 2019.
120 For such an approach see Maryam Hoseinkhah, *Unfinished Story – Mothers and Families of Khavaran: Three-Decade Search for Truth and Justice* (2015).
121 For example, see Mansoureh Behkish, "Mr. Rouhani, please hear our voice!" (2013), available at www.mpliran.net/2013/08/blog-post_7.html, accessed October 23, 2019; also see Parvaneh Milani, "Mr. Rouhani, Do you know that Mr. Pourmohammadi made many families grieve for their loved ones?" (2013), available at https://exilesactivist.wordpress. com/2013/08/19, accessed October 26, 2019.

4. Those who are responsible for the massacres of the 1980s should be held accountable.[122]

However, the families did not receive a response from any of the presidents.

The reaction to the changes was not unanimous among the families or with those who became active in supporting their requests for truth and justice. Some of the families thought that any public action, such as sending letters to officials, might intensify the government's pressure on the families. Others, who were silent throughout the 1980s and 1990s because of fear of possible state reaction to their radical political positions, found space to speak about the atrocities. They argued that, when possible, it is necessary to speak about the beliefs of the victims, because their *beliefs* were the main reason for their having been killed. Although they raise an important point, many of the families were not in agreement about publicly speaking about the ideals and beliefs of the victims in Khavaran cemetery.[123] They argued that any harsher reaction by the government, including preventing the families from going to Khavaran or holding commemoration ceremonies in Khavaran and/or their residences, would have a significant impact on the morale and emotions of the families,[124] weakening the justice-seeking movement.[125] Therefore, finding common ground among the families and political and social activists was, and still is, a difficult task.[126]

The efforts made by the bereaved families were eventually recognized. In 2008, the Iranian Women's Studies Foundation selected the Mothers of Khavaran as the "Women of the Year" at their nineteenth annual conference. The organizers announced that, "We are proud that after 20 years of honorable efforts for justice and against amnesia made by the 'Mothers of Khavaran,' we have selected them as the women of the year."[127]

---

122 Mothers of Khavaran, "The Complaint Letters of the Families of the Executed in the 1980s" (1988–2003), republished in Bidaran and available at www.bidaran.net/spip. php?article25, accessed October 26, 2019.

123 Personal communication with six participants in the commemoration.

124 Fernando J. Bosco, "Emotions that Build Networks: Geographies of Human Rights Movements in Argentina and Beyond" (2007) *Tijdschrift voor economische en sociale geografie*, 98, pp. 545, 550.

125 Mansoureh Behkish, "What Happened in Khavaran?" *Iran-e Emrooz* (2006), available at https://khawaran.wordpress.com/2016/02/27/k-4201, accessed October 26, 2019.

126 It is important to mention that the most famous human rights activists never went to Khavaran cemetery. They kept themselves at a safe distance from this important movement.

127 Golnaz Amin, "Preface," in *The Essential Needs of the Iranian Women Today* (2008), p. 4.

Since 1988, other families of the victims of the IRI's atrocities, such as the families of the victims of the "chain assassinations" (see p. 310), those detained and tortured after the disputed election in June 2009, and families of the activists of social movements, specifically workers' and students' movements, have joined the struggle for truth and justice.

Beginning in June 2009, peaceful demonstrations against the fraudulent presidential election were crushed by military and paramilitary forces. Dozens of protestors were killed on the streets or inside prisons, and thousands more were arrested. Neda Agha Soltan and Sohrab A'rabi, who were killed on the streets of Tehran in June 2009, became icons for protestors[128] inside and outside Iran.[129] Their families have announced that they have filed their grievances with the judicial system.[130]

In Tehran, after an invitation by several women's rights activists in late June 2009, relatives of victims, women rights activists, and their supporters gathered in Laleh Park, a well-known park in the center of Tehran. They gather every Saturday afternoon for a one-hour silent vigil, wearing dark clothing and holding candles in their hands. They are known as the Mourning Mothers of Iran or, later, as the Mothers of Park Laleh.[131] After a few weeks, the families of the victims of the 2009 suppression were threatened by the authorities in order to stop them from attending the vigil. This vigil attracted some support inside and outside Iran. The vigil in Laleh Park continued for seven months without the presence of the families of the victims. Some of the families of the victims of the atrocities of the 1980s did participate in the vigil to show their support and to emphasize that ultimately united action by the victims' families would be successful.[132]

The authorities attacked the vigil several times and arrested several participants on December 5, 2009, and January 9, 2010, keeping them in

---

128 The Islamic reformists' presidential candidates, Mir Hossein Mousavi and Mehdi Karroubi, and the former president, Mohammad Khatami, went to the homes of the victims of the protest movement to give their support and condolences to the families of the victims. Parvin Fahimi, mother of one of the young victims, also spoke in the Tehran city council to explain what happened to her son.

129 One of the popular slogans used by the people inside Iran was, "Our Sohrab [a student martyr] is not dead, it is the government that is dead."

130 There has been no report on the result of these claims.

131 See Mourning Mothers' Facebook and weblog, available at www.facebook.com/pages/Mourning-Mothers-of-Iran/121906523071, accessed October 27, 2019.

132 Personal communication with the participants of the vigil.

detention centers or Evin prison for several days.[133] They also arrested five of the supporters of the Mourning Mothers in early February 2010 and kept them in Evin prison for approximately forty days.[134]

Today, the knowledge that Iranians have about the atrocities that have taken place since February 1979 is more comprehensive than it has ever been. The victims' families have played a vital role in spreading this knowledge. The pain and agony felt by the families has motivated them to search for truth and justice. Their demand to know why, where, when, and by whom and under whose order the atrocities were committed has resulted in the mobilization of other activists and has challenged the policies of oppression and denial on the part of the IRI. The victims' families, along with other social and political activists, became a strong force for the promotion of human rights and for preventing the same atrocities from happening again in Iran.

THE MYKONOS TRIAL[135]

In the first decade after the 1979 Revolution, tens of thousands fled the country. The regrouping of the opposition outside Iran was a concern for the IRI.[136] Although state-sponsored terrorism had been used by the IRI from the beginning of its rule and the first assassination had taken place on December 7, 1979, in Paris,[137] it was after the 1988 Massacre and on into the late 1990s that such terrorism became one of the dominant oppressive measures used against opposition figures and groups both inside and outside Iran.[138] The intention was to eliminate the leaders and cadres of opposition groups

---

133 See "'Mourning Mothers' Arrested at Protest in Tehran," available at www.iranhumanrights.org/2009/12/mothers-arrested; also see "Detention of 33 Iranian Mothers Sparks Protest, Group Says," available at www.cnn.com/2010/WORLD/meast/01/10/iran.mourning.mothers/index.html; both accessed October 27, 2019.

134 Human Rights Watch, "Iran: Free 'Mourning Mothers' Supporters," March 5, 2010, available at www.hrw.org/news/2010/03/05/iran-free-mourning-mothers-supporters, accessed October 27, 2019.

135 In April 1992, IRI killers assassinated four prominent Iranian dissidents in the Mykonos Restaurant in Berlin. The trial of the perpetrators became known as the Mykonos Trial.

136 Iran Human Rights Documentation Center, "No Safe Haven: Iran's Global Assassination Campaign," 3 (2008), available at https://iranhrdc.org/no-safe-haven-irans-global-assassination-campaign, accessed October 27, 2019.

137 Iran Human Rights Documentation Center, "No Safe Haven," 2.

138 Mehran Payandeh, Abbas Khodagholi, and Hamid Nowzari, *Es Gibt Noch Richter in Berlin – Mykonos: Der Anschlag und der Prozess* (There Are Still Judges in Berlin: The Attack and the Trial) (Berlin: Nima Verlag, 2000), p. 16.

as well as prominent intellectuals.[139] During this period, the IRI intelligence services outside Iran assassinated more than a hundred opposition figures.[140] In most cases, the assassins were never caught.[141]

On September 17, 1992, Sadeq Sharafkandi and two other leaders of the Democratic Party of Iranian Kurdistan, and Nouri Dehkordi, an exiled Iranian political activist, were assassinated in the Mykonos Restaurant in Berlin. Shortly after the assassination, with leads from outside sources, the police were able to arrest several suspects.[142] The trial of the five Mykonos suspects opened on October 28, 1993, in the Berlin Court of Appeals, and the court issued its judgment, after a total of 246 sessions, on April 10, 1997.[143] Shohreh Badiei, the widow of Nouri Dehkordi, one of the victims, was dressed in black and was present for almost all the court sessions.[144] Her emotional testimony demonstrated that the assassinations were not only a political loss, but were also catastrophic for the families of the victims.[145] Other families of the victims also participated in all or some of the court sessions.[146] The presence of the victims' families and the contribution of their lawyers demonstrates the importance of active participation of the families in the search for truth and justice. Four men were convicted of the killings, while the fifth, a Lebanese man, was acquitted. Kazem Darabi, an Iranian, was convicted of organizing the killings on behalf of Iranian security forces.[147] The court found that Iran's political leaders, through a "committee for special operations," had ordered the killings. Members of the committee included Ali Khamenei (then Supreme Leader of the IRI), Ali Akbar Hashemi Rafsanjani (then President), Ali Akbar Velayati (then Foreign Minister), Ali Fallahian (then Minister of Intelligence), and other intelligence officials.[148] It is important to

---

139 Ibid., p. 15.
140 For a list of the victims of the IRI-sponsored terrorism outside Iran, see https://iranhrdc.org/no-safe-haven-irans-global-assassination-campaign, 3 (2008), accessed October 27, 2019.
141 See https://iranhrdc.org/no-safe-haven-irans-global-assassination-campaign, 3.1 (2008), accessed October 27, 2019.
142 Payandeh *et al.*, *Es Gibt Noch Richter in Berlin*, p. 52.
143 Iran Human Rights Documentation Center, *Murder at Mykonos: Anatomy of a Political Assassination* (2007), p. 13.
144 Payandeh *et al.*, *Es Gibt Noch Richter in Berlin*, p. 86.
145 Ibid.
146 Ibid., p. 156.
147 Amnesty International, "Iran: 'Mykonos' Trial Provides Further Evidence of Iranian Policy of Unlawful State Killings" (1997), available at www.amnesty.org/download/Documents/164000/mde130151997en.pdf, accessed October 27, 2019.
148 Amnesty International, "Iran: 'Mykonos' Trial Provides Further Evidence of Iranian Policy of Unlawful State Killings."

mention that there were some diplomatic efforts by the IRI and its allies to prevent a trial of the suspects of the Mykonos assassinations or at least limit the police and court investigation only to the individuals, not to the Iranian government.[149] In contrast to Shapour Bakhtiar's case in France, although the German government tried hard to prevent the judicial system from naming the IRI as the main suspect, there was an intention in Germany's judiciary and some media to bring the perpetrators, including high-ranking Iranian officials, to justice.[150]

The European Union (EU) released a statement on the same day that the court issued its verdict, and as a result, for the first time in recent history, EU members recalled their ambassadors from Tehran.

The Mykonos court's warrants and verdict were a catastrophic defeat for the IRI. Hossein Mousavian, Tehran's ambassador to Berlin at the time of the assassination and trial, wrote: "The consequence of the Mykonos verdict was therefore grave: Namely that for the first time since the Second World War there was no dialogue between Europe and Iran."[151] The IRI had never been so isolated from the rest of the world. It was also a significant defeat for the security forces and Islamic Revolutionary Guards Corp (IRGC), and it is reasonable to assume that top authorities of the IRI thought seriously about stopping overseas operations of their forces after the release of the verdict in the Berlin court.[152]

The Mykonos court's warrants and verdict were a significant triumph for the victims' families, human rights advocates and activists, and for Iranian opposition groups who, from the very first assassination of an IRI opponent outside of Iran, made it clear that the IRI was responsible for the killings; however, they did not take advantage of this opportunity to pursue the issue of gross human rights violations in Iran.

Furthermore, the verdict of the Mykonos trial might have influenced the outcome of the presidential election on May 23, 1997. The decision was specifically a defeat for the hardliners who, after the death of Ayatollah Khomeini,

---

149 Thomas Sancton, "Iran's State of Terror," *Time*, November 1996, p. 78, cited by Iran Human Rights Documentation Center, in *Murder at Mykonos: Anatomy of a Political Assassination* (2007), p. 13.

150 Mehran Payandeh, Abbas Khodagholi, and Hamid Nowzari, *Es Gibt Noch Richter in Berlin – Mykonos: Der Anschlag und der Prozess* (There Are Still Judges in Berlin: The Attack and the Trial) (Berlin: Nima Verlag, 2000), pp. 187–190.

151 Hossein S. Mousavian, *Iran–Europe Relations: Challenges and Opportunities* (Oxfordshire, UK: Routledge, 2008), p. 113.

152 After the Mykonos court issued warrants for the minister of intelligence, the assassination campaign in Europe was suspended until recently.

controlled the security forces and IRGC. The verdict led to the international isolation of the IRI for a short period of time.[153] As such, the defeat may have paved the way for the agenda of the "reformist" faction and the victory of Mohammad Khatami, their presidential candidate for the May 1997 election.

The outcome of the Mykonos trial demonstrates that, when justice is carried out properly and, in the process, at least some important aspects of truth are revealed and formally acknowledged, the cycle of violence may effectively break, thus building a more humane society. This, in turn, would help victims and their families, as well as society at large, to come to terms with the atrocities of the state and the losses suffered as a result.

JUSTICE DENIED: POLITICAL ASSASSINATIONS AFTER THE 1980S MASSACRES

In this section, the murder of several influential political activists and prominent intellectuals, known as "chain assassinations"[154] of 1998, one of the high-profile cases in the history of the IRI, is reviewed. The author shows the importance of this case in three respects:

- It was the first time that the IRI acknowledged a political crime committed by its officials.
- The victims' families were able to speak out and, for a short period of time, newspapers were allowed to provide coverage of the case.
- It was the first time that citizens were able to file their grievances in the judicial system against the officials of the IRI for political crimes.

In June 1999, when the student movement was crushed by the IRI, the balance of power changed toward the hardliners and, as a result, public media inside the country became completely unreachable. Furthermore, even though there was impunity for those who ordered the crimes, the case raised public awareness about the importance of basic civil and political rights.

---

153 The ambassadors of all but one EU country returned to Iran after the election of Khatami. Germany, however, delayed sending its ambassador back to Tehran in protest of the Mykonos verdict. It was only after President Khatami went against protocol and requested the return of the German ambassador that the high German presence was reestablished in Iran. See Hossein S. Mousavian, *Iran–Europe Relations: Challenges and Opportunities* (Oxfordshire, UK: Routledge, 2008), p. 202.

154 The author uses "chain assassinations" instead of "chain murders" to emphasize the political nature of the crimes.

On November 22, 1998, the shocking news of the brutal killing of Parvaneh Majd Eskandari (Forouhar) and Dariush Forouhar, two influential opposition figures, circulated in Tehran and then around the world. On December 2, 1998, Mohammad Mokhtari, a well-known author, secular intellectual, and one of the six members of the consulting committee of the Iranian Writers' Association (IWA),[155] disappeared, and on December 8 of that year he was declared murdered by the coroner's office, having been found suffocated. On the same day, Mohammad Jafar Pouyandeh, another well-known author, translator, and member of the consulting committee of the IWA, also disappeared. His body was found near Tehran on December 12, 1998; he had also been suffocated.[156]

The role of the security forces was clear in these crimes. More than twenty thousand people participated in the funeral ceremony of Parvaneh and Dariush Forouhar.[157] The people were chanting anti-government slogans such as "The murderers of the Forouhars are under the leader's cloak," a slogan that directly accused the Supreme Leader of protecting the killers or of authorizing the killings. Political and civil activists, intellectuals, and many ordinary citizens knew that these killings were an attempt by the hardliners to overshadow the people's demand for radical change.

Many of the high-ranking reformists and Mohammad Khatami's cabinet members came from the intelligence services, the judiciary system, or the IRGC.[158] Therefore, it is a reasonable assumption that they knew *who* was doing *what* in the Ministry of Intelligence and the IRGC. It is important to note that the assassination campaign started in the first decade after the 1979 Revolution when present-day reformists had the upper hand in the intelligence community.[159]

---

155 The intention of the consulting committee was to revive the Iranian Writers' Association, which had been campaigning for freedom of expression for more than thirty years.

156 While the government wants to limit the number of victims of the chain assassinations to these four, the actual number of victims is much higher. See Nasser Mohajer, "Crime and Punishment" (1999), available at www.ketabfarsi.org/ketabkhaneh/jostejoo/html/01081.htm, accessed October 28, 2019.

157 Personal communication with Parastou Forouhar, daughter of Parvaneh and Dariush Forouhar.

158 Mahmoud Zahedi, "Some Critiques on Ahmadinejad's Cabinet Which Are Not Valid" (2005), available at http://news.gooya.com/politics/archives/035139.php, accessed October 29, 2019.

159 Iran Human Rights Documentation Center, "No Safe Haven: Iran's Global Assassination Campaign," 3 (2008), available at https://iranhrdc.org/no-safe-haven-irans-global-assassination-campaign, accessed October 27, 2019.

The hardliners and Ayatollah Khamenei, the Supreme Leader, blamed "foreign powers" for the assassinations and said that "the enemy" was creating instability in order to undermine the progress of Iran's Islamic system.[160] They tried hard to block any serious investigation of the assassinations, but in December 1998, President Khatami appointed an investigation committee.

A compromise was reached between two factions of the IRI and, on January 6, 1999, the Ministry of Intelligence issued a statement admitting that "some of the rogue members of the Ministry had committed the crimes."[161] The case of the chain assassinations became the center of attention for the media as well as the public. The pro-reformist newspapers gave substantial coverage to the case and uncovered many other aspects that had not been mentioned in the Ministry's statement.[162] Akbar Ganji and Emadeddin Baghi, who had close ties with former high-ranking intelligence officials, published articles and books (which became best sellers) claiming that Ali Fallahian, the former Minister of Intelligence, Qurban Ali Dorri Najafabadi, the Minister of Intelligence at the time of the killings, and other high-ranking clerics, such as Mesbah Yazdi, had ordered and authorized the killings.[163]

The victims' families filed their cases with the judicial system just after the killings. The files were transferred to the judiciary organization of the armed forces in order to limit the access of victims' families and their lawyers. They wrote a letter to Ayatollah Shahroodi, then head of the judicial system, and asked him to reveal who was in charge of the case. Parastou Forouhar, daughter of Parvaneh and Dariush Forouhar, met with the designated judge to find answers to the questions of the victims' families about the factual circumstances surrounding the commission of the crimes, but none of her questions were answered.[164]

160 BBC, "Arrests Made in Iran Murder Case" (1998), available at http://news.bbc.co.uk/2/hi/middle_east/234954.stm, accessed October 29, 2019.
161 Nahid Mousavi, "A Review of Serial Murders" (1999), *Zanan Social & Cultural Magazine*, 58, available at http://archive.li/v1VrC, accessed October 28, 2019.
162 The publishers and editors of most pro-reformist newspapers were former high-ranking intelligence officials in the 1980s and 1990s. Akbar Ganji had a close relationship with several of these individuals including Saeed Hajjarian, one of the former deputies of the Ministry.
163 Akbar Ganji, *Ghosts' Darkhouse: Pathology of Transition to the Developmental Democratic State* (Tehran: Tarh-e No, 1999), in Farsi.
164 Parastou Forouhar, "Report to the Nation" (2002), available at www.iranrights.org/english/document-516.php, accessed October 29, 2019.

The brutal suppression of the student uprising of July 1999 and the mass closure of pro-reformist newspapers showed that the hardliners in the political establishment had reorganized after recovering from the shock of the 1997 election and the uncovering of the chain assassinations. They decisively used any means available to them for the suppression of the reform movement, including the use of military and paramilitary forces, parallel intelligence services, and the judicial system.

The judicial system reorganization after the 1979 Revolution was intended to move toward a more centralized Islamic system with power in the hands of the Supreme Leader.[165] This structure facilitates suppression of all opponents and critics, and prevents citizens from filing grievances against high-ranking officials, clerics, and other influential figures.[166]

Based on a deep understanding of the inherent biases and ineptitude of the judicial system, and with the intent to protest this mockery of justice, the families of the victims and their lawyers boycotted the trial. The trial of the perpetrators was launched by the military court behind closed doors on December 23, 2000, and was completed on January 19, 2001, after thirteen sessions.

The judicial system and the state decided to sacrifice some intelligence officers, including one of the deputy ministers, to protect those who had issued the fatwa labeling the victims as *Mortad* (atheist) or *Nasebi* (those who denigrate the Prophet Mohammad and the imams).[167] Because it was not beneficial to either faction of the government to accuse clerics of the killings,[168] the investigation committee appointed by President Khatami was also not willing to look beyond Saeed Emami, a deputy of the Ministry of Intelligence, who served as the link between the masterminds and operatives. Emami was found dead in custody under suspicious circumstances. The court's verdict only mentioned that "rogue elements" of the Ministry of Intelligence had carried out the crimes without any involvement on the

---

165 Forouhar, "Report to the Nation," p. 209.

166 Majid Mohammadi, *Judicial Reform and Reorganization in 20th Century Iran: State-building, Modernization and Islamicization* (2010), pp. 81–90; also see "Iran Document: The Tajzadeh Criticism and the Reformist Way Forward. Statement: *Father, Mother, we have been accused again*" (2010), available at http://enduringamerica.com/2010/06/18/iran-document-the-tajzadeh-criticism-and-the-reformist-way-forward-sahimi, accessed October 29, 2019.

167 Kazem Kardavani, "Chain Killings: A National Case" (2009) *Arash*, 86, January/February 2004, p. 36.

168 Parastou Forouhar, "Report to the Nation" (2002), available at www.iranrights.org/english/document-516.php, accessed October 29, 2019.

part of clerics, for example, Dorri Najafabadi, a high-ranking cleric and then Minister of Intelligence, who, according to Saeed Emami's confessions, was one of the clerics who had issued the fatwa.[169]

It was not surprising that the appointed investigation committee employed the same approach as hardliners given that its members consisted entirely of high-ranking intelligence officers and officials.[170] In this respect, the attempts made by the families of victims, human rights activists, journalists, some opposition groups and personalities, a number of intellectuals (including the IWA), some reformist politicians, and many citizens, had failed. Justice was denied.

In July 1999, the victims' families, with the help of lawyers and intellectuals, established the Committee for the Defense of the Rights of the Victims of the Chain Assassinations. The committee's goals were to: (a) investigate all murders related to the case, (b) bring all responsible parties before the courts, (c) research the social basis for these crimes, and (d) cooperate with human rights advocacy organizations.[171] The objectives of the committee were very broad, and it is not clear what plans they had to achieve these goals. The committee published a report[172] of its activities in November–December 2000. The report was silent about what they had accomplished given their goals.[173]

While it might seem that the active advocacy for truth and justice had failed,[174] the present author argues that the case was an important success for the victims' families, human rights advocates, and pro-democracy forces in Iran. First, the operational team of the assassination campaign was torn

---

169 The court did convict fourteen of the accused and acquitted three others. Three of the accused were sentenced to *qesas* (retribution), four to life imprisonment, one to 10 years, one to 6 years, and five others to 2.5–4 years. The families of the victims were against the death penalty and any cruel punishment and rejected *qesas*.

170 Akbar Ganji, "The Red Eminence and the Gray Eminences" (2000), 69, available at https://mamnoe.files.wordpress.com/2009/06/alyjenab-sorkhposh.pdf, accessed October 29, 2019.

171 Letters and Statement by the Committee for the Defense of the Rights of the Victims of the Chain Assassinations (2000), available at www.irhumanrights.com/paik9.pdf, accessed October 29, 2019.

172 Committee for the Defense of the Rights of the Victims of the Chain Assassinations (2000).

173 Akbar Ganji, on the first anniversary of the killings, suggested that a "National Truth Committee" be established. He proposed that the committee include the victims' families, independent jurists, independent national figures, and journalists. But his call was not heeded.

174 Cited by Parastou Forouhar in a personal communication.

apart, and the main security officers involved in the operation were arrested.[175] Moreover, those clerics who issued the fatwa for the killings distanced themselves from the assassination campaign to avoid exposure of the involvement of high-ranking officials in the killings; therefore, the hardliners were forced to halt their assassination campaign inside Iran.[176]

Second, the case brought human rights issues to the center of attention to a significant portion of city dwellers. Those involved in the case, including attorneys for the families of the victims, became prominent social figures in Iran, and this inspired other young activists to promote human rights in Iran. The attempts by the families and their lawyers to find truth and justice encouraged other lawyers to pursue fair political trials in Iran and to stand for victims' rights, despite the threats and pressure exerted by the government.

Third, the chain-assassinations case was an example of how the pursuit of justice and truth, which was the goal of victims' families, human rights activists, and civil society, resulted in city dwellers engaging in the debate about accountability, human rights, and critiques of the discriminatory and inhumane laws—a debate which would strengthen the bid for democracy. And finally, rejection of *qesas*, that is, the death penalty and all types of cruel punishment, heated up the sensitive debate around the death penalty, torture, and cruel punishment in society.

The case demonstrated that when the balance of power favors justice and openness, and when there is some freedom of speech, the mobilization of the public for truth and justice, as well as intense debate about the atrocities, is possible, and this in turn could force an oppressive government to acknowledge crimes committed by its officials and operatives.

POLITICS OF MEMORY AND JUSTICE IN CONTEMPORARY IRAN

This section briefly reviews the discourse among Iranians about justice and truth when a transition to democracy will be realized. First, it reviews the politics of justice and memory after the 1979 Revolution, the role of different

---

175 Mohammad Reza Sardari, "Chain Murders: Continuation of the 1988 Massacre" (2017), available at www.radiozamaneh.com/309920, accessed October 29, 2019.

176 On March 12, 2000, Saeed Hajjarian, one of the main figures among the supporters of President Khatami and member of the Tehran city council, was assassinated by Saeed Asghar, a member of one of the paramilitary groups sponsored by the IRI after the 1979 Revolution. Asghar was sentenced to fifteen years imprisonment but was released after one year.

actors in this period, and the atrocities that took place against the personalities of the *ancien régime*. Then, it briefly discusses how the politics of memory and justice have evolved since February 1979.

In recent years, a heated debate has raged among scholars and activists on how society should face the systematic and widespread human rights violations and brutalities by a dictatorial regime in order to facilitate a more peaceful transition to democracy.[177] Four main points help explain the current debate:

1. It has been argued that citizens' ignorance about the criminal acts of the IRI paved the road for the perpetrators to commit the same crimes again.
2. Survivors, victims' families, and growing numbers of human rights activists are seeking justice and truth.
3. It is claimed that "reformist leaders" are among those who must be held, directly or by deputy, responsible for the massacres as well as systematic and gross human rights violations of the 1980s.
4. Many opposition figures argue that if the perpetrators feel that they will face a trial and punishment for the past atrocities, the chance of a negotiated and peaceful transition will diminish.

Justice and "Public Opinion" After the 1979 Revolution

The 1979 Revolution was a great victory for Iranians after the long reign of a repressive regime. The Revolution was mainly peaceful, but toward the end, several acts of brutality were carried out against agents of the Shah's regime. As a result, Ayatollah Taleghani, a moderate cleric and one of the leaders of the Revolution, asked for a general amnesty, which was rejected by Khomeini.[178] Yet two days after seizing power, Ayatollah Khomeini appointed three clerics as the shari'a judges of the revolutionary tribunal[179] and directed

---

177 International Center for Transitional Justice, available at www.ictj.org/about/transitional-justice, accessed October 29, 2019.
178 Ebrahim Yazdi, "The Death Penalties Issued by Ayatollah Khomeini" (2008), available at www.tarikhirani.ir/fa/news/8099, accessed October 31, 2019.
179 According to Amnesty International, there were revolutionary tribunals in sixty-four cities around the country. See the Amnesty International report after their only visit to Iran following the 1979 Revolution from April 12 to May 1, 1979: "Law and Human Rights in The Islamic Republic of Iran, 1980" (1980), pp. 44–5, available at www.amnesty.org/download/Documents/200000/mde130031980en.pdf, accessed October 29, 2019.

them to follow shari'a law.[180] From February 1979 to June 1981, 757 people were executed by the tribunals.[181]

Shortly after Ayatollah Khomeini appointed the judges, it became clear that Mehdi Bazargan, the appointed provisional Prime Minister (from February to November 1979), did not agree with the tribunals' proceedings and verdicts.[182] He was not against the death penalty, but he wanted to have a proper trial for the accused.[183] In addition to Mehdi Bazargan, moderate clerics voiced some objections to the revolutionary tribunals. Ayatollah Shariatmadari, a grand ayatollah, also objected to the tribunals.[184] Sadeq Khalkhali, one of the appointed judges, accused Shariatmadari and Bazargan of being nonrevolutionaries.[185]

Most clerics, IRI officials, opposition groups, and even some lawyers and "human rights activists" shared the same opinion as Sadeq Khalkhali about brutally treating the ruling personalities of the Shah's regime.[186] Even the Iranian Bar Association only objected to arbitrary arrests and summary trials of opposition groups' members, not the Shah regime's officials.[187] There are only a few reports about the objection to the revolutionary tribunal's procedure and verdicts by intellectuals and human rights lawyers.

Some opposition groups requested that the tribunals expand their mandate

---

180 The three appointed judges were Hojat al-Islam Khalkhali, Hojat al-Islam Anvari, and Hojat al-Islam Jannati; however, the last two were not actively involved in the proceedings of the tribunal. See Sadeq Khalkhali, *Memoirs of Ayatollah Khalkhali: The First Religious Judge of the Revolutionary Tribunals* (Tehran: Sayeh Publications, 2000), p. 291. Khalkhali "brought to his job as Chief Justice of the revolutionary courts a relish for summary executions... that earned him a reputation as Iran's hanging judge." See *Daily Telegraph*, November 28, 2003.

181 Iran Human Rights Documentation Center, "A Faith Denied: The Prosecution of Baha'is in Iran" (2006), available at www.iranhrdc.org, accessed October 22, 2019; also see www. amnesty.org/download/Documents/200000/mde130031980en.pdf, accessed October 29, 2019.

182 Mehdi Bazargan, *Iran: Revolution in Two Steps* (Tehran: Mazaheri, 1984).

183 Ebrahim Yazdi, "The Death Penalties Issued by Ayatollah Khomeini" (2008), available at www.tarikhirani.ir/fa/news/8099, accessed October 31, 2019.

184 Amnesty International, "Law and Human Rights in The Islamic Republic of Iran, 1980" (1980), p. 52, available at www.amnesty.org/download/Documents/200000/mde130031980en.pdf, accessed October 29, 2019.

185 Amnesty International, "Law and Human Rights in The Islamic Republic of Iran, 1980," p. 52.

186 Monireh Baradaran – Soheila A., "Left and Capital Punishment", *Noghteh*, 7 (1997).

187 Amnesty International, "Law and Human Rights in The Islamic Republic of Iran, 1980," p. 31.

to cover landlords and capitalists.[188] They thought that democracy and human rights were not necessary for a fair and just society. After a short time, the tribunals expanded their mandate to include "counterrevolutionary activities" of the political opposition and religious minorities.[189] Followers of Khomeini supported and facilitated the move, but the opposition groups strongly opposed the revolutionary tribunals' verdicts against minorities and activists.

Meanwhile, there were no attempts to document the "truth" about the past atrocities. The request by a few in the provisional government to give time to the accused to reveal the truth about past wrongdoings was not welcomed by Ayatollah Khomeini and his followers.[190] There were only a few trials, which were held publicly, for the Shah's security service torturers.[191] The judges issued their verdicts, which were all death sentences, after only a few sessions.[192]

The discourse on "justice" and public opinion at that time was completely in favor of summary trial and execution. The only objections, apart from those raised by the supporters of the past regime, came from some intellectuals and human rights lawyers, some cabinet members of the provisional government, and some of the moderate clerics.

Politics of Memory

Since the 1980s atrocities, the victims and their families have acted, individually or collectively, against the IRI policy of denial and amnesia. They want the *absolute truth* about the atrocities to be revealed. However, the IRI, like other dictatorial regimes,[193] claims that suppression is a necessary measure for national unity, the welfare of citizens, and the safeguarding of the moral

---

188 For example, see *Omat*, a magazine of the "Militant Muslims' Movement," an Islamist-nationalist group: *Omat*, 2, available at www.iran-archive.com/sites/default/files/sanad/00002-1358-02-05.pdf, accessed October 30, 2019.

189 For example, see *Kar*, 30, available at www.iran-archive.com/sites/default/files/sanad/kar-ta-ensheaab_1-60-030.pdf, accessed October 30, 2019.

190 Ebrahim Yazdi, "The Death Penalties Issued by Ayatollah Khomeini" (2008), available at www.khandaniha.eu/items.php?id=274.

191 Some of the opposition groups objected to some of these public trials as a plan by the followers of Ayatollah Khomeini to use the SAVAK interrogators against their opposition.

192 Amnesty International reported two public trials in Tehran and one in Tabriz, but most of the other trials were behind closed doors.

193 Andreas E. Feldmann and Maiju Perälä, "Reassessing the Causes of Nongovernmental Terrorism in Latin America," *Latin American Politics and Society*, 46, 2 (2004), p. 108.

and religious beliefs of people. The denial of any wrongdoing is the formal policy of the IRI.

In the following paragraphs, the author briefly explains, using the Schirmer approach, how the politics of memory have been developed in Iran and shows that there is a sensitive political challenge regarding how to make sure that truth prevails and serves as the political foundation for Iran's future.[194]

The IRI used all of its power to silence the victims and their families after 1981. State media[195] only promoted the IRI's so-called version of the truth; however, the situation in Iran is rather complicated. Followers of Khomeini, who had the upper hand in all government branches in the 1980s,[196] were the perpetrators of gross human rights violations. Their version of the truth regarding the atrocities of the 1980s is identical to that of the hardliners. They claim that their actions during that period were based on democratic codes of conduct;[197] however, hardliners and some opposition groups have challenged their position. On the one hand, hardliners asked: If followers of Khomeini are honest about their condemnation of the recent arrests, trials, and executions, why are they still justifying the mass arrests and executions of the 1980s?[198] On the other hand, some opposition groups have said that reformists are responsible for the atrocities of the 1980s and they should be held accountable for those atrocities. Some of the reformists, in response to these allegations, have decided to come forward and condemn the wrongdoings and ask for forgiveness.[199] Although the condemnation was welcomed by some victims and their families, by using Gibney's approach, one can argue

---

194 According to Jennifer Schirmer, a political anthropologist and the author of many books on political violence, there are questions about the extent to which "truth" is in the telling: whether truth varies with the form of the narrative, with the understanding of those who do the telling, or with the listeners who must *decide* what is true. "If the final story of the truth depends on who you chose to speak with—and believe—then we need to speak and listen to many...we cannot assume that we already know what the truth is, especially if that truth is to serve as the political baseline for the future" of a nation. See Jennifer Schirmer, "Whose Testimony? Whose Truth? Where Are the Armed Actors in the Stoll-Menchu Controversy?," *Human Rights Quarterly*, 25, pp. 60–73.

195 The few independent magazines that existed were not allowed to publish anything about the past atrocities.

196 Mustafa Tajzadeh, "*Matn va hashiyeh*," *Cheshmandaz-e Iran*, 26 (2005).

197 Ibid.

198 Mohammad J. Larijani, Debate between Larijani (deputy of judicial system) and Kavakebian (leader of Hezb-e Mardomsalari), 2009.

199 Mustafa Tajzadeh, in "Iran Document: The Tajzadeh Criticism and the Reformist Way Forward. Statement: *Father, Mother, we have been accused again*" (2010), available at http://enduringamerica.com/2010/06/18/iran-document-the-tajzadeh-criticism-and-the-reformist-way-forward-sahimi, accessed October 29, 2019.

that it is not a genuine request because the reformists did not talk about what had happened in the 1980s and their roles therein.[200]

Some other reformists have asked for a national repentance. They have argued that opposition groups, the IRI, and even all citizens who were silent should be held responsible for the atrocities.[201] Some of the opposition figures have also followed the same approach and put the burden on all political actors.[202] By using Arendt's methodology, one can argue that if all citizens are seen as being "collectively guilty" of the wrongdoings, then individual actors and institutions responsible for the crimes committed by the IRI since February 1979 are hidden and normalized. Who is guilty?[203] Most other groups have also based their reactions regarding the past atrocities on their rather narrow political agendas instead of an understanding of human rights codes of conduct.

As for collective memory, one may ask: Is it possible to have a unique and all-inclusive collective memory? Although most Iranians, especially the young generations, are not informed about the atrocities of the past, those who know about the atrocities are deeply divided on what has happened. According to Mohammed Reza Nikfar,[204] it seems that there are competing collective memories and there is no possibility of eliminating other versions

200 Marc Gibney and Rhoda E. Howard-Hassmann, Canadian social scientists who specialize in international human rights, argue that if we assume apology is an effort to build a bridge between victims and perpetrators of the state atrocities or between past, present, and future, then the truth shall be revealed first. It should be very clear who is apologizing to whom and for what. Without truth, without acknowledging that wrongs have happened in the past, there would not be any apology. Based on this reasoning, they presume that political apologies pertain to democratic societies. A case in point is the aboriginals in Canada. Without an effective public inquiry into what happened to the first peoples of Canada, any government apology would be only an empty word. An apology without truth hurts victims more. See Mark Gibney et al. (eds.), The Age of Apology: Facing Up to the Past (Philadelphia: University of Pennsylvania Press, 2007), pp. 1–9.

201 Ali Reza Alavitabar, "30th of Khordad 1360, Non-tolerable Regime, Totalitarian Opposition" (2003), available at www.meisami.net/ch19/34-47.htm, accessed October 31, 2019.

202 Y. Reza Fani, "For Setup of the Truth Commission" (2009), available at www.rezafani.com/index.php?/site/comments/truth, accessed October 31, 2019.

203 According to Hannah Arendt, "When all are guilty, no one is; confessions of collective guilt are the best possible safeguard against the discovery of culprits, and the very magnitude of the crime the best excuse for doing nothing." However, she distinguishes between political responsibility and collective guilt. See her book, On Violence (Orlando, Florida: Houghton Mifflin Harcourt, 1970), p. 65.

204 Mohammad Reza Nikfar (b. 1956) is a renowned Iranian political scientist and essayist. He lives in Köln, Germany, and is currently the chief editor of the Persian-language Radio Zamaneh (based in Amsterdam).

of what has happened in the past.[205] One of the major intentions of transitional justice, Barahona argues, is to replace the version developed by the dictatorial regime with a version that is more in favor of the victims who have suffered from the atrocities.[206] Although Iran is not in a transitional period to democracy, the struggle to overcome the IRI's official truth have started already: the survivors, victims' families, human rights activists, and opposition groups are trying hard to influence the hearts and minds of younger generations born in the IRI era.

Politics of Justice

The call for democracy is the central demand of many Iranians. Currently, many of the activists and intellectuals are facing the following crucial questions:

- If the transition to democracy is to be realized, what should be the response to the atrocities of the IRI?
- What form of justice could fulfill the moral, political, and social obligations of a transitional government?
- Do the legitimate requests of the survivors, victims' families, and human rights activists for the trial of those responsible for the past atrocities undermine the equally legitimate requests of many Iranians for peace, stability, and democracy?

There are no clear-cut answers to these questions; not because the demand for justice is not legitimate, but because society in its transitional period faces serious challenges. It is not clear where the balance of power will fall and what forces will play pivotal roles during the transitional period.[207] The way a society faces past atrocities is also determined by the culture, tradition, and historical experience of each nation including their religious and ethical beliefs.

It is also clear that a transitional regime will face an unsympathetic judiciary dominated by the supporters of the *ancien régime*.[208] In this matter, the

---

205 Mohammad Reza Nikfar, *The Memory of That Summer* (2008).

206 "Introduction," in *The Politics of Memory: Transitional Justice in Democratizing Societies* (Alexandra Barahona De Brito *et al.*, eds.), 2001, pp. 1–39.

207 Neil Kritz *et al.*, *Transitional Justice: How Emerging Democracies Reckon with Former Regimes* (Washington: United States Institute of Peace, 1995), pp. 65–81.

208 Robert I. Rotberg and Dennis Thompson, *Truth v. Justice: The Morality of Truth Commissions* (Princeton University Press: Princeton, New Jersey, 2000), p. 75.

author agrees with Judge Baltasar Garzon who advocates (a) investigation of all perpetrators from the top to the bottom, (b) marshaling of sufficient personnel and material means for a complete investigation, and (c) if it is not possible to sanction *all* perpetrators, then seeking reconciliation for the inferiors and *not* for the superiors, as they are the ones who are *truly* responsible.[209]

Many political activists who are trying to reform the IRI consider the demand for the trial and punishment of those responsible for the past crimes as an act of revenge.[210] Taqi Rahmani, who spent fourteen years in prison, wrote to the victims' families that "the trial and conviction of perpetrators does not help to break the cycle of revenge and violence, and powerless people will be the losers."[211] It is not clear why the trial and conviction of the wrongdoers in a proper court of law might ignite violence in Iran again.[212] Without a doubt, the terrible experience of "wild justice" after the 1979 Revolution, which replaced justice with retaliation and revenge, may have influenced the opinions of these political activists. However, they may have missed the fact that, contrary to the demand for the execution of the Shah's officers after the 1979 Revolution, most of the survivors and victims' families are against the death penalty and any sort of cruel punishment and retaliation.[213]

The appeal to abolish the death penalty and cruel punishment in Iran is not limited to the victims' families. Most of the opposition groups have proclaimed that they are against capital punishment.[214] This development among the opposition of the IRI, provides some hope for the possibility of a peaceful transition to democracy without repetition of the bloodshed following the 1979 Revolution. At the same time, the reformists' faction of the IRI has not been willing to commit to the abolition of the death penalty and other forms of cruel punishment.[215]

---

209 Daniel Rothenberg, "Let Justice Judge: An Interview with Judge Baltasar Garzon and Analysis of His idea." *Human Rights Quarterly*, 24 (2002), p. 948.

210 Taqi Rahmani, "Mothers of Pain and Wait" (2009), available at www.kar-online.com/node/1149, accessed October 31, 2019.

211 Ibid.

212 The request to avoid acts of revenge is not only limited to Iranians: Archbishop Desmond Tutu, head of the Truth and Reconciliation Committee in South Africa, also requested that the victims and their families avoid the act of revenge based on the teachings of Christianity.

213 Stated in Parvaneh Milani's acceptance speech for The Gwangju Prize for Human Rights on behalf of the Mothers of Khavaran (2013).

214 For example, see Nader Rafiienejad, *Execution: The Tool for Mullahs to Stay in Power* (Ashraf, Iraq: Amirkhiz, 2005), p. 19.

215 Emadeddin Baghi, in his letter to Mohsen Mirdamadi, the secretary-general of Jebheh-ye Mosharekat-e Iran-e Eslami, on August 28, 2007.

Those who claim that the trial and punishment of wrongdoers are acts of revenge that will cause the escalation of violence in Iran ask victims and their families to forgive the perpetrators.[216] The author agrees with Shadi Sadr, a human rights lawyer, when she asks: How is it possible to ask a mother to forgive her child's killers when she doesn't know how her child was murdered and where he or she was buried? Isn't this another form of brutality?[217] These individuals also ignore the fact that the act of forgiveness by itself has no advantage, at least in its ability to reconcile both sides of a conflict or dispute, without the wrongdoers genuinely asking for forgiveness and acknowledging (that is, revealing the truth about) their past wrongdoings.[218]

Furthermore, some of these political activists and intellectuals have observed the experiences of selective countries in which transitions have happened through reform or negotiation, and have concluded that, in order to facilitate a peaceful transition in Iran, the opposition must assure the IRI officials that there will not be any sort of trial and punishment for the perpe-trators of the atrocities.[219] As a result, these individuals try hard to convince the victims and their families to forgive the perpetrators in order to have a moral justification for amnesty. They are ready to sacrifice justice in exchange for peaceful transition to democracy. But there is no indication that the IRI in its entirety (that is, all of its political factions) is ready to agree with any group of the opposition on the transition to democracy; all the facts indicate that the IRI is going the other way.

On the other side of the political spectrum, there are some who seem to employ seeking justice for their own political agenda.[220] These groups hold commemorations for the victims of the atrocities of the 1980s[221] mainly to expose the IRI. In their eyes, the ceremony is primarily an opportunity to condemn the IRI, not to promote human rights in Iran.

---

216 Reza Alijani, "Upside-Down Peace in Mandela's Forgiveness" (2008), available at http://talar.shandel.info/thread-437.html#pid2293, accessed October 31, 2019.
217 Shadi Sadr, "On the Meaninglessness of Forgiveness" (2010), available at www.akhbar-rooz.com/article.jsp?essayId=26449, accessed October 31, 2019.
218 Robert I. Rotberg and Dennis Thompson, *Truth v. Justice: The Morality of Truth Commissions* (Princeton University Press: Princeton, New Jersey, 2000), pp. 179–82.
219 Akbar Ganji, *What We Should Do with the IRI* (2010).
220 For example, see "Campaign to Set Up an International Court to Investigate the Massacres of Political Prisoners in Iran" (2009) in *Iran Tribunal: International People's Tribunal* (Sweden: Iran Tribunal Publication, 2013).
221 It is interesting to note that those "leftists" who support reformists within the IRI almost never held any commemorations for the atrocities of the 1980s until Ahmadinejad came to power.

It is accurate to state that the appeal by the victims, their families, and human rights activists for justice and truth is a form of resistance to the dictatorial regime.[222] But, to the author's understanding, it is more than anything an attempt to force government officials to admit their wrongdoings and follow international norms that help protect all people everywhere from severe political, legal, and social abuses, which in and of itself is a strong form of resistance against the dictatorial regime. However, it is neither the request of many of the victims' families in Iran and abroad nor that of human rights activists to use the issue of accountability as a tool to overthrow the government. Mohammad Reza Moini, who lost his brother in the 1988 Massacre, wrote:

> Seeking justice for the victims of the 1988 prison massacre is not only a legal destiny; seeking justice is not only the pursuit of the punishment of the wrongdoers and compensation for the victims. Punishment is only part of justice, which acknowledges the rights of the victims and stops impunity... the significance of the court verdict is the formal acknowledgment of the [crimes] that were carried out and denied by formal history.[223]

Language of Memory and Justice

The author must briefly touch on the subject of language, which has been used in the transitional-justice discourse. In the 1980s and early 1990s, the language of memory and justice was mostly overshadowed by a radical political language. There was no independent discourse on memory and justice due to a weak human rights movement, few published prison memoirs, and no strong voice from the victims' families.

In the 1990s and first decade of the twenty-first century, the number of prison memoirs increased dramatically. More importantly, the *language* employed by the authors experienced a dramatic change. In the early memoirs, the language used was more similar to political reports and analyses, but in later memoirs the language became more colorful and more personal.[224]

222 Alexandra Barahona De Brito *et al.* (eds.), *The Politics of Memory: Transitional Justice in Democratizing Societies* (2001), p. 119.
223 Mohammad Reza Moini, "Seeking Justice is a Campaign for Today" (2008), available at www.bidaran.net/spip.php?article167, accessed October 22, 2019.
224 Azam Kiakejouri, *Prison Memoirs: A Linguistic View* (Sweden: Baran Publications, 2005), pp. 8–9.

The memoirs also evolved from a narrative about the relationships between prisoners and prison guards to narratives which focused more on the relationships between prisoners.[225]

The other important development, as described in the first and third sections, was that victims' families became more vocal. As it developed, the voice of the victims' families in Iran became more independent and more vibrant in comparison with the language used by political activists. This development had a great impact on how the language of memory and justice separated itself from tough political language.

The brutalities that took place in Iran after the 1979 Revolution, and the inception of the IRI, were targeted against a very diverse population. This diversity and the large number of victims might lead to the assumption that a strong movement for truth and justice in Iran would result. But during the first two decades of the IRI, most of the survivors and victims' families were silent and not willing to confront the government. In the first decade, there was no space for those survivors and the victims' families who wanted to raise their voices for justice and truth. However, some of them, despite all the threats and pressure of the authorities, continuously went to Khavaran cemetery, other cemeteries, and also held commemoration services for the victims in their residences. Furthermore, they went to the authorities and wrote letters demanding truth and justice for the 1980s massacres, other political killings that had occurred since February 1979, and also to ask for improvement in prison conditions for those still imprisoned.

Furthermore, at that time, most prominent human rights lawyers and activists inside Iran distanced themselves from the atrocities of the 1980s. The official policy of all factions of the IRI was, and continues to be, denial and cover-up. Moreover, opposition groups were not able to form a strong voice for justice and truth. Inside Iran, opposition groups were brutally suppressed and, in exile, they were divided. Those in favor of forming some sort of coalition with the IRI in the hope of transitioning to democracy were against any activity that could jeopardize their own political agenda.

This situation changed in 1997 when the verdict of the Mykonos trial apparently put a halt to the terrorist operations of the IRGC and of the intelligence services outside of Iran. The disclosure of the chain assassinations and the efforts made by the victims' families, journalists, and human rights lawyers, as well as the support and resolve of motivated citizens,

---

225 Majid Khoshdel, interview with Nasser Mohajer, *Prison Memoirs Review* (2008), available at www.goftogoo.net/matlabPage1.php?id=34, accessed October 31, 2019.

seemed to put an end to the extrajudicial killings by the IRGC and intelligence services.

During this time, some of the survivors and victims' families became very vocal and active. Their presence in Persian media abroad, whenever possible, challenged the policy of denial and amnesia. Iranians in exile also became more active and started to hold ceremonies in commemoration of the 1980s atrocities, the Mykonos killings, and the chain assassinations. As a result of all these changes, many Iranians in exile became more involved in human rights activities and gained a stronger voice for justice and truth. Although those human rights activists who are connected to, or sympathetic to, Islamic reformists remain reluctant to support the movement for truth and justice, specifically the Mothers of Khavaran, changes since 1997 have empowered more radical approaches among human rights activities inside and outside Iran.

The new political atmosphere after the disputed presidential election of June 12, 2009, as well as large and widespread protests against the IRI in late 2017 and early 2018, has led to further brutal suppression of dissents. The reality of dozens of protestor casualties, detainment of thousands, and the forced exile of activists who are more in favor of *radical change* in Iran instead of piecemeal reforms led by the Islamic reformists have all provided a new space in which to talk about the atrocities of the past.

The balance of power is gradually turning in favor of justice.

Appendix A

Unearthing a Crime Against Humanity in Bits and Pieces[1]

KAVEH YAZDANI[2]

In what follows, we will delve into how the "Great Massacre" of 1988 was reported, reflected upon and reacted to by Amnesty International, the United Nations, and Western parliaments (such as the European Parliament and the Canadian House of Commons), as well as a number of newspapers and international news agencies such as *The New York Times, The Washington Post, The Christian Science Monitor, The Independent, Le Monde, L'Humanité, TAZ (Die Tageszeitung), Neues Deutschland,* the Associated Press, and Reuters.[3]

Other than Ayatollah Ruhollah Mousavi Khomeini's first fatwa and

1 I would like to express my sincere gratitude to Siavush Randjbar-Daemi for kindly providing us with important sources that greatly enhanced the quality of this section, and also for his fine translations of some important documents from Italian into English. Nasser Mohajer also deserves an abundance of gratitude for carefully reading this manuscript and making invaluable suggestions and additions. Without his initiative, encouragement, and criticisms, the writing of this article would not have been possible. I would also like to thank Laura Gaurjance for her careful and valuable additions, as well as Naima and Kimberly Bright for their helpful corrections and suggestions.

2 Kaveh Yazdani received his Ph.D. degree at the University of Osnabrück in 2014 (*summa cum laude*). He was granted the Prince Dr. Sabbar Farman-Farmaian Fellowship at the International Institute of Social History (IISH) in Amsterdam in 2015 and a Mellon Postdoctoral Research Fellowship at the Centre for Indian Studies in Africa (CISA), University of the Witwatersrand, Johannesburg, South Africa between 2015 and 2017. He is currently a lecturer in economic history at the University of Bielefeld and a research associate at CISA. He is the author of the monograph *India, Modernity and the "Great Divergence": Mysore and Gujarat (17th to 19th C.),* Leiden 2017 and co-editor of a recent volume entitled *Capitalisms: Towards a Global History,* Oxford 2020.

3 A considerable number of these documents can be consulted on the following website: https://www.noghteh.org/en/massacre-1988-iran/.

edict (see "Theocracy Memos," p. 360, at the end of this appendix),[4] and also the correspondence between Ayatollah Khomeini and Ayatollah Hossein Ali Montazeri—the second in command in the Islamic Republic of Iran's Shi'ite hierarchy—these records represent Europe and North America's first exposure to one of the most atrocious crimes in the last quarter of the twentieth century. They also reveal how the trickling information on the executions was gradually acknowledged in Europe and North America.

AYATOLLAH KHOMEINI'S FATWA AND EDICT, AND AYATOLLAH MONTAZERI'S LETTERS

The Islamic Republic of Iran (IRI) accepted UN Security Council Resolution 598, stipulating a ceasefire between Iran and Iraq, on July 20, 1988. Three days after this astounding event, the National Liberation Army (NLA)—the armed wing of the People's Mojahedin Organization of Iran (PMOI), an exiled Iranian opposition group based in Iraq—crossed the western borders of Iran. Its self-proclaimed intention was to eliminate the "Reactionary Islamic Regime." As the IRI's position seemed to be weakened due to the unexpected ceasefire, the Mojahedin believed that the Iranian people would join its military attack to overthrow the state. However, the people in Iran did not follow the PMOI's call to revolt, and the NLA suffered a crushing defeat by the combined armed forces of the IRI.[5]

The massacre of political prisoners began a few days after the PMOI's incursion, following the fatwa and edict issued by Ayatollah Khomeini. Neither the fatwa nor the edict was dated. Although it is unknown exactly when they were written, we now know that the fatwa was implemented on July 28, 1988.[6] This date has been corroborated by Ayatollah Montazeri

---

4 On July 9, 2017, Ali Fallahian, Iran's former Minister of Intelligence, confirmed to the state-affiliated Tarikh Online website that a fatwa by Ayatollah Khomeini in the summer of 1988 called for the eradication of all affiliates of the strongest Iranian opposition group, the People's Mojahedin Organization of Iran (PMOI also referred to as MEK). https://iran1988.org/ali-fallahian-former-intelligence-minister-iran-says-khomeini-ordered-execution-pmoi-affiliates-1988-massacre/.

5 See Nasser Mohajer, "The Mothers of Khavaran" (this volume) for more details.

6 This information is based on Ayatollah Montazeri's memoirs and on many testimonies, including those of Hossein Ali Nayyeri, who acted as religious judge in Tehran's Death Commission of 1988 and, on August 15, 1988, revealed to Ayatollah Montazeri that since July 15, 1988, they had already executed 750 prisoners in Tehran and planned to kill 200 more. See www.hamneshinbahar.net/article.php?text_id=418. A number of

and Hossein Ali Nayyeri, the religious (shari'a) judge and board member presiding over the inquisition tribunal. Additionally, a UN report of the Economic and Social Council stipulated that on July 28 about 200 political prisoners were murdered in Evin prison.[7] The fact that on July 28 executions were carried out, more or less simultaneously in various cities throughout the country suggests that the decision was most probably centrally planned some time before Ayatollah Khomeini issued the fatwa and edict.[8]

According to Ayatollah Montazeri and some other sources, a second fatwa or edict was issued later ordering the execution of "non-religious and communist" political prisoners. But this document has never been unearthed or revealed.[9]

By December 1988, "the evidence for mass executions was... indisputable" as it became known that "the true total could run into thousands."[10] However, high officials of the IRI either denied the accusations or justified the executions by suggesting that they were wiping out Iranian pawns and mercenaries of the belligerent Iraqi state arrested at the borders. It is important to note that Ayatollah Montazeri was the first and only prominent personality of the theocratic state who diverged from the official narrative and in three letters voiced some opposition to the executions of political prisoners. The first two letters were dated July 31 and August 4, 1988, and were directed to Ayatollah Khomeini. The third letter, dated August 15, 1988, was addressed to the four-member board presiding over the inquisition tribunals: Hossein

recently published reports also confirm this assertion. See, for example, Report of an Inquiry Conducted by Geoffrey Robertson QC, published as *The Massacre of Political Prisoners in Iran, 1988*, Abdorrahman Boroumand Foundation, April 4, 2011: https://www. iranrights.org/attachments/library/doc_118.pdf, pp. 7–8; Justice for the Victims of the 1988 Massacre in Iran (JVMI), *The 1988 Massacre in Iran*, Second Report, October 2017, prepared by Tahar Boumedra and Azadeh Zabeti assisted by a team of representatives of the families of the victims, www.iran1988.org, p. 47; Amnesty International, *Blood-soaked secrets: Why Iran's 1988 prison massacres are ongoing crimes against humanity* (London: Amnesty International), pp. 9–10, 140–66.

7 Ayatollah Hossein Ali Montazeri, *Khaterat-i Ayatollah Montazeri. Majmu'eh-i Payvastha va Dastnevisha* [Memoirs of Ayatollah Montazeri] (2000), https://amontazeri.com/book/khaterat/volume-1/623; UN Report: A/43/705, October 13, 1988, p. 12.

8 See Assad Saif, "Executions in the Provinces" and Appendix C in this volume. See also Iran Human Rights Documentation Centre, *Deadly Fatwa: Iran's 1988 Prison Massacre*, 2009, p. 10; Amnesty International, *Blood-soaked secrets*, pp. 92–5, 140–66.

9 Montazeri, *Memoirs*, https://amontazeri.com/book/khaterat/volume-1/639; Amnesty International, *Blood-soaked secrets*, pp. 99–100.

10 Amnesty International (AI) Index: MDE 13/31/88, December 13, 1988, pp. 1–2.

Ali Nayyeri, the religious judge; Morteza Eshraghi, the prosecutor general of Tehran; Ebrahim Raisi, the deputy prosecutor general of Tehran, and Mostafa Pourmohammadi, a representative of the Ministry of Intelligence. On March 25, 1989, the Persian service of BBC Radio disclosed the three letters, which had been leaked by the first President of the IRI, Abolhassan Banisadr, shortly before.[11] The very next day, on March 26, Ayatollah Khomeini dismissed Ayatollah Montazeri as his heir apparent.

THE FIRST SIGNS

Months before the beginning of the execution of political prisoners, the Tudeh Party of Iran was warning against the serious threat that jeopardized the lives of political prisoners. The Tudeh Party was one of the few opposition groups that initiated an international campaign to raise consciousness about this "imminent danger." As early as March 2, 1988, Tudeh's weekly journal *Mardom* announced, "Worrisome news is reaching us from prisons in Iran about the death sentence of 70 political prisoners."[12] Almost five months later, on July 27, 1988, the Central Committee of the Tudeh Party released a press communiqué on the execution of two of its party members and a Feda'i sympathizer. Moreover, it revealed that 55 other political prisoners were on the verge of being killed. The Tudeh Party appealed to all democratic-minded and freedom-loving political organizations, parties, and personalities to denounce this heinous crime and take immediate measures to prevent bloodshed in prisons across Iran.[13] Consequently, as early as August 3, in a letter to the British foreign minister the Communist Party of Great Britain asked him to make a protest against the July 20 execution of four Iranian leftists by the Iranian regime, as well as the transfer of 55 political prisoners "to solitary confinement in the so-called 'Death Cells,' awaiting execution."[14]

---

11 However, as Nasser Mohajer has pointed out (in "The Mothers of Khavaran," p. 217, in this volume), Banisadr had already referred to Ayatollah Montazeri's letters in *Enghelabe Eslami* (in exile), no. 187, October 10–23, 1988. For the first edition in Persian of the first letter see no. 198, March 13–26, 1989. For the first edition in Persian of the second and third letters see no. 199, March 27–April 9, 1989.

12 *Nameh Mardom*, no. 192, March 2, 1988.

13 Ibid., no. 218, August 2, 1988.

14 Letter by Ian McKay, national organiser of the Communist Party of Great Britain, to Sir Geoffrey Howe, MP, House of Commons, August 3, 1988, FRO: NBP 243/1. See also the chronology, "Appendix C" in this volume.

The survivors of the massacre and the bereaved families of the executed prisoners of conscience spread the word about the carnage, and were the first to pass on the information both inside and outside the country. At the time, there may have been over one million Iranians in Europe and North America.[15] A good number of them had left Iran in 1981 in the wake of a massive government crackdown on all opponents of Ayatollah Khomeini's theocratic rule, which culminated in the imprisonment of many thousands of dissidents and the execution of many hundreds of "non-conformists." The vast majority of the exiles landed in big cities in Europe and North America as political refugees. Many of them were engaged in political and human rights activism against the IRI, hoping for its demise and immediate downfall. Thus, when the news reached the Iranian diaspora, contact was made with international media, human rights organizations such as Amnesty International, civil society groups, workers' unions and political parties. As a result, on August 16, 1988, Amnesty International wrote about the existing evidence of political executions.[16] At that time, nobody outside certain circles within the regime had heard the slightest hint of the magnitude of the massacre, and as such Amnesty International reported on isolated incidences of ca. 30 executions.

As Nasser Mohajer has correctly pointed out, an underground formation named Feda'ian (Minority) was the first Iranian political organization to report on the "new wave of executions" as early as late July or August 1988. In September 1988, it announced that "In the past months, hundreds of political prisoners have been executed."[17] This also seems to have influenced

15 In the late 1980s, Iranians were the tenth largest group of refugees around the world. About 270,100 Iranian refugees had to flee their country in the late 1980s (World Refugee Survey, 1988 in Review, Table 4). There were 637,500 Iranians in Europe and North America, according to national population censuses of the receiving countries (1990). In the US, for example, the number of Iranians more than doubled from 121,500 in 1980 to 285,000 in 1990. Mehdi Bozorgmehr, "Diaspora: viii. Diaspora in the Post-Revolutionary Period," in *Encyclopaedia Iranica* (2011 [1995]).

16 AI Index: MDE 13/13/88, August 16, 1988.

17 Quoted in Nasser Mohajer, "The Mothers of Khavaran" (this volume). Through 1988 and 1989, the expression "wave of executions" reappeared in a number of European and North American newspapers and news agency reports. See, for example, Ahmad Vahdatkhah, "Tehran's butcher is back in business," *The Independent*, September 24, 1988; Ed Blanche, "Iranian Rebels Claim Tehran Executes 300 More Dissidents," Associated Press, October 24, 1988; Paul Lewis, "UN Says Human Rights Abuses Are Continuing Throughout Iran," *The New York Times*, November 3, 1988; *The Financial Times*, "Iran Re-examines Some of its 'Crude Aspects'," November 29, 1988; *The New York Times*, "Amnesty Reports Wave of Executions in Iran," December 13, 1988; *Le Monde*, "Iran: Amnesty International dénonce une 'vague d'exécutions politiques'," December 14, 1988; Elaine Sciolino, "Tehran Finds War Was Easier to Make Than a Stable Peace," *The New*

subsequent reports by Amnesty International. On September 2, this human rights organization averred that:

> the continuing ban on family visits to political prisoners in Evin prison in Tehran and elsewhere... has fuelled speculation that hundreds of political prisoners may have been executed... The executions have reportedly been carried out predominantly on members and supporters of the People's Mojahedin Organization of Iran (PMOI), but about 20 supporters of other political opposition groups are also reported to have been executed. Amnesty International does not have sufficient information to estimate the number of political executions.[18]

As this quotation shows, although Amnesty International exercised caution in citing numbers, within less than three weeks—between mid-August and the beginning of September 1988—its estimations changed from about thirty to hundreds of executed political prisoners. As Amnesty International explained,

> Since these events took place, Amnesty International has interviewed dozens of relatives of execution victims, and a number of former political prisoners who were in prison at the time when the mass killings were taking place. It has received written information from many Iranians who believe that their friends or relatives were among the victims.[19]

On September 9, the Associated Press reported on an Iranian in New York who "poured gasoline over his head and critically burned himself Friday as hundreds of other Iranians rallied a few blocks away to denounce the execution of dissidents in their homeland."[20] As *The New York Times* pointed out: "In a

---

York Times, January 2, 1989; Harvey Morris, "'1,000 dead' in Iran Executions Spree," *The Independent*, January 30, 1989; *The New York Times*, "Rights Group Reports 1,000 Iran Executions," January 30, 1989; Patrick E. Tyler, "Wrong Ways on a 'Righteous Path'," *The Washington Post*, February 20, 1989; *The Financial Times*, "Rift Deepens As Khomeini's Heir Steps Aside," Iran, March 30, 1989; *The Guardian*, "Iran After Khomeini: Revolutionary decade dominated by war," June 5, 1989.

18 AI Index: MDE 13/14/88, September 2, 1988.

19 AI: Iran: Violations of Human Rights 1987–1990, MDE 13/21/90, p. 11.

20 "Mehrdad Imen, thirty-two, burned himself outside the United Nations building at 42nd Street and First Avenue in New York at about noon as his compatriots held a protest in a park across from the UN, police said." Peter James Spielmann, "Iranians protest executions in their homeland; Protester burns self," The Associated Press, September 9, 1988.

statement handed to reporters, the organizers said they were protesting 'the massacre of thousands of political prisoners, and the hanging and execution of hundreds of innocent citizens by the Khomeini regime in recent weeks.' The statement said 860 political prisoners had recently been executed."[21]

The September edition of the *Enghelabe Eslami* newspaper (in exile), published by the ex-president of the IRI Abolhassan Banisadr, was among the first to reveal that on August 17 and 18, 1988, Ayatollah Khomeini induced the execution of 500 political prisoners, "300 of them were Mojahedin Khalq's sympathizers and the rest were members of the left-leaning groups."[22] It is now an established fact that, at the time, the mass execution of leftist prisoners had not yet started, and throughout the bloody month of August the IRI was set to wipe out the "hypocrites" as a prelude to the liquidation of the atheists and "apostates."

On September 13, *Le Monde* mentioned a report by Amnesty International, published on September 9, condemning Iran for having executed political prisoners. The killings were said to have been conducted during the previous month following the incursions of the PMOI from Iraqi territories between July 25 and 28. The French newspaper also noted that the League for the Defense of Human Rights in Iran, located in Paris, indicated that the death sentence against 55 political prisoners had been recently confirmed.[23] On September 16, *The Christian Science Monitor* noted that:

> Observers of Iran are concerned by a wave of political executions... Because access to Iran is denied [to] many Westerners, details are difficult to establish. But enough evidence is accumulating... to suggest that hundreds of political prisoners may have been executed.[24]

Furthermore, *The Christian Science Monitor* reported that two members of the House Foreign Affairs Committee, from California and Ohio, "have asked for action from the United Nations. In a letter to [the] Secretary General...

---

21 Dennis Hevesi, "Man Sets Himself Afire Outside United Nations," *The New York Times*, September 10, 1988. See also *The Christian Science Monitor*, "Iran's revenge on its 'dissidents'," September 16, 1988.

22 *Enghelabe Eslami* (in exile), no. 184, August 29 – September 11, 1988, quoted in Nasser Mohajer, "The Mothers of Khavaran" (this volume).

23 *Le Monde*, "Amnesty International condamne les exécutions politiques en Iran," September 13, 1988.

24 John Hughes, "Iran's revenge on its 'dissidents'," *The Christian Science Monitor*, September 16, 1989.

they urge sending a UN mission to inspect 'Iranian prisons and torture chambers'."[25] It was pointed out that:

> in a Friday prayer speech last month [August 5], monitored by Western sources, Iran's chief justice, Ayatollah Mousavi Ardebili, said the people are so angry at the dissidents that the "judiciary is under great pressure from public opinion, which questions why we even try them. There is no need for any trial. The crime is clear, the verdict is clear, and the punishment is also clear. There is no need for [a] trial... the people do not accept it when we say we must have proof, we must have evidence... the people say they should all be executed."[26]

By mid-October 1988 there was little evidence concerning the extent of the executions. After Iranian activists and their international cohorts, journalists, lawyers, intellectuals, human rights advocates and political organizations, as well as some media outlets, called attention to the execution of political prisoners in Iran, a few international institutions felt compelled to address and condemn the atrocities of the Iranian regime. One of the most important reactions was the UN report on October 13, which acted on the assumption that hundreds of political prisoners had perished over a few months in detention centers across Iran. It made clear which opposition groups were affected by the massacre and also hinted at the country-wide scope of the executions. Indeed, it indicated that it was a thorough purge and a sort of cleansing of all relevant opposition groups, including the most important leftist organizations:

> On 26 August 1988 it was alleged, that on 28 July 1988, 200 persons described as political prisoners, sympathizers of the Mojahedin organization, had been massacred in the central hall of Evin prison... from 14 to 16 August 1988, 800 bodies of "executed political prisoners" had been transferred from Evin prison, in Tehran, to Behesht Zahra cemetery... Most... were reported to be members of the People's Mojahedin Organization, but some 20 supporters of other opposition groups, such as the Tudeh party and the People's Feda'ian Organization of Iran (Majority) [Rah-e Kargar and members of Kurdish opposition

---

25 Ibid.
26 Ibid. This statement was first published in the Iranian newspaper *Ettela'at* (August 6, 1989).

groups] were also reported to have been executed... approximately 80 members of the People's Mojahedin Organisation, mostly prisoners or former prisoners, were allegedly executed in early August 1988 in the towns of Mashhad, Kermanshah, Arak and Varamin, and in the prison[s] of Evin, Shiraz and Malayer. Some of them were reported to have been publicly hanged.[27]

By October 15, 1988, Ayatollah Montazeri's statement to the annual meeting of the Association of Muslim Students held earlier in October reached the media as the British *Independent* reproduced the following passage: "People have complained to me that their relatives, while serving short prison sentences for political offences, have been executed without any explanation. This is not how our Islamic justice should operate."[28]

On October 20, Amnesty International merely added that information on further political executions in Orumiyeh and Tabriz in northwestern Iran and elsewhere had been obtained.[29]

THE EVIDENCE

Again, as Nasser Mohajer brought to light, the October edition of *Enghelabe Eslami* was the first media outlet to reveal that not hundreds, but thousands of political prisoners were executed in the summer of 1988. The journal, relying on inside information, reported that "the number of the executed exceeds 2500 people."[30] Nonetheless, this information was ignored by the mainstream media in Western Europe and North America. Meanwhile, by the end of November and beginning of December, most of the bereaved family members realized the extent of the death and devastation.[31]

On the basis of a UN report published on November 2, *The New York Times* quoted Reynaldo Galindo Pohl, the UN special rapporteur of the Commission on Human Rights in Iran, stating that his findings "justify

---

27 UN Report: A/43/705, October 13, 1988, pp. 12, 15. *The Financial Times* also pointed out that members of the Kurdish Democratic Party were executed. *Australian Financial Review*, "Iran re-examines some of its 'crude aspects'," November 29, 1988.
28 Quoted in AI Index: MDE 13/17/88, October 20, 1988.
29 AI Index: MDE 13/17/88, October 20, 1988.
30 *Enghelabe Eslami* (in exile), no. 187, October 10–23, 1988, quoted in Nasser Mohajer, "The Mothers of Khavaran" (this volume).
31 AI: "Iran: Violations of Human Rights 1987–1990," MDE 13/21/90, pp. 12–13; AI Index: MDE 13/18/92 (October 1992), p. 3.

international concern" about the human rights situation in Iran.[32] The newspaper also stressed that:

> The report said 200 Mojahedin supporters were believed to have been killed in Evin prison in Tehran on July 28. The bodies of 860 more "executed political prisoners" were reported to have been taken from the same prison to the Behesht Zahra cemetery from August 14 to 16. The report lists numerous other executions of Government opponents in the summer.[33]

Ironically, *The New York Times* mentioned that "Iran's military setback and its decision to accept a ceasefire also seems to have unleashed a backlash of revenge inside the country against anyone suspected of disloyalty to the government, diplomats say."[34] On November 8, Amnesty International reported that:

> Some opposition groups put the figure at over 2,000 while a wide range of opposition opinion agrees that hundreds of executions have taken place... There have been reports from witnesses of large numbers of bodies being discovered in shallow graves in the area of Behesht Zahra cemetery in Tehran usually reserved for executed political prisoners, and in other parts of the country.[35]

On November 26, *The New York Times* revealed that, as a result of public criticism by the UN bodies,

> Iran announced today that it was ready to cooperate with a United Nations investigation into allegations that it is responsible for widespread human rights violations... in return, Iran is asking a General Assembly committee to tone down a draft resolution highly critical of its human rights record.[36]

---

32 Paul Lewis, "UN Says Human Rights Abuses Are Continuing Throughout Iran," *The New York Times*, November 3, 1988. See also *The New York Times*, "What Iran Wants Ignored," November 30, 1988.
33 Ibid. The UN later repeated these findings. See UN Report, E/CN.4/1989/25, February 6, 1989, p. 30.
34 Ibid.
35 AI Index: MDE 13/20/88, November 8, 1988.
36 Paul Lewis, "Iran Says It Will Aid UN on Human Rights Study," *The New York Times*, November 26, 1988.

The same article noted that: "Iran is the only country that has consistently refused to cooperate with United Nations human rights investigations since it was first accused of violations in 1985."[37] Apart from that, *The New York Times* mentioned the French government's intention to send Roland Dumas—as the first French Foreign Minister since the inception of the IRI—to visit Tehran next year.[38] On November 27, an article by *Le Monde* correspondent Jean Gueyras was printed in the *Guardian Weekly* (first published in *Le Monde* on November 20). It was a report on a National Liberation Army release in Baghdad that reiterated that "hundreds of political prisoners [had been] shot or hanged in recent weeks." Gueyras added, "Since early October the repression, which is also directed against left-wing organizations—Tudeh or the People's Feda'ian—has spread to non-conformist members of the Iranian clergy close to Ayatollah Montazeri."[39] A day later, the Associated Press reported: "The dissident Iranian factions have said that more than 1,100 activists were executed before the ceasefire took effect Aug. 20."[40]

On November 30, *The New York Times* pointed out that the effect of Iran's "canny" response to the UN's concern about mass killings of political prisoners

> has been to divide its General Assembly critics by offering for the first time to open its borders to a special representative of the UN. In return, Iran wants the UN to scrap a draft resolution

---

37 Ibid.

38 Ibid.

39 Gueyras added that: "Scores of religious and political figures were arrested early in October in Qom and Tehran, without any reasons being given for the measures, which have moreover not been announced officially. Eleven of those arrested—five members of the Islamic clergy and six lay persons attached to Qom's theological centres—were summarily executed. The victims included a former *Majles* member, Hojat al-Islam Fathollah Omid Najafabadi, one of Ayatollah Montazeri's aides...The four other religious figures executed—Hojat al-Islam Hosseini Arab, Sharaf al-din Mashkur, Ghayur and Khavari Langerudi—were also part of Montazeri's close circle, as were the six lay persons, most of them former Revolutionary Guards who had been dismissed." Jean Gueyras, "Rash of executions in Iran a warning to Montazeri," in *Guardian Weekly*, November 27, 1988; Idem, "IRAN: la poursuite de la répression. Onze personnalités proches de l'ayatollah Montazeri ont été exécutées," *Le Monde*, November 20, 1988. However, two months later Youssef Ibrahim rightly cautioned: "It is true that over the last decade the ruling Iranian clergy has executed hundreds of opponents. But it is also true that virtually all of the victims were not clergymen." Youssef M. Ibrahim, "The world; clerics and politics: why there are no 'moderates' in Iran," *The New York Times*, February 26, 1989.

40 Anwar Faruqi, "Dissidents claim Iran executions part of political purge," the Associated Press, November 28, 1988.

deploring the wave of summary executions of political prisoners. Thus Iran wants a pat on the back for complying with the most rudimentary rules... Since this summer, at least 1,000 people are believed to have been shot, and thousands imprisoned, most on charges of supporting an armed insurgency, the People's Mojahedin. The UN report finds "a nucleus of veracity" in accounts of these killings and of ill treatment of prisoners... Iran does not wholly scorn the UN or its resolutions—or else it would not haggle over censorious words.[41]

On the same day, British Labour Party MP Jeremy Corbyn, during a short debate in the House of Commons, asked the secretary of state for foreign and Commonwealth affairs, William A. Waldgrave, what representations had been made to the government of Iran concerning the recent spate of executions of political prisoners. Waldgrave responded that the reports of executions were a matter of concern to the government.[42] On December 1, *The New York Times* reported that an "attempt to send a United Nations team into Iran for an investigation of the human rights situation there collapsed today in a dispute over the wording of a General Assembly resolution criticizing the Tehran Government's record."[43] It added that: "Advocates of the condemnation said they could not accept Iran's proposal on principle: Iran is the only country that has refused to cooperate with a United Nations Human Rights Commission investigation... Iran could not be given exceptional treatment, these countries argued."[44] On December 2, *Le Monde* reported that Tudeh Party members in exile announced that the majority of their Central Committee and Politburo members had been executed during the past weeks. They had been detained in Iranian prisons since February 1982 and were murdered "as they refused to sign deeds of renunciation." Furthermore, on the basis of the information furnished by family members, Tudeh published a list of thirty-one communists who had either been shot or hanged. However, *Le Monde* mentioned that the list was far from being exhaustive as some estimate that more than two

41 *The New York Times*, "What Iran Wants Ignored," November 30, 1988.
42 Short Debate in the Lords: Human Rights, December 7, 1988, and December 12, 1988, FRO: NBP 240/1.
43 Paul Lewis, "Deal for UN Rights Inquiry in Iran Crumbles," *The New York Times*, December 1, 1988.
44 Ibid.

hundred Tudeh members had been "liquidated."[45] On the same day, the main point-person of the Italian Communist Party (PCI) for the Middle East throughout the 1980s, Giancarlo Lannutti, reported in *L'Unità*, the official newspaper of the PCI, that:

> The former representative in Italy of the Tudeh (Communist) Party of Iran, Feri Farjad, a tireless protagonist of the fight for freedom in his country, has been killed in cold blood in Evin prison in Tehran after six years of incarceration... it is impossible for us to comprehend what his "guilt" was, other than being a communist.[46]

As a direct result of these increasing accusations, it is telling that Iran's then-President and current Supreme Leader, Seyyid Ali Hosseini Khamenei, reportedly said at a meeting in Tehran University, "As regards the mass executions... those in prisons who had contacts with the *Monafeqin* [PMOI], who mounted an armed incursion against the Islamic Republic... are condemned to death and must be executed" (Tehran radio, December 5, 1988).[47]

On December 7, *Le Monde* noted that the Committee in Solidarity with Political Prisoners in Iran (*le comité de solidarité avec les prisonniers politiques en Iran*) released a statement in Paris, announcing the execution of "hundreds" of political prisoners in the past two weeks. They published a list of about 150 executed political prisoners, including 24 members of the Feda'ian (Majority).[48] On the same day, *The Independent* reported that more than 1,000

---

45 *Le Monde*, "La répression en Iran: La plupart des membres du comité central et du bureau politique du Parti communiste ont été executes," December 2, 1988. Less than a week later, *The Independent* also noted that the Tudeh Party reported, "more than 30 of its top leaders have been executed in recent weeks. Among them was a man of more than 80." Harvey Morris, "More executed in purge of political opponents; Iran," *Sydney Morning Herald*, December 7, 1988.

46 Giancarlo Lannutti, "La repressione in Iran. Feri Farjad, comunista, è stato assassinato nel carcere di Teheran" (Repression in Iran. Feri Farjad, a Communist, has been assassinated in the prison of Tehran), *L'Unità*, December 2, 1988.

47 JVMI, *The 1988 Massacre in Iran*, p. 4. See also *Resalat*, December 7, 1988, pp. 2 and 11; *The New York Times*, December 13, 1988; "The Killing Fields of Iran," *The Christian Science Monitor*, January 25, 1989; AI Index: MDE 13/18/92 (October 1992), p. 2; "Official statements about the executions of the 1980s," BBC Persian radio service, September 12, 2013, www.bbc.com/persian/mobile/iran/2013/09/130912_25_anniversary_authoriteis_speech_nm.shtml. As AI correctly points out, "a large number of those executed either had no links with the PMOI, or had already been in prison for some years." AI Index: MDE 13/18/92 (October 1992), p. 2.

48 *Le Monde*, "Iran: Des exécutions en série," December 7, 1988.

people had been executed since Iran signed a ceasefire with Iraq in August. This report was based upon the information published by the British-based Committee for the Defence of the Iranian People's Rights.[49]

On December 8, the UN General Assembly expressed its grave concern that "there was a renewed wave of executions in the period of July–September 1988 whereby a large number of persons died because of their political convictions."[50] On December 10, the Associated Press reported that the PMOI "has said 12,000 political prisoners, including large numbers of their activists and sympathizers, have been executed in Iranian prisons in recent months."[51] This news was replicated at different times, by different groups and on different occasions.[52]

At that time, the dispatches of the different commissions of the UN, appeals to "Urgent Actions" by Amnesty International, as well as mounting international pressure and media coverage, prompted the Iranian regime to seek to deflect the attention of the world community from its ferocious atrocities. Based on reports of the official IRI News Agency, on December 10 the Associated Press reported on Chief Justice Ayatollah Abdolkarim Mousavi Ardebili's announcement of Iran's intention to free prisoners in February, on the tenth anniversary of the IRI.[53] As the German newspaper *TAZ* reported a few days later:

> The wave of executions that followed Iran's approval of the UN ceasefire resolution [598]... obviously aims at annihilating the most active cadres and members of the opposition parties prior to the amnesty... so that they do not pose a threat to the regime anymore. This is supposed to lay

49 Harvey Morris, "More executed in purge of political opponents; Iran," *Sydney Morning Herald*, December 7, 1988.

50 "43/137: Situation of human rights in the Islamic Republic of Iran (A/43/868), 8.12.1988," in *Resolutions and Decisions adopted by the General Assembly during its Forty-Third-Session, Vol. 1, 20 September – 22 December 1988. General Assembly. Official Records: Forty-Third Session. Supplement No. 49 (A/43/49)*, New York 1989, p. 211.

51 Ed Blanche, "Iran says it will free some prisoners," Associated Press, December 10, 1988.

52 See, for example, Matt Rees, "Amnesty: Iranian executions increasing," *United Press International*, December 12, 1988; E. A. Wayne, "Iran executing hundreds, human rights group says," *The Christian Science Monitor*, December 14, 1988; Harvey Morris, "Khomeini orders an end to wave of political executions," *The Independent*, January 27, 1989; *Le Monde*, "Iran: nouvelles exécutions?" February 11, 1989.

53 Ed Blanche, "Iran says it will free some prisoners," Associated Press, December 10, 1988.

the groundwork for liberalization which the regime, due to economic reasons, deems necessary.[54]

On December 12, *L'Humanité* reported that the French Minister of Foreign Affairs, Roland Dumas, declared the resumption of normal relations with Iran. As a result, the president of the communist faction in the National Assembly, André Lajoinie, called for an "immediate condemnation" by the French government of the "unprecedented wave of executions" of political prisoners in Iran, or otherwise to cancel the planned trip of the Foreign Minister to Tehran the next year. The delegate minister, Edwige Avice, responded that the government was "deeply concerned and moved" by the political executions and announced communications with the twelve members of the European Economic Community (EEC) "to find means for adequate action."[55]

Between November and December Amnesty International was writing with more certainty, issuing over a dozen "Urgent Actions" and reporting a "new wave of executions" carried out since July 1988. At that time, the human rights organization was still uncertain about the scope of the killings and oscillated between the execution of "hundreds," "many hundreds," or "thousands" of political prisoners.[56] By mid-December, Amnesty International was more confident in its allegations. On December 12 and 13, it held that "the evidence for mass executions was now indisputable, with evidence coming from many sources, including relatives of executed prisoners and recent statements by the authorities themselves." Amnesty International claimed that the Iranian authorities "have been carrying out the biggest wave of secret political executions since the early 1980s," that the exact number of executions could run into the thousands and that many executed prisoners had been tortured while in detention. It pointed out that the victims included prisoners from all walks of life: they ranged from secondary school students seized in the 1981 and 1982 witch-hunts to medical doctors, teachers, social scientists, manual workers, as well as lawyers and journalists.[57] Indeed, the

54 "Iran liquidiert Opposition," *TAZ* (*Die Tageszeitung*), December 13, 1988.
55 "André Lajoinie interpelle le Gouvernement sur L'Iran," *L'Humanité,* December 12, 1988.
56 See, for example, AI Index: MDE 13/21/88, November 10, 1988; AI Index: MDE 13/25/88, November 28, 1988; AI Index: MDE 13/29/88 (December 1988); AI Index: MDE 13/33/88, December 12, 1988; AI Index: MDE 13/31/88, December 13, 1988, p. 1.
57 AI Index: MDE 13/29/88, December 1988, p. 2; AI Index: MDE 13/31/88, December 13, 1988, pp. 1–2. Amnesty International also mentioned that "mullahs suspected of

political prisoners included people of different ages, professions, religious persuasion, social stratification, political affiliation and gender. It thus became crystal clear that the executed prisoners had not been POWs arrested during the Mojahedin's military incursions, as claimed by IRI authorities. According to Amnesty International, "the evidence was overwhelming. Many details on the executions had come from opposition groups and close relatives of those executed. The sources covered a wide range and their information had been cross-checked."[58] As Vahe Petrossian poignantly formulated in *The Guardian*, "thousands of government opponents are reportedly being massacred behind prison walls in a final settling of political accounts."[59] On December 13, the Netherlands' foreign ministry spokesman made public that the country "has taken note with great concern of recent reports of large scale executions in Iran of alleged opponents of the regime."[60] On the same day, the ambassadors of the twelve members of the EEC in Tehran wrote a "restricted" report in which they stated:

> According to the persisting rumours and the published information, as well as unconfirmed reports from usually reliable sources, an undefined number of people were executed on account of their political activities, including even mere membership of opposition groups. The majority of the executed are reported to be supporters of the Mojahedin Khalq Organization. Also a certain number of the Tudeh Party (communist) supporters have been supposedly executed. Some of the executions were carried out secretly, among them a considerable number allegedly took place in Iranian prisons.[61]

supporting Ayatollah Montazeri designated to succeed Ayatollah Ruhollah Khomeini" had been executed. Parts of AI's report were reproduced in a number of sources, including Audrey Woods, "Amnesty International reports hundreds of executions in Iran," Associated Press, December 12, 1988; Matt Rees, Amnesty: "Iranian executions increasing," *United Press International*, December 12, 1988; "Amnesty Reports waves of executions in Iran," *The New York Times*, December 13, 1988; "Iran: Amnesty International dénonce une vague d'exécutions politiques," *Le Monde*, December 14, 1988; E. A. Wayne, "Iran executing hundreds, human rights group says," *The Christian Science Monitor*, December 14, 1988.
58 AI Index: MDE 13/31/88, December 13, 1988, p. 2.
59 Vahe Petrossian, "Iranian rumour-mill goes into overdrive," *The Guardian*, December 12, 1988.
60 Human Rights Situation in Iran/Amnesty International Report, December 13, 1988, p. 1, FRO: CPE HAG 611.
61 Report by the Ambassadors of the Twelve in Tehran on Political Executions in Iran, December 13, 1988, p. 1, FRO: CPE/PRES/ATH/644.

At the same time, they cautioned that:

> embassies of the European Community in Tehran are hindered in their
> efforts to obtain evidence concerning alleged massive political execu-
> tions, which they can thus neither confirm nor deny. Consequently,
> it is unanimously felt that the elements available are not enough to
> justify an official complaint to the Iranian authorities.[62]

In the same spirit, as late as December 14, Charles E. Redman, the US assistant
secretary of state for public affairs claimed during a regular briefing of the
State Department that he did not have any information on recent executions
in Iran.[63] On the same day, *Le Monde* reported on a demonstration organized by the French Human Rights League against "the massacre of political
prisoners in Iran" on that day.[64]

Mid-December, however, was a turning point in the disclosure of the
dimensions of the massacre. The evidence that had surfaced bit by bit in
the past weeks and months left very little doubt that more than a thousand
political prisoners had been secretly executed in the midsummer of 1988.
Nevertheless, as we shall see in the following pages, this was often not
reflected in the European and American mainstream media as influential
outlets continued to write of "hundreds" of executed political prisoners.
Having said that, after several intercontinental campaigns, supported by an
array of democratic-minded individuals, progressive political organizations
and human rights activists, and despite the inclination of the EEC's ambassadors in Tehran "to exercise caution" about events in Iran, the European
Parliament adopted a resolution at the Plenary Session in Strasbourg on
December 15, 1988. It stated that the European Parliament was "horrified
at reports that thousands of opponents of the Khomeini regime, including members of the Feda'ian, the Tudeh Party, the Mojahedin, dissident
clergy and others have been executed in Iran over the course of the last
four months."[65] A day later, *L'Humanité* reported on hundreds of protesting individuals "of all origins," including Iranian exiles, gathering at the

---

62 Ibid., p. 2.

63 "State Department, regular briefing. Briefer: Charles Redman," Federal News Service,
December 14, 1988.

64 "Iran: La ligue française des droits de l'homme appelle à un rassemblement," *Le
Monde*, December 14, 1988.

65 European Parliament Joint Resolution replacing Docs. B2-1127 and 1149/88 Resolution
on Iran, December 15, 1988, p. 6 (A).

aforementioned December 14 demonstration in Paris and calling for an end to the massacre. The French newspaper also reported that the Iranian ambassador in the French capital refused to receive a delegation of demonstrators.[66] On December 17, two days after the resolution of the European Parliament and with reference to Amnesty International, the French newspaper *L'Humanité* pointed out that the biggest wave of secret political executions since the early 1980s had taken place in Iran.[67] The French daily further added that:

> according to testimonies by Iranian travelers who had recently arrived in France, a large portion of the executions had taken place in August and September even though the news only reached the families one or two months later... the administration refused to hand over the corpses to the families or to inform them about the burial site... Certain prisoners who were released conditionally were required to show up in prison once a month. They were blindfolded and had to give an account of their contacts and activities.[68]

On December 27, the German weekly magazine *Die Weltbühne*, appearing in East Berlin, published an in-depth piece on the executions. It published a letter, written on May 6, 1987, by a doctor of medicine, Ahmad Danesh, who was killed during the Great Massacre. Dr. Danesh was a Tudeh member and in 1978 had been the first person to successfully perform a kidney transplant in Iran. The article included a short introduction and concluding remarks by his son Stefan Parvis Töpelmann, who had grown up in the German Democratic Republic. It must be noted that *Die Weltbühne* was the only East German media outlet that wrote in detail on the Great Massacre in Iran.

Five days later, on January 2, 1989, *The New York Times* reported that, according to US State Department estimates, Tehran had executed between several hundred and two thousand people between late July and early September. It added that most of them were members of the Mojahedin, but some were senior officials in the Tudeh Party who had been imprisoned since 1982, others were Kurdish rebels, and there were even six clerics. This was an important official reappraisal of the public statements made by the

---

66 *L'Humanité*, December 16, 1988.
67 "Nouveaux témoignages sur les éxecutions en Iran: Prison de la mort," *L'Humanité*, December 17, 1988.
68 Ibid.

State Department two weeks earlier. Significantly, *The New York Times* also made it public that:

> Although the State Department expressed its "deep concern" about the executions, it has not made an official protest through the Swiss, who represent American interests in Tehran. American officials and Western diplomats said the executions would not hinder a move toward better relations.[69]

On January 11, Canada's *The Globe and Mail* reported that the day before the Mojahedin had listed names of 1,107 executed political prisoners.[70] Two days later, *The Independent* wrote that Amnesty International "has spoken of 600 people killed in the past few months, while the Iranian opposition has claimed more than 2,000 deaths." The same article published passages from a letter supposedly addressed to the Minister of Justice and Ayatollah Khomeini himself, in which Ayatollah Montazeri complained: "It appears that in most cases those executed have been serving short prison sentences for minor political offences. I declare my opposition to these sentences, and I am sure there are a good number of people in this country who would share this [sentiment] with me." The London-based newspaper also quoted Ayatollah Montazeri's following statement: "For what valid reasons or on what basis has our judiciary approved these executions, which can result in nothing but damaging the face of our revolution and the system."[71] Although

69 Elaine Sciolino, "Tehran finds war easier to make than a stable peace," *The New York Times*, January 2, 1989. By December 13, in a "restricted" report, the ambassadors of the twelve members of the EEC had already indicated that the Iranian authorities had announced the execution of a group of nine persons, including six mullahs condemned to death by a religious court. Report by the Ambassadors of the Twelve in Tehran on Political Executions in Iran, December 13, 1988, p. 1, FRO: CPE/PRES/ATH/644.

70 "Iranian opposition lists names of 1,107 executed by Khomeini," *The Globe and Mail*, January 11, 1989. The same number of executed political prisoners was also mentioned in *The Christian Science Monitor* ("The Killing Fields of Iran," January 25, 1989).

71 Ahmed Vahdatkhah and John Bulloch, "Khomeini's heir denounces regime over executions," *The Independent*, January 13, 1989. Right after the publication of the aforementioned letter, Ayatollah Montazeri was "under virtual house arrest in the holy city of Qom... According to reports from Tehran, Mr Montazeri's house is kept under constant surveillance by Revolutionary Guards. Though there is no official ban on him moving about or leaving Qom, he has decided not to do so because of the climate of intimidation built up by the regime." Safa Haeri, "Montazeri is held 'under virtual house arrest' in Qom," *The Independent*, January 14, 1989. On January 29, *The Washington Post* quoted from Ayatollah Montazeri's letter that had been reported in *The Independent* and published more than two weeks earlier: "This month, in an open letter to Khomeini

the translation of the reported letter is not quite accurate and seems to be a free translation of Ayatollah Montazeri's first letter to Ayatollah Khomeini, yet it was the first time that the non-Iranian press reported on the confirmation of the recent wave of executions by one of the leading figures of the IRI, Ayatollah Khomeini's heir apparent himself.

On January 18, *Neues Deutschland*, the official party newspaper or central organ of the Socialist Unity Party of [ex-East] Germany, referred to a statement issued in Paris by the Tudeh Party, about "the mass executions in Iran." The newspaper added that "Many of their party members also fell victim to the executions; amongst whom we can find members of the Politburo of the Central Committee."[72] This was an important indication and probably a defining moment as the Soviet bloc ascertained and admitted reports about atrocious events in Iran which the Western European news outlets had been disseminating since August.

On January 26, the UN Special Representative on the human rights situation in Iran "challenged Iran's 'global denial' of the wave of executions." He submitted a list of 1,084 names to the authorities, asking for information on their fate and whereabouts and noted that "there were in all probability several thousand victims."[73] In response to this diplomatic paradigm shift, the masterminds and policymakers of the IRI concluded that the tenth anniversary of the Iranian Revolution should be used as a smokescreen and a springboard to change the criminal image of the Iranian regime abroad. Thus throughout January and early February they undertook planning and preparation for orchestrating a fanfare with the rhetoric of "amnesty" and the release of political prisoners through the "mercy" of Ayatollah Khomeini and the "compassionate Islamic Republic of Iran."[74]

In spite of the new political line propagated by the Iranian authorities and its spokespersons, the international media and news outlets continued

---

and the minister of justice, Montazeri decried as 'sins' and 'bloodletting' the political executions that were carried out in the wake of last summer's cease-fire." Patrick E. Tyler, "Ten years later, Iran struggles to rebuild; revolution endures despite war, malaise," *The Washington Post*, January 29, 1989.

72 *Neues Deutschland*, "Erklärung der Volkspartei Irans" (Tudeh), January 18, 1989.

73 Amnesty International, *Blood-soaked secrets*, p. 13. Nonetheless, as late as January 28 *The Washington Post* reported: "Estimates of the number killed ranged from 300 to 2,400." Patrick E. Tyler, "Ten years later, Iran struggles to rebuild," *The Washington Post*, January 28, 1989.

74 Some Western media outlets wrote about the IRI's amnesty plans. See, for example, Harvey Morris, "Khomeini orders an end to wave of political executions," *The Independent*, January 27, 1989.

to report on the number of victims of the Great Massacre. On January 30, *The New York Times* reported, "More than 1,000 political prisoners [mostly Mojahedin but also members of other left-wing groups] had been shot or hanged in Iran over the past six months in the biggest wave of executions there since the early 1980s."[75] On February 1, the Associated Press wrote that Amnesty International had evidence of over 1,100 executed political prisoners.[76] The next day, the BBC mentioned that the Central Committee of the Communist Party of the Soviet Union had expressed serious concern over the executions in Iran of representatives of the Tudeh Party, the Feda'ian (Majority), and other organizations (as reported on Soviet television on January 31).[77] On the same day (reported by *Le Monde* on February 4), the French Socialist Party (PS) expressed its "indignation in view of the wave of executions in Iran" and voiced the desire that "an international mission obtains a possibility to visit the Iranian prisons."[78] On February 5, *Le Monde* referred to a UN report that had been made public two days earlier. The French newspaper pointed out that, according to Reynaldo Galindo Pohl, the special rapporteur of the Commission of Human Rights on Iran, thousands of political prisoners had been killed between July and December 1988. *Le Monde* also noted that most of the prisoners were members of the Mojahedin, Feda'ian, and Tudeh Party, while at least eleven religious authorities had also been executed. Significantly, the French newspaper alluded to the UN report's emphasis that a great number of the victims of the wave of executions had either been in prison for years or were former prisoners who had been rearrested. *Le Monde* concluded that "it seems improbable that these prisoners had been involved in violent actions against the State."[79]

---

75 *The New York Times*, "Rights Group Reports 1,000 Iran Executions," January 30, 1989. Similarly, *The Independent* reported that Amnesty International "will today present the United Nations Human Rights Commission in Geneva with the names of 1,000 political prisoners reported to have been shot dead or hanged in Iran in the past six months." Harvey Morris, "1,000 dead in Iran executions spree," *The Independent*, January 30, 1989.
76 Ed Blanche, "Bells peal across Iran to mark decade of revolution," Associated Press, February 1, 1989.
77 "Soviet concern over executions in Iran," BBC Summary of World Broadcasts, February 2, 1989. See also *The New York Times*, "The Cruelty that Isolates Iran," February 10, 1989.
78 *Le Monde*, "IRAN: indignation et inquiétude du Parti socialiste français," February 4, 1989. The PS further asked Roland Dumas, the Minister of Europe and Foreign Affairs, who visited Iran on February 5, to protest against the executions. *Le Monde*, "Le voyage de M. Dumas à Téhéran," February 5–6, 1989.
79 *Le Monde*, "Un rapport accablant pour l'Iran est présenté à la commission des droits de l'homme de l'ONU," February 5, 1989. See also UN Report, E/CN.4/1989/25, February 6, 1989, p. 30.

The next day, February 6, 1989, the UN released a report that reinforced the earlier findings published on November 2, 1988.[80] However, on February 9 *The New York Times* reported that several thousand political prisoners would be released on the tenth anniversary of the Iranian Revolution. The same newspaper reported that nine hundred opponents of the state—especially from the PMOI—accused of murder and other serious crimes would not be freed. Although *The New York Times* did not disclose the number of those to be released, "officials and experts" assumed three thousand and perhaps as many as ten thousand prisoners would be freed. A report by Youssef Ibrahim, senior Middle East correspondent for *The New York Times*, reveals something of what was going on behind closed doors in the UN, as well as in the State Departments of European capitals and the United States:

> The amnesty decision follows strong evidence of many executions carried out since August against hardened political opponents... Nevertheless, the decision was largely viewed by foreign diplomats and many Iranians as a significant new step in a policy of gradual liberalization in domestic and foreign policy that started last summer.[81]

Ibrahim continued that the decision to release political prisoners "was made today by Ayatollah Khomeini, Iran's supreme leader, in response to a request

---

80 UN Report, E/CN.4/1989/25, February 6, 1989, p. 30. Following the repeated assertions and allegations about the massacre in Iran, in February 1989 Ali Akbar Hashemi Rafsanjani, then the second man in command, appeared on a French TV program and claimed that only "certain" imprisoned opponents had been killed: "We have discovered that certain imprisoned hypocrites in Iran were in contact with their fighting friends in Iraq," Rafsanjani said in reference to the rebels, "We killed them, but there certainly were not 1,000. Any competent jurisdiction can easily prove it." Quoted in Associated Press, February 28, 1989. See also Associated Press, February 13, 1989. According to the BBC, Rafsanjani even alleged that "some of those who assisted the *Monafeqin* in their attack on our country have been punished, but they represented only a few cases." "Rafsanjani interviewed on Franco-Iranian relations, executions claims, succession to Khomeini," BBC Summary of World Broadcasts, February 15, 1989.

81 Youssef M. Ibrahim, "Iran will release certain prisoners for anniversary," *The New York Times*, February 9, 1989. We do not have any reliable information on the number of prisoners at that time, nor do we know how many prisoners were actually released in the wake of the amnesty. The previous day, the Associated Press wrote that, "Khomeini's latest amnesty followed a wave of executions in which hundreds of political prisoners and captured anti-Khomeini activists have been reported slain." It was added that AI "said last week that it knows of more than 1,500 executions in that period." "Khomeini pardons Iranian political prisoners," Associated Press, February 8, 1989.

from Iran's Minister of Intelligence Affairs, Mohammad Reyshahri"![82] On February 10, *Le Monde* confirmed *The New York Times'* news. The French newspaper quoted Mohammad Reyshahri, who described this decision as a sign of "consolidation" of the IRI which, as he explained, was no longer threatened by certain factions who were, moreover, "on the brink of total extinction."[83] This statement was a clear message that the ruling theocracy in Iran was not going to succumb to world powers, abandon its fundamental tenets or negotiate with its adversaries from a position of weakness. From this moment on, the discourse of possible "liberalization" of the IRI lost momentum, and the Great Massacre, with the number of men and women who lost their lives in that bloodbath, resurfaced in European and North American newspaper editorials and diplomatic circles.

On February 10, *The New York Times* noted that Amnesty International "has gathered more than 1,000 names of political prisoners believed to have been killed, some for belonging to the armed resistance, others jailed years ago for such offenses as distributing leaflets."[84] On February 12, the Associated Press reported that the UN and Amnesty International "estimate there have been 1,000 executions."[85] The same day, United Press International noted that "Human rights groups have charged Iran with executing 1,500 political prisoners in the last six months."[86] On February 15, *The Washington Post* alluded to a sermon by Ayatollah Montazeri in Qom "early this month" where he preached "about the simple life of Mohammad, who, Montazeri declared in sharp tones, did not abide 'prisons or massacres or killings and executions'."[87] Two days later, *The Washington Post* referred to a speech Ayatollah Montazeri had given a week before, where he said that "People in the world got the idea that our business in Iran is just murdering people."[88] On February 27, *Newsweek* reported that "at least 1,000 of the regime's opponents have been executed since the end of the war last August—one of the bloodiest phases of Khomeini's revolution."[89] The next day, the Associated Press noted that on Tuesday, UN Secretary-General

82 Ibrahim, "Iran will release certain prisoners for anniversary."
83 *Le Monde*, "Iran: Large amnistie pour des prisonniers politiques," February 10, 1989.
84 "The cruelty that isolates Iran," *The New York Times*, February 10, 1989.
85 Alex Efty, "Khomeini's heir calls for the end to extremism, questions who won war," Associated Press, February 21, 1989.
86 Lee Stokes, "Khomeini's successor calls for new Iranian image," United Press International, February 12, 1989.
87 Patrick E. Tyler, "Khomeini says writer must die; Book publishers also condemned," *The Washington Post*, February 15, 1989.
88 Shaul Bakhash, "What's Khomeini up to?" *The Washington Post*, February 17, 1989.
89 "A satanic fury," *Newsweek*, February 27, 1989.

Javier Peréz de Cuéllar received a PMOI list of the names of 1,634 executed Mojahedin prisoners.[90] On March 25, 1989, the Persian service of BBC Radio broadcast three letters, previously leaked by the ex-president of Iran Abolhassan Banisadr, written by the then Deputy Supreme Leader, Ayatollah Montazeri, which criticized the executions of the People's Mojahedin prisoners as "malicious" and "vengeful." Amnesty International stated that:

> The publication of these three leaked letters in the media sent shock waves across Iran and globally, and exposed the Iranian authorities, who had worked hard to keep the nature and scale of the mass killings secret. A day after they were published, Ruhollah Khomeini wrote a harsh letter to Hossein Ali Montazeri, dismissing him as his successor and rebuking him for criticizing the executions.[91]

Significantly, on March 29, 1989, Reuters once again quoted Ayatollah Montazeri's letter to Ayatollah Khomeini, in which he wrote of "thousands of executions in a few days," saying that many are "innocent" and "minor offenders who were executed following your last order."[92] Soon after, portions of Ayatollah Montazeri's letters to Ayatollah Khomeini were reproduced in other media outlets, including *The Guardian* and the German newspaper *TAZ*, which printed two of Ayatollah Montazeri's letters almost in their entirety.[93]

On May 8, the Associated Press reported that:

> Since its ceasefire with Iraq, Iran has become a killing ground of executions... It is the biggest wave of executions in Iran since

---

90 "Interior Minister denies saying political prisoners executed," Associated Press, February 28, 1989.

91 Amnesty International, *Blood-soaked secrets*, pp. 95–6. Ayatollah Khomeini wrote: "From now on, do not write to me and do not allow *monafeqin* to pass on every state secret that there is to foreign radios." Ibid. For the full text of the letter, see Fars News Agency, "Imam's letter dismissing Mr Montazeri," March 26, 2017, www.bit.ly/2RIPcpf.

92 Quoted in AI: "Iran: Violations of Human Rights 1987–1990," MDE 13/21/90, p. 6. A number of other newspapers also reported on Ayatollah Montazeri's letters. See, for example, Hazhir Teimourian, "Khomeini accepts resignation of his chosen successor; Ayatollah Hosain Ali Montazeri," *The Times*, March 29, 1989; David B. Ottaway, "Khomeini's designated heir resigns amid purge in Iran," *The Washington Post*, March 29, 1989; Martin Woollacott, "Commentary: The passing of Montazeri and reality," *The Guardian*, March 30, 1989; Youssef M. Ibrahim, "The world: Montazeri's evolution; an heir is gone," *The New York Times*, April 2, 1989.

93 Paul Webster, "Montazeri's sought end to executions," *The Guardian*, March 30, 1989; Taz. *Die Tageszeitung*, "Montaseri: 'Massaker ohne Gerichtsverfahren'," April 28, 1989.

1980–81…[PMOI] has given out the names of 1,600 it says have been victims.[94]

On July 10, the Associated Press reported that the PMOI had sent the UN secretary-general a list of 2,023 political prisoners executed since the ceasefire in the Iran–Iraq war.[95] More importantly, sometime between August and September 1989, *The Center to Support Political Prisoners (Inside Iran)*—mostly consisting of the families of the executed sympathizers of the communist Tudeh Party and the Feda'ian (Majority)—independently published a list of the political prisoners who were murdered in the summer of 1988. It contained the names of 1,345 victims of the Great Massacre. *Bang-e Raha'i* (Cry for Freedom), the organ of the Center, underscored that the list contained only the names of some of the thousands of victims.[96] These publications had tangible repercussions as they provided hard evidence that helped to raise awareness about the massacre.

In spite of all this, no UN condemnation or authorized investigation took place. As an Amnesty International report from 2018 calls to mind:

> On 2 November 1989, the UN Special Representative spoke of the mass prisoner killings of July–September 1988 no longer as an allegation but as a verified fact. Despite this, the UN failed to take appropriate action. Not only was there no condemnation from or investigation authorized by the then UN Commission on Human Rights and no referral by the UN General Assembly to the Security Council, the General Assembly did not even follow up on its resolution of 8 December 1988.[97]

In effect, geopolitical considerations and economic interests, as well as the imperatives of global and regional powers, prevented the UN from taking even such basic measures as the dispatch of a fact-finding commission to Iran to look into the existing evidence on the ground.

---

94 Ed Blanche, "Iran a killing ground of executions since cease-fire with Iraq," Associated Press, May 8, 1989. It was also reiterated that "The United Nations, Amnesty International and the US State Department estimate that about 1,000 political prisoners have been executed, although they acknowledge that the true figure is probably far higher." Ibid.
95 Kerin Hope, "Opposition says 2,000 detainees executed since cease-fire, deputy arrested," Associated Press, July 10, 1989.
96 Quoted in Nasser Mohajer, "The Mothers of Khavaran" (this volume).
97 Amnesty International, *Blood-soaked secrets*, p. 77; UN Report: A/44/620, November 2, 1989.

Yet the ensuing policy of silence about this heinous crime in the final quarter of the twentieth century did not last long. The year 1990 was a second turning-point, as both Amnesty International and the Human Rights Commission of the UN released new evidence on the number of political prisoners slaughtered during the midsummer of 1988. In 1990, Amnesty International confirmed that more than two thousand political prisoners had been secretly executed between July 1988 and January 1989.[98] Amnesty International also conceded that "Even now, two years after these events, it is still not clear how many people died during the six-month period from July 1988 to January 1989."[99] That said, Amnesty International added, accounts by family members and friends of the executed, as well as accounts by former political prisoners, "taken together with statements by Iranian Government personalities, have convinced Amnesty International that during this six-month period the biggest wave of political executions since the early 1980s took place in Iranian prisons."[100] Amnesty International also reported on the treatment of the family members of the executed political prisoners and alluded to the systematic character of the mass executions in different regions of the country and suggested that there had been a diktat from the center of power:

> [The families of the executed political prisoners were] required to sign undertakings that they would not hold a funeral or any other mourning ceremony. Family members were not informed where their relatives were buried, and even if they managed to find out they were not permitted to erect a gravestone... This suggests to Amnesty International that the massacre of political prisoners was a premeditated and coordinated policy which must have been authorized at the highest level of government.[101]

Around the same time, a UN report also pointed out that:

> in various parts of Iran, several thousand persons had been executed without trial or with a trial of an extremely summary nature... A list of 2,023 names of persons executed in 1988, allegedly for political

98 AI: "Iran: Violations of Human Rights 1987–1990," MDE 13/21/90, pp. 2, 6.
99 Ibid., p. 11.
100 Ibid.
101 Ibid., p. 13.

reasons, and lists of 404 names of persons executed between January and August 1989, had been received by the Special Rapporteur... Among those executed were allegedly prisoners who had been serving prison terms or persons whose sentences had expired but who had remained in detention, as well as prisoners who had never been tried or sentenced. Several victims were said to have been rearrested after they had been released. The executed allegedly included women and minors below 18 years of age.[102]

From 1990 to 1992 no new statistics surfaced on the number of men and women who lost their lives in the Great Massacre. However, in October 1992 Amnesty International released a report stating that between July 1988 and January 1989, it "recorded more than 2,500 political prisoners who were executed, including prisoners of conscience."[103]

From 1992 to 2000, once again, a period of silence prevailed regarding the 1988 massacre and the number of executed political prisoners. However, the publication of Ayatollah Montazeri's *Memoirs*, in the year 2000 was a third turning point in the disclosure of this monstrous crime against humanity. This was a crucial juncture that caused an international stir, leaving not the slightest shadow of doubt about the reality of this abominable massacre. Now all skepticism and speculation was doomed to fade away. Indeed, Ayatollah Montazeri's *Memoirs* revealed that thousands of political prisoners were slain in the wake of fatwas and edicts decreed by Ayatollah Khomeini and that the massacre had been systematically planned throughout the country. From this time on, the approximation of the number of executions of political prisoners in 1988 was bolstered to between 2,800 and 3,800.[104] In the following year, the PMOI published a list of the names of 3,208 Mojahedin prisoners who were executed in 1988. This disclosure took place on the threshold of a new phase.[105]

---

102 UN Report, E/CN.4/1990/22, January 23, 1990, p. 57. The release of this UN report coincided with UN Special Representative on Human Rights Reynaldo Galindo Pohl's first visit to Iran between January 21 and January 28, 1990.
103 AI Index: MDE 13/18/92 (October 1992), p. 1. It was added that, "Former political detainees who witnessed the massacre have told Amnesty International that they believed the overall number of those executed during that period was between 5,000 and 10,000, including around 2,000 in Tehran alone." Ibid., p. 2.
104 Hossein Ali Montazeri, *Memoirs*, https://amontazeri.com/book/khaterat/volume-1/620.
105 National Council of Resistance of Iran Foreign Affairs Committee, Crime Against Humanity..., Auvers-sur-Oise 2001.

A fourth phase evolved in the early 2000s, when a good number of survivors of the Great Massacre—who had fled Iran and found refuge in the cities of Europe and North America—began writing their memoirs about the gruesome events they had witnessed. Some of them embarked on calculating the number of prisoners who were taken to the gallows in their wards. Based on these calculations, a new estimate emerged. Now, most of the estimations were around four to five thousand political prisoners executed in the midsummer of 1988.[106] The true death toll will remain obscured while the theocracy is in power and continues to block any independent investigations, keeping the details of the Great Massacre a state secret. Nonetheless, these memoirs also influenced and informed further reports by Amnesty International and other human rights organizations. In 2008, for example, Amnesty International alleged that "In all between 4,500 and 5,000 prisoners are believed to have been killed."[107] Most recently, in a thorough report, Amnesty International reiterated that:

> To date, the exact number of those killed is unknown but minimum estimates put the death toll at around 5,000. The real number could be higher, especially because little is still known about the names and details of those who were rearrested in 1988 and extrajudicially executed in secret soon after arrest.[108]

---

106 See, for example, Iraj Mesdaghi, *Neither Life nor Death. Memoirs of Prison (1981–1991), Vol. 3: Restless Raspberries*, Stockholm 2004, p. 356 (around 4,000 executed political prisoners); Mehdi Aslani, *The Crow & the Red Rose. Memoirs of Prison*, Arash Books and Magazine: Germany 2009, pp. 400–5 (around 4,000). One of the early books that was published on the subject was Nima Parvaresh, *Nabardi Nabarabar, Guzarishi-i Haft Sal Zendan, 1361 ta 1368* (Unequal Battle, Report on Seven Years' Imprisonment, 1982 to 1989) (Andeesheh va Peykar Publication: Germany, 1995); Nima Parvaresh, "What Happened to Us in 1988?," Paris: The ad-hoc committee on the anniversary of massacre of the political prisoners in Iran 1995, p. 26 (between 4,500 and 5,000).

107 AI Index: MDE 13/118/2008, August 19, 2008, p. 1. Similarly, in 2011, Geoffrey Robertson wrote that by mid-August 1988 up to five thousand Mojahedin had been murdered. Report of an Inquiry Conducted by Geoffrey Robertson, p. 115.

108 Amnesty International, *Blood-soaked secrets*, p. 11. The Committee for the Defence of Human Rights in Iran recorded the names of 4,672 persons from various political affiliations killed during the mass prisoner killings in 1988. As Amnesty International points out: "This is a minimum number and does not include the hundreds of arrests that are believed to have taken place in the weeks leading to the armed incursion of the PMOI on 25 July 1988 or shortly after it." Moreover, a list compiled by PMOI, titled "Crimes Against Humanity," records the full names of 4,969 Mojahedin prisoners who were allegedly killed during the mass executions. Ibid., p. 23.

These are important, though minor, steps in raising awareness of the most sinister cleansing in recent Iranian history, about which we still know little—especially when it comes to the provinces. According to Amnesty International, as a direct result of the fatwa decreed by Ayatollah Khomeini, the massacre was conducted in thirty-two cities. Nonetheless, information could not be obtained for fourteen of these cities.[109]

Although a considerable number of Iranian exile communities and pro-democracy collectives made relentless efforts to raise awareness and call attention to the mass executions of the summer of 1988, by and large the killings remained unrecognized and received little media coverage. Western economic and geopolitical interests, especially endeavors to open the Iranian market to foreign investors, partially explains why states and parliaments around the globe, most notably in North America and Western Europe, long kept silent about this colossal crime. After the European Parliament issued a resolution on December 15, 1988, that silence lasted twenty-five years until in 2013 the Canadian House of Commons became the second parliament in the world to condemn "the mass murder of political prisoners in Iran in the summer of 1988 as a crime against humanity." The silence then lasted another four years before the US Congress took some measures to address the atrocities. On March 9, 2017, the US House of Representatives introduced a draft bill condemning the government of the IRI for the 1988 massacre of thousands of political prisoners and calling for justice for the victims. However, the bill was never voted on.[110] On January 31, 2017, the Piemonte provincial council in Italy also issued a resolution that condemned the 1988 massacre, stating that:

> In the summer of 1988, the Iranian regime conducted the summary
> and extra-judicial execution of tens of thousands of political prisoners

---

109 For a list of the thirty-two cities, see Amnesty International, *Blood-soaked secrets*, p. 19. See also pp. 140–66.
110 H.Res.188 – Condemning the Government of the Islamic Republic of Iran for the 1988 massacre of political prisoners and calling for justice for the victims. 115th Congress (2017–18). It was ascertained that "over a 4-month period the victims included thousands of people, including teenagers and pregnant women, imprisoned merely for participating in peaceful street protests and for possessing political reading material...prisoners were executed in groups, some in mass hangings and others by firing squad according to Amnesty International." Ibid. However, it should be noted that we possess too little proof about the number of teenagers among the executed, and the prisoners were mostly hanged and not shot by firing squads, as the massacre was conducted in secret and the authorities wanted to avoid suspicious noise.

who were jailed in prisons across the country, on the basis of a religious decree (fatwa) emitted by the then-Supreme Leader of the regime, Ayatollah Khomeini... the 1988 massacre in Iran remains one of the darkest moments of recent human history, and one of the lesser known and debated ones... [It] [c]ompels the Italian Government to firmly condemn the 1988 massacre of political prisoners in Iran.[111]

On April 26, 2018, the US House of Representatives passed the Iran Human Rights and Hostage-Taking Accountability Act (H.R. 4744). The text contains the following passage: "Over a 4-month period in 1988, the Iranian regime carried out the barbaric mass executions of thousands of political prisoners by hanging and firing squad for refusing to renounce their political affiliations and in some cases for possessing political reading material."[112]

The perpetrators of the Great Massacre are still venerated and continue to hold the highest positions in the state apparatus. To this day, no touch of remorse or acknowledgment of the sufferings of the executed prisoners' families is visible among the power holders of the Islamic hierocracy, who continue to cover up and support the slaughterers of 1988. These include Iran's current Minister of Justice, Alireza Avaei, in 1988 the prosecutor general of Dezful in Khuzestan Province and a member of the Death Commission in that city; Hossein Ali Nayyeri, the current head of the Supreme Disciplinary Court for Judges, who acted as religious judge in the Tehran Death Commission; Mohammad Hossein Ahmadi, currently a member of the Assembly of Experts and in 1988 member of the Death Commission in Khuzestan; Mostafa Pourmohammadi, Justice Minister between 2013 and 2017, who represented the Ministry of Intelligence in the Tehran "death commission;" and Ebrahim Raisi, the current chief justice of Iran who was among the miniscule number of presidential candidates—only 0.37% of applicants were accepted—who were allowed to run for the presidency in 2017. Raisi was the deputy prosecutor general of Tehran in 1988 and ordered the extrajudicial executions of thousands of political prisoners murdered during the Great Massacre.

---

111 http://www.cr.piemonte.it/mzodgfo/legislatura/10/atto/985/documento/5074/visualizza.
112 The victims included prisoners of conscience, teenagers, and pregnant women. H.R.4744 – Iran Human Rights and Hostage-Taking Accountability Act. 115th Congress (2017–18).

Last but not least, as the UN reported in August 2017:

> In August 2016, an audio recording of a meeting held in 1988 between high-level State officials and clerics was published. The recording revealed the names of the officials who had carried out and defended the executions, including the current Minister of Justice, a current high court judge, and the head of one of the largest religious foundations in the country and candidate in the May presidential elections. Following the publication of the audio recording, some clerical authorities and the chief of the judiciary admitted that the executions had taken place and, in some instances, defended them.[113]

---

113 UN Report: A/72/322, August 14, 2017, pp. 4, 15. For the original Persian transcript of the audio recording of the meeting that took place on August 15, 1988, see www. hamneshinbahar.net/article.php?text_id=418.

THEOCRACY MEMOS

Ayatollah Khomeini's Fatwa

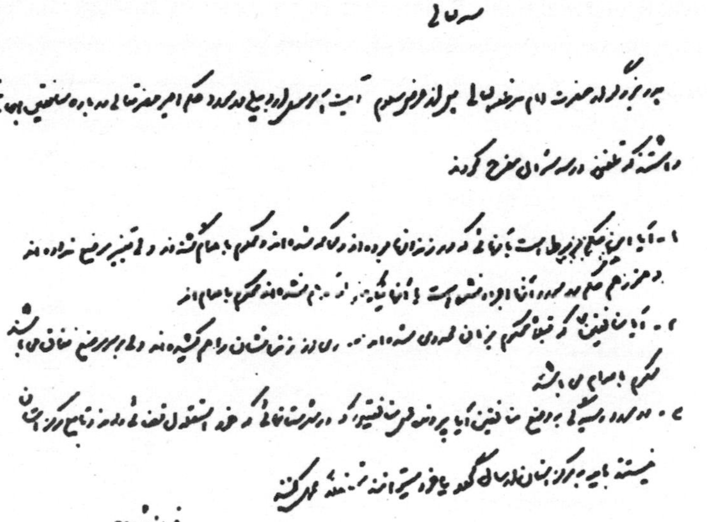

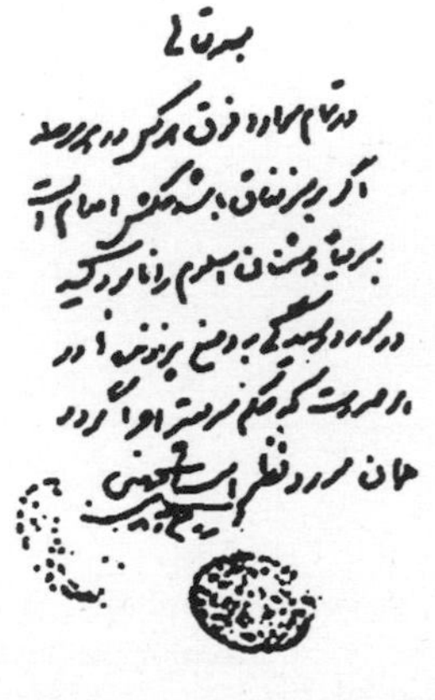

In the name of God,

Exalted father, Your Eminence Imam, may your high shadow be lasting,

After greetings, Ayatollah Mousavi Ardebili is in need of some clarifications about your recent fatwa about *Monafeqin* [hypocrites] and posed three questions via telephone in this regard:

1. Is this order about those who have been in jail, have been tried and have been sentenced to death [but their sentences have not been carried out] and who remain in their hypocritical positions? Or those who have not yet been tried but are nevertheless sentenced to death?
2. Are the hypocrites who have been sentenced to prison terms and passed part of their sentences but still insist on their hypocritical positions sentenced to death?
3. Do cities and counties who have judicial independence and are not judicially subject to the Provincial Capitals need to send the cases of the hypocrites to the Capital of their Province or can they independently take action in these cases?

Your son, Ahmad

In the name of God,

In all cases mentioned above, if anybody, at any stage, insists on a hypocritical position, they are to be condemned to death. Liquidate the enemies of Islam rapidly. Regarding the method of reviewing the cases, whichever is faster should be considered.

Ruhollah Mousavi Khomeini

Ayatollah Khomeini's Edict

بسم الله الرحمن الرحیم

از آنجا که منافقین خائن به هیچ وجه به اسلام معتقد نبوده و هر چه می‌گویند از روی حیله و نفاق آنهاست و به اقرار سران آنها از اسلام ارتداد پیدا کرده‌اند، با توجه به محارب بودن آنها و جنگهای کلاسیک آنها در شمال و غرب و جنوب کشور با همکاریهای حزب بعث عراق و نیز جاسوسی آنان برای صدام علیه ملت مسلمان ما و با توجه به ارتباط آنان با استکبار جهانی و ضربات ناجوانمردانهٔ آنان از ابتدای تشکیل نظام جمهوری اسلامی تاکنون، کسانی که در زندانهای سراسر کشور بر سر موضع نفاق خود پافشاری کرده و می‌کنند، محارب و محکوم به اعدام می‌باشند. و تشخیص موضوع نیز در تهران با رأی اکثریت آقایان حجت الاسلام نیری دامت افاضاته (قاضی شرع) و جناب آقای اشراقی (دادستان تهران) و نماینده‌ای از وزارت اطلاعات می‌باشد، اگر چه احتیاط در اجماع است. و همین‌طور در زندانهای مراکز استان کشور رأی اکثریت آقایان قاضی شرع، دادستان انقلاب و یا دادیار و نمایندهٔ وزارت اطلاعات لازم الاتباع می‌باشد. رحم بر محاربین ساده‌اندیشی است. قاطعیت اسلام در برابر دشمنان خدا از اصول تردیدناپذیر نظام اسلامی است. امیدوارم با خشم و کینهٔ انقلابی خود نسبت به دشمنان اسلام رضایت خداوند متعال را جلب نمایید. آقایانی که تشخیص موضوع به عهدهٔ آنان است وسوسه و شک و تردید نکنند و سعی کنند اشداء علی الکفار باشند. تردید در مسائل قضایی اسلام انقلابی نادیده گرفتن خون پاک و مطهر شهدا می‌باشد. والسلام

روح الله الموسوی الخمینی

In the name of God, the Compassionate, the Merciful,

Since the treacherous hypocrites (*Monafeqin*) [Mojahedin] do not believe in Islam and whatever they say stems from their deception and hypocrisy, and since their leaders have confessed that they have become heretics to Islam, and since they wage war against God and are engaging in classical warfare on the western, northern, and southern fronts and collaborating with the Ba'athist Party of Iraq, as well as their spying for Saddam [Hossein, Iraq's former president] against our Muslim nation, and since they are tied to the World Arrogant Hegemonists [US and Western powers] and have inflicted cowardly blows upon the Islamic Republic since its establishment up to the present time, those in prisons throughout the country who insist on their position of hypocrisy (*nifaq*) are considered to be waging war against God (*Mohareb*) and are condemned to be executed.

In Tehran, this determination shall be made based on a majority vote by [shari'a judge] Hojat al-Islam Nayyeri, may his blessings be continued, Mr. Eshraghi and a representative of the Ministry of Intelligence, though unanimity is the preferred cautionary option. In the prisons of provincial capitals in the country, the views of a majority of [a trio consisting of] the shari'a judge, the revolutionary prosecutor general or assistant prosecutor, and the ministry of intelligence representative must be obeyed.

It is naive to show mercy to those who fight against God (*Mohareb*). The decisiveness of Islam before the enemies of God is among the unquestionable tenets of the Islamic regime. I hope that you satisfy God Almighty with your revolutionary rage and hatred against the enemies of Islam. The gentlemen who are responsible for making the decisions must not hesitate, nor show any doubt or concerns and they must be the "harshest on non-believers." To hesitate in the judicial process of revolutionary Islam is to ignore the pure and clean blood of the martyrs, and Peace.

Ayatollah Montazeri's First Letter to Ayatollah Khomeini

بسم الله الرحمن الرحیم

محضر مبارک آیة الله العظمی امام خمینی مدظله العالی

پس از سلام و تحیت بعرض میرساند راجع به دستور اخیر حضرتعالی مبنی بر اعدام منافقین موجود در زندانها: اعدام بازداشت شدگان حادثه اخیر را ملت و جامعه پذیرا است و ظاهراً اثر سوئی ندارد ولی اعدام موجودین از سابق در زندانها اولاً در شرائط فعلی حمل بر کینه توزی و انتقامجوئی میشود. و ثانیاً خانواده های بسیاری را که نوعاً متدین و انقلابی هستند ناراحت و داغدار میکند و از نظام جدا و آزرده میشوند. و ثالثاً بسیاری از آنان سر موضع نیستند ولی بعضی از مسئولین تند با آنان معامله سر موضع میکنند. و رابعاً در شرائط فعلی که با فشارها و حملات اخیر صدام و منافقین ما در دنیا چهره مظلومی بخود گرفته ایم و بسیاری از رسانه ها و شخصیتها از ما دفاع میکنند صلاح نظام و حضرتعالی نیست که یکدفعه تبلیغات علیه ما شروع شود. و خامساً افرادی که بوسیله دادگاهها با موازینی در سابق محکوم بکمتر از اعدام شده اند اعدام کردن آنان بدون مقدمه و بدون فعالیت تازه ای بی اعتنائی به همه موازین قضائی و احکام قضات است و عکس العمل خوب ندارد. و سادساً مسئولین قضائی و دادستانی و اطلاعات ما در سطح مقدس اردبیلی نیستند و اشتباهات و تأثر از جو بسیار و فراوان است و با حکم اخیر حضرتعالی بسا بیگناهان و یا کم گناهانی هم اعدام میشوند. و سابعاً ما تاکنون از کشتنها و خشونتها نتیجه ای نگرفته ایم جز اینکه تبلیغات را علیه خود زیاد کرده ایم و جاذبه منافقین و ضد انقلاب را بیشتر نموده ایم بجاست مدتی با رحمت و عطوفت برخورد شود که قطعاً برای بسیاری جاذبه خواهد داشت. و ثامناً اگر فرضاً بر دستور خودتان اصرار دارید اقلاً دستور دهید ملاک اتفاق نظر قاضی و دادستان و مسئول اطلاعات باشد نه اکثریت، و زنان هم استثناء شوند مخصوصاً زنان بچه دار.

و بالاخره اعدام چند هزار نفر در ظرف چند روز هم عکس العمل خوب ندارد و هم خالی از خطا نخواهد بود.

و بعض از قضاة متدین بسیار ناراحت بودند و بجاست این حدیث شریف مورد توجه واقع شود:

«قال رسول الله (ص): ادرؤوا الحدود عن المسلمین ما استطعتم فان کان له مخرج فخلوا سبیله فان الامام ان یخطئ فی العفو خیر من ان یخطئ فی العقوبة.» والسلام علیکم و ادام الله ظلکم ۶ ذی الحجه ۱۴۰۸ - ۶۷/۵/۹

In the Name of God, the Compassionate, the Merciful,

To His Auspicious Presence, the Grand Ayatollah Imam Khomeini, may his Exalted Shadow be prolonged

With Greetings, regarding Your Eminence's recent order about the executions of *Monafeqin* [Mojahedin] who are in prisons, the execution of those arrested in the recent incident would be acceptable by the nation and by society and apparently would not have any ill effects. But the execution of those prisoners still in prison from before the incident, under the present conditions, will be perceived, first, as acts of vengeance and vendetta. Second, many of their families who are generally pious and revolutionary will be aggrieved, distressed and discouraged. Third, many of the prisoners are not insisting on their previous positions, but they are treated as if they were. Fourth, now that with attacks and pressures from Saddam and *Monafeqin* [Mojahedin] we have gained a reputation as the oppressed and many of the media and the personalities defend us, it would not be advantageous for the regime and Your Eminence if, all of a sudden, propaganda began against us. Fifth, to execute, without justification, those who have previously been sentenced to less than execution by the courts and who have subsequently carried out no new activities is to disregard all judicial principles and rulings by judges and will not reflect well on us. Sixth, our judicial officials, prosecutorial and intelligence apparatuses are not infallible like Moghaddas Ardebili [Ardebili, the Saint]. Mistakes and influences resulting from the prevailing atmosphere are numerous and with your recent order it is quite possible that the innocent or individuals with lesser charges will be executed. Seventh, we have not benefitted from violence and killings so far, but we have stirred more propaganda against ourselves and created more attraction for *Monafeqin* [Mojahedin] and counter revolution. It is appropriate to use mercy for a while, which definitely will have more attraction for many. And eighth, if you insist that your order will be carried out, at least give the order that there should be a unanimous decision by the judge, the prosecutor and the intelligence official rather than a majority decision.

Women should be excepted from execution, especially women with children. Lastly, executing several thousands in a few days is not going to create a good reaction and will not be free of errors. Some pious judges are very distressed.

Hossein Ali Montazeri
Date: July 31, 1988

Ayatollah Montazeri's Second Letter to Ayatollah Khomeini

بسمه تعالی

تاریخ ٦٧/٥/١٣
شماره

بسم الله الرحمن الرحیم

محضر مبارک آیة الله العظمی امام خمینی مدظله العالی

با عرض سلام و تحیت   پیرو نامه مورخه ٦٧/٥/٩ برای رفع مسئولیت شرعی از خود مجدداً می‌رسانم:

سه روز قبل رئیس شرع یکی از استان‌های کشور در مورد اختلافی می‌باشد با بنده راجع از نحوه اجرای فرمان اخیر حضرتعالی به قم آمده بود و می‌گفت: مسئول اطلاعات یا دادستان - تردیدم از این است - از یکی از زندانیان برای تفتیش احکام سر موضع است یا نه پرسید: تو فتوی را از قافته را را حکم کنی؟

گفت: آری، پرسید، حاضری مصاحبه کنی، گفت: آری، پرسید: حاضری برای جنگ

با عراق کیسه بردی، گفت: آری، پرسید: حاضری روی مین بردی؟

گفت: اگر همه مردم حاضر به روی مین بروند دانمی از ترس تا این حد نیست و دوست نیست.

گفت: معلوم می‌شود تو هنوز سر موضعی و با او بعداً علیه سر موضع اعدام داد.

و این قاضی شرع می‌گفت: من هر چه اجرا کردم پس علاوه بر اتفاق آراء باید با رأی دادستان پذیرفته نشد

و فقیر باسمی را هم این مسئول اطلاعات دارد و دیگران علاوه تحت تأثیر می‌باشند.

حضرتعالی ملاحظه فرمایید که کل بنا به دیدی مسئول اعدام فرا از موقع حضرتعالی قم بنا به هزاران نفر

مربوط به هست، می‌باشند و السلام علیکم و رحمة الله و برکاته

August 4, 1988

In the Name of God, the Compassionate, the Merciful,

To His Auspicious Presence, the Grand Ayatollah Imam Khomeini, may his Exalted Shadow be prolonged

After Greetings, following my letter dated July 31, 1988, in order to fulfill my religious duty I would like to report that three days ago the religious judge of one of the provinces, whom I trust, had come to Qom and was distressfully complaining about the method of implementing Your Eminence's order and was saying that either the intelligence official or the prosecutor—the confusion is on my part—in order to determine whether a prisoner was still holding his position asked the prisoner: "Are you ready to condemn the *Monafeqin* [Mojahedin] Organization?" The prisoner answered "Yes." He asked the prisoner: "Are you ready to participate in a public interview?" The answer was "Yes." Question: "Are you ready to go to the war front against Iraq?" The answer again was "Yes." He asked: "Are you ready to go over the minefields?" The prisoner answered "Is everybody ready to go over the minefields? Moreover, one should not expect from a newly converted Muslim so much." Then the questioner said, "This makes it clear that you are still holding your position," and dealt with him as he was still holding his position [the prisoner was killed]. This religious judge was saying that my insistence that the decision should be unanimous and not only by majority was not accepted. Everywhere, the main role is played by the intelligence official and the others are under his influence.

Your Eminence, see what kind of people, with what points of view, are responsible for implementing your important order which deals with the lives of thousands of individuals.

Ayatollah Montazeri's Letter to the Board of Four

بسمه تعالی

خطاب به آقایان نیری و اشراقی و رئیسی و پورمحمدی

تاریخ ۷۶/۵/۲۲

۱ –

۲ –

۳ –

۴ –

۵ –

۶ –

۷ –

۸ –

۹ –

۱۰ –

Date: August 15, 1988
To: Messrs:

Nayyeri [religious judge],
Eshraghi [prosecutor],
Raisi [deputy prosecutor],
Pourmohammadi [Intelligence Ministry representative],

In the Name of God, the Most High

1. I have suffered more blows from the *Monafeqin* [Mojahedin] than any of you, whether in prison or outside of it—they martyred my son—and if we were to go with vengeance I should have been first to go, but I consider the expediency of Islam, revolution and the country, as well as the prestige of the *Velayat-e faqih* [the guardianship of the Islamic Jurists] and the Islamic State. I consider the judgment of history and posterity.

2. This kind of massacre of prisoners without any trial will certainly benefit them [*Monafeqin* (Mojahedin)] and encourage them into further armed struggle and the world will condemn us. It is wrong to fight an idea with killing.

3. Look at the conduct of the Prophet with regard to his enemies in the conquest of Mecca and in the Battle of Hawazen and see how he showed mercy and forgiveness and God bestowed him with the title of "the Mercy of both worlds." Consider the way "the Commander of Muslims" [Ali, the first imam of the Shi'ite Muslims] treated his enemies after defeating them in the Battle of Jamal.

4. The hardening of the position of many prisoners is the result of the interrogators and jailers' behavior. Otherwise these prisoners would have been more flexible.

5. The mere notion that these prisoners would rejoin the *Monafeqin* [Mojahedin] if they were released is not reason enough to call them *Mohareb* [one who wages war on God] or *Baghi* [a mutineer against God]. "The Commander of Muslims" [Ali] did not punish Ibn Moljem [his assassin] before he committed the crime, although he said he will be my assassin.

6. The mere belief does not make a person *Mohareb* or *Baghi*, and

the heresy of the leaders does not, necessarily, make their sympathizers heretics.

7. Judgment and sentencing should be carried out in a proper atmosphere and without emotion. These days, with provocations and sloganeering, the social atmosphere is not proper. We are distressed by the crimes of *Monafeqin* [Mojahedin] in the west [of Iran] but we are taking it out on the prisoners and former prisoners. Executing them when they have not carried out any new activities will cast doubt on all judges and all previous judgments. According to what criteria do you execute someone who had been sentenced to a lesser punishment? At the present time you have cut off all prison visits and telephone calls—how will you answer the prisoners' families tomorrow?

8. More than anything else, I am thinking about the prestige and the reputation of His Eminence Imam and *Velayat-e faqih*. I don't know how and in what manner they have presented things to him. Were all those discussions in fiqh [Islamic jurisprudence] about caution in dealing with people's lives and blood and properties wrong?

9. I have met several wise and pious judges who were distressed and were complaining about the extremism and the way the order is being carried out. They cited many cases of people who were executed without any justification.

10. At the end, Mojahedin Khalq [People's Mojahedin] are not [only] individuals, they are a school of thought, an interpretation and a manner of logic, and wrong logic should be answered by right logic and killing does not solve the problem.

May God help you to success,
Hossein Ali Montazeri

THE GREAT MASSACRE IN THE WESTERN PRESS

amnesty international

INTERNATIONAL SECRETARIAT
1 Easton Street London WC1X 8DJ
United Kingdom

EXTERNAL (for general distribution)

UA 219/88   Death Penalty   16 August 1988

IRAN: Political Executions

URGENT ACTION

AI Index: MDE 13/13/88
Distr: UA/SC

Amnesty International is concerned by evidence that a new wave of political executions is taking place in Iran.

In recent weeks the official Iranian media have continued to report the execution of government opponents. These include 10 "counter-revolutionaries and Iraqi spies" executed on 10 July, seven members of the outlawed People's Mojahedine Organization of Iran hanged in public in Bakhtaran on 1 August and another member of that organization hanged in public in Ilam on 3 August. Approvals by the Supreme Judicial Council of death sentences on members of opposition groups also continue to be reported.

Amnesty International has also received reports that three leading members of the Tudeh Party, Kiumars Zarshenas, Simin Fardin and Sa'id Azarang, and a member of the People's Fedaiyan Organization of Iran (Majority), Farsamarz Sufi, were executed by firing squad in Evin Prison on 20 July. It is alleged that up to eight others were executed at the same time, and that death sentences have been confirmed on 55 more political prisoners who are now awaiting execution.

Amnesty International opposes the death penalty in all cases as a violation of the right to life and the right not to be subjected to cruel, inhuman or degrading treatment or punishment, as proclaimed in the Universal Declaration of Human Rights. In the case of Iran it is particularly concerned by the lack of provisions for fair trial in political cases, and the lack of any procedure for prisoners sentenced to death to appeal against conviction or sentence.

RECOMMENDED ACTION: Telegrams/telexes/airmail letters:

- expressing deep regret at these executions and asking for details of the procedures by which death sentences are being passed and approved;

- urging the commutation of all outstanding death sentences and an end to executions in Iran.

The New York Times

THE NEW YORK TIMES, THURSDAY, NOVEMBER 3, 1988

U.N. Says Human Rights Abuses Are Continuing Throughout Iran

By PAUL LEWIS
Special to The New York Times

UNITED NATIONS, Nov. 2 — A United Nations report said today that serious human rights violations were continuing in Iran. It said the violations included a wave of executions of political prisoners in July, August and September after Tehran accepted a cease-fire in the war with Iraq.

The author of the report, Reynaldo Galindo Pohl of El Salvador, the Special Representative for Iran of the United Nations Commission on Human Rights, said his findings "justify international concern" about the rights situation in that country. He called on the Iranian authorities "to redress abuses and prevent their recurrence."

The United Nations Human Rights Commission has been examining the human rights situation in Iran since 1985, issuing a series of annual reports, all of which have found evidence of widespread abuses.

The report today drew attention to a "wave of executions" that it said occurred in Iran over the summer and were carried out mainly against "members of various opposition groups" including the Mujahedeen National Liberation Army fighting the Tehran Government from bases in Iraq and other dissident groups.

The report said such executions "justify international concern" that the Iranian authorities are in breach of their obligations under the United Nations Human Rights Covenants. It noted that another United Nations human rights official investigating summary and arbitrary executions sent telegrams to the Iranian Foreign Minister in July and August expressing concern about the executions.

Officials at the Iranian Mission to the United Nations said that they had not yet received a copy of the report and that they would have no comment at this time.

The new report will be debated this month by the third committee of the United Nations General Assembly, which deals with social, cultural and humanitarian questions.

The report said 200 Mujahedeen supporters were believed to have been killed in Evin Prison on July 28. The bodies of 860 more "executed political prisoners" were reported to have been taken from the same prison to the Beheshti Zahra cemetery from Aug 14 to 16. There report lists numerous other executions of Government opponents in the summer.

The wave of executions described in the report today came after a series of military successes by the Iraqi Army and the Mujahedeen forces that analysts say swung the tide of the gulf war in Baghdad's favor, prompting Iran to accept the cease-fire urged on both sides by the United Nations.

But Iran's military setback and its decision to accept a cease-fire also appears to have unleashed a backlash of revenge inside the country against anyone suspected of disloyalty to the Government, diplomats say.

The report expressed concern about widespread reports of beatings and torture in Iranian prisons as well as trials at which the prisoner is prevented from offering a defense. It spoke of "poor and insufficient food," "lack of medical treatment and "extremely poor sanitary prison conditions."

The report also expressed concern at reports that all family visits to political prisoners in Evin Prison and other detention centres have been suspended since August

---

Le Monde
ENGLISH SECTION

Rash of executions in Iran a warning to Montazeri

CONTRARY to what could have been reasonably expected, the ceasefire in the Gulf war has not put an end to political repression in Iran.

Executions of People's Mujahidin members are continuing unabated. They began in August following an abortive incursion into Iranian territory by Masud Rajavi's Iraqi-financed and supplied National Liberation Army. The rate of executions even seems to have gone up, according to a National Liberation Army release in Baghdad which speaks of "hundreds of political prisoners shot or hanged in recent weeks." Since early October the repression, which is also directed against leftwing organisations — Tudeh or the People's Fedayin — has spread to non-conformist members of the Iranian clergy close to Ayatollah Montazeri, the man who has been named to succeed Imam Khomeini.

Scores of religious and political figures were arrested early in October in Qom and Tehran, without any reasons being given for the measures, which have moreover not been announced officially. Eleven of those arrested — five members of the Islamic clergy and six lay persons attached to Qom's theological centres — were summarily executed. The victims included a former Majlis member, Hojatoleslam Fathollah Umond Najafabadi, one of Ayatollah Montazeri's aides.

Najafabadi was very actively involved in working among the disadvantaged (mustazafin). After the 1979 revolution, he was a judge at the Isfahan revolutionary court, where he made a name for himself through his work for the socially deprived. At the time he earned the enmity of former representatives of the Shah's re-

By Jean Gueyras

gime by systematically expropriating their possessions. In 1986 he was arrested along with Ayatollah Montazeri's son-in-law, Mehdi Hashemi, the top man of a hardline dogmatic "Islamic world revolution" movement who was executed in September 1987. Najafabadi was spared only because Khomeini's heir-apparent intervened personally.

The four other religious figures executed — Hojatoleslam Husseini Arab, Sharufeddin Mashkur, Ghayur and Khavari Langerudi — were also part of Montazeri's close circle, as were the six lay persons, most fo them former Revolutionary Guards who had been dismissed

following the Mehdi Hashemi affair.

The accusations would appear to be a warning to Montazeri who, taking his role as Khomeini's heir-apparent seriously, sent out on October 1 a series of instructions to the country's top officials in which he made a severe indictment of government action since the ceasefire came into effect. In doing that he was voicing the grievances of a public disappointed that peace with Iraq had not brought with it any relaxation of the system.

In these directives, publication of which was censored by the official media, Montazeri blamed the country's stagnation on leaders in Tehran, whom he accused of "intransigence, incompetence and lack of imagination". He also attacked the Revolutionary Guards, the Martyrs' Foundation and other revolutionary bodies which he accused of being responsible for the paralysis and disorganisation of economic life".

The ayatollah advocated a degree of economic liberalisation, saying that "even the socialist countries have realised their mistakes and have opted for a policy of opening out in this area." Even more serious was the suggestion that the men in power, "all those who have turned statism into sterile dogma", be fired from their jobs and replaced by new, more "broad-minded" men.

Montazeri also hit out at the intelligence services and security committees and bodies, pointing out that "nothing can be achieved through mindless repression and the proliferation of death sentences", which he said were measures against the spirit of Islam "the religion of pardon and tolerance" and they were "deepening the country's political isolation". In addition, he proposed an "unequivocal" general amnesty which would enable two million Iranians who fled Iran after the revolution to come home "as they could take part in rebuilding the economy by the injection of a new dynamism".

Ayatollah Montazeri finally called for "openness" in government. The Iranians were an "adult people", he said, and "they are entitled to know what's happening in the upper circles of the government. Iranian leaders should stop behaving as if they are above the law. Newspapers should reflect the viewpoints of the various trends present in the country and lawful opponents should have their say in running the country."

But his demands are apparently considered unacceptable by the Iranian authorities who once again appear to have opted for arbitrary repression to silence voices that do not echo the official line.

(November 20/21)

Fact and fiction mingle in revolutionary Iran

The Tehran rumour-mill has gone into overdrive. **Vahe Petrossian** reports

Iran's powerful parliamentary speaker, Hashemi Rafsanjani, whose opponents say him dodged bullets in at least two assassination attempts

THE INDEPENDENT

Friday 13 January 1989

Khomeini's heir denounces regime over executions

By Ahmed Vahdatkhah and John Bulloch

THE MAN designated the successor to Ayatollah Khomeini as leader of Iran published an open letter yesterday calling the continuing executions of political prisoners "sins", and declaring his opposition to what was going on.

Ayatollah Hussein Ali Montazeri, increasingly the focus of dissent in Iran, wrote in his letter of the "blood-letting" going on in Iran, where a wave of executions has followed the truce in the Gulf war. Amnesty International has spoken of 600 people killed in the past few months, while the Iranian opposition has claimed more than 2,000 deaths.

In his letter, Ayatollah Montazeri confirmed one of the claims of Iranian exiles. "It appears that in most cases those executed have been serving short prison sentences for minor political offences," he wrote. "I declare my opposition to these sentences, and I am sure there are a good number of people in this country who would share with me —"

Ayatollah Khomeini, whose grip on reality is slipping as his life fades away, chose his old friend and contemporary Montazeri as a malleable heir. But Ayatollah Montazeri has shown himself to be tougher and more single-minded than expected, and willing to challenge the regime at all levels. It is widely held that Ayatollah Montazeri knew of the violent activities of his kinsman, Mehdi Hashemi, who was executed after his attempts to disrupt the US-Iranian arms-for-hostages deal went astray.

In his letter, addressed to the Minister of Justice as well as to Ayatollah Khomeini himself, Ayatollah Montazeri chose theological as well as practical grounds for his objections to what is going on in Tehran. "If these executions have been carried out in the name of observing the retribution law, then where are the members of the families of those victims in whose name an act of revenge has been authorised?" he asked. Under Sharia law, the families of victims can choose whether to commute a death sentence for murder to payment of compensation.

"For what valid reasons or on what basis has our judiciary approved these executions, which can result in nothing but damaging the face of our revolution and the system," he wrote.

According to reports from Tehran, and from Amnesty and other organisations, supporters of the left-wing opposition Mujahedin and Fedayin organisations, as well as members of the Tudeh Communist party, have been among the recent victims, many buried in mass graves. Exile sources claimed that hundreds were killed when an explosion was arranged at Evin prison, and say they believe that the aim is to decimate the opposition before an amnesty is declared to mark the tenth anniversary of the Islamic revolution later this year

NEUES DEUTSCHLAND

Proletarier aller Länder, vereinigt euch!

ORGAN DES ZENTRALKOMITEES DER SOZIALISTISCHEN EINHEITSPARTEI DEUTSCHLANDS

18 Januar 1989

Erklärung der Volkspartei Irans (Tudeh)

Parteikader wurden Opfer von Massenhinrichtungen

Paris (ADN). In einer Erklärung, die in Paris herausgegeben wurde, hat das Zentralkomitee der Volkspartei Irans (Tudeh) zu Massenhinrichtungen in Iran Stellung genommen, denen auch viele Mitglieder ihrer Partei zum Opfer gefallen sind. Unter ihnen befinden sich die Mitglieder des Politbüros des ZK Manoutcher Behzadi, Esmail Zolghdar und Rafaat Mohamedzadeh sowie der bekannte Mediziner Ahmed Danesh, der als erster Arzt in Iran Nierentransplantationen durchführte. Wie aus den Informationen der Partei hervorgeht, gibt es über die tatsächliche Zahl der Hinrichtungen keine genauen Angaben. Die vor sechs Jahren inhaftierte Gruppe von Tudeh-Mitgliedern sei unter Ausschluß der Öffentlichkeit verurteilt worden.

In der Erklärung wird darauf verwiesen, daß hervorragende Vertreter der Volkspartei sowie anderer revolutionärer und progressiver Organisationen hingerichtet wurden, denen weder ein ordnungsgemäßer Prozeß noch die Möglichkeit der Verteidigung ihrer Anschauungen ermöglicht wurde. Vor der Öffentlichkeit werde der Versuch unternommen, diese Tatsachen und ihre Hintergründe zu verschweigen. Das iranische Volk und die revolutionäre Bewegung des Landes, so stellt die Volkspartei Irans fest, habe eine Anzahl ihrer bewußtesten und erfahrensten Söhne und Töchter verloren. Dies sei zu einem Zeitpunkt erfolgt, als der Waffenstillstand im Golfkrieg zustande kam.

Bei den hingerichteten Kadern der Partei sowie anderer progressiver Kräfte habe es sich um Menschen gehandelt, die aus Liebe zu ihrem Volk den Kampf gegen Imperialismus und Reaktion, für Frieden, Unabhängigkeit und soziale Gerechtigkeit führten.

The Washington Post

Weather

SUNDAY, JANUARY 29, 1989

Ten Years Later, Iran Struggles to Rebuild

Revolution Endures Despite War, Malaise

By Patrick E. Tyler
Washington Post Foreign Service

TEHRAN, Jan. 28—The Iranian Revolution, born a decade ago when a religious cleric little known in the West incited a mass revolt with his vision of a benevolent Islamic society, remains an unpredictable movement striving to rebuild from a devastating eight-year war.

Though many Iranians have been demoralized by the effects of the long and bloody conflict with Iraq, by revolutionary excesses at home and by the severe economic strain of the last 10 years, a number of Iranian sources and western analysts interviewed here this week report that a strong resiliency continues to enable this population of 50 million to cope with immense hardship.

The revolutionary bond is fed by religion, nationalism and the shared legacy of having backed Ayatollah Ruhollah Khomeini in an uprising to overthrow Shah Muhammad Reza Pahlavi and the monarchy that existed here for 2,500 years.

The flags, bunting and posters are going up for what has been entitled the "Ten Days of Dawn"

On the wall of the old U.S. Embassy compound in Tehran, the slogans of a decade of confrontation still carry Ayatollah Ruhollah Khomeini's defiant threat to the "Great Satan": "We will deliver a severe defeat to America."

festival that begins Wednesday to commemorate Khomeini's triumphant return from exile on Feb. 1, 1979, and the collapse of the shah's last government on Feb. 11, 1979.

The occasion of this 10th anniversary comes at a time when the country is struggling to revive itself following Iran's acceptance last July of a cease-fire in its war with Iraq. Some Iranian intellectuals say the government is making the most of the upcoming celebrations to rebuild morale and rekindle the revolutionary pride of the swelling population of young people.

But in a sign of the times, President Ali Khamenei, pointing to the war-damaged electrical system that is straining under the country's postwar power demands, asked Iranian citizens in a message this week not to turn too many decorative lights on during the upcoming anniversary celebrations to avoid overtaxing the system.

For Americans, this anniversary is an uncomfortable reminder of American lives lost and hostages taken as U.S.-Iranian relations disintegrated over the past 10 years. Many political

See IRAN, A32, Col. 1

30p
Wednesday
March 29
1989
Published in London
and Manchester

The Guardian

Khomeini's heir asks to quit

David Hirst in Nicosia

WITH disarray gaining ground among Iran's revolutionary leadership, Ayatollah Khomeini's anointed heir yesterday announced that he no longer wanted the post.

According to the official Iranian news agency, Ayatollah Hussein Ali Montazeri, whose criticisms of officials and policies have grown increasingly outspoken in recent months, informed Khomeini of his intentions in a letter on Monday.

"I beg your excellency to order the Council of Experts to firmly have in mind the future interests of Islam, the revolution and the country and . . . permit me, as an insignificant and humble theology student, to teach and carry out scholarly activities in the service of Islam and the revolution under your excellency's wise leadership."

The Ayatollah replied: "As you have written, leading the Islamic Republic is a difficult task and a grave responsibility requiring more endurance than yours," adding that he and Montazeri had from the start opposed his appointment as successor.

"But the Assembly of Experts had reached this conclusion and I did not want to interfere in their legal sphere . . . Everyone knows that you are the fruit of my life and I intensely like you," the Ayatollah said. "In order not to repeat the past mistakes I advise you to clean up your house from dishonest people and seriously keep away opponents of the system who masquerade as supporters of Islam and the Islamic Republic."

"Theological students, prayer leaders, newspapers and radio and television should make this simple fact known to people, that in Islam the interests of the system come first and we should all obey them."

The resignation was made public after Khomeini held a rare meeting with the Assembly of Experts, the august body of Islamic scholars one of whose tasks is to choose his successor.

If no one person is deemed fit to assume the responsibilities of Velayet e-Fakih, or the Guardianship of the Religious Jurisprudent — as the supreme office of the Islamic Republic is known — it can be assigned to a group of three or five persons.

Montazeri had been criticised by hardliners for his pragmatism in foreign policy.

Although he has not much of an organised power-base, he had been growing in moral authority as a scourge of the existing order.

He had made himself a systematic critic of the two principal factions, the "pragmatists" led by the House Speaker, Hashemi Rafsanjani, and the "radicals" typified by the Prime Minister, Mir-Hussein Mousavi, who are now vying for Khomeini's favour, and are likely to engage in an uninhibited power struggle when he finally goes.

Montazeri has made a sweeping arraignment of the corruption and incompetence of the system, and the failure of the revolution to meet people's aspirations.

Appendix B

POLITICAL PARTIES
AND ORGANIZATIONS
OF 1980S IRAN

Arman-e Mostaz'afin

NASSER MOHAJER

The Ideal of the Downtrodden Organization (آرمان مستضعفین or *Arman-e Mostaz'afin*) was the ideological-political organ of the Organization of the Vanguard Fighters of the Downtrodden (سازمان رزمندگان پیشگام مستضعفین ایران or *Sazeman-e Razmandegan Pishgam-e Mostaz'afin-e Iran*).

The group was founded in 1977 by Mohammad Bagher Barzooie in the city of Dezful, in the south of Iran. Barzooie was an adherent of Dr. Ali Shariati, who "advocated a fresh reading of Islamic scripture in order to reconstruct Islam's concepts into a modern, progressive ideology of mobilization to enfranchise and empower the masses."[1] The group opposed revolutionary praxis, concentrating on studying the role Shi'ite clergy played in the under-development of Iran and raising consciousness about the relationship between church and state in the contemporary history of the country.

Following the February 1979 revolution in Iran, Arman-e Mostaz'afin transformed itself from an array of study groups scattered in Iran's big cities to a robust and disciplined political organization. It declared itself to be against the backward-looking, fundamentalist Shi'ite clergy who had embarked on reviving obsolete rules and regulations, and in favor of lay Muslim men and women adhering to an "adaptable Islam" that aspired to a modern and pro-gressive Islamic society (*Ummah*). This discourse became popular amongst segments of the urban Islamic youth, who abhorred the Shi'ite clergy and perceived them as a stumbling block in the development of a modern Iranian society. Such a discourse made the security forces of the Islamic Republic of Iran (IRI) more sensitive to the activities of Arman-e Mostaz'afin and eventually led to waves of arrests of its members in the early months of the Revolution and the closure of their headquarters on April 4, 1980. After the

---

1 Shariati, Ali, *The Oxford Dictionary of Islam*, (ed.) John L. Esposito, Oxford University Press, 2003, p. 289.

all-out repression of June 1981 and the inception of armed struggle by the People's Mojahedin Organization of Iran (PMOI), Arman-e Mostaz'afin split and roughly half of its members and sympathizers joined ranks with the PMOI. Soon after, the organization's branches in Tehran, Mashhad, Dezful, Rasht, Hamadan, Isfahan, and Sabzevar were attacked by the armed forces of the IRI and members of the group were arrested and detained. Consequently, the Organization of the Vanguard Fighters of the Downtrodden was wiped out from the political and intellectual scene.

While all leaders and many members of the organization who had joined ranks with the PMOI perished in prison, none of the members of the other faction, even Bagher Barzooie himself, were executed; all were ultimately released after the Great Massacre.

The Feda'ian, Majority, Minority...

NASSER MOHAJER

BEFORE THE REVOLUTION OF 1979

An attack on a gendarmerie post in Siahkal, Gilan, on February 8, 1971, marked the beginning of urban guerrilla warfare against the Shah Mohammad Reza Pahlavi's autocracy in Iran. The Siahkal operation was planned and executed by the initial nucleus of a group that would later be known (23 Day 1350 / January 13, 1972) as Cherikha-ye Feda'i-ye Khalq (چریک‌های فدایی خلق) or People's Feda'i Guerrillas). The emergence of the Feda'i Guerrillas should be understood as part of a larger worldwide trend of urban guerrilla warfare against military dictatorships in the 1960s and 1970s. The core philosophy and basic strategy of the Feda'i Guerrillas relied on "armed propaganda" to challenge the unmitigated repression of the Shah's regime and remove obstacles in the way of organizing the working class, youth and intelligentsia. The fact that the People's Feda'i Guerrillas survived and grew into a formidable force despite relentless repression by SAVAK (the notorious secret police of the Shah Mohammad Reza Pahlavi) indicates the existence of favorable conditions for this growth. In particular, it was sustained by the support it gained from the politically conscious segments of society, especially university students and progressive intellectuals.

The People's Feda'i Guerrillas came together in early 1972 through the unification of two groups with different historical and political roots. The first group, founded by Bijan Jazani and Hassan Zia Zarifi and known as Jazani-Zarifi (Group One), arose from within the ranks of the Youth Organization of the Tudeh Party and the student movement of the 1960s and early 1970s. The second group, formed by Masoud Ahmadzadeh, Amir Parviz Pouyan, and Abbas Meftahi and called Ahmadzadeh-Pouyan-Meftahi (Group Two), was primarily composed of university students coming from the northern and northeastern cities of Mashhad and Babol. These two groups had independently concluded that the political impasse in Iran could only be broken through armed struggle. It is noteworthy that the legendary Hamid Ashraf, who helped coordinate the unification of the two groups and was the contact person from Tehran with the Siahkal team and subsequently led the Feda'ian for years to come, was a member of the Jazani-Zarifi group.

The emergence of the Feda'i Guerrillas and their perseverance in armed struggle was not inconsequential. Many revolutionaries and university students who joined the Feda'ian were politically conscious and not only highly educated but at the top of their class, and knowingly faced one of the most brutal and suppressive regimes of the time. Scores of sympathizers of the guerrilla movement, both men and women, endured imprisonment and unprecedented torture in detention centers, and were later executed by firing squads. Furthermore, many were killed in armed confrontations on the streets of major Iranian cities, subsequent to the Siahkal incident, and in raids on underground safe houses. Remaining steadfast in their ethics, beliefs, and humanistic values in the face of these atrocities and under the scrutiny of unjust military tribunals left a profound impact on the psyche of Iranian intellectuals, political personalities, and ordinary people. For each member of the movement killed by the armed hand of the regime, there were many who would volunteer themselves to join the Fedai'an. Through persistent struggle against the Shah's dictatorship, they challenged the invincibility of the tyrannical regime, and the illusion that Iran was an "island of peace and stability" in the Middle East. Deeply believing in and advocating an independent, democratic and progressive Iran, they opposed dependence on foreign powers, especially the United States, which was the main supporter and patron of the Shah's regime. The Feda'ian also distanced themselves from the Soviet Union, East European Bloc, and the People's Republic of China. However, firmly believing in the international solidarity of revolutionary and progressive forces, they wholeheartedly supported national liberation movements and democratic revolutions such as the Palestinian Resistance Movement, the Vietnamese struggle for independence, or the Dhofar Liberation Front in Oman. Their military operations and political line were based on the Leninist principle of "concrete analysis of concrete situations." While not necessarily homogenous and united on every major issue regarding the anti-dictatorial struggle, the Feda'ian strongly adhered to certain fundamental principles, such as an uncompromising fight against the Shah's regime, the importance of the working-class movement for radical social transformation, and identifying the political bloc that could help lead the Iranian revolution to victory.

The Feda'i Guerrillas gave importance to raising the awareness of their supporters and the masses in general. Their military operations mainly targeted the symbols and instruments of repression. The operations were followed by the distribution of detailed leaflets, pamphlets, and at times booklets, exposing the repressive nature of the target under attack, and explaining the logic and reasoning behind each particular armed action. The Feda'i Guerrillas also produced seven issues of a well-known journal, *Nabard-e Khalq* (People's Struggle), as well as various translations of works published by other national liberation movements, progressive organizations, and Marxist thinkers, and also multiple domestic studies, ranging from the agrarian question in Iran to the particularities of dependent capitalist development.

In the sixth issue of *Nabard-e Khalq* (May 1975), the People's Feda'i Guerrillas added the word "Organization" to the beginning of their name. By the time the seventh and last issue was published, the word "Iran" had also been added, making it the Organization of Iranian People's Feda'i Guerrillas (OIPFG). The changes in the name highlighted the transformation of the Feda'ian from a small, autonomous group of revolutionaries into a centralized, nationwide organization.

THE REVOLUTION AND OIPFG

It became imperative for the SAVAK secret police to crush the ever-growing OIPFG. In July 1976, the security forces finally succeeded in tracking down and killing Hamid Ashraf, the charismatic overall leader of the time, after a shootout in the South Mehrabad area of Tehran, where he and a dozen other senior members of the group were holding a meeting. Together with the execution of the group's main ideological mentor, Bijan Jazani, in a staged execution on the hills outside Evin prison the previous year, the death of Ashraf could have led to the extinction of the organization. However, the survivors of the various Feda'i cells reorganized under a collective three-person leadership and spent the next two years ensuring the organization's survival. They occasionally printed communiqués and carried out demonstrative armed actions against regime targets. The rise to power of Jimmy Carter in 1977 and his "human rights" discourse induced the Shah to release some veteran members of the initial groups at the end of their decade-long sentences. On their release they joined the OIPFG and progressively helped to restore links between the underground organization and its broader public support base, particularly among the liberal professions and on university campuses.

In 1978, facing a rampant economic crisis and foreign pressure to reduce human rights abuses, Iran witnessed a resurgence of social protests. The urban poor, intellectuals, students, youth and later the Bazaar merchants, clergy, teachers, and white- and blue-collar workers took to the streets in mass rallies, demonstrations and strikes, crying "Death to the Shah" and "Free all political prisoners" as their main rallying slogans. The release of many political prisoners and the relative opening up of the political atmosphere were concessions made by the Shah to an ever-growing mass movement. This helped the OIPFG to reconstruct and revive itself, facilitating intervention in the political process and enabling it to play a noticeable role in the struggle to overthrow the Shah's regime. The OIPFG was initially wary about the likelihood of a drift towards restrictions on social and political freedoms under Ayatollah Khomeini and aired its concerns in an open letter which was published in the weeks prior to Ayatollah Khomeini's return to Iran on February 1, 1979.

The Provisional Revolutionary Government and its Prime Minister Mr. Mehdi Bazargan, who was appointed by Ayatollah Khomeini, had to reckon with the OIPFG as a major political force leading hundreds of thousands of supporters all over the country, as well as proposing a new political agenda, taking positions on national issues and offering solutions in the new dynamics of Iranian politics. It was at this historical juncture that the OIPFG transformed itself from an underground revolutionary guerrilla organization into an overt political force, actively involved in the day-to-day politics of Iranian society.

However, the leadership of OIPFG was not able to unite on a clear and concrete political platform. Different factions swiftly formed within the OIPFG. The first faction that eventually broke away was led by Ashraf Dehghani and Mohammad Hormatipour, who had spent most of the 1970s as key members in the OIPFG's overseas branch. They deeply distrusted the existing leadership, opposing its viewpoints and alarmed by its political tendency to compromise with the "advocates of Imam Khomeini's line" (*Khat-e Imam*). Dehghani and her comrades, who were steadfast believers in the theses of Masoud Ahmadzadeh, took issue with the loose recruitment policies that opened the door to those who rejected armed struggle and the revolutionary traditions of the organization. They adopted a radical position against the IRI, which they considered to be all but a puppet of "imperialism," and while they did not openly advocate armed struggle at the start, they refused to lay down their arms and become involved in solely political activities. Dehghani "first decided to stay in the organization as a regular member and start an ideological struggle with the new leadership. Later... she, along with other comrades, severed ties with this organization" in April 1979, forming an offshoot which is still known as the People's Feda'i Guerrillas.[2]

The second and largest split was between Aksariyat (Majority, اکثریت) and Aqaliyat (Minority, اقلیت). These terms derive from factions that formed within the Central Committee following the OIPFG's first plenum in September–October 1979. Events such as the central government's armed suppression of the Kurdistan uprising in the summer of 1979, divergence over the occupation of the US embassy in Tehran, and differing appraisals of the nature of the emerging Islamic state, resulted in a deep rift in the organization. Most of the leadership of the Majority characterized the new regime as progressive, "anti-imperialist," pro-poor and the disinherited. The Minority on the other hand believed the IRI to be anti-democratic and reactionary, representing the traditional clergy and merchant bourgeoisie in a tactical alliance with the liberal bourgeoisie. The OIPFG-Minority called for the overthrow of the IRI through the struggle of the working people, ethnic groups, youth, and students under the leadership of the "conscious proletariat." The split formally came about in June 1980, after a dispute over the layout and content of a special supplement of the OIPFG's official organ, *Kar* (labor), led to both factions publishing their own editions of *Kar*, effectively implementing the split.

A third split, this time within the OIPFG-Majority, took place in September 1980 in the wake of the Iraq–Iran war, resulting in the emergence of the OIPFG-Left Wing (سازمان چریک‌های فدایی خلق ایران «اکثریت» جناح چپ).

This group was comprised of a member of the Aksariyat (Majority) leadership, Mostafa Madani, as well as cadres such as Vida Hadjebi Tabrizi and many members and sympathizers who had sided with revolutionary and progressive movements, believing Ayatollah Khomeini to be backward-looking and reactionary. Quite distinct from the Majority and Minority, they characterized the new government as neither a popular progressive government, nor (like the Minority) a clerical-bourgeoisie government. Rather, they viewed the IRI as the agent of the pre-modern classes and strata led by the traditional petit bourgeoisie and their historical allies and representatives, the Shi'ite clergy.

---

2 "A Brief Biography of Comrade Ashraf Dehghani," www.ashrafdehgani.com/biography, accessed October 21, 2019.

While the Left Wing had major ideological and political differences with the Minority, it still allied with them in the face of the Majority, led by Farrokh Negahdar, Jamshid Taheripour, Mehdi Fatapour, and Ali Keshtgar. Through its publications, the Left Wing expressed its strong viewpoint about a "crisis of identity" that existed within the landscape of the Iranian left, openly taking positions against Stalinism, Soviet revisionism, and Maoism. While the Majority believed that the Islamic Republic symbolized the struggle of the oppressed against imperialism and was on the path of "non-capitalist development," the Left Wing argued that the struggle against imperialism in our era cannot be detached from the struggle for the democratization of society, which it considered to consist of freedom of thought, press, and assembly, women's equal rights with men, workers councils, autonomy for various Iranian nationalities, and the realization of social justice, as preconditions for a truly democratic evolution of Iranian society. The Left Wing assessed the very existence of the IRI to be a defeat of the ideals of the Iranian revolution and called for the "continuation of the Bahman [February 1979] Revolution."

The Majority's leadership enthusiastically backed the IRI's repression of the opposition forces following the dismissal of Abolhassan Banisadr from the presidency. In a communiqué released after the 7 Tir [June 28, 1981] bombing that resulted in the assassination of some seventy members of the Islamic Republic Party (IRP), the Majority leadership called upon its members and sympathizers to report all members of the radical left groups who called for resistance first to the IRP and only subsequently to the Majority organization itself. This initiative caused disquiet and dissent, and was partly the cause for another split, led by Manouchehr Halilroudi and Ali Keshtgar, which took place within the Majority on 16 Azar 1360 (December 6, 1981). The new group, called the adherents of the 16 Azar Manifesto, conditionally supported the IRI, encouraging its "anti-imperialist" policies and criticizing the anti-democratic course of actions against pro-democracy forces. The main cause of their split was, however, the publicly announced intention of the Majority leadership to merge with the pro-Soviet Tudeh Party.

After the events of spring and summer 1981, the ensuing all-out repression, the eradication of the remnants of democratic freedom, and the suppression of all pro-democracy groups and activists, the radical offshoots of the initial OIPFG were attacked one by one by the repressive forces of the IRI. In less than a year, even conformist factions came under attack from the regime and faced torture, imprisonment, and exile. The Majority was the last part of the Feda'i family to suspend its overt political activities. Its leadership, by and large, fled Iran in the wake of the suppression of the Tudeh Party in the spring of 1983. But the vast majority of the imprisoned members of the Majority, like the jailed members of the Tudeh Party, were executed in the Great Massacre of 1988.

Other than the OIPFG-Left Wing and the adherents of the 16 Azar Manifesto, all the other factions have survived in exile with some regroupings and continue their struggle through publications, propaganda, and acts of political agitation.

Kumeleh

SAED WATANDOST

Kumeleh (کومه‌له or *Komala*) was originally created by a number of Kurdish nationalists and intellectuals in Mahabad, a year after the fall from power of Reza Shah. In the Kurdish language, the term "Kumeleh" is similar to *Jameh-e* in Persian, meaning either "Society" as a whole, "Organization," or "Association" (e.g. The Teacher's Association). Kumeleh's activities came to an end with the suppression of the Kurdish Republic of Mahabad in 1946.

Kurdish opposition to the Shah Mohammad Reza Pahlavi's autocracy revived in the mid-1960s. In step with their counterparts across Iran, and under the influence of local and global trends, Kurdish intellectuals prepared for armed struggle against the Shah's regime. Most of these Kurdish intellectuals had studied at universities across the country, such as Tehran, Tabriz, and Orumiyeh, and had gravitated towards Marxism–Leninism. Others considered themselves either Maoist, or "Kurdish Nationalist," uniting with like-minded young radicals across the country, jointly rejecting what they considered to be the reformist or passive attitude of the National Front and the Tudeh Party in the face of the reigning repression. Together, they engaged in debate and discussion over the best possible answer to the crucial question of the time: "What is to be done?"

After a period of intense debate and discussion, a group of Kurdish intellectuals with close knowledge of Kurdish issues agreed on the creation of a circle that could provide a response to the pressing political, militant, historical, and class issues of Kurdistan. Its communiqués, such as the one produced for the celebrations of the 2,500th anniversary of the Persian Empire in 1971 and distributed in the Kurdish major city of Sanandaj, were signed with generic names such as *tashkilat* (organization), or *rowshan-fekran* (intellectuals), in order to evade the scrutiny of the SAVAK. The founders of this radical circle included Fuad Mostafa Soltani, Mohammad Hossein Karimi, and Abdollah Mohtadi, all of whom were university students, and

Yadollah Biglari, Fateh Sheykholeslami and Saed Watandost, who had already completed their studies.

The intellectual principles of the circle were based upon Marxism–Leninism, but Mao's Thought and to some extent the model of the Chinese Revolution were also alluring. However, the core belief of the latter, i.e. "the siege of cities through the rural areas," was not accepted by many of Kumeleh's members, as the founders had aspired to eventually becoming part of a broader Iranian and global communist movement. Therefore, from this perspective, Kumeleh was not a stand-alone party, but rather a formation that sought to contribute to the creation of a nationwide Communist Party in Iran.

The research material used by Kumeleh members was mostly Marxist literature and selections from Lenin and Mao. Additionally, they made use of *Tudeh*, the theoretical organ of the Revolutionary Organization of the Tudeh Party (precursor of the Ranjbaran Party). The circle's preferred method of action was political agitation, and organizing the struggle of the "masses." Kumeleh's members aspired to live amongst urban workers, peasants, and toilers, and succeeded in forming small circles of members in the major Iranian Kurdish towns.

Between 1970 and 1979, the circle organized and participated in various initiatives, such as worker strikes at the Bukan Dam in 1974, and taking part in the peasant and workers protest in Marivan. From 1974 onwards they occasionally produced leaflets containing strongly worded attacks upon the Shah's regime. Like all opposition groups active inside the country, the circle had to face SAVAK repression. From 1973 onwards, a considerable number of the circle's members were apprehended by the Shah's secret police, but the group managed to engage in limited activities outside jail.

During the revolutionary turmoil of 1978–79, the circle expanded its public activities and signed leaflets that started with the invocation: "For our struggling compatriots." Between November and December 1978, ten veteran members held a long congress-like meeting lasting over a month, which led to better organization and a clearer structure with respect to membership expansion and goals.

On February 15, 1979, one of the key members of the circle, Mohammad-Hossein Karimi, lost his life during an attack on the gendarmerie station in the city of Saqqez. It was at that stage that the circle decided to announce its open existence as an organization named "The Revolutionary Organization of Kurdistan Toilers—Kumeleh" (سازمان انقلابی زحمتکشان کردستان کومەلە) or

Sazeman-e Enghelabi Zahmatkeshan-e Kurdistan—Kumeleh). This day has been remembered ever since as "Kumeleh Day."

Despite its recent surfacing, Kumeleh played an integral role in efforts to defuse the increasing tensions between Kurdish organizations and the central government during the Norouz festivity of March 1979. It agreed to the creation of a City Council in Sanandaj, which came into existence through the first elections of the post-revolutionary era. Kumeleh succeeded in obtaining one of the six seats on the City Council for Youssef Ardalan, and soon engaged in the publication of a *Khabarnameh* (newsletter), and a considerable number of pamphlets regarding social and political issues concerning Iranian Kurdistan. However, the young organization was soon confronted by both the Kurdistan Democratic Party of Iran headed by Abdul Rahman Qassemlou, and the central government.

In mid-August 1979, Ayatollah Khomeini ordered the full use of force to re-establish central government control over Kurdistan after the KDPI and Kumeleh together besieged the town of Paveh between August 13 and 19. After seeking to capture the garrison of the newly-formed Islamic Revolutionary Guards Corps (IRGC) in the town of Marivan, one of Kumeleh's most charismatic leaders, Fuad Mostafa Soltani (1948–79), led a remarkable act of civil disobedience and defiance consisting of virtually the entire population of Marivan leaving the town as a protest against the presence of the IRGC and the central government's decision to resort to violence. Soltani was killed by the army on August 28. Nevertheless, Kumeleh carried on its political and military struggle. It remained steadfast in its secularism, defense of the right to national autonomy, Marxism, and the notion of opening its membership to all layers of Kurdish society, including women, for whom it sought full legal equivalence with men. Women always formed a bedrock in Kumeleh's military and political activities.

When the rising tide of repression against non-Islamist political movements reached Kurdistan in 1980, Kumeleh sought the cooperation of other political movements in order to ensure its survival. At its third congress in Spring 1982, it endorsed the platform of the Communist Party of Iran, which was formed on September 2, 1982. In 1991 in Europe, however, the Communist Party's leading cadres, including Mansoor Hekmat (1951–2002) and Kourosh Modaresi, broke away from the Party and formed the Workers' Communist Party of Iran. This led to further splits within the Kumeleh, now mainly based outside Iran.

At present, there are four different formations which claim a common heritage from the original organization of 1979: the Kurdistan Branch of the Communist Party of Iran (Kumeleh); The Revolutionary Organization of the Toilers of Kurdistan (also known as the Kumeleh Party); The Organization of Kurdistan Workers Kumeleh; and The Kumeleh Socialist Process.

TRANSLATED BY SIAVUSH RANDJBAR-DAEMI

Mojahedin

SHAHRAM AGHAMIR

The origins of the People's Mojahedin Organization of Iran (سازمان مجاهدین خلق ایران or *Sazeman-e Mojahedin-e Khalq-e Iran*, PMOI) lie in the 1961 formation of the Liberation Movement of Iran (*Nehzat-e Azadi-ye Iran*), a nationalistic liberal and lay-religious organization formed by a group of supporters of former Prime Minister Mohammad Mossaddeq.

The suppression of anti-government protests by the Shah's regime on June 5, 1963, ushered in a split in the Liberation Movement over how to fight the regime. Consequently, three young members of the organization, Mohammad Hanifnezhad, Said Mohsen and Ali Asghar Badizadegan, formed a secret circle in search of ways to continue the struggle against the regime. They were the founding members of the Mojahedin. Two years later, the trio brought together some twenty trusted friends and started a study group, which concentrated on reading and discussing religious texts, modern Iranian history, revolutionary theory and literature on the Russian, Chinese, Cuban, and Algerian revolutions. September 6, 1965, the date of this group's first meeting, has been recognized as the date that the People's Mojahedin Organization of Iran was founded.

The Mojahedin's ideology was an amalgamation of Islam with Marxist thought. Their early writings form a radical interpretation of Shi'ite Islam, but the Mojahedin unequivocally denied being Marxists or even socialists. As Rouhani and Haghshenas, veteran members of the organization at the time, recounted several years later: "Our original aim was to synthesize the religious values of Islam with scientific thoughts of Marxism... for we were convinced that true Islam was compatible with the theories of social evolution, historical determinism and the class struggle."[3]

---

3 Ervand Abrahamian, *The Iranian Mojahedin* (New Haven: Yale University Press, 1989), p. 92.

For the Mojahedin the main contradiction in Iranian society was the irreconcilable contradiction between the masses on the one hand and the US-led world imperialism together with its client state, i.e. the Shah's regime, on the other. In the age of the Cuban and Algerian revolutions and the intensification of guerrilla warfare in Vietnam, Palestine, and Latin America, it was unsurprising that the Mojahedin chose urban guerrilla warfare as their paramount strategy for fighting the Shah's regime and its patron. Therefore, beginning in 1968, their members went to camps run by the Palestinian Liberation Organization (PLO) for training.

In 1971, the Mojahedin decided to launch their first military operation with the ambitious goal of inflicting a blow on the Shah's lavish celebration of twenty-five centuries of monarchy, but the regime's secret police foiled the planned operation and arrested dozens of their members. Consequently, sixty-nine men, nearly half of the Mojahedin's members, including eleven of the sixteen members of the Central Cadre, were tried in military tribunals. Those eleven men were handed death sentences, and the other fifty-eight militants were given prison sentences. Masoud Rajavi, who would become the prominent leader of the Mojahedin in the 1980s, and another member had their death sentences commuted, but the other nine members, including the three founders of the Mojahedin, were subsequently executed.

The survivors changed the structure of the organization and continued the armed struggle. They also issued a proclamation in February 1972 in which, for the first time, they unveiled the name "People's Mojahedin of Iran." Previously, the Mojahedin had been referring to themselves only as "our group" or "our organization."

The Mojahedin's arduous attempts to synthesize Islam and Marxism became more complicated in September 1975 when the organization published a manifesto declaring that it had dispensed with Islam, which was "unscientific," "idealistic," and a "petit bourgeois ideology," and had adopted Marxism–Leninism as the path to the liberation of human beings. The majority of the Mojahedin had abandoned Islam in favor of Marxism–Leninism by the spring of 1975, and the manifesto simply memorialized an earlier split in the organization. Alas, the split was not peaceful. In an armed confrontation in May 1975, a leading member of the organization who opposed this conversion was killed by the rival faction, while his right-hand man was wounded and subsequently executed when the doctor attending him turned him over to the regime. After the split, both factions continued fighting the regime in separate organizations until the 1979 revolution.

The 1978–79 revolutionary upheaval accelerated the release of political prisoners by the Shah. Since the Muslim Mojahedin had mainly survived inside prisons, Masoud Rajavi and his circle in prison formed the core of leadership of the revived PMOI once they were free.

Following the fall of the *ancien régime* on February 11, 1979, the Mojahedin pursued a strategy of non-confrontation with the two main factions of the ruling bloc. Their objective was to not alienate either the provisional government of Prime Minister Bazargan or the clerical establishment, which had created a parallel power structure through its control of Kommittehs (people's committees), Revolutionary Tribunals and Revolutionary Guards. The Mojahedin were also concerned for their radical and anti-imperialist credentials, and did not wish to be outshone by other leftist organizations.

The Mojahedin did not deviate from their non-confrontational policy and tried to be an opposition force within the framework of the Islamic Republic even when Mohammad Reza Sa'adati, a leading member of PMOI, was arrested and unscrupulously charged with spying for the Soviet Union, when their offices and their rallies were attacked, and when Rajavi was barred from running as candidate in the presidential election held in January 1980.

In their pursuit of this strategy, PMOI did not actively support women or ethnic minorities when the regime was trampling on their rights. They did not protest when Islamist thugs attacked dissenting newspapers, the offices of the opposition groups and gatherings organized by them, or when the broad-based constituent assembly promised by Khomeini during the revolutionary uprising was substituted by a 73-man Assembly of Experts, with the implication that the new constitution would be drafted by "religious experts." Mojahedin's reasoning for their silence and inaction was that the imperialists would capitalize on internal divisions if the nation did not stand beside Ayatollah Khomeini, whom they referred to as "our great father." Masoud Rajavi and the Mojahedin leadership later claimed that they had always known that Ayatollah Khomeini and the clerics supporting him were "reactionaries," but had decided to avoid an immediate showdown because of imperialist threats as well as Khomeini's popularity among the masses.

The takeover of the US embassy on November 4, 1979, provided Ayatollah Khomeini with the opportunity to use his populist rhetoric to rally the public around a nationalist and anti-imperialist flag. It allowed the clerical faction and their Islamic Republic Party (IRP) to consolidate their power within the ruling bloc by having their clerical draft Constitution ratified and by purging Bazargan's cabinet and the liberals from the power structure. PMOI initially supported the students who had seized the embassy and called for national mobilization against a possible invasion by US imperialism.

The *Majles* elections in the spring of 1980 was a turning point in the Mojahedin's attempts to operate as a loyal opposition group within the political structure of the Islamic Republic. They did not win a single seat in spite of garnering nearly twenty percent of the vote. They exposed the IRP and its thugs who had attacked their offices, election rallies, printing presses, closed down the polling stations at the last minute, and destroyed ballot boxes.

In June 1980, Khomeini avoided using the word Mojahedin and said, "The *Monafeqin* [hypocrites] are more dangerous than the infidels." By early 1981, the clerical faction of the regime had closed down PMOI's offices, banned their newspapers and rallies, and issued arrest warrants for some of their leaders. For their part, the Mojahedin responded by denouncing the regime for rigging elections, attacking rallies and meetings, outlawing newspapers, trampling on the rights of ethnic minorities, imprisoning and torturing activists, closing down the universities for a "Cultural Revolution," monopolizing power, and hijacking the revolution. At the same time, Mojahedin moved closer to President Abolhassan Banisadr and formed an alliance with him. Banisadr, the first president in post-revolutionary Iran, was entangled in a power struggle with the IRP over a range of political and economic issues. Once the Iraqi military invaded Iran in September 1980, the issue of the role of the regular army and how to conduct the war became additional bones of contention between Banisadr and the IRP.

By early 1981, the question of democracy and political freedoms had found an eminent place in PMOI's public discourse. In what can be characterized as a political U-turn, Masoud Rajavi argued that only democracy could protect the country against US imperialism.

On June 12, 1981, Banisadr went into hiding with the PMOI leadership. On June 18, Khomeini reiterated the ban on public demonstrations and warned that defying the ban would be construed as acts against God. On June 19, PMOI and Banisadr defied the ban on public demonstrations and called on the public to pour into the streets the next day to protest against the IRP "monopolists" and their "coup" against President Banisadr.

On June 20, mass demonstrations were held in Tehran and many provincial cities. In Tehran the crowd was estimated to be over half a million (PMOI's estimate is over a million.) The regime deployed the Islamist Hezbollahi thugs as well the Revolutionary Guards in the streets and responded with brute force, using live ammunition. They killed more than fifty protestors and injured and arrested hundreds, including teenagers.

In the wake of the June 20 demonstrations, the state unleashed a wave of terror against the PMOI and also the radical opposition. The PMOI responded with a campaign of assassinations and attacks that targeted the regime's officials, prominent clerics, the Revolutionary Guards, and the Kommittehs. Earlier, in its May 7 open letter to Ayatollah Khomeini, the PMOI had warned that it would resort to armed struggle if all peaceful avenues were closed off.

On July 29, Rajavi and Banisadr landed in Paris, announced the formation of a National Council of Resistance of Iran (NCRI) and invited all "democratic" Iranians to join it. The NCRI also strove for international recognition, particularly in Europe and North America. Some secular and leftist groups as well as prominent figures heeded the call and joined the NCRI, but the coalition was short-lived. Beginning in 1984, Banisadr, the Kurdish Democratic Party, nearly all the left-wing groups of the coalition, and most of the renowned intellectuals of Iran announced their resignation. By mid-1985, the NCRI was no longer a broad coalition.

Once it became clear that PMOI's insurrectionary tactics of June 1981 and its ensuing urban guerrilla warfare were not going to bring about the downfall of the regime, the Mojahedin leadership changed its strategy and restructured the organization to be inward-looking. In January 1985, Rajavi announced an "ideological revolution," which resulted in the restructuring of the organization to be even more leader-oriented. The new structure designated Rajavi's new wife Maryam Azodanlu as his co-equal leader. The PMOI's new slogan "Iran is Rajavi, Rajavi is Iran" epitomized a new notion of leadership and the formation of a cult of personality in PMOI. As a result of the "ideological revolution," a number of the members left the PMOI.

In 1986, after the French government made a deal with Tehran for the release of French hostages held by the Hezbollah in Lebanon, the PMOI moved its headquarters to Iraq and established the National Liberation Army of Iran (NLA) to fight the IRI. In 1988, the NLA, which was armed and equipped by the Iraqi regime, had up to seven thousand fighters in its ranks, most of whom were PMOI members.

On July 20, 1988, the IRI announced its acceptance of the UN-brokered ceasefire resolution. Six days later, the NLA launched an ambitious military operation with the support of the Iraqi Air Force. The NLA forces crossed the Iran–Iraq border and had some initial success inside Iran, but as its fighters advanced further, it suffered heavy casualties and its fighters had to retreat to their base in Iraq.

The PMOI's failure in its grandiose endeavor in July 1988, coupled with the weakening of the Iraqi regime as a result of the military attacks and the United Nations Security Council sanctions on the country in the aftermath of Saddam Hossein's military occupation of Kuwait, appears to have convinced the Rajavis that the only way that the PMOI could replace the Iranian regime would be by winning the support of outside powers. Hence the PMOI intensified its efforts to woo the politicians in Europe and North America and moved increasingly to the right. Whereas in the early 1980s the PMOI had garnered the support of a large number of socialist and communist parties in Europe, starting in the 1990s it courted some notorious right-wing elements within the political establishment in the States. After the 2003 occupation of Iraq, the PMOI found new allies in the Bush administration among the neoconservatives behind the invasion and occupation of Iraq. This alliance with right-wing politicians, media, and institutions still continues, with Mojahedin cherishing a good rapport with some key figures in the Trump administration as well as with the Republican Party in the US. The PMOI appears to have found new allies among some regional powers as well. A gathering of the PMOI in July 2016 had as one of the speakers a member of the Saudi royal family and the former head of Saudi Arabia's intelligence agency.

After the new Iraqi government with close ties to the IRI announced that PMOI was not welcome in the country and violently attacked its members, the Mojahedin militia had to leave their bases in Iraq and relocate to Albania in a process that began in 2012 and ended in 2016.

Peykar

MOHAMMAD MOBARAKEH

The historical roots of the Peykar Organization for the Emancipation of the Working Class (سازمان پیکار در راه آزادی طبقه کارگر) or *Sazeman-e Peykar dar rah-e Azadi Tabaqeh Kargar*, or simply Peykar) reach back to the People's Mojahedin Organization of Iran (PMOI), which was created by some leading members of the Islamic Students Association, who were aspiring to modernize Islamic thought, culture, politics and society. They became an attractive movement on university campuses in the second half of the 1960s. One of the characteristics of this movement was their attempt to re-interpret the Quran, Shi'ite epistemology and mythology, based on historical materialism and Marxist thought.

The imprisonment and execution of many first-generation Mojahedin by the SAVAK in 1971 produced a situation conducive to some of the remaining leaders of the group radically shifting towards Marxism–Leninism. This was followed by the publication of the *Manifesto of the Ideological Positions of the People's Mojahedin* (November 1976), which was authored by the mentor figure of Peykar and a leading member of the central nucleus of the PMOI leadership, Mohammad Taqi Shahram. The subsequent purge of the Muslim members of the organization was an act condemned by a handful of veteran Iranian Marxists of the time and the OIPFG. The next step taken by the Marxist Mojahedin was to renounce urban guerrilla warfare, attack the Tudeh Party as a stooge of the "social-imperialist" Soviet Union, distance themselves from the OIPFG, and declare war against the "traditional" forces of the society, whom they deemed the bedrock of Islamist ideologies. Most notable was their emphasis on organizing the day-to-day struggle of the workers and toilers against the Shah's regime and its main supporters, "US Imperialists." Unlike the Muslim wing of the PMOI, which was virtually bereft of any meaningful activity outside the Shah's prisons, the Marxist wing succeeded in maintaining a minimal form of activism inside the country and established ties with regional radical groups, particularly the Popular Front for the Liberation of Oman and the Arabian Gulf (PFLOAG). Members of the Marxist wing traveled to Oman to fight on the side of PFLOAG.

In the summer of 1978 another important shift occurred within the Marxist Mojahedin. Some leaders, many cadres, and a few members convened an assembly in Paris to assess their recent record. Their critical self-evaluation led them to denounce the way in which they had undertaken their previous ideological transformation following the misappropriation of an originally Muslim organization through a bloody purge. The assembly also restored the honor of purged Mojahedin members such as Majid Sharif-Vaqefi, who had been falsely accused of collaborating with the SAVAK. This same assembly resulted in the deposition of Taqi Shahram, and the abandonment of the "Mojahedin" label in favor of a new name for the organization. Ultimately, the remaining members of the Marxist wing split into three factions, most notably the Peykar Organization for the Emancipation of the Working Class, as well as the Unity for the Ideal of the Working Class, and the Struggle for the Emancipation of the Working Class.

In the months leading up to the 1979 February revolution, Peykar was a significant leftist player in the struggle to topple the Shah, raising the demands of the working class and advocating for their acceptance. Emphasizing the unity of all Marxist–Leninist currents against "American imperialism" and "Soviet Social-Imperialism," refuting urban guerrilla warfare as a deviation and distraction from organizing the working class, defending the right of self-determination for "ethnic minorities," and perceiving the working class as the heart of struggle against the newly established theocracy and the existing ruling bloc, made Peykar a popular and significant force within the emerging Third Tendency (*Khat-e 3*). While Peykar boycotted the referendum held to institute the Islamic Republic of Iran in April 1979, the group participated in the election of the Assembly of Experts, a replacement for the Constitutional Assembly, and also took part in the election of the Islamic Parliament (*Majles-e Eslami*). Peykar also actively opposed the Iran–Iraq war, citing its detrimental effects on society and working people, and claiming that both belligerent states were reactionary and self-serving. Peykar went so far as to call for the transformation of the external war with Iraq into an internal war against the IRI. This organization was also one of the pillars of resistance against the closing of universities during the so-called "Cultural Revolution" (June 1980). It denounced the crackdown on the free press, and participated in demonstrations against the closing down of the *Ayandegan* newspaper.

The Peykar Organization published a weekly political journal, *Peykar*, totaling 127 issues, the first of which appeared in May 1979. The group also produced pamphlets and periodicals, targeting local and ethnic populations, workers, and college and high school students. Two leading members, Torab Haghshenas and Hossein Rouhani, became the first members of the emerging leftist opposition to challenge Ayatollah Khomeini's theory and praxis of governance and his lack of support for revolutionary struggle against the Shah's regime by publishing a long interview in several issues of *Peykar*. In it they recalled their encounter with Khomeini in Najaf in February 1972, when they had traveled there on behalf of the PMOI to enlist the Ayatollah's support for armed struggle against the Shah's regime.

Peykar ended publication in December 1981, after resistance to the outright repression that had started in June 1981 became impossible. This eventually led to the disintegration of the organization, which divided into factions and had to grapple with a severe internal crisis. In a short span of time many of its leaders and some 450 of its cadres, members, and sympathizers, 30 percent of whom were women, were executed. Hundreds more were either imprisoned or forced into exile. A few remnants of Peykar founded *Andeesheh va Peykar* in Europe. The group made available a vast archive of its publications, and has actively produced new material in recent decades and published it on the www.peykarandeesh.org website.

TRANSLATED INTO ENGLISH BY PARI FARROKH

Rah-e Kargar

SIAVUSH RANDJBAR-DAEMI

The Workers' Path (راه کارگر or *Rah-e Kargar*) was officially established on June 25, 1979, as a Marxist initiative primarily founded by radical former political prisoners who had repudiated the vanguards' armed struggle. During their time in the Shah's jails, they had reached the conclusion that urban guerrilla action had failed in practical terms. Many of the group's founders had previously advocated Amir Parviz Pouyan's thesis of "The Necessity of Armed Struggle and the Refutation of the Theory of Survival" or supported Masoud Ahmadzadeh's "small engine, big engine" proposition (meaning that a small guerrilla force can mobilize huge masses of people).

Prominent founding members of The Workers' Path included Mohammad Reza Shalgouni and Hedayat Soltanzadeh from the "Palestine Group," Alireza Shokoohi, Ali Mehdizadeh, and Dr. Gholam Reza Ebrahimzadeh of the Red Star Group, die-hard sympathizers of Masoud Ahmadzadeh such as Dr. Mehran Shahab-edin, Ruben Makarian, and Ali Asghar Izadi, and also former members of Mojahedin-e Khalq, such as Taqi Ruzbeh, Ebrahim Avakh, and Mehdi Khosroshahi, who were influenced in both strategy and tactic by Ahmadzadeh's principle of armed struggle. Other founders included independent Marxists such as Shahab Borhan. After being part of the Feda'i prisoner commune and retaining support for Masoud Ahmadzadeh's ideas, Izadi parted company with the Feda'ian from his prison cell in 1976.

All of the Rah-e Kargar founding figures had therefore distanced themselves from the views of groups such as the Feda'i and Mojahedin organizations, which never discarded the principle of urban guerrilla warfare until the victory of the revolution in February 1979. The Rah-e Kargar founders were to be released from the Shah's jails between December 1978 and January 1979. As the name of the group suggests, Rah-e Kargar attached great importance to developing and maintaining a constant presence within worker communities, and not with the masses at large, as other Iranian Marxist groups aspired to at the time.

Rah-e Kargar's most tangible contribution to the public scene in the first two years of its existence consisted of inquisitive and highly original articles which sought to provide a broader theoretical backdrop to its analysis of contemporary Iranian politics and society. These usually came in the form of booklets compiled from the organization's weekly organ, *Rah-e Kargar*, the first issue of which was published on November 29, 1979. The religious background of some of its founders enabled Rah-e Kargar to produce an in-depth analysis of Ayatollah Khomeini's *Velayat-e Faqih*, which bore the same name. The *Rah-e Kargar* periodical furthermore introduced Iranian readers to prominent Marxist intellectuals such as Nicos Poulantzas, and adopted a position on the major issues of the international communist movement of the time that was outside the bloc and not doctrinaire. It was neither pro-Soviet nor pro-Chinese; instead it was inspired by localized socialist experiences such as Angola or Vietnam. This was conducive to Rah-e Kargar assuming a position which, according to the aforementioned categorization of the Iranian Left of the time, made it a member of the *Khat-e 4* ("Fourth Tendency"), separate from the First (Tudeh Party), Second (Feda'i Movement and its splinters), or Third (Maoist formations).

Rah-e Kargar was the first movement within the Iranian Marxist Left to announce that the ideals which had brought about the revolution of 1979 had become a spent force, even before the removal from power of President Banisadr in June 1981, which marked the end of pluralism. This view was reflected in the most famous series published by Rah-e Kargar in its early stages, *Fascism, Kabus ya Vaqeiyat?* (Fascism: Nightmare or Reality?) which warned, as early as the winter of 1979, of the impending authoritarian turn of the nascent Islamic Republic following the downfall of the Provisional Revolutionary Government of Mehdi Bazargan. Rah-e Kargar's attitude towards the short-lived presidential administration of Abolhassan Banisadr was based on the premise that both main factions (the "liberal" one led by Banisadr and the "fictitious radicals" composed of the Islamic Republic Party) were to be opposed, and the Iranian Left should not approve of any of them and should instead periodically attack both. In another famous booklet it defined the emerging ruling establishment as a "Governmental Caste" and warned about the emergence of Bonapartist rule in Iran. In this regard, Rah-e Kargar differed from other organizations such as the Ranjbaran Party, the Tudeh and the Feda'ian Majority, which eventually sided with one of these governmental factions. Rah-e Kargar also broke with these and other organizations in not siding with any of the main trends in international communism.

As with the rest of the Iranian Marxist groups of the early 1980s, few reliable statistics exist on the extent of Rah-e Kargar's membership and popularity. Izadi ran for office during the first parliamentary elections of Spring 1980, and obtained around fifty thousand votes in the Tehran constituency, a figure comparable or higher than most of the Tudeh leadership, including the first secretary Noureddin Kianouri.

As with many other smaller leftist groupings, Rah-e Kargar's destiny was ultimately intertwined with broader political developments. Despite not adopting urban armed struggle against the Islamic Republic following Abolhassan Banisadr's dismissal from office in June 1981, Rah-e Kargar was soon forced to suspend overt political activities, and did so openly in the last issue of its organ, in order to prevent further repression against its followers after the arrest of many prominent members, including Shokoohi and Khosroshahi. Nevertheless, its leadership was forced to transfer to Kurdistan, where it ran a radio station named Seda-ye Kargar (The Voice of the Worker) which operated until 2001 and subsequently relocated to Europe.

Once in exile, Rah-e Kargar went through a name change and adopted the name *Sazeman-e Kargaran-e Enqelabi-ye Iran (Rah-e Kargar)* (the Organization of Revolutionary Workers of Iran—Rah-e Kargar) in August 1983, once the new series of the organ started publication. It has maintained the ethos of its previous phase by continuing to publish theoretical and current journals throughout the past three decades. In between various congresses, Rah-e Kargar joined forces in 1984 with members of another seminal group dedicated to theoretical and analytical output, Rah-e Feda'i, but parted ways with them later. At various points during the 1980s members of other prominent groups, such as the Tudeh Party and the Feda'ian Majority, joined Rah-e Kargar.

Rah-e Kargar's first congress took place in the summer of 1991 in Europe and was mostly dedicated to procedural issues deriving from internal differences during the late 1980s and to an analysis of the reasons behind the collapse of the Soviet bloc. It reaffirmed the organization's socialist slant, whilst retaining the belief that Soviet-style bureaucratic socialism was not the right pathway towards the fulfilment of its aspirations. As with previous stances, Rah-e Kargar confirmed its opposition to urban guerrilla warfare even in exile, and sought instead to retain contact with working-class sympathisers and lower-level members in Iran and abroad through regular publications and bulletins addressed to them. To this day it retains its initial view that Marxism in Iran will prevail once it is able to achieve hegemony within the working class.

In 1994 Rah-e Kargar sought to join forces primarily with an array of communist political groups, from ex-Majority Feda'i, Minority and Ettehad-e Feda'ian groups of the Feda'i movement, to Marxist–Leninist–Maoists, Trotskyites and the Communist Party of Iran, and to form the Ettehad-e Chap-e Kargari, or "Worker Left Union." In later years, as that coalition of twenty-four groupings faded away and ceased operation, it resumed its autonomous operation.

Today, Rah-e Kargar operates independently, with its key members spread across two factions due to a split in the summer of 2009 in the wake of its 14th congress and the 30th anniversary of its foundation. For a few years one faction, formed by, amongst others, Mohammad Reza Shalgouni and Ruben Makarian, operated under the name of Political Bureau, while the other, whose prominent members were Hassan Hessam and Ebrahim Avakh, chose the Executive Committee name. Some of the older cadres, such as Asghar Izadi and Ardeshir Mehrdad, have taken up a position which is independent of these two factions. To avoid confusion, Hessam and his comrades switched back to the original Rah-e Kargar name at their 16th congress in 2011.

Ranjbaran

ALI HOJAT

The Toilers' Party of Iran (حزب رنجبران ایران or *Ḥezb-e Ranjbarān-e Īrān*, or simply *Ranjbaran*) is a Marxist–Leninist party in exile and one of the main proponents of Maoism in Iran.

It was established in December 1979 through a founding congress featuring nine groups and organizations of similar persuasion. The most prominent of these was the *Sazemān-e Enqelābi-ye Ḥezb-e Tudeh-e Iran*, or Revolutionary Organization of the Tudeh Party, which was formed in the mid-1960s as a consequence of the emergence of a strong Maoist tendency within the Tudeh Party in exile, as well as the departure of up to ninety percent of Tudeh Party cadres and sympathizers, who were then active mainly in Western Europe.

All of the founding groups of the Ranjbaran Party supported the revolution of February 1979, and most of them adopted a pro-Khomeini stance in the months following the demise of the Shah's regime until the December 1979 congress.

The Ranjbaran Party, advocating anti-imperialism (USA and its European partners) and anti-social imperialism (ex USSR, and other Eastern European countries), became the key element of the "Third Tendency," or "*Khat-e 3*," within the Iranian post-revolutionary left, which consisted of political organizations who considered themselves distinct from the historic Tudeh Party ("First Tendency"), as well as various components of the Feda'i movement ("Second Tendency").

Before and after the December congress, Ranjbaran aligned itself with Abolhassan Banisadr, the first President of the Islamic Republic, and maintained a presence within his office. It also began to indirectly assume positions against Ayatollah Khomeini and his most ardent supporters when tensions began to rise between them and Banisadr. The Ranjbaran Party's overt activities were stifled from the summer of 1980 onwards. Its members and sympathizers were arrested by the Revolutionary Guards and the security forces of the state. By the end of 1980, the Ranjbaran leadership and main cadres were forced underground, and resumed political activity covertly.

After the all-out repression imposed in the immediate aftermath of Banisadr's impeachment and removal from office on June 20, 1981, a score of Ranjbaran members were arrested and summarily executed. The party then adopted the line of seeking to overthrow the IRI and strategically participated in regional armed struggle against the regime, notably in Mazandaran, Fars, and later in Iranian Kurdistan.

While almost all its leading members were arrested or forced into exile, a small group of committed activists continued operating for several years in Kurdistan (mostly Iraqi Kurdistan). Yet by the end of the 1980s all surviving members had taken refuge in Europe or North America.

The Ranjbaran's main press organ from 1979 to 1982 was the weekly *Ranjbar* (Toiler), which was published in broadsheet format and carried frequent analyses and commentaries on the major political developments of the time. To this day it maintains a presence in the Iranian left's exiled communities and maintains an active official website, http://www.ranjbaran.org.

Razmandegan

SIAVUSH RANDJBAR-DAEMI

The Organization of Militants for the Freedom of the Working Class (سازمان رزمندگان آزادی طبقه‌ی کارگر) or *Sazeman Razmandegan Baraye Azadi Tabaqeh Kargar*) was a Marxist–Leninist group formed in late 1978. It was active until the summer of 1981. The first nucleus of Razmandegan was formed inside the Shah's jails by the political prisoners who were not adherents of guerrilla movements and adamant in their opposition to the Tudeh Party. Jamshid Nushzad, who had been released from jail in 1974, established contact with worker and intellectual cells in some factories in Tehran, Karaj, and Khuzestan and also sought to create such cells elsewhere. Another prominent member was Reza Ghorashi, who encountered other members of the group in jail after being imprisoned in 1973 following several acts of civil disobedience against the regime in the late 1960s and early 1970s. Together with other imprisoned leftists of the same persuasion, he became a prominent member of the "Political Labour" circle which settled on a position which was distinct and contrary to both the Tudeh Party and the guerrilla organizations. Ghorashi and others were gradually released from detention from 1977, when international pressures on the Shah's regime brought about a loosening of political repression throughout the country.

The activities of the initial nucleus were severely affected by the arrest or death of its members, particularly Nushzad, who died accidentally whilst cleaning his personal firearm. However, the popular revolt of 1978–79 against the Shah's dictatorship allowed remaining cadres to regroup and expand, and to form the "Razmandegan Organization for the Freedom of the Working Class" in late 1978. Razmandegan succeeded in joining forces with "struggle in the path of the ideals of the working class," one of the off-shoots of the Marxist Mojahedin, and other groups such as the Daneshjuyan-e Mobarez, or Militant University Students, in cities such as Isfahan, Rasht, and provinces like Mazandaran and Fars. It was in this period that the group published the

Razmandegan periodical, the first issue of which came out on February 20, 1980. Publication would carry on until the winter of 1980.

The occupation of the US embassy by the "Students Following the Line of the Imam" marked the first instance of theoretical discord between the Razmandegan leadership and its rank and file. It revolved around the extent to which the newly formed Islamic Republic regime was considered to be anti-imperialist and how to confront it. The Iran–Iraq war expanded differences within the organization. Some in the organization were of the view that the nature of the conflict between the two belligerent governments was neither revolutionary nor anti-revolutionary. They argued that the two governments were simultaneously anti-imperialist and anti-revolutionary. The same view was held concerning the nature of the IRI. Razmandegan's leaders also maintained a diversity of views about the Soviet Union. On the one hand, they held a firm view on the Soviet Union's policies vis-à-vis countries such as Poland and Afghanistan, and considered it to be usurping and "anti-proletarian" in nature. Whilst believing that the Soviet Union's leadership pursued an imperialist foreign policy, a majority of the Razmandegan leadership was of the view that the Soviet Union needed to be studied better and refrained from employing the derogatory "social-imperialist" term widely used by many Maoist groups at the time. Razmandegan was a key participant in the "Unity Conference" which was held in the latter half of 1979 with the aim of bringing about the fusion of twelve different groups, circles and organizations into a single movement which would become the flagbearer of the *Khat-e 3*, or "Third Tendency." Such efforts were not successful.

The lack of a common, single viewpoint on many theoretical and political issues, including the class nature of the IRI, however, led the Razmandegan Organization to the precipice of splits, which occurred in March 1981. Part of the leadership went on to join the OIPF (Majority), while another group joined some *Khat-e 3* formations by the autumn of that year. Lastly, a third faction became part of the Communist Party of Iran, which was formed by the Sahand Group and the Kumeleh Organization. By the end of 1981, Razmandegan had ceased significant political activity, as many of its members were imprisoned, executed or had to escape Iran.

Sahand and the Union of Communist Militants (UCM)

MOHAMMAD MOBARAKEII

The formation of the Sahand Cell (هسته سهند or *Hasteh Sahand*) was announced in late 1978 as a support group of the Union to Struggle for the Cause of the Working Class, briefly called the Union.

Mansour Hekmat, Hamid Taghvaie, and Iraj Azarin were the principal founding members of Hasteh Sahand, while they lived and studied in England during the years leading up to the Iranian Revolution. They heeded the call of Taqi Shahram, the then leader of Marxist Mojahedin, who had come to reject urban guerrilla warfare, portrayed the Iranian national bourgeoisie as a comprador bourgeoisie, and deemed the contradiction between wage laborers and capital as the principal contradiction of Iran as a capitalist society.

At the brink of the Iranian Revolution of 1979, the Sahand Cell and all its sympathizers moved to Iran and took part in the struggle against the dictatorial regime of the Shah. Even though the focal point of their work was theoretical, their few members also took part in the debates between university professors and student activists fighting for the democratization of academia. They also stayed in close contact with the Union to Struggle for the Cause of the Working Class, a splinter group of Marxist Mojahedin. However, following a split in the Union, Hasteh Sahand withdrew support for the political grouping in December 1980. Hasteh Sahand then formed the Union of Communist Militants, or UCM, based on the views expressed in two of their pamphlets: "The Iranian Revolution and the Role of the Proletariat: Main Views," and "The Myth of the National and Progressive Bourgeoisie." Both pamphlets unequivocally proclaimed that the main goal of the UCM was to create a new Iranian Communist Party based on revolutionary Marxism, by building an organic relationship with the Iranian proletariat and uniting other revolutionary leftists.

To promote exchange of thought and theoretical cooperation, in the early fall of 1982 Kumeleh invited the UCM to hold its first congress in one of the Kumeleh-controlled regions of Kurdistan. Accepting this invitation, the UCM decided to engage in practical attempts to form a new Communist Party by joining forces with Kumeleh, a few leftist cells, and some Marxist individuals.

On September 2, 1983, these efforts culminated in the conception of the Communist Party of Iran through the merger of the UCM, Kumeleh, and a few ex-members of the Peykar and the original Feda'ian. The UCM itself formally dissolved after this merger. In 1991 the Communist Party of Iran changed its name to the Workers' Communist Party of Iran, at the cost of Kumeleh breaking ranks with the rest of the party. Finally, with the death of Mansour Hekmat on July 4, 2002, the Workers' Communist Party of Iran split into many small groups scattered throughout Europe and the USA. In the diaspora, they are still engaged in political propaganda against the Islamic Republic of Iran.

Tudeh Party

CYRUS BAHRAMIAN

The Tudeh Party of Iran (حزب توده ايران or *Hezb-e Tudeh-e Iran*) literally meaning the Party of the Masses of Iran, was founded in September 1941 by a number of Marxist intellectuals from diverse political backgrounds and the shared experience of imprisonment during the reign of Reza Shah Pahlavi. Advocating a democratic and reformist platform, the Tudeh Party was openly pro-Soviet Union. Its anti-fascist, anti-colonialist, and progressive discourse attracted to its ranks not only the educated and intellectuals of Iranian society, but also the workers and laboring poor. This modern and well-organized party cultivated and constructed a vast social and political network throughout the country, encompassing women's groups, youth organizations, workers societies, and trade unions, as well as a covert military organization.

In 1944, eight party candidates, with seventy percent of votes in their constituencies, were elected to the *Majles* (Parliament), masterfully employing this arena to support the immediate demands of the working class and the oppressed. Two years later, at the peak of its power and political influence, the party claimed to have the loyalty of 300,000 workers, and by its second convention in 1948, some Marxist–Leninist principles were incorporated into the party charter.

Apprehensive about the growing influence of the party, the regime outlawed the Tudeh Party after a failed attempt to assassinate Mohammad Reza Shah Pahlavi, though the reality of this is still unknown. Consequently, the party continued its activities covertly, as well as through front organizations (*Jam'iyat-e Melli-ye Mobareze ba Estemar, Jam'iyat-e Irani-ye Havadar-e Solh*, multiple youth organizations, etc.) and an array of newspapers (*Shahbaz, Besu-ye Ayandeh, Razm*).

With the premiership of Dr. Mohammad Mossadegh (1951–53) the party resumed open political activity, fiercely criticizing the nationalist government by portraying it as pro-American. This political line radically changed after the resignation of Dr. Mossadegh in protest at the Shah's "unconstitutional and conspiratorial" maneuvers. The ensuing mass uprising of July 16, 1952, against the Shah's nominee for Prime Minister, Ahmad Qavam, strengthened this change of heart. From then on, the Tudeh Party supported Dr. Mossadegh, now re-appointed by the Shah, and tried its best to forge an alliance with his National Front. This became a pretext for the concerted effort of MI6 and the CIA to organize the August 1953 coup d'état against the government of Dr. Mossadegh, even though he considered the Tudeh Party treacherous and a lackey of the Soviet Union.

The party faced fierce suppression after the 1953 coup; its military network was crushed, a number of its leaders were executed, and thousands of its members were detained, while thousands more took refuge, mainly in Soviet bloc countries.

In the post-coup years, the party was effectively dismantled in Iran and lost its influence throughout the country. In exile, supported by the Soviet Union, the party maintained its strong organization with a number of newspapers, theoretical journals, and a radio station which broadcast news and analyses of current affairs from Sofia/Bulgaria. Its publishing house in Leipzig, Germany, produced numerous books on a variety of subjects, including the translation of Marx's *Capital* and the selected works of Lenin.

In January 1979, in the wake of the downfall of the Shah's regime, Tudeh Party leaders met in Leipzig, and Iraj Eskandari, the then general secretary of the party, who was an ardent secularist and against any kind of alliance with the Shi'ite clergy, was replaced with Noureddin Kianouri, who considered Ayatollah Khomeini an anti-imperialist and a progressive cleric. At the end of the same meeting, the party announced its full support for Ayatollah Khomeini's leadership of the "anti-dictatorial movement of the masses of the Iranian people."

With the downfall of the Shah the Tudeh Party moved back to Iran with all its apparatus, leaders, cadres, and hundreds of dedicated members. Contrary to the majority of the left-leaning groupings, it participated in the undemocratic referendum of April 1 and voted for the establishment of the Islamic Republic of Iran. Months later, the Tudeh Party voted for the Islamic constitution and newly founded institutions of a Shi'ite theocracy. The disillusionment of the modern strata of Iranian society, especially the urban middle class, with the Islamic Republic's backward, anti-democratic, and misogynic mindset and the upsurge of the anti-dictatorial movement did not have an impact on the political line of the Tudeh Party. On the contrary, on September 22, 1980, a central committee communique encouraged party members to report groups and individuals opposing the regime to the security forces and the Revolutionary Guards.

Despite all of this, the very existence of a pro-Soviet Communist Party with hundreds of seasoned cadres and sympathizers could not be tolerated by a totalitarian theocracy. In 1982 the state targeted the Tudeh Party, arresting almost all the leadership and scores of its activists throughout Iran. Many Tudeh Party activists were tortured and forced into false confessions on their activities as "spies of the Soviet Union" and "agents of the KGB." Sentenced to long years of imprisonment, many of them perished in the mass executions of 1988. A few party leaders and cadres who were abroad at the time, along with hundreds of members who managed to escape Iran and take refuge in European countries, rebuilt the party under the leadership of Ali Khavari. But the party soon underwent a profound crisis, intensified by the fall of the Soviet Union, which culminated in a split and the formation of the short-lived Democratic Party of Iranian People.

Union of Iranian Communists

NASSER MOHAJER

The Union of Iranian Communists (اتحادیه کمونیست‌های ایران or *Ettehadiyeh Communisthaye Iran*) was formed in 1977 through the integration of the Organization of Revolutionary Communists (ORC) and some remnants of what was known as the Palestine Group, the name given to a number of Iranian university students who had attempted to leave for Palestine in order to receive military training.

The ORC was formed in 1970. Its known founders, Siamak Za'im, Hamid Kossari, and Parviz Shokat, were students, political activists, and members of the Berkeley (Northern California) branch of the Iranian Students Association, which was itself a member of the World Confederation of Iranian Students (National Union). ORC's monthly organ was called *Communist*. The group followed "Mao Zedong Thought" and aimed to implement the Chinese model of revolution in Iran. This contributed to an initial sympathy towards "The Revolutionary Organization of the Tudeh Party" (ROTP). However, insistence on organizational independence and differences in methods of work prevented this group from joining ranks with the ROTP. Over time, the ORC increasingly distanced itself from the ROTP.

In June 1976, unity between the ORC and the *Pouya Group* (remnants of the "Palestine Group" based in Baghdad) under the leadership of Hossein Riahi and Behrouz Sotudeh was a high point for the ORC. In October 1976, after the death of Mao, who was considered by the organization as the "Teacher and Great Leader of the World Proletariat," the ORC took a critical position vis-à-vis the foreign policy of the People's Republic of China, while also exposing "Soviet Social Imperialism." It is at this time that *Haghighat* (Truth) replaced the previous monthly organ, *Communist*, and began its publication as the organ of a newly formed organization, "The Union of Iranian Communists" (UIC).

The task of *Haghighat* was to pave the road for the emergence of a "True Communist Party," aiming to:

1. "Ruthlessly expose the crimes and treasons" of the... Pahlavi Regime and "enflame the gunpowder depot of the people's wrath."
2. Bestow socialist consciousness on the working classes and raise revolutionary awareness in the masses of the people through "propaganda and agitation."
3. Conclude "the process of ideological struggle among different points of view," "seeking the theory of Iranian revolution... through various perspectives as related to the day to day struggles of the people and specific conditions of Iranian society."
4. Become "the connecting link between all Marxist–Leninist organizations, groups, cells and elements over this vast land, whose contact has become difficult due to the brutal fascism of the Pahlavi Regime." [4]

With the rise of the Iranian people's movement against the Shah's regime in 1978, the UIC lost its political cohesion. Despite an ever-growing crisis, the UIC leadership dispatched many of its cadres to Iran. Directly facing the tangible problems of society intensified the crisis within the organization. A series of articles in *Haghighat* under the heading "On the Path to Create the Party" were reflections on the crisis among the cadres and members of the UIC. Some of those who thought that the establishment of the Communist Party without any link to the working class would be impossible, split from UIC at the cusp of the 1979 revolution. They published their organ, called *Zahmat* (Toil), in June of 1979, after the publication of thirteen issues of *Haghighat* (second series). Although *Zahmat* was the organ of the "Revolutionary Unity for the Emancipation of Labor" (*Ettehad Enghelabi Baraye Rahaee Kaar*), the group itself came to be known as Zahmat. This group only attracted a few cadres and members of the UIC, and was unsuccessful in making a coalition with other revolutionary left groups. Zahmat activists also published a short-lived newspaper, *Neda-ye Azadi* (The Voice of Freedom), on May 26, 1979, which was closed by the government nearly a year later on May 12, 1980. Soon after, the life of the Zahmat group came to an end. It should be noted that the political line of Zahmat towards the Islamic Republic of Iran

---

4 *Haghighat*, The Organ of the Union of Iranian Communists, October 1976.

was more cohesive and persistent than that of the UIC, who in contrast to Zahmat supported the occupation of the US embassy in Tehran and appraised the resignation of the first Prime Minister of the IRI, Mehdi Bazargan, as a big step in "deepening the revolution."

With the escalation of tension between Ayatollah Khomeini and Abolhassan Banisadr, the first President of the Islamic Republic of Iran, the UIC pointed its arrow of attack at Khomeini and by the beginning of the total repression on June 20, 1981, had joined the movement to overthrow the IRI. After a few months of preparation in the northern jungles by the Caspian Sea, UIC armed militias, called *Sarbedaran* ("those ready to be hanged"), broke the government encirclement and entered the city of Amol in Mazandaran Province in the early hours of Monday, January 25, 1982 and took over the city.[5] This operation, undertaken in hope of sparking a chain of uprisings against the ruling theocracy in other northern cities, instead encountered the immediate dispatch of armed forces to Amol by the government and after two days of bloody clashes *Sarbedaran* had to retreat to the jungle. The government conquered the city on January 27, and executed tens of *Sarbedaran*, as well as the Amoli youth who had joined the militia after they entered the city. On the same date, Siamak Za'im and some other *Sarbedaran* were entrapped and arrested. From that day on, the government hunted down the leadership, cadres and members of the UIC and arrested many of them in the "general attack" of July 1983. Hossein Riahi and twenty-one others were all executed on January 25, 1984. Siamak Za'im, after months of brutal and constant torture in jail, was killed on January 25, 1985, exactly a year later.

Despite all these blows, the arrest of its leaders, the imprisonment of hundreds of its sympathizers, and the escape of many members and cadres and the UIC to Europe and the United States, the ORC has continued its struggle against the Islamic Republic of Iran. UIC convened its founding convention abroad in 2003, calling itself the "Communist Party of Iran (Marxist–Leninist–Maoist)" and restarted publishing *Haghighat* as its organ.

TRANSLATED FROM PERSIAN BY ALI HOJAT

---

5 *Haghighat*, March 20, 1982

Vahdat-e Komunisti

ESKANDAR SADEGHI-BOROUJERDI

The Organization of Communist Unity (سازمان وحدت کمونیستی or *Sazman-e Vahdat-e Komunisti*) was a Marxist–Leninist organization known for its advocacy of Tricontinentalism and logistical operations inside the Arab world, its sterling defense of internal party democracy, and its foresight vis-à-vis the perils of blindly embracing Ayatollah Khomeini's political leadership following the fall of the *ancien régime*.

The genealogy of the Organization of Communist Unity is multi-faceted and complex. The nucleus of the group arose out of student activist circles with one-time links to the Tudeh Youth Organization and, more importantly, the National Front of Iran (*Jebheh-ye melli-ye Iran*), who over time grew disillusioned with both of these organizations and decided to set upon a more radical path. The Tudeh Party had come to be seen as hopelessly dependent on the Soviet Union, while the Second National Front of the early 1960s came to be regarded as conservative, ineffective, and pursuing a dead-end strategy. The core militants emerged out of the student movement in Europe and the United States, and many participated in the activities and governing structures of the Confederation of Iranian Students (National Union) which became a bane of the Shah's rule throughout the 1960s and 1970s, as well as the amorphous Organizations of the National Front Abroad (*Sazman-ha-ye jebheh-ye melli kharej az keshvar*).

These radicalized activists in the Organizations of the National Front Abroad (within which there were several splits and reconciliations) had, much like their compatriots in the nascent People's Feda'i Guerrillas, given up on electoral politics and civil resistance and embraced the politics of armed struggle. The examples of Algeria, Cuba, the Palestinian Liberation Organization, and Uruguay were uppermost in their minds. In 1970, in the aftermath of several organizational permutations, a core group of militant activists decided to dispatch cadres to Beirut and Baghdad in order to receive guerrilla training. This was done under the aegis of the Organizations of the National Front Abroad, Middle East Branch, which published its own run of *Bakhtar-e emrouz* from the region, as well as an Arabic language publication entitled *Iran al-thawra* (Iran's Revolution).

These Organizations of the National Front Abroad (Middle East Branch) were the public face of another clandestine organization by the name of the Star Group (*Guruh-e setareh*), which entered into discussions with the better-known Iranian People's Feda'i Guerrillas (OIPFG) from 1973 to 1976. The aim of the discussions was to determine the conditions under which the Star Group would join and incorporate itself into the OIPFG. The importance of the Star Group for the OIPFG resided in its extensive contacts within the Middle East and its ability to facilitate the OIPFG's development of its relations with fellow militants in the region. The famous debates between representatives of the Star Group and OIPFG, often referred to as the "homogenization process" (*poroseh-ye tajanos*), ultimately reached an impasse and the anticipated incorporation of the Star Group was never realized. Following the failure of the "homogenization process," a further group called the Communist Alliance Group (*Goruh-e ettihad-e kommunisti*) was established in 1977 and found its final form in the 1979 revolution as the Organization of Communist Unity.

Both during the revolution and in subsequent years the Organization of Communist Unity would write several notable pamphlets and publish a journal, *Raha'i*, that tackled many of the leading theoretical and political questions of the day. They engaged with topics ranging from the history of Islamism in Iran, to the critique of Stalinism and the nature of socialist revolution, to the question of women's rights and the abolition of capital punishment in Iran. A number of members of the organization would later join the guerrilla movement against the Islamic Republic itself, while others slipped off the radar and entered premature political retirement, abandoning political activism altogether.

After 1982, the organization was decisively crushed because many of its members were either forced into silence, executed or driven into exile, where the last active vestiges of Communist Unity published the journal *Andisheh-ye raha'i*. Finally, after the arrest of its leadership inside Iran, the organization decided to disband itself in 1990.

Appendix C

Chronology of the Massacre

FATEMEH JOKAR

1988

Monday, July 18
- International news agencies report that Hojat al-Islam Ali Khamenei, the President of the Islamic Republic of Iran (IRI), has expressed Iran's willingness to accept UN Resolution 598. Ayatollah Khomeini's telegram to the UN secretary-general, Mr. Javier Peréz de Cuéllar, comes as a surprise to political observers as the IRI had vowed to continue the war until the overthrow of President Saddam Hossein and the establishment of an Islamic Republic in Iraq.

Wednesday, July 20
- In a message to the Iranian people, Ayatollah Khomeini states: "I have accepted UN Resolution 598... I feel terrible that I have to accept the UN Resolution while I am still alive... Making this decision was more deadly than taking poison. I submitted myself to God's will and drank this chalice of poison."

Monday, July 25
- The People's Mojahedin Organization of Iran (PMOI) dispatches their National Liberation Army to the western borders of Iran. Nearly 1,620 Mojahed are killed and tens more are taken as prisoners of war.

Tuesday, July 26
- In Gohardasht prison, visiting rights are suddenly canceled.

Wednesday, July 27
- At Evin prison, families of political prisoners are denied the right to visit their husbands, wives, sons and daughters, fathers and mothers.
- In Gohardasht prison, family visits and time off in the yard (*havakhori*) are canceled. Prison authorities take the TV sets out of prison cells and stop delivering newspapers to prisoners.

Thursday, July 28
- An undated and secret fatwa—most probably written after July 20—is issued by Ayatollah Khomeini.
- Chief Justice Mousavi Ardebili craftily asks Ayatollah Khomeini for some clarifications on his order of killing political prisoners throughout Iran. Ayatollah Khomeini's answer is: "In all cases mentioned above, if anybody, at any stage, insists on a hypocritical position, they are to be condemned to death. Liquidate the enemies of Islam rapidly. Regarding the method of reviewing the cases, whichever is faster should be considered."
- His deadly, secret fatwa is undated.
- A commission consisting of a religious judge, Hasan Ali Nayyeri; the prosecutor general of Tehran, Morteza Eshraghi; the deputy prosecutor general of Tehran, Ebrahim Raisi; the representative of the Ministry of Intelligence, Mostafa Pourmohammadi; and the head of Gohardasht prison, Mohammad Moghisseh (Nasserian) begins the inquisition of political prisoners at Evin prison.
- The prisoners call the commission the "Death Commission."
- The execution of about 200 Mojahedin political prisoners begins in Evin prison.
- According to a UN report, 50 PMOI sympathizers are executed in Mashhad.

Friday, July 29
- The execution of political prisoners at Evin prison continues.
- Separation of Mojahedin prisoners from their leftist inmates begins in Anzali prison.

Saturday, July 30
- The Death Commission moves its activities from Evin to Gohardasht prison.
- Summary executions start in Gohardasht prison.
- In Rasht prison, the executions start in the evening. They last for a week.

Sunday, July 31
- Execution of Mojahed prisoners continues.
- Ayatollah Montazeri writes his first letter to Ayatollah Khomeini stipulating that "women should be excepted from execution, especially women with children" and noting that "several thousand prisoners" have been executed "in a few days."

Monday, August 1
- The Death Commission returns from Gohardasht to Evin prison. The inquisition tribunals and issue of death sentences continue.
- Between seven and ten members of the PMOI are hanged in public in Bakhtaran.

Tuesday, August 2
- The massacre of political prisoners in Evin continues.

Wednesday, August 3
- The Death Commission returns to Gohardasht prison and begins the second wave of executions of Mojahed prisoners.
- A PMOI member is hanged in public in Ilam.

Thursday, August 4
- Ayatollah Montazeri writes his second letter to Ayatollah Khomeini.

Friday, August 5
- In a Friday prayer speech Iran's Chief Justice, Ayatollah Mousavi Ardebili, focuses on the issue of political prisoners: "There is no need for trial... the people do not accept it when we say we must have proof, we must have evidence... the people say they should all be executed."

Sunday, August 14–Tuesday, August 16
- 860 bodies of executed political prisoners are covertly transferred from Evin prison, in Tehran, to Behesht Zahra cemetery.

Monday, August 15
- Ayatollah Montazeri meets with Hossein Ali Nayyeri, the religious judge, Morteza Eshraghi, the Prosecutor General of Tehran, Ebrahim Raisi, the Deputy Prosecutor General of Tehran, and the representa-

tive of the Ministry of Intelligence, Mostafa Pourmohammadi, in his abode.

- Nayyeri reveals to Ayatollah Montazeri that since July 28, 750 political prisoners have been executed in Tehran.

Tuesday, August 16–Friday, August 26
- There is a stay of execution of political prisoners in Evin and Gohardasht prisons.

Saturday, August 27
- Inquisition tribunals for arxist political prisoners begin in Evin prison.
- A second fatwa is issued by Ayatollah Khomeini for the execution of "non-religious and communist" political prisoners. (This document was never made public and was only exposed by Ayatollah Montazeri in his *Memoirs*. The date of the fatwa is equally unknown.)

Sunday, August 28
- Inquisition tribunals of leftist political prisoners begin in Gohardasht prison.
- The Death Commission stops work for three days.

Wednesday, August 31
- Summary executions of leftist political prisoners in Evin and Gohardasht prisons resume.
- Lashing of the leftist women political prisoners begins in Gohardasht prison. Five times a day, at each prayer time, Marxist women who do not wish to pray are punished with five lashes by the prison guards.

Friday, September 23
- Newspapers and TV sets are allowed back in the prison wards. The lashing of leftist women stops.

Saturday, December 10
- On the basis of a news broadcast by the official IRI News Agency, Western press reports on Chief Justice Ayatollah Abdolkarim Mousavi Ardebili's announcement that prisoners would be freed in February, on the tenth anniversary of the IRI.

1989

Wednesday, February 8
- It is announced that several thousand political prisoners would be released on the occasion of the tenth anniversary of the February Revolution of 1979. "This does not include the 900 opponents of the government accused of murder" and other "serious crimes."

Sunday, February 12
- Newspapers announce that participation in the Bahman 22 march (the anniversary of the February 1979 Revolution) is a condition for amnesty to male political prisoners in Tehran. They also indicated that Ayatollah Khomeini is considering granting amnesty to political prisoners.

Thursday, February 23
- State-owned newspapers announce: "The first group of political prisoners who received amnesty from Imam Khomeini were released this morning on the occasion of the glorious anniversary of the victory of the Islamic Revolution...230 prisoners, including 24 women, were released from Evin prison yesterday."
- According to state-run media: "A great number of prisoners who were released from Evin prison yesterday were those who had received death sentences or life imprisonment for committing serious crimes." Reportedly, they were of all ages and members of various political groups.

Saturday, March 25
- The BBC Persian radio service broadcasts the three letters by Ayatollah Montazeri, leaked by the first President of the IRI, Abolhassan Banisadr.

TRANSLATED FROM PERSIAN BY HEDAYAT MAHDAVI

Glossary

Adelabad: Central prison of the city of Shiraz. The name Adelabad originally comes from the name of a village in the southern vicinity of the city of Shiraz where the prison was originally constructed. With the urban development of the city in the 1960s, the prison became part of the city center and also the main detention center for political opponents of the Shah M.R. Pahlavi. In the 1980s, many political prisoners were kept in the excruciating conditions of this prison. Today, this colossal facility is old, dilapidated, and devoid of modern facilities.

Ahmadinejad, Mahmoud (b. 1956): The sixth President of the Islamic Republic of Iran. He served two terms from 2005 to 2013.

Ahvaz: Capital of Khuzestan province in southwestern Iran. This ancient city was built on the banks of the Karun River. It is the eighth most populous city of the country, composed of various ethnic groups such as Arabs, Lurs (Bakhtiaris), Dezfulis, Shushtaris, and so forth.

Amoozeshgah: Literally, "teaching center"; the name of a three-story building, part of the Evin prison compound located on the slopes of Evin hills. It comprises six saloons.

Asayeshgah: Literally, "rest house"; a ward in Evin prison that was built by prisoners used as forced laborers during the years 1981–1983. This section of Evin prison is allocated as individual cells only.

Ashura: "Tenth day of the Muslim month of Moharam. Commemoration of the martyrdom in 680 of Hossein ibn Ali, Mohammad's grandson and the third Imam of Shi'ite Islam. Shi'i communities annually reenact the tragedy in a passion play, including self-mortification and displays of sorrow and remorse intended to unite them in Hossein's suffering and death as an aid to salvation on the Day of Judgment..." (*The Oxford Dictionary of Islam*, p. 27).

Assembly of Experts for the Leadership (*Majles-e Khobregan-e Rahbari*): According to the IRI Constitution, Article 107, "the responsibility for designating the leader shall be with the Assembly of the Experts who are appointed by the people. The Experts jointly evaluate the qualifications of the jurisprudents as discussed in Articles 5 and 109. The qualifications for the choice of the leader comprises knowledge with regard to the rules and subjects of jurisprudence, political and social issues, popularity, or prominence in other areas indicated in Article 109. In case none of the candidates are found suitable, the law allows for one of the Experts to be chosen and declared as the leader of IRI." Article 111 states that if the "leader will be dismissed from his position in case he is incapable of performing his legal responsibilities, becomes deficient in one of the qualifications mentioned in Article 5 and 109; or it becomes evident that from the offset [*sic*] he has been lacking in some of the qualifications... or in case of the death, resignation, or dismissal of the leader, the Experts are responsible for designating a new leader as soon as possible." Article 108 states, "The law on the number [83] and qualifications of the Experts, the manner of their selection, and the internal guidelines of their meetings in the first term must be prepared by the jurisprudents of the first Guardian Council. It must be ratified by their majority vote, and submitted to the leader for the final approval. Whence, any change or review of this law and approval of the regulations related to the responsibilities of the Experts falls within the authority of the Experts themselves."[1]

Ayatollah: "Sign of God. Honorific title in Twelver Shi'i Islam. Popularly assigned to outstanding legal scholars. General use of the title appeared in the late Qajar period in Iran [1880s]... An ayatollah must be a fully qualified mujtahid, serve as Marja al-taqlid (reference for emulation serving as role model for religious matters as well as daily affairs), and assert authority over peers and followers. The leading Iranian Ayatollah is known as Ayatollah al-uzma, reflecting the temporal and spiritual power initially held by Ayatollah Ruhollah Khomeini." (*The Oxford Dictionary of Islam*, p. 30).

Azadi-ha: Those who have refused the regime's ideological and political demands as the condition for their release upon serving their prison sentence (i.e., public denunciation of their beliefs and political affiliations, demonstrating their allegiance to the IRI, or signing a letter of revulsion).

Baha'i: The Baha'i religion has its roots in the Babi movement which was born in Iran in 1844 and immediately gained recognition and popularity among people from all walks of life, especially the youth and the learned. Its charismatic leader, Seyyid Ali Mohammad Shirazi (1819–50), was a brilliant Shi'ite clergyman and merchant who was influenced

---

1 Translation by the International Society for Iranian Studies.

by earlier unorthodox, reform-minded Muslim theologians. His original and modern interpretations of the verses of the Quran called for the reformation of Shi'ite Islam. Implying that he is the Bab (literally, "door") to the twelfth imam of the Shi'ite creed who is believed to live in occultation, and claiming to be inspired by his revelations, rendered more credibility to his teachings. However, the movement that he led was crushed by an alliance of the state and church (orthodox Shi'ite clergy) in a bloody conflict.

After the execution of Seyyid Ali Mohammad Shirazi (July 1850), a ferocious repression ensued culminating in the slaughter of thousands of Babis and the migration of many of his followers to neighboring countries, mainly Greater Syria and Iraq. It was in exile that one of the disciples of the Bab, Mirza Hossein Ali Nouri (1817–92), better known as Baha'u'llah, assumed the leadership of the Babis. Baha'u'llah declared his teaching had superseded that of the Bab, proclaimed himself a new prophet and announced the creation of the Baha'i religion. There were about 100,000 Baha'is in the 1880s and they grew to nearly 200,000 by the 1950s, thus becoming probably the largest religious minority in Iran prior to the 1979 Revolution.

Baha'is, in particular Baha'i women, were mostly well educated and well represented in the professional and entrepreneurial arenas. Some Iranian Baha'is also played a noticeable role in establishing modern schools, medical centers, and public facilities in the early and mid-twentieth century. The Baha'is suffered recurrent waves of persecution instigated by the traditional Shi'ite clergy who systematically portrayed them as renegades and apostates. But their conditions improved and they were, in effect, accepted as citizens and more or less integrated into civil society and its institutions. Some even assumed prominent positions among the business elite during the Pahlavi reign.

It was after the 1979 Revolution and the establishment of the IRI that a more regressive trend commenced and vicious waves of persecution were launched against the Baha'i communities throughout Iran. The theocratic state ordered the shutdown of Baha'i institutions; engaged in the destruction of sacred Baha'i sites; confiscated their endowments, companies, and properties; expelled followers from all State institutions; and even banned their children from attending institutions of higher education. Furthermore, hundreds of Baha'is were arrested, tortured, and imprisoned. Thousands more had to flee the country. It is well documented that during the first seven years of the IRI, about two hundred Baha'is were executed by the state.

Baluchistan: A province in southeastern Iran bordering Pakistan and Afghanistan with an estimated population of 2.8 million. The Baluchis speak a distinct language, abide by the Sunni denomination of Islam, and adhere to their own culture and traditions.

Basij: Literally, "mobilization"; full name: *Sazman-e Basij-e Mostaz'afin* (The Organization for the Mobilization of the Oppressed). It is one of the five branches of the Islamic Revolutionary Guard Corps, a paramilitary volunteer militia established after the Iran–Iraq War, originally consisting of civilian volunteers who were urged by Ayatollah Khomeini to volunteer and fight in the war fronts.

Basiji: A member of the *Basij*.

Behesht Zahra: Literally, "the Paradise of Zahra" (daughter of Prophet Mohammad). It is the largest cemetery in Iran, located in the southern part of metropolitan Tehran. It was built in the late 1960s and inaugurated in 1970.

Caravan-e Azadi: Literally, "freedom caravan"; refers to those male survivors of Gohardasht and Evin prisons who were forced to attend the first Friday prayer of Tehran upon their release on the tenth anniversary of the 1979 Revolution.

Chador: "Veil"; a full-length garment covering a woman from head to foot, typically black in color; not mandated by the Quran, yet common among traditional Muslim women. Historically worn by urban upper-class women for protection, honor, and distinction.

Chelcheragh Operation: Chelcheragh, meaning "Chandelier" in Farsi, was one of the most spectacular military operations of the PMOI in spring–summer 1988. The operation started in the evening of June 18, 1988, with the artillery attack of the Mojahedin's National Liberation army on the Revolutionary Guards and Army positions around the city of Mehran in Ilam province, located at the Iran–Iraq border. By 10:30 a.m. the next day Mehran had fallen, and by June 21 Mojahedin forces had captured one thousand square kilometers of land, as well as tanks, military transport vehicles, weapons, and ammunition. Mojahedin forces then pulled back behind the Iraqi border with "about fifteen hundred soldiers" including some officers who had surrendered to them.

Dadsara: Public prosecutors' offices.

Darbasteh: Closed-door wards.

Darmangah: Infirmary.

Dastgerd: A city in Isfahan province; also the name of a major prison in that province which was constructed for five thousand inmates in the middle of an arid desert.

Eid-e Ghadir Khumm: (Literally, "Feast of pool of Khumm"); "the name of a pool near a small oasis along the caravan route between the cities of Mecca and Medina... According to Shi'ites, this is the site at which the Prophet Mohammad announced the authority of Ali ibn Abi Taleb over the Muslim Community on... March 632, as he was returning from the Farewell Pilgrimage... to Mecca. Many Sunnite authorities likewise consider Ghadir Komm [*sic*] the site of Prophetic announcement regarding Ali, but do not recognize it as a political appointment..."[2]

Eid-e Qurban: "Feast of the Sacrifice... Celebrated at the end of the annual pilgrimage to Mecca... Unblemished animals are sacrificed in commemoration of the sheep substituted by God when Abraham was commanded to sacrifice his son, Ishmael, as a test of faith. Only a portion, usually one-third, of this animal's meat is to be consumed by the family offering the sacrifice. The rest is to be distributed to the poor. For those not on pilgrimage, the celebration includes visits to mosques and to the graves of relatives. It lasts for three days and includes the distribution of gifts and sweets as well as receiving and visiting extended family." (*The Oxford Dictionary of Islam*, p. 131).

Enzejarnameh: Literally, "letter of revulsion." The IRI's prison officials used to demand signing of an *enzejarnameh* by political prisoners to ensure their total abstinence from future political activities. This document also serves as a means for the prisoners to express their abhorrence toward the political organizations with which they were affiliated.

Evin prison: The most infamous prison of Iran, constructed in the 1960s near the village of Evin in the north of Tehran and on the slopes of Alborz mountains. It replaced Qasr prison as the main detention center of political opponents of the ruling regime starting in 1972. More modern than any other prison in the country, sophisticated corporal and psychological tortures were first introduced in its chambers. A number of political prisoners were killed under such tortures, among them Behrooz Dehghani. Some of the most heinous atrocities of SAVAK (the Shah's notorious secret police) occurred on the hills

---

2 *Encyclopaedia Iranica*, vol. 10, p. 246.

of Evin too, notably the murder of Bijan Jazani, the historic leader of OIPFG, six other members of his group, and two of the leading Mojahedin—all in cold blood. After the 1979 Revolution, Evin briefly became a site open to the public to visit, attracting thousands. The IRI did not heed the popular demand to turn Evin into a museum and resumed running it as the main top-security prison in the land. Mohammad Borujerdi was the first IRI warden of Evin. He was replaced by Mohammad Kachouyi.

It was after the assassination of the latter in June 1981 that Assadollah Lajevardi, the chief prosecutor of Tehran, was appointed as its warden. After the all-out repression of June 1981, the number of its detainees increased to exceed fifteen thousand and it became the main slaughterhouse of the IRI, where up to sixty people were executed nightly. It is noteworthy that the wards of Evin prison are divided between the Judiciary, the Intelligence Ministry, and the Intelligence Bureau of the Revolutionary Guards, each independently administrating their own particular sections. After Lajevardi's tenure, Hossein Mortazavi became the director of Evin, but he did not last long in that position and Maisam (pseudonym for Davoud Bayat) took the helm from 1986 to 1987. However, he was replaced by Seyyid Hossein Mortazavi Zanjani who presided over the 1988 Great Massacre and was the chief warden of Evin until October 1988.

Ezterari: Literally, "emergency." Prisoners with health issues regarding their kidneys or bladders were called "emergency" as they needed to urinate and/or have bowel movements more often than normal. However, "emergency" prisoners were typically not allowed to use the bathrooms on an as-needed basis.

Farhadians: Farhad was a working man known in ancient Iranian mythology to have had fallen in love with Shirin, the Queen of Armenia. He became famous for having had the likeness of his beloved carved in stone. He has been portrayed as a role model and an icon of dedication and perseverance.

Fars mountains: Located in the province of Fars, in southern Iran; a traditional hideout for rebels, bandits, and local tribes defying the government forces.

Fatwa: "Authoritative legal opinion given by a legal scholar in response to a question posed by an individual or a court of law. A fatwa is typically requested in cases not covered by the fiqh literature." (*The Oxford Dictionary of Islam*, p. 83).

Forough-e Javidan: Eternal Light (Operation). Name of the military excursions of the People's Mojahedin Organization of Iran (PMOI) to Iran's western borders, a week after the IRI accepted UN Security Council resolution 598 and ceasefire with Iraq. The PMOI's National Liberation Army (NLA) crossed the borders to deal the "final blow" to the "Reactionary Islamic Regime." Yet, neither in Tehran nor anywhere else in Iran did people heed the Mojahedin's call to take to the streets. Ignored by the masses and cornered in the western zone, the NLA was swiftly and brutally crushed in Karand and Eslamabad by the combined forces of the *Pasdaran* (Revolutionary Guards), the *Basij* (the Islamic militia), and other irregular armed bands and vigilantes of the IRI. Some 1263 NLA militants were killed in what the regime called the Mersad Operation. Dozens of Mojahedin were captured and immediately executed on the spot and some dispatched to Evin and Gohardasht prisons. See also Mersad.

Ghasr-e Shirin: A city in Kermanshah Province.

Ghazvin: The capital of the province of Ghazvin, located 150 km northwest of Tehran. The city was a capital of the Safavid dynasty for over forty years (1555–98).

Gohardasht: A prison located in Gohardasht on the outskirts of the city of Karaj, approximately twenty kilometers west of Tehran. It is now called Rajai Shahr prison.

Haj/Haji: A title given to a Muslim who has made his or her dutiful pilgrimage to Mecca.

Halva: Literally means "sweet." It is a dense pastry made of flour and butter, mixed with syrup of sugar, saffron, rosewater, and cardamom, which gives it a pleasant taste and aroma.

Halwaie, Mojtaba: Not much is public knowledge about Haj Mojtaba's past. However, it is certain that at the beginning of the sweeping crackdown of June 1981, he was serving in the Revolutionary Guards at Evin prison, and was among Lajevardi's inner circle, performing the coup de grâce. He was one of the members of Evin's Task Force (*Goruh-e Zarbat*), actively participating in the arrest of the members and sympathizers of opposition groups. He was also an operating member of the death squads.

Mojtaba Halwaie was promoted to the deputy director of Evin's disciplinary and security department after the removal of Assadollah Lajevardi as the chief prosecutor of Tehran and the chief warden at Evin prison. As deputy director of Evin from 1986 to 1988, he played a major role in identifying and subjugating an array of detained opponents of the IRI, launching a night attack on prison wards, beating prisoners, and destroying their belongings. During the Great Massacre of 1988, he played a central role in Evin prison. It was he who forced the prisoners who survived the inquisition tribunals to say the prayers. At the end of the 1988 Great Massacre, Mojtaba Halwaie (Asghar) left Evin prison forever for unknown reason(s).

Hamedan: Name of a western province of Iran, as well as one of the most ancient cities of Persia.

Havakhori: "Breathing fresh air." In the context of prison, it refers to walking around the prison courtyard.

Hojat al-Islam: An honorific title meaning "authority on Islam" or "proof of Islam."

Hosseiniyeh: A Shi'ite place of worship. It served as an auditorium in the IRI's detention centers.

Iftar: "The breaking of the fast every evening after sunset during Ramadan... According to the example of the Prophet, the fast should be broken by eating dates or salt." (*The Oxford Dictionary of Islam*, p. 133).

Ilam: One of the provinces located in western Iran. It shares 425 km of border with Iraq and also borders on the provinces of Kermanshah, Lurestan, and Khuzestan. The provincial capital is the city of Ilam.

Imam: "One who stands in front; a role model for the Muslim community in all its spiritual and secular undertakings... Historically, Muslim rulers used to appoint the imam for the official function of leading the Friday prayers and services in the main mosque of capital cities... In Shi'i Islam the imam is the divinely appointed successor of Mohammad and is regarded as infallible, with the ability to make binding decisions in all areas of their disciples' daily activities. In Twelver Shi'ism, following the disappearance of the twelfth and last imam, the jurists (*foqaha*) have assumed the title imam. Hence, Khomeini after the Iranian revolution in 1979 was given the title imam, following the practice of the Arab Shi'is, who have always called their religious authorities imams." (*The Oxford Dictionary of Islam*, p. 135).

Interview: In the context of IRI prisons, it pertains to staged video confessions of political prisoners to be broadcast on state television or kept within the prison archives. The television recantations of the opponents of IRI were, and are, typically extracted by force and under ferocious torturing of the prisoners.

Isfahan: A city in central Iran, located 406 km south of Tehran, and the capital of the province of Isfahan. It is the third largest city of the country and was one of the world's largest cities in the sixteenth and seventeenth centuries. It became the capital of Persia for the second time during the Safavid dynasty, under Shah Abbas the Great. Isfahan is famous for its architecture, bridges, palaces, mosques, minarets, and traditional artisanship.

Kanoon: Headquarters of the Revolutionary Guards in the city of Karaj.

Karaj: The capital of Alborz Province in northern Iran, in the vicinity of Tehran.

Karbala: Name of a city in Iraq, holy to the Shi'ites of the world as their third imam, Hossein ibn Ali, lost his life in the fight against Yazid ibn Moavieh in 680 and was interred in Karbala.

Kargah: Literally means "workshop." A room or a number of rooms in the basement or another section of prisons where a group of repentant or nonprisoners were, or are, put to work sewing, knitting, and woodworking earning meager wages.

Kermanshah: Also known as Bakhtaran. It is the capital of Kermanshah Province, in western Iran, and located 525 km west of Tehran.

Khavaran: A cemetery in southeastern Tehran, originally known as *La'nat-abad* ("place of the damned"). It was designated for the burial of apostates and atheists right before the total onslaught of the IRI on its leftist opponents in June 1981. The regime never permitted Khavaran to become a cemetery in the true sense of the word, as none of the graves are allowed to have gravestones, signs, and/or marks. It is known that there are four mass graves in Khavaran containing interred corpses of the political prisoners executed in the 1980s. From the late 1990s until 2009, the agents of the IRI have bulldozed the area repeatedly. The last two rounds took place on December 25, 2008, when the regime demolished the graveyard, removed some topsoil, added fresh soil, and planted trees on individual and mass graves to eradicate this very important sight of their crime against humanity.

Between January 9 and 16, 2009, the authorities, once again, bulldozed the mass gravesites and destroyed grave markings made by the families. The Garden of Khavaran, as it is called by the pro-democracy opposition, has been one of the most significant symbols and sites of resistance to the ruling theocracy in Iran and the place for commemoration of those who lost their lives fighting against the IRI.

Khiabani, Mousa: Born in Tabriz on September 29, 1947. His father was an affluent and devout merchant in the Bazar of Tabriz, the second economic epicenter of Iran prior to the 1962 Shah's White Revolution. Mousa Khiabani was a devoted Muslim who frequently participated in the religious processions in the month of Moharam. Upon graduation from high school, he won a state scholarship to study physics at Tehran University, where he joined the avant-garde Islamists, later called the People's Mojahedin Organization of Iran (PMOI). In September 1971, Khiabani was arrested along with thirty-three members of the incipient group and immediately underwent severe torture and interrogation. The death sentence the military court issued for him in May 1972 was reduced to life imprisonment as a result of an international campaign to save his life. During his incarceration, he remained one of the leaders of the PMOI. He was one of the last political prisoners of Mohammad Reza Shah Pahlavi to be released on January 20, 1979.

Upon his release, he joined Masoud Rajavi in leading the growing organization and acted as one of its main speakers. The IRI's crackdown on the peaceful march of June 20, 1981; the alliance of Banisadr, Mojahedin, and an array of pro-democracy groups; the spectacular flight of Rajavi and Banisadr from Tehran to Paris; and the establishment of the National Council of Resistance of Iran made Khiabani the effective commander in chief of the PMOI inside the country. On February 18, 1982, forces of the Islamic Revolutionary Committee surrounded Mousa Khiabani's safe house, which contained Khiabani, his wife (Azar Rezaie), Ashraf Rabiei, Rajavi's wife, and several other leading members of that organization. After a gun battle of several hours, the house was captured with all twenty-three occupants killed.

Kommitteh: Persian word for "committee." Originally, during the final months of the Iranian Revolution, spontaneous task forces emerged to protect neighborhoods and provide people with the necessities of life. After the revolution, it evolved into an informal police task force.

Lajevardi, Assadollah (1935–98): A former lingerie peddler who joined the Islamic Coalition Party in the early 1960s and took part in the assassination of Prime Minister Hassan Ali Mansour in 1966. After having served eighteen months in prison, he resumed his political–religious activities and was arrested again for attempting to blow up the Tehran office of El Al (the Israeli airline). After the 1979 Revolution, he was named the chief prosecutor of Tehran and in 1981 the warden of Evin prison. Discharged in 1984, he was appointed as the head of the Organization of Iran's Prisons. Lajevardi was assassinated by PMOI sympathizers in Tehran Grand Bazaar on August 23, 1998, on the tenth anniversary of the Great Massacre of 1988.

La'natabad: "The Cemetery of the Damned," Khavaran.

Lashkari, Davoud (Agha Taqi Adeli): Known as Haj Davoud, he was born in 1958 in Imamzadeh Hassan, one of Tehran's most traditional neighborhoods. He was tall and had large, strong hands. Haj Davoud played an active role in organizing marches in support of Islamic fundamentalists. After Ayatollah Khomeini seized power, he joined the Revolutionary Guards and was sent to Gohardasht prison to monitor, interrogate, and torment political prisoners. Because of his cruel initiatives and the special methods of extracting information from detainees (for example, he masterminded the "grave" or "coffin" method of torture), he was continually promoted. In 1984, he became the deputy director of the prison Security and Discipline section.

After the dismissal of Lajevardi as the warden of Evin prison, he became the interim director of the prison. But with the change in the directorship of the country's prisons, he was again placed in charge of security and discipline in Gohardasht. Prior to the Great Massacre of 1988, he divided prisoners into three groups—red, yellow, and white—based on his evaluation of their state of mind and militancy. He was one of the major players in the Great Massacre in Gohardasht.

Long: A rectangular fabric made of cotton and hemp, with black stripes on a red background, usually used in bathhouses.

Mahram: "Forbidden, inviolable, holy, sacred. Traditionally used to refer to that part of the Bedouin tent, or bayt, reserved specifically for women, where cooking was done and provisions stored. The plural, *maharim*, is used to refer to a man's close female relatives. In Islamic law, mahram connotes a state of consanguinity precluding marriage." (*The Oxford Dictionary of Islam*, p. 187).

Mashhad: The second most populous and one of the richest cities in Iran, and the capital of Khorasan-e Razavi Province. It is located in northeastern Iran, sharing borders with Turkmenistan and Afghanistan. It is an important pilgrimage site as the imam of the Shi'ites is buried in Mashhad in a colossal mausoleum.

Mass'oul-e band: Literally means "person in charge of the ward." He or she is either a repentant prisoner appointed by prison officials or elected by prisoners themselves. *Mass'oul-e band* is in charge of organizing and coordinating the internal affairs of the ward and communicating with prison authorities. His or her job as a day laborer includes grooming, obtaining and distributing meals, washing dishes, and so forth.

Mehrieh: Husband's pledge to pay a pre-agreed amount of dowry money, property, goods, or gifts to his spouse upon her request.

Mellikesh: Prisoners who, despite having served their sentences, were not released and remained incarcerated against their will.

Mersad: Literally means "ambush." It is the name the IRI utilized for the military operation to contain and crush the military incursion of the NLA affiliated with the PMOI. The operation took place in Chaharzebar canyon, some thirty-five kilometers west of the city of Kermanshah. See also *Forough-e Javidan* (Eternal Light).

Moghisseh, Mohammad (Nasserian): He was born in a village near the city of Sabzevar, in the province of Khorasan. Prior to the 1979 Revolution, he attended the Seminary of Qom but was not involved in political activities. When regressive Shi'ite forces joined the movement against the Shah's dictatorship, he became politically active. Upon the victory of the Revolution, he was absorbed into the religious–political factions of the state and started working with the Islamic Revolution Prosecution Office in 1981. In the same year, he took charge of interrogation and extraction of information from political prisoners in Branch Three of Evin prison.

In winter 1984, Moghisseh began to work as an assistant to the prison supervisor at Qezel Hesar prison, along with Hossein Shariatmadari. After the transfer of Qezel Hesar prisoners to Evin and Gohardasht in 1986, he was assigned to Gohardasht as an assistant to the prison supervisor. In summer 1987, in the absence of the head of the prison, Mortazavi, he temporarily took charge of Gohardasht prison. During the Great Massacre of 1988, he was one of the main officials actively authorizing and encouraging the executions. Moghisseh believed that not a single PMOI sympathizer should be spared, and he insisted on maximizing the number and rate of the executions.

Mohareb: Enemy combatants against Islam (both men and women). For the leftists, the term used by the IRI is *Mortad* (apostates).

Moharebin: Plural of *Mohareb*.

Mojahed: "One who engages in jihad." It often translates as "warriors of God." In the Iranian context, it means a member or sympathizer of the PMOI.

Mojahedin: Plural for Mojahed and the abbreviated name for the PMOI.

Monafeq: "A polemical term applied to Muslims who possess weak faith or who profess Islam while secretly working against it. In the Quran, the term applies to a specific group of people headed by Abd-Allah ibn Ubaiy, whose lukewarm support of Mohammad at critical moments, such as the Battle of Uhud and the Battle of Trench caused a great strain for the early Muslim community. The Quran equates hypocrisy with lack of belief (kufr) and condemns hypocrites to hellfire for their failure to fully support the Muslim cause financially, bodily, and morally." (*The Oxford Dictionary of Islam*, p. 121).

Mortad: Apostate.

Namaz: "Prayer, worship... The second pillar of Islam is the prayers required of Muslims. In Shi'i Islam prayers are performed five times daily: daybreak... noon... midafternoon... sunset... and evening." (*The Oxford Dictionary of Islam*, p. 275).

National Liberation Army (**NLA**): The military wing of the National Council of Resistance affiliated with the PMOI, based in Iraq.

Nazarabad: The capital of Nazarabad County, Alborz Province, in northern Iran.

Nifaq: Hypocrisy, discord, and dissension (gerund of *Monafeq*).

Orumiyeh: The largest city in West Azerbaijan Province in northwestern Iran, and the capital of Orumiyeh County. The tenth most populated city in Iran, harboring one of the world's largest salt lakes located east of the city. Toward the west, Orumiyeh borders the Turkish mountains.

Pahlavi (dynasty): The last Iranian Kingdom reigning between 1925 and 1979. The dynasty was founded by Reza Shah Pahlavi in 1925 through a coup d'état. In 1941, the British forced him to abdicate following the Anglo-Soviet invasion of the country. Reza Shah was succeeded by his son, Mohammad Reza Pahlavi, the last Shah of Iran.

Pasdar: Member of the Islamic Revolutionary Guard Corps (plural: *Pasdaran*).

Prison's Dialogue: The journal named *Prison's Dialogue* was initiated in 1997 by a collective of former political prisoners of the IRI living in exile. *Prison's Dialogue* has also published books documenting the experiences of political prisoners who have survived the IRI's jails. As of writing, this unique review has published eighteen Persian-language publications and two books in German. Since 2005, *Prison's Dialogue* has been organizing a biennale, "Global Gatherings on the Massacre of Political Prisoners in Iran," in collaboration with other Iranian activists. The three-day event takes place every two years in a European country.

Qaramatian: "The popular nickname of a group of Ismai'li Shi'is who founded a state in the ninth century. Initially, the Qaramita challenged the Abbasids in Iraq and Syrian deserts. Although defeated in 906... the Qaramita carried out extensive raiding in western Arabia and Iraq and stole the Black Stone of the Kaaba. The Qaramita state of Bahrain finally collapsed in 1077." (*The Oxford Dictionary of Islam*, p. 253).

Qezel Hesar: Literally means "red wall" or "red enclosure"; one of the largest prisons in Iran operating until 1984. Located in the region of Kian Mehr on the outskirts of Karaj, it was built in 1964 during the reign of Mohammad Reza Shah Pahlavi. The prison was divided into two buildings (the northern and southern penitentiaries).

Quarantine: A prison cell in open-door wards where the prisoner is detained at his or her arrival for a certain amount of time, depending on the allegations against them and his or her behavior prior to their transfer to a long-term cell and/or ward. In Qezel Hesar prison "quarantine" referred to wards where the doors were kept closed at all times, except when the prisoner needed to use the bathroom, take a bath, or get some fresh air.

Quran: The sacred text of Islam which Muslims believe to be an oral revelation from God (Allah) to the Prophet Mohammad.

Rafsanjani, Ali Akbar Hashemi: (1934–2017) A student of Ayatollah Khomeini in one of the most prestigious seminaries in the city of Qom. He was active in the 1963 uprising against the Shah's "White Revolution" that led to the exile of Ayatollah Khomeini to Iraq. He was one of the main supporters of Khomeini among the Iranian clergy and his associates in Qom and Tehran. His religiopolitical activities against the Shah's autocracy and for the establishment of an Islamic hierocracy brought about his imprisonment many times, the last one in 1975. Hashemi Rafsanjani was one of the key members of the Council of Islamic Revolution and a founding father of the IRI. He was the speaker of the Islamic *Majles* (Parliament) during the turbulent years of 1980–1989, the President of the IRI from 1989 until 1997, chairman of the Expediency Council (which became much more influential than the office of presidency during his chairmanship), and the chairman of the crucial Assembly of Experts which, after the death of Ayatollah Khomeini in 1989, elected Ayatollah Ali Khamenei at the open request and recommendation of Rafsanjani.

Rafsanjani fell out of favor with Ayatollah Khamenei in the early 2000s and became the target of the Mahmoud Ahmadinejad defamation campaign during Ahmadinejad's rigged presidential election of 2009 and his two-term presidency until 2016. Rafsanjani's defense of the Green movement, which protested the rigged election and the presidency of Ahmadinejad, resulted in his further estrangement from Ayatollah Khamenei; however, his popularity increased in society at large. Rafsanjani remained one the most influential politicians of the IRI until his death on January 8, 2017.

Rahmani, Davoud: An ironsmith born in 1955 into a political family in a working-class neighborhood of Tehran. After the revolution, he joined one of the Revolutionary Kommittehs of Tehran. As a result of his acquaintance with Lajevardi, the chief prosecutor of Tehran, he became the head of Qezel Hesar prison between 1981 and 1984. He was laid off from this position after Lajevardi's dismissal and returned to his previous occupation in Tehran Grand Bazaar.

Rajavi, Masoud: Masoud Rajavi was born in 1948 in Tabas, an ancient town in the province of Khorasan. He attended Tehran University and studied political science. Rajavi became a sympathizer of the Freedom Movement and joined the radical wing of that movement, later called the People's Mojahedin Organization of Iran. Rajavi was arrested in 1971 and sentenced to life in prison. After the execution of the founding fathers of the PMOI, he became one of the leaders of his fellow incarcerated Mojahedin. Upon his release from prison in 1979, he played a key role in reorganizing the PMOI and, along with Mousa Khiabani, facilitated its transition to a mass movement.

At the outset of nationwide repression in summer 1981, the PMOI joined forces with Abolhassan Banisadr, the ousted President of the IRI, and an array of political organizations, personalities, and progressive intellectuals in an alliance named The National Council of Resistance of Iran (NCRI). Simultaneously, the PMOI launched urban guerrilla warfare against the IRI. Rajavi left Iran for France on July 29, 1981, to lead the NCRI (see Appendix B). Upon the PMOI's failure to incite urban warfare against the IRI, and the departure of many key members from the NCRI, Rajavi founded the Iraqi-based National Liberation Army in June 1987.

Ramadan: "In Islam fasting is required during Ramadan, the ninth month of the Muslim lunar calendar, during which all Muslims are required to abstain during daylight hours from eating, drinking, or engaging in sexual activity." (*The Oxford Dictionary of Islam*, p. 83).

Rasht: The capital city of Gilan Province in northern Iran. It is the most densely populated city of the country and the largest city along the Caspian

Sea coast. It is a major trade center between Caucasia, Russia, and Iran using the port of Bandar-e Anzali.

Sahari: "Last meal prior to daybreak during the month of Ramadan. Marks the beginning of the fast. After sahari, Muslims abstain from food, drink, and sex until the sun sets." (*The Oxford Dictionary of Islam*, p. 303).

Saqat al-Islam: The lowest-level cleric in Shi'ite Islam.

Sar-e moze-i: Literally means "persistent in one's point of view." Refers to prisoners who are steadfast, noncomplying, and uncompromising.

SAVAK: Abbreviation for *Sazeman-e Ettela'at va Amniyat-e Keshvar* (National Organization for Security and Intelligence). It was the secret police agency found after the 1953 coup against Dr. Mossadegh. It served as an intelligence service, domestic security, and secret police. SAVAK was established with the help of the US Central Intelligence Agency and developed by the Israeli Mossad. It operated from 1957 until the 1979 Revolution, and was dissolved by the order of Prime Minister Shapour Bakhtiar on February 6, 1979. As a result of its practice of torturing and executing opponents of the Shah's regime, SAVAK was one of Iran's most hated and feared institutions prior to the revolution.

Senfi: Prison idiom. *Senf* means "guild," so *senfi* can be translated "guild-ish." All the day-to-day issues relating to the prisoners such as quality of food, lack of milk and dairy products, medicine for the sick and pregnant women, to special needs of mothers and children, were called "*senfi* problems."

Sepah Pasdaran: Abbreviation for *Sepah-e Pasdaran-e Enghelab-e Eslami*, literally, "Army of Guardians of the Islamic Revolution or Islamic Revolutionary Guard Corps." It is a branch of the Iranian Armed Forces, founded after the 1979 Revolution by the order of Ayatollah Khomeini. The statute of this most powerful military and economic institution of the IRI defines its major role as the defendant of the Islamic Republic in the face of foreign interference, machinations of internal enemies, and "deviant movements."

Shah: A title given to the emperors and kings of Persia. Some Persian rulers regarded themselves as the *Shahanshah* (King of Kings) or *Padishah* (Master King).

Shari'a: Canonic law or "God's eternal and immutable will for humanity, as expressed in the Quran and Mohammad's example (Sunnah), considered binding for all believers; ideal Islamic law." (*The Oxford Dictionary of Islam*, p. 287).

Shi'ite (Shi'ism): Members of one of the main denominations of Islam differentiated from the majority Sunni.

Shiraz: The fifth most populous city of Iran and the capital of Fars Province located in the southwest of the country. It had been a regional trade center for over a thousand years. Shiraz is one of the oldest cities of Persia and is known as the city of poets, literature, wine, flowers, and gardens.

Sorkhe-Hesar: See Qezel Hesar.

Tabriz: Located in the northwest, Tabriz is the sixth most populous city in Iran and the capital of East Azerbaijan Province.

Talaba/Talabeh: Seminary student.

Tavab: "A major theme of the Quran, mentioned over seventy times and with an entire surah (9) titled for it. Usually described as turning toward God, asking forgiveness, and being forgiven... In case of sin against another person, restitution is required. In case of sin against God, repentance, remorse and resolution to change one's behavior are considered sufficient." (*The Oxford Dictionary of Islam*, pp. 261–2). The *tavabs* throughout the IRI's detention centers collaborated with the prison establishment to different degrees and were one of the main tools of discipline and punishment of prisoners.

Tooman: Former Iranian currency unit before being replaced by Rial in 1932 by the Central Bank of Iran during Reza Shah's reign.

UNESCO prison: In the late 1960s UNESCO (United Nations Scientific and Cultural Organization) established headquarters in the southern city of Dezful to combat illiteracy and provide care for the children of the poor. This educational–health center became part of the Bureau of Education of the city of Dezful in the early 1970s and later turned into a teachers' club. After the overthrow of the Shah, the club was transformed into a detention center by the IRI, imprisoning opponents. With the intensification of the struggle against the ruling theocracy in the early 1980s, UNESCO prison was expanded and evolved into one of the most horrendous prisons of the country, famous for its savage interrogators and sophisticated methods of torture. UNESCO prison has been replaced by a larger prison located in the center of Dezful City.

Vakilabad prison: When it was built in the late 1960s, it was outside the city of Mashhad, in a resort, but following Mashhad's expansion, the prison is now almost at the city's center. Vakilabad prison was rebuilt and modernized after the 1979 Revolution. From 1983 to 1984, at the pinnacle of repression, a few wards were added to this two-story construction.

Velayat-e faqih: Literally, "Rule of Guardianship by Islamic Jurists and/or Supreme Jurisprudence." According to Article 5 of the Constitution of the Islamic Republic of Iran, adopted in December 1979, the state has to be run by Shi'i jurists (*foqaha*). "The sovereignty of the command [of God] and religious leadership of the community [of believers] is the responsibility of the jurisprudent who is just, pious, courageous, knowledgeable about his era, and a capable administrator, and is recognized and accepted by the majority of people as leader."[3] According to Article 107 of the Constitution of 1979, *Velayat-e faqih is* a "source of imitation" (*marja'-e taqlid*), qualified to decree fatwas. However, after the death of Ayatollah Khomeini and the ensuing revision of the Constitution in 1989, the low-ranking cleric *Hojat al-Islam* Khamenei became the Supreme Leader of the IRI in 1989.

The *Velayat-e faqih*, as conceptualized by Ayatollah Khomeini in his years of exile in Najaf (Iraq), is the Supreme Jurist who exercises leadership until the return of the hidden imam (Mehdi) in the Shi'i creed. The *Velayat-e faqih* in the IRI is appointed by the Assembly of Experts (*Majles-e Khobregan*). In turn, the *Velayat-e faqih* names religious jurists to membership in the Guardian Council (*Shura-ye Negahban*). He also appoints the senior officers of the military, the Revolutionary Guards (*Pasdaran-e Enqelab*), and the highest authority of the judiciary. He is exclusively responsible for the declaration of war and is the commander in chief of Iran's armed forces. Significantly, the Supreme Leader decides on the general direction of the IRI's policies in all domains. He is in a position to dismiss the president, supervise the three branches of government, and grant amnesty or issue death sentences for the blasphemous. In effect, *Velayat-e faqih,* or Supreme Leader, as he is officially called in Iran, stands above all laws of the land.

Zanjan: The capital of Zanjan Province in Azerbaijan, northern Iran. It is located 298 km northwest of Tehran and is the twentieth largest city of the country. The population of Zanjan consists mostly of Iranian Azeris.

Zir-e Hasht: Prison idiom. It is where the ward guards are stationed in the prison along with the control desk.

---

3 Translation by the *International Society for Iranian Studies.*

Index